W9-BIQ-440

SHORT STORY WRITERS

SHORT STORY WRITERS

Volume 1
Alice Adams — Hamlin Garland

edited by
FRANK N. MAGILL

consulting editor
Charles E. May

SALEM PRESS, INC.
Pasadena, California   Englewood Cliffs, New Jersey

Essays originally appeared in *Critical Survey of Short Fiction, Revised Edition,* 1993; new material has been added.

∞ The paper used in these volumes conforms to the
American National Standard for Permanence of Paper
for Printed Library Materials, Z39.48-1984.

Library of Congress Cataloging-in-Publication Data
Short story writers / edited by Frank N. Magill ; consulting editor, Charles E. May.
    p.   cm. — (Magill's choice)
    Includes index.
    ISBN 0-89356-950-X (set : alk. paper). — ISBN
0-89356-951-8 (v. 1 : alk. paper). — ISBN 0-89356-952-
6 (v. 2 : alk. paper). — ISBN 0-89356-953-4 (v. 3 : alk.
paper)
    1. Short story. 2. Short stories—Bio-bibliog-
raphy—Dictionaries. 3. Novelists—Biography—Dictionaries. I. Magill, Frank Northen, 1907-1997.
II. May, Charles E. (Charles Edward), 1941-   . III.
Series.
   PN3373.S398   1997
   809.3'1'03—dc21
   [B]   97-23079
                                     CIP

First Printing

PRINTED IN THE UNITED STATES OF AMERICA

Publisher's Note

Short Story Writers surveys 102 of the most important authors of short fiction: the most taught, most read, most acclaimed, and most researched in the American library. These essays, culled from the *Critical Survey of Short Fiction, Revised Edition* (1993) and then updated, provide an essential look at the best in short-fiction writing in an easy-to-use format. Although every list of contents in a work such as this is subjective and the inclusion of any one author over another is open for debate, we have attempted to cover the core curriculum, presenting at least the authors who are common to every basic reading list.

The contents focuses on the modern short story, with a brief nod to the classic work in the 1300's of Giovanni Boccaccio (*The Decameron*) and Geoffrey Chaucer (*The Canterbury Tales*); then to the influence of the *contes* or *Märchen*, represented here with the Grimm Brothers and *Grimm's Fairy Tales*. By the mid-1800's, two distinct types of short fiction existed: the tale and the essay-sketch. The modern short story brings together the best of these two traditions. Although the debate is lively about how, when, and where short fiction developed, most scholars of the genre agree that the modern short story began in the United States and through the person of Washington Irving; it is often conceded that "Rip Van Winkle" is the first *great* modern short story.

Irving has been called the "inventor of the short story," however, the modern short story appeared almost simultaneously in Russia, France, Germany, and the United States. The moniker "father of the modern short story" has been attributed to Nikolai Gogol, Prosper Mérimée, Nathaniel Hawthorne, and Edgar Allan Poe. Of these four, Poe stands out because he not only wrote short stories but also wrote about the short story in theory. He addressed it as a distinct genre, advancing the thesis that a story should have a unifed effect and be compact—principles that still guide short-story criticism.

Many outstanding craftsmen of the genre have followed, and the remaining authors covered in this set reflect the range and diversity of nineteenth and twentieth century short story writing. More than half of the authors (57) are from the United States, reflecting the strength of the genre in its birthplace, of these five are African Americans. The second largest national grouping is England (16), added to which are the great authors of Ireland (7) and Scotland (3). The user will also find some of the cornerstone short fiction writers of Canada, the Continent, Russia, Asia, Africa, and

South America. Women authors have excelled in the genre, and 28 are surveyed in these volumes, from Kate Chopin (1851-1904) to Alice Walker (born 1944).

The essays are arranged alphabetically in the three volumes, and their concise and accessible formats follow an easy-to-use template. Each begins with the author's name, birth date and place, death date and place when appropriate, and a chronological list of the subject's major publications of short fiction. The text of the essay is divided into four subsections: "Other literary forms" is a paragraph describing other genres in which the author has worked; "Achievements" addresses what the author has contributed to the genre, as well as mentions important honors and awards; "Biography" provides a summary of the author's life; and the main body of the text is devoted to "Analysis," an in-depth look at the author's short-story writing, usually taking three or four individual stories to help explicate the author's work. The back matter of each essay includes "Other major works," which lists the author's publications in genres other than the short story, and a solid annotated bibliography.

Volume 3 concludes with a glossary of more than 150 terms and techniques commonly used in the study of short fiction and a comprehensive index. A list of the many scholars who contributed their time and knowledge to writing the articles appears on the following page.

List of Contributors

Thomas P. Adler
Purdue University, Indiana

Marilyn Arnold
Brigham Young University, Utah

Robert W. Artinian
Independent scholar

Stanley S. Atherton
Independent scholar

Bryan Aubrey
Fairfield, Iowa

Jane L. Ball
Wilberforce University, Ohio

Mary Baron
Independent scholar

Bert Bender
Independent scholar

Carol Bishop
Indiana University Southeast

Lynn Z. Bloom
Williamsburg, Virginia

Julia B. Boken
Indiana University Southeast

Jerry Bradley
New Mexico Tech

Harold Branam
Savannah State College, Georgia

Gerhard Brand
Seattle, Washington

Laurence A. Breiner
Independent scholar

Kieth H. Brower
Dickinson College, Pennsylvania

Louis J. Budd
Independent scholar

Rebecca R. Butler
Dalton College, Georgia

Edmund J. Campion
University of Tennessee, Knoxville

Warren J. Carson
Universtiy of South Carolina, Spartanbury

Thomas J. Cassidy
South Carolina State University

Hal Charles
Eastern Kentucky University, Richmond

Bill Delaney
San Diego, California

Joan DelFattore
University of Delaware, Newark

Grace Eckley
Golden, Colorado

Wilton Eckley
Colorado School of Mines

Robert P. Ellis
Worcester State College, Massachusetts

Thomas L. Erskine
Salisbury State University, Maryland

Walter Evans
Augusta College, Georgia

James Feast
Baruch College, New York

John W. Fiero
University of Southwestern Louisiana, Lafayette

Edward Fiorelli
St. John's University, New York

James K. Folsom
Independent scholar

Carol Franks
Portland State University, Oregon

Timothy C. Frazer
Western Illinois University

Terri Frongia
University of California, Riverside

Jean C. Fulton
Maharishi International University, Iowa

Kenneth Funsten
Independent scholar

Linda S. Gordon
Worcester State College, Massachusetts

Peter W. Graham
Virginia Tech, Blacksburg

Julian Grajewski
Tucson, Arizona

James L. Green
Arizona State University, Tempe

David Mike Hamilton
Los Altos, California

Terry Heller
Coe College, Iowa

Archibald E. Irwin
Indiana University Southwest

Eunice Pedersen Johnston
North Dakota State University, Fargo

Karen A. Kildahl
South Dakota State Universtiy, Brookings

Sue L. Kimball
Methodist College, North Carolina

Cassandra Kircher
Elon College, North Carolina

Carlota Larrea
Pennsylvania State University

Eugene S. Larson
Pierce College, California

Donald F. Larsson
Mankota State University, Minnesota

Mary S. LeDonne
Orangeburg, South Carolina

Leon Lewis
Appalachian State University, North Carolina

R. C. Lutz
University of the Pacific, California

Richard D. McGhee
Arkansas State University, Jonesboro

Victoria E. McLure
Texas Tech University

Bryant Mangum
Independent scholar

Barry Mann
San Diego, California

Patricia Marks
Valdosta State College, Georgia

Karen M. Cleveland
Marwick
Herts, England

Paul Marx
University of New Haven, Connecticut

Laurence W. Mazzeno
Alvernia College, Pennsylvania

Kenneth W. Meadwell
University of Winnipeg, Canada

Ann A. Merrill
Emory University, Georgia

Vasa D. Mihailovich
University of North Carolina, Chapel Hill

Paula M. Miller
Biola University, California

Robert W. Millett
Independent scholar

Robert A. Morace
Daemen College, New York

Sherry Morton-Mollo
Claremont Graduate School, California

Earl Paulus Murphy
Independent scholar

Brian Murray
Youngstown State University, Ohio

William Nelles
University of Massachusetts, Dartmouth

Evelyn Newlyn
Virginia Polytechnic Institute and State University, Blacksburg

Emma Coburn Norris
Troy State University, Alabama

George O'Brien
Georgetown University, Virginia

Cóilín Owens
George Mason University, Virginia

Janet Taylor Palmer
Caldwell Community College, North Carolina

Robert J. Paradowski
Rochester Institute of Technology, New York

Leslie A. Pearl
San Diego, California

Susan L. Piepke
Bridgewater College, Virginia

Constance Pierce
Independent scholar

Mary Ellen Pitts
Western Kentucky University, Bowling Green

Victoria Price
Lamar University, Texas

Norman Prinsky
Augusta College, Georgia

Jere Real
Lynchburg College, Virginia

Mary Rohrberger
University of Northern Iowa, Cedar Falls

Paul Rosefeldt
Delgado Community College, Louisiana

Ruth Rosenberg
Brooklyn, New York

David Sadkin
Niagara University, New York

Chaman L. Sahni
Boise State University, Idaho

Victor A. Santi
University of New Orleans, Louisiana

D. Dean Shackelford
Concord College, West Virginia

Jan Sjåvik
Universtiy of Washington

Ira Smolensky
Monmouth College, Illinois

Katherine Snipes
Eastern Washington University, Spokane

Jean M. Snook
Memorial University of Newfoundland, Canada

George Soule
Carleton College, Minnesota

Madison V. Sowell
Brigham Young University, Utah

Sandra Whipple Spanier
Independent scholar

Louise M. Stone
Bloomsbury University of Pennsylvania

W. J. Stuckey
Purdue University, Indiana

Alvin Sullivan
Southern Illinois University, Edwardsville

James Sullivan
California State University, Los Angeles

Catherine Swanson
Austin, Texas

Terry Theodore
University of North Carolina, Wilmington

Lou Thompson
Texas Woman's University

Christine Tomei
Allegheny College, Pennsylvania

Dennis Vannatta
University of Arkansas, Little Rock

Patricia A. R. Williams
Texas Southern University, Houston

Michael Witkoski
Columbia, South Carolina

Anna M. Wittman
University of Alberta, Edmonton, Canada

Mary F. Yudin
Pennsylvania State University

Contents – Volume 1

Complete List of Contents

Contents — Volume 1

Contents — Volume 2

Contents — Volume 3

ALICE ADAMS

Born: Fredericksburg, Virginia; August 14, 1926

Principal short fiction · *Beautiful Girl*, 1979 · *To See You Again*, 1982 · *Molly's Dog*, 1983 · *Return Trips*, 1985 · *After You've Gone*, 1989

Other literary forms · Though Alice Adams was first successful in short fiction, she has also published several novels: *Careless Love* (1966), *Families and Survivors* (1974), *Listening to Billie* (1978), *Rich Rewards* (1980), *Superior Women* (1984), *Second Chances* (1988), and *Caroline's Daughters* (1991). In addition, her story "Roses, Rhododendrons" has appeared as an illustrated gift book.

Achievements · Adams did not publish her first collection of stories until she was in her fifties, but she has quickly assumed a place among the leading practitioners of the genre. Her stories frequently appear in *The New Yorker* and have been selected for annual collections of outstanding short fiction. Like writers as diverse as Ann Beattie and Raymond Carver, Adams is a chronicler of contemporary life. Her fiction deals with interpersonal relationships. Frequently, her heroines develop from young women involved in destructive relationships to well-rounded middle-aged adults whose priorities include satisfying work and friendships. Her tone is characteristically understated, often ironic, yet currents of emotion flow beneath the surface of her stories.

In 1982, Adams received the O. Henry Special Award for Continuing Achievement, given for only the third time; her predecessors were Joyce Carol Oates (in 1970) and John Updike (in 1976).

Biography · Alice Boyd Adams was born in Fredericksburg, Virginia, on August 14, 1926, the daughter of Nicholson Adams, a professor, and Agatha (née Boyd) Adams, a writer. Shortly after her birth, the family moved to Chapel Hill, North Carolina, where Adams spent her first sixteen years. After receiving her B.A. degree from Radcliffe College in 1946, she married Mark Linenthal, Jr. Two years later, they moved to California, and in 1951, their only child, Peter, was born. Their marriage ended in divorce in 1958, following which Adams held a number of part-time clerical, secretarial, and bookkeeping jobs while rearing her son and writing short stories.

It was not until 1969 that she broke into the magazine market when *The New Yorker* bought her story, "Gift of Grass." Since then, her stories have continued to appear in *The New Yorker* as well as *Redbook, McCall's*, and *The Paris Review*. In 1976, Adams received a grant from the National Endowment for the Arts and in 1978, a Guggenheim Fellowship. In addition, Adams has taught at the University of California at Davis, the University of California at Berkeley, and Stanford University.

Analysis · Most of Alice Adams' stories revolve around common themes, and her characters, mostly educated, upper-middle-class women, are defined by a set of common traits and situations which reappear in somewhat different combinations. They find their lives flawed, often by unhappy relationships with lovers, husbands, parents, friends, sometimes with combinations of these, usually with a living antagonist, occasionally with one already dead. Often, they resolve these problems, but sometimes they do not.

Frequently, the tensions of Adams' plots are resolved when her central, female characters learn something new or find a new source of strength, which enables them to part from unsatisfactory husbands, lovers, or friends. Claire, in "Home Is Where" (in *Beautiful Girl*), leaves both an unsatisfactory marriage and a miserable love affair in San Francisco, where she feels "ugly–drained, discolored, old," to spend the summer with her parents in her North Carolina hometown, where she had been young and "if not beautiful, sought after." Refreshed and stimulated by the sensual landscape and a summertime affair, Claire returns to San Francisco to divorce her husband, to take leave of her unpleasant lover, and, eventually, to remarry, this time happily. Cynthia, in "The Break-In" (*To See You Again*), finds herself so different from her fiancé, Roger, when he automatically blames the burglary of his home on "Mexicans," that she leaves him without a word, "going home." The narrator of "True Colors" (*To See You Again*) discovers, in Las Vegas, David's ugly side as an obsessive gambler and leaves him: "From then on I was going to be all right, I thought." Clover Baskerville in "The Party-Givers" (*To See You Again*) leaves behind her malicious friends when she realizes that she need not call them if she does not want to see them. All these characters have learned that "home is where the heart" not only "is" but also chooses to be.

Adams' heroines must also sometimes free their hearts from painful entanglements with the dead. In "Lost Luggage" (*To See You Again*), a widow unable to get on with her life loses her luggage, which contains a notebook she has kept as therapy to deal with her husband's death, even though they did not love each other much and he had little time for her. Her life begins again when she starts a new notebook which "will fit easily" into a "carry-on traveling bag." Charlotte O'Mara's visit after many years to "Berkeley House" (*To See You Again*) helps to rid her of her obsession with both the house and the memory of her dead parents' unhappy marriage. In "Legends" (*To See You Again*), Jane Phelps's exhaustive but therapeutic discussion of her long affair with the late legendary Randolph Clavell helps her to decide that enough has been said about Clavell, and she and her interlocutor agree to direct the interview toward her own work as a sculptor. In "Sintra" (*Return Trips*), Arden Kinnel finally frees herself from the memory of her dead lover Luiz when she learns to live with being alone. For the women in these stories, a dead past is luggage that must be lost before they can live in the present or face the future with confidence.

Sometimes the renewal of Adams' characters gives them the strength not to escape from unhappy relationships and situations but to live with them. In "Time in Santa Fe" (*Return Trips*), Emma, worried by everyone around her, her mother, her husband, her daughter, even her ailing cat, visits her old friend David, who comforts her despite his own pain over the possible terminal illness of his lover Jeffrey; from their friendship, she returns to face her troubles feeling "rich." The narrator in "Return Trips," from the title story of that collection, traveling to her husband's homeland in Greece (he is uninterested in her past), feels less alone and isolated as they drive near the place in Yugoslavia where in her youth she was loved by Paul, a young poet.

Adams' heroines sometimes reach out from their lonely and isolated lives to find sympathetic bonds with poor or troubled people from other cultures. In "Greyhound People" (*To See You Again*), a divorced, middle-aged woman's discovery of kinship with her (mostly black and poor) fellow commuters, along with her discovery that her commuter ticket will take her anywhere in California, is so liberating that she can finally break free of her repressive, domineering roommate and friend, Hortense. In "Verlie I Say unto You" (*Beautiful Girl*), Jessica Todd's sensitivity to her black maid Verlie's humanity underscores a fundamental difference between herself and her insensitive husband (see also "The Break-In" in this regard). In "Mexican Dust" (*To See You Again*), Marian comes to prefer the company of the Mexican peasants to that of her husband, friends, and other Americans as they bus through Mexico on vacation; she abandons her party and returns to Seattle, where she plans to study Spanish, presumably to prepare for a return to Mexico alone. In fact, one sign of a strong character in Adams' stories is a marked sensitivity to other cultures. Elizabeth, in the story of that name, purchases her Mexican beach house in the name of her Mexican servant Aurelia and leaves Aurelia in full possession of the house

at her death. The central focus in "La Señora" (*Return Trips*) is the friendship between a wealthy, elderly American woman who vacations annually
at a Mexican resort, and Teodola, the Mexican maid in charge of her hotel
room. Adams' own concern for the human plight of those of other cultures
can be seen in "Teresa," in *Return Trips*, a story about the privation, terror,
and grief of a Mexican peasant woman.

At the same time, Adams' stories also show the restraints between
people that can result from regional and class differences. In "New Best
Friends" (*Return Trips*), Sarah and Jonathan, a Northern couple trans-
planted to the South, after failed attempts to find new friends and an
especially painful rejection by the very Southern McElroys, find that
"we're low, very low, on their priority list." In "A Southern Spelling Bee"
(*To See You Again*), Avery Todd, a young girl taken in by her father's relations
while her own family is much in trouble, is still, years later, though grown
up, married, brilliant, and successful, trying to win the approval of her
relations, to overcome their unfair prejudice against her in the Southern
spelling bee she endured as a child. "Truth or Consequences" (*To See You
Again*) recounts the class bias among Southern whites. As a penalty for
losing the game referred to in the title of the story, young Emily is required
to kiss Carstairs Jones, one of the "truck children" from uneducated
families who are bused to school from the countryside. Though the incident prompts Jones himself to academic achievement, social mobility, and,
ultimately, celebrity status across the nation, the trauma of the incident and
the ribbing that she took from her upper-middle-class schoolmates haunt
Emily for years.

In two of Adams' most effective stories, female protagonists learn to live
confidently with themselves: "Molly's Dog" (*Return Trips*) and "A Public
Pool" (*Return Trips*). In the former, Molly returns with her homosexual
friend Sandy to a small oceanside cabin, where she experienced a love
affair so intense she cannot think of it without weeping. A friendly dog
attaches itself to them on the beach and follows them as they leave; Molly
pleads with Sandy to go back, but he drives faster, and the dog, though
running, falls back and shrinks in the distance. Molly and Sandy quarrel
over the dog, and Molly, realizing that she is much too dependent on men,
comes to see less of Sandy back in San Francisco. She finally learns to think
of the dog without pain but cannot forget it, and the place by the ocean
becomes in her memory "a place where she had lost, or left something of
infinite value. A place to which she would not go back."

In "A Public Pool," the protagonist, though working-class, neither part
of the literary or artistic world nor so well educated as many of Adams'
women characters, shares with many of them a dissatisfaction with her

body and a sense of being cut off and alone. She cannot bear to meet people or even look for a job ("we wouldn't even have room for you," she imagines an employer saying), so that life at age thirty is a grim existence in a cold apartment with a penurious mother. Though swimming offers an escape from home and a chance for meeting new people, it also has its fears: exposing her body in the locker room and enduring the rebukes of strangers–of the faster swimmers whose lane she blocks, of the blond-bearded man who goes by so swiftly that he splashes her, and of a large black woman who tells her that she should stay by the side of the pool. After a few months of lap swimming, her body changes and her fear of others lessens. An early remark of the blond-bearded man made her babble nervously, but now she responds to his conventional questions with brief assent. On the day the black lady compliments her on her stroke and they leave the pool together, she is finally able to find a job and thinks of moving out of her mother's apartment. She walks happily about the neighborhood, thinking that she and the black woman might become friends. At that moment, she meets in the street the blond-bearded man, who smells of Juicy Fruit and is wearing "sharp" clothes from Sears. He invites her for coffee, but, "overwhelmed" by the smell of Juicy Fruit and realizing that "I hate sharp clothes," she makes her excuses. Like other Adams women, she has felt loneliness, but also like many other women in these stories, she finds new strength that will mitigate her isolation by giving her independence. Yet here it is primarily achieved by herself, and, appropriately, Adams' always masterful use of language here is especially striking. As Adams' character goes off independently from the blond-bearded man, she says confidently, "I leave him standing there. I swim away."

Not all of these stories, however, end so conclusively; in others, it is unclear whether the heroines' chosen resolutions to the problems confronting them will be satisfactory. The young housewife of "You Are What You Own: A Notebook" (*Return Trips*) lives in a house crammed with her domineering mother's furniture, which the girl seems doomed to polish for all eternity. Her boring graduate student husband complains that she does not polish the furniture enough and even starts to do it himself. She escapes in fantasy, fictionalizing the artists who live in a house down the street from her, assigning them her own names (not knowing their real ones), and indulging with them in imagined conversations. At the end of the story–recorded in her notebook–she tells her husband in a letter that she is leaving him the furniture and leaving to look for a job in San Francisco. Did she go? Is she capable? Similarly, the lonely young wife in "To See You Again" uses the image of a beautiful adolescent boy in her class to re-create the image of her husband as he was when they fell in love—slim and energetic, not as he is now, overweight and frequently paralyzed by chronic, severe depression. The story ends with her fantasizing that somehow she has escaped her grim life with him, that things are as they once were, her husband somehow reclaimed in the body of the young student.

The story plots summarized here raise a possible objection to Adams' fiction—that many of her female characters are too obsessed with the attention of men, even to the point where the women's own highly successful careers seem to matter little. This issue, however, must be placed in historical perspective. Most of the women in her stories, like Adams herself, grew up and entered adulthood during the period after World War II, when women's roles in American society were constricted, when women were sent home from their wartime jobs to take on what seemed then an almost patriotic duty, submitting themselves to the roles of wife and mother. From this point of view, Adams' female characters are victims of that culture, dependent on men and falling desperately in love with them because they were expected to do just that. Given these crushing expectations, it is no wonder that Adams' heroines feel lost when bereft, by divorce or widowhood, of the men in their lives. The young people in these stories often reach out to surrogate parents, usually mothers, when the incredible strain on the postwar nuclear family cracks and splinters it (someone in "Roses, Rhododendrons," in *Beautiful Girl*, says "we all need more than one set of parents—our relations with the original set are too intense, and need dissipating").

Emblematic of the plight of this generation is Ardis Bascombe in "Beautiful Girl," an ironic title because Ardis, though in her youth beautiful and popular, is now fleshy, drinking herself to death in her San Francisco apartment, failed as a wife and, as her filthy kitchen attests, failed as a homemaker. She had been independent enough to leave her unhappy, marriage, but like other women of her generation, despite her intelligence, idealism, courage, and sophistication, she was unable to make a new life. The life of this beautiful girl demonstrates graphically the destructive pressures on postwar women.

Adams' stories, then, present a composite portrait of women struggling with the pressures and pain of a particular moment in history. In their intensely personal ways, they accommodate themselves to their circumstances, but with varying degrees of success. The time frames of Adams' stories and Adams' own writing career, moreover, suggest that with the passage of time comes hope. "Beautiful Girl," after all, in which one finds the helplessness of Ardis Bascombe's middle age, is from the earliest volume of stories, while "A Public Pool" is from a later volume and depicts a woman of a later generation. Looking at Alice Adams' stories together teaches one that women, and American society in general, have emerged from the grim reality of Ardis' grimy kitchen to that extraordinary moment when the woman from "A Public Pool," once almost pathologically shy, considers a man's offer of a cup of coffee and exercises a splendid freedom in refusing.

Other major works

NOVELS: *Careless Love*, 1966; *Families and Survivors*, 1974; *Listening to Billie*, 1978; *Rich Rewards*, 1980; *Superior Women*, 1984; *Second Chances*, 1988; *Caroline's Daughters*, 1991; *Almost Perfect*, 1993; *A Southern Exposure*, 1995; *Medicine Men*, 1997.

NONFICTION: *Mexico: Some Travels and Some Travelers There*, 1990.

Bibliography

Adams, Alice. "PW Interviews Alice Adams." Interview by Patricia Holt. *Publishers Weekly* 213 (January 16, 1978): 8-9. In talking about her life with interior designer Robert McNee, Adams emphasizes the importance of her work as the foundation for the self-respect necessary in a long-term relationship.

Blades, L. T. "Order and Chaos in Alice Adams' *Rich Rewards*." *Critique: Studies in Modern Fiction* 27 (Summer, 1986): 187-195. In an issue devoted to four women writers—Adams, Ann Beattie, Mary Gordon, and Marge Piercy—Blades explores the artificially imposed order created by Adams' female characters and the world of chaos that threatens it. Like Jane Austen's characters, Adams' women enter into unstable relationships but eventually realize that they must concentrate on work and friendships, not romance, to have a healthy self-respect.

Chell, Cara. "Succeeding in Their Times: Alice Adams on Women and Work." *Soundings* 68 (Spring, 1985): 62-71. Work is the catalyst that enables Adams' characters to realize their self-worth. Chell provides an interesting treatment of this theme throughout Adams' career.

Flower, Dean. "Picking Up the Pieces." *The Hudson Review* 32 (Summer, 1979): 293-307. Flower sets Adams among other American storytellers who look to the past for explanations and intensification of feelings. He explores how this orientation leads to a preoccupation with growing old.

Pritchard, William H. "Fictive Voices." *The Hudson Review* 38 (Spring, 1985): 120-132. Pritchard examines Adams' narrative voice in the context of other contemporary writers. Though the section on Adams is not long, it provides a useful approach to analyzing her stories.

Upton, Lee. "Changing the Past: Alice Adams' Revisionary Nostalgia."
Studies in Short Fiction 26 (Winter, 1989): 33-41. In the collection of
stories *Return Trips*, Adams' female characters turn to memories of the
past as their most valued possessions. Upton isolates three different
relationships with the past and shows how each enables Adams' characters to interpret nostalgic images so that they produce more satisfying
relationships with the present.

Timothy C. Frazer
(Revised by *Louise M. Stone*)

CONRAD AIKEN

Born: Savannah, Georgia; August 5, 1889
Died: Savannah, Georgia; August 17, 1973

Principal short fiction · *Bring! Bring! and Other Stories*, 1925 · *Costumes by Eros*, 1928 · *Among the Lost People*, 1934 · *Short Stories*, 1950 · *Collected Short Stories*, 1960 · *Collected Short Stories of Conrad Aiken*, 1966

Other literary forms · Best-known as a poet, Conrad Aiken published dozens of volumes of poetry from 1914 until his death in 1973. He also published novels, essays, criticism, and a play. In addition, he edited a considerable number of anthologies of poetry.

Achievements · Aiken's reputation as a writer of short fiction rests on two frequently anthologized short stories: "Silent Snow, Secret Snow," which has twice been adapted to film, and "Mr. Arcularis," which was adapted to a play. Although he published several collections of short stories–they were collected in one volume in 1950–he did not contribute significantly to the development of the short story. Instead, the fictional "voice" so closely approximates Aiken's poetic "voice" that the stories are often seen as extensions of his more famous poems. Both are "poetic" expressions of characters' psychological states. "Silent Snow, Secret Snow," in fact, is often read as the story of a creative artist, a "poet" in a hostile environment. His Freudian themes, his depiction of a protagonist's inner struggle and journey, and his portrait of the consciousness–these are perhaps better expressed in lengthy poetic works than in prose or in individual poems, which are rarely anthologized because they are best read in the context of his other poems.

Biography · When Conrad Aiken was eleven, his father killed his mother and then committed suicide. This incident could very well have influenced the subject matter of a great number of his stories, where one step more may take a character to an immense abyss of madness or death. Graduating from Harvard University in 1911, Aiken became a member of the famous Harvard group which included T. S. Eliot, Robert Benchley, and Van Wyck Brooks. He published his first volume of poems in 1914. A contributing editor of *The Dial* from 1917 to 1919, Aiken later worked as London correspondent for *The New Yorker*. Through the course of his career he was the recipient of many awards, including the Pulitzer Prize in 1930 for *Selected Poems* (1929), the National Book Award in 1954 for *Collected Poems* (1953), and the Bollingen Prize in Poetry in 1956. He died in 1973 at the age of eighty-four.

Analysis · In "Silent Snow, Secret Snow," a story once included in almost every anthology of short fiction, Aiken describes a young boy's alienation and withdrawal from his world. The story begins one morning in December when Paul Hasleman, aged twelve, thinks of the postman, whom the boy hears every morning. The progress of the postman as he turns the corner at the top of the hill and makes his way down the street with a double knock at each door is familiar to the boy, and, as he slowly awakens, he begins to listen for the sounds on the cobblestones of the street of heavy boots as they come around the corner. When the sounds come on this morning, however, they are closer than the corner and muffled and faint. Paul understands at once: "Nothing could have been simpler—there had been snow during the night, such as all winter he had been longing for." With his eyes still closed, Paul imagines the snow—how it sounds and how it will obliterate the familiar sights of the street—but when he opens his eyes and turns toward the window, he sees only the bright morning sun. The miracle of snow has not transformed anything.

The moment and his feelings about the snow, however, remain with him, and later in the classroom as his geography teacher, Miss Buell, twirls the globe with her finger and talks about the tropics, Paul finds himself looking at the arctic areas, which are colored white on the globe. He recalls the morning and the moment when he had a sense of falling snow, and immediately he undergoes the same experience of seeing and hearing the snow fall.

As the days go by, Paul finds himself between two worlds—the real one and a secret one of peace and remoteness. His parents become increasingly concerned by his "daydreaming," inattentive manner, but more and more he is drawn into the incomprehensible beauty of the world of silent snow. His secret sense of possession and of being protected insulates him both from the world of the classroom where Deidre, with the freckles on the back of her neck in a constellation exactly like the Big Dipper, waves her brown flickering hand and from the world at home where his parents' concern and questions have become an increasingly difficult matter with which to cope.

Aiken's presentation of the escalation of Paul's withdrawal is skillfully detailed through the use of symbols. The outside world becomes for Paul fragmented: scraps of dirty newspapers in a drain, with the word Eczema as the addressee, and an address in Fort Worth, Texas; lost twigs from parent trees; bits of broken egg shells; the footprints of a dog who long ago "had made a mistake" and walked on the river of wet cement, which in time had frozen into rock; the wound in an elm tree. In the company of his parents Paul neither sees them nor feels their presence. His mother is a voice asking questions, his father a pair of brown slippers. These images cluster together in such a way as to foreshadow the inevitable and relentless progress of Dr. Howells down the street to Paul's house, a visit which replicates the progress of the postman.

The doctor, called by the parents because their concern has now grown into alarm over Paul's behavior, examines the boy, and, as the examination and questioning by the adults accelerate, Paul finds the situation unbearable. He retreats further into his secret world where he sees snow now slowly filling the spaces in the room—highest in the corners, under the sofa—the snow's voice a whisper, a promise of peace, cold and restful. Reassured by the presence of the snow and seduced by its whisperings and promises, Paul begins to laugh and to taunt the adults with little hints. He believes they are trying to corner him, and there is something malicious in his behavior:

> He laughed a third time—but this time, happening to glance upward toward his mother's face, he was appalled at the effect his laughter seemed to have upon her. Her mouth had opened in an expression of horror. . . . This was too bad! Unfortunate! He had known it would cause pain, of course—but he hadn't expected it to be quite as bad as this. . . .

The hints, however, explain nothing to the adults, and, continuing to feel cornered, Paul pleads a headache and tries to escape to bed. His mother follows him, but it is too late. "The darkness was coming in long white waves," and "the snow was laughing; it spoke from all sides at once." His mother's presence in the room is alien, hostile, and brutal. He is filled with loathing, and he exorcises her: "Mother! Mother! Go away! I hate you!" With this effort, everything is solved, "everything became all right." His withdrawal is now complete. All contact with the real world is lost, and he gives himself over to a "vast moving screen of snow—but even now it said peace, it said remoteness, it said cold, it said sleep." Paul's withdrawal is, as the snow tells him, a going inward rather than an opening outward: "it is a flower becoming a seed," it is a movement toward complete solipsism and a closure of his life.

"Strange Moonlight," another story of a young boy's difficulty in dealing with the realities of life and death, could be a prelude to "Silent Snow,

Secret Snow." In "Strange Moonlight" a young boy filches a copy of Edgar Allan Poe's tales from his mother's bookshelf and in consequence spends a "delirious night in inferno." The next day the boy wins a gold medal at school which he later carries in his pocket, keeping it a secret from his mother and father. The desire to keep a secret recalls Paul's need to keep from his parents his first hallucination of snow. The gold medal is "above all a secret," something to be kept concealed; it is like a particularly beautiful trinket to be carried unmentioned in his trouser pocket.

The week's events include a visit to a friend's house where the boy meets Caroline Lee, an extraordinarily strange and beautiful child with large pale eyes. Both Caroline Lee and the house in which she lives with its long, dark, and winding stairways excite and fascinate him. Within a few days, however, the boy learns that Caroline Lee is dead of scarlet fever. He is stunned: ". . . how did it happen that he, who was so profoundly concerned, had not been consulted, had not been invited to come and talk with her, and now found himself so utterly and hopelessly and forever excluded—from the house as from her?" This becomes a thing he cannot understand.

The same night he is confronted with another disturbing mystery. He overhears an intimate conversation between his father and mother. Filled with horror, the boy begins at once to imagine a conversation with Caroline Lee in which she comes back from the grave to talk with him. The next day his father unexpectedly takes the family to the beach, and the boy wanders away and finds a snug, secret hiding place on a lonely hot sand dune. He lies there surrounded by tall whispering grass, and Caroline's imagined visit of the night before becomes real for him. Rather than ending in unreality as one would expect, however, Aiken inexplicably brings the boy back to reality without resolving any of the problems set up in the story. He thus leaves a gap between the protagonist's conflicts with sexuality, reality, and unreality, and their final resolution.

In another story, however, "Your Obituary, Well Written," Aiken presents a young man identified only as Mr. Grant who confronts a similar circumstance. Told in the first person by the protagonist, Mr. Grant, the story repeats what is basically the same pattern of events. Although supposedly a portrait of Katherine Mansfield to whom Aiken is strongly indebted for the forms his stories take, the character of Reiner Wilson is also strongly reminiscent of Caroline Lee, the little girl in "Strange Moonlight." The narrator says of Reiner Wilson: "I was struck by the astonishing frailty of her appearance, an otherworld fragility, almost a transparent spiritual quality—as if she were already a disembodied soul." Knowing from the first that she is not only married but also fatally ill, he manages to see her one time and fall in love with her, and then he almost simultaneously withdraws. "At bottom, however, it was a kind of terror that kept me away. . . . The complications and the miseries, if we did allow the meetings to go further might well be fatal to both of us."

The same conflicts which Paul, the child in "Silent Snow, Secret Snow," experienced are again faced by the man who is not able to resolve the riddles of sex and love, life and death. The narrator never sees Reiner again, and at her death he is left on a park bench under a Judas tree wanting to weep, but unable to: "but Reiner Wilson, the dark-haired little girl with whom I had fallen in love was dead, and it seemed to me that I too was dead." Another similarity between "Silent Snow, Secret Snow" and "Your Obituary, Well Written" is Aiken's use of a natural element as a major metaphor. In "Your Obituary, Well Written," rain functions in the same manner that snow does in "Silent Snow, Secret Snow." During Grant's one meeting alone with Reiner Wilson, the room had suddenly darkened and rain fell, sounding to him as though it were inside the room. The sensations the man feels in response to the rain are similar to those Paul feels in response to the snow. Grant tells Reiner about a time when as a boy he went swimming and it began to rain:

> The water was smooth—there was no sound of waves—and all about me arose a delicious *seething*. . . . [T]here was something sinister in it, and also something divinely soothing. . . . I don't believe I was ever happier in my life. It was as if I had gone into another world.

Reiner calls Grant "the man who loves rain," and her estimate of him is correct. Unable to open up himself, unable to make himself vulnerable and live in the real world, he is at the end of the story as withdrawn from reality as is Paul who chooses the silent and secret snow.

Besides dealing with various subconscious desires projected by means of hallucinating visions, many of Aiken's stories reflect preoccupations of the times in which the stories were written. Chief among these themes is the changing roles of women and sexual mores of the 1920's. In most of Aiken's stories, these conflicts are presented through the male point of view.

"Thistledown," a first-person narrative told by a man who is married and living with his wife, opens with private musings of the narrator, wherein he associates a young woman named Coralyn with thistledown which is being swept in every direction by the wind but which is ultimately doomed for extinction. Coralyn had been his wife's secretary, and, attracted to her, Phillip, the narrator, became bent on seduction. Far from being "frighteningly unworldly," Coralyn is a "new woman" who has had numerous lovers. He finds her cynical and detached, she finds him an old-fashioned and sentimental fool. The affair is brief. Coralyn leaves, and as the years pass she is in and out of his life, until she disappears altogether, leaving him bitter, disappointed, and angry. The irony that marks "Thistledown" is characteristic of the stories in which Aiken examines the conventional sexual mores, holding a doublefaced mirror to reflect the double standard by which men and women are judged.

In "A Conversation," this theme of double standards is examined within the framework of a conversation between two men, probably professors, taking place on a train in a sleeping car. The conversation is overheard by a visiting lecturer at the University who occupies the adjacent sleeping car. The lecturer is tired of "being polite to fools" and wants desperately to go to sleep; but the conversation he overhears keeps him awake, as do clock bells that ring marking every quarter hour. The conversation concerns the fiancé of one of the men, and the other is trying to convince his friend that the woman is not as innocent as she looks; indeed, she has been "manhandled." The engaged man keeps trying to protect his own views of the woman: her central idealism, her essential holiness—views that attach themselves to women who are not prostitutes. By the end of the story, however, the point is made; the engagement will not last, and the woman will be put aside like a used razor or a cork that has been tampered with, images used earlier in the story. The clock bells do not ask a question; they simply continue to toll. In the end, the men cannot accept a female sexuality which is not exclusively directed toward a husband although there is never a question about their own sexual behavior.

Other major works

NOVELS: *Blue Voyage*, 1927; *Great Circle*, 1933; *King Coffin*, 1935; *A Heart for the Gods of Mexico*, 1939; *Conversation: Or, Pilgrim's Progress*, 1940; *The Collected Novels of Conrad Aiken*, 1964.

PLAYS: *Fear No More*, 1946; *Mr. Arcularis: A Play*, 1957.

POETRY: *Earth Triumphant and Other Tales in Verse*, 1914; *Turns and Movies and Other Tales in Verse*, 1916; *The Jig of Forslin*, 1916; *Nocturne of Remembered Spring and Other Poems*, 1917; *The Charnel Rose*, 1918; *Senlin: A Biography and Other Poems*, 1918; *The House of Dust*, 1920; *Punch: The Immortal Liar*, 1921; *Priapus and the Pool*, 1922; *The Pilgrimage of Festus*, 1923; *Changing Mind*, 1925; *Priapus and the Pool and Other Poems*, 1925; *Prelude*, 1929; *Selected Poems*, 1929; *John Deth: A Metaphysical Legend, and Other Poems*, 1930; *Gehenna*, 1930; *The Coming Forth by Day of Osiris Jones*, 1931; *Preludes for Memnon*, 1931; *And in the Hanging Gardens*, 1933; *Landscape West of Eden*, 1934; *Time in the Rock: Preludes to Definition*, 1936; *And in the Human Heart*,

1940; *Brownstone Eclogues and Other Poems*, 1942; *The Soldier: A Poem by Conrad Aiken*, 1944; *The Kid*, 1947; *Skylight One: Fifteen Poems*, 1949; *The Divine Pilgrim*, 1949; *Wake II*, 1952; *Collected Poems*, 1953, 1970; *A Letter from Li Po and Other Poems*, 1955; *The Fluteplayer*, 1956; *Sheepfold Hill: Fifteen Poems*, 1958; *Selected Poems*, 1961; *The Morning Song of Lord Zero*, 1963; *A Seizure of Limericks*, 1964; *Cats and Bats and Things with Wings: Poems*, 1965; *The Clerk's Journal*, 1971; *A Little Who's Zoo of Mild Animals*, 1977.

NONFICTION: *Skepticisms: Notes on Contemporary Poetry*, 1919; *Ushant: An Essay*, 1952; *A Reviewer's ABC: Collected Criticism of Conrad Aiken from 1916 to the Present*, 1958; *Selected Letters of Conrad Aiken*, 1978.

ANTHOLOGIES: *A Comprehensive Anthology of American Poetry*, 1929, 1944; *Twentieth Century American Poetry*, 1944.

Bibliography

Aiken, Conrad. *Selected Letters of Conrad Aiken*. Edited by Joseph Killorin. New Haven, Conn.: Yale University Press, 1978. Killorin includes a representative sample of 245 letters (from some three thousand) written by Aiken. A cast of correspondents, among them T. S. Eliot and Malcolm Lowry, indexes to Aiken's works and important personages, and a wealth of illustrations, mostly photographs, add considerably to the value of the volume.

Butscher, Edward. *Conrad Aiken: Poet of White Horse Vale*. Athens: University of Georgia Press, 1988. This critical biography emphasizes Aiken's literary work, particularly the poetry. Butscher's book nevertheless contains analyses of about fifteen Aiken short stories, including his most famous ones, "Silent Snow, Secret Snow" and "Mr. Arcularis." Includes many illustrations, copious notes, and an extensive bibliography that is especially helpful in psychoanalytic theory.

Hoffman, Frederick J. *Conrad Aiken*. New York: Twayne, 1962. The best overview of Aiken's short fiction. Hoffman's volume contains careful analyses of several individual stories, including "Mr. Arcularis," which receives extensive discussion. Hoffman, who believes Aiken's short stories are more successful than his novels, stresses Aiken's attitude toward New England, his obsession with "aloneness," and his concern about human relationships. Contains a chronology, a biographical chapter, and an annotated bibliography.

Lorenz, Clarissa M. *Lorelei Two: My Life with Conrad Aiken*. Athens: University of Georgia Press, 1983. Lorenz, Aiken's second wife, discusses the 1926-1938 years, the period when he wrote his best work, including the short stories "Mr. Arcularis" and "Silent Snow, Secret Snow." She covers his literary acquaintances, his work habits, and the literary context in which he worked. The book is well indexed and contains several relevant photographs.

Seigel, Catherine F. *The Fictive World of Conrad Aiken.* DeKalb, Ill.: Northern Illinois University Press, 1993.

Spivey, Ted R., and Arthur Waterman, eds. *Conrad Aiken: A Priest of Consciousness.* New York: AMS Press, 1989. Though their focus is on Aiken's poetry, Spivey and Waterman include essays on the short stories and a review of criticism of the short stories. Contains an extensive chronology of Aiken's life and a lengthy description of the Aiken materials in the Huntington Library.

Mary Rohrberger
(Revised by *Thomas L. Erskine*)

HANS CHRISTIAN ANDERSEN

Born: Odense, Denmark; April 2, 1805
Died: Copenhagen, Denmark; August 4, 1875

Principal short fiction · *Eventyr*, 1835-1872 (*The Complete Andersen*, 1949; also *Fairy Tales*, 1950-1958; also *The Complete Fairy Tales and Stories*, 1974) · *It's Perfectly True and Other Stories*, 1937 · *Andersen's Fairy Tales*, 1946 · *Hans Andersen's Fairy Tales*, 1953

Other literary forms · Hans Christian Andersen's first publication was a poem in 1828, and his first prose work, a fantasy of a nightly journey titled *Fodreise fra Holmens Canal til Østpynten af Amager* (1829; a journey on foot from Holman's canal to the east point of Amager), was an immediate success. He wrote six novels, of which *Improvisatoren* (1835; *The Improvisatore*, 1845) securely established his fame. His nine travel books began with *En digters bazar* (1842; *A Poet's Bazaar*, 1846) and mainly concern his European travels. Other works are *Billebog uden billeder* (1840; *Tales the Moon Can Tell*, 1855) and *I Sverrig* (1851; *In Sweden*, 1852). His autobiographies are *Levnedsbogen, 1805-1831* (1926; *Diaries of Hans Christian Andersen*, 1990), discovered fifty years after his death; *Mit Livs Eventyr* (1847; *The Story of My Life*, 1852); and the revised *The Fairy Tale of My Life* (1855). Other publications include his correspondence, diaries, notebooks and draft material, drawings, sketches, paper cuttings, and plays.

Achievements · Although hailed as the greatest of all fairy-tale writers in any language, throughout most of his life, Andersen considered his fairy tales to be of far less importance than his other writings. He considered himself much more of a novelist, playwright, and writer of travel books. It was his fairy tales, however, that spread his fame across Europe and, immediately upon publication, were translated into every European language. Andersen was much more famous, courted, and honored abroad than in his native Denmark. In his later years, however, his own compatriots did at last recognize Andersen's greatness. He became a friend and guest to royalty, was made a state councillor, and had a touching tribute paid to him in the form of the statue of the Little Mermaid, which sits in the Copenhagen harbor.

Biography · The son of a shoemaker, who died when Hans Christian Andersen was eleven, and an illiterate servant mother, Andersen from his early childhood loved to invent tales, poems, and plays and to make intricate paper cuttings; he loved to recite his creations to any possible listener. Later he yearned to be a *Digter*, a creative writer of divine inspiration, and to be an actor. In 1819 he journeyed to Copenhagen where he lived through hard times but developed a talent for attracting benefactors. Among them was Jonas Collin, whose home became Andersen's "Home of Homes," as he called it, who acted as a foster father, and whose son Edvard became a close friend. Through Jonas' influence and a grant from the king, Andersen attended grammar school (1822-1827) and struggled with a difficult headmaster as well as with Latin and Greek. Andersen never married, although he was attracted to several women, among them the singer Jenny Lind. Although he was very tall and ungainly in appearance, with large feet, a large nose, and small eyes, and although he was sentimental and exceptionally concerned with himself, his fears and doubts, Andersen enjoyed the company of Europe's leading professionals and nobility, including kings and queens; in later life many honors were bestowed upon him. His last nine years he lived at the home of the Moritz Melchiors, just outside Copenhagen, and he died there on August 4, 1875.

Analysis · Following publication of his 1844 collection of tales, Hans Christian Andersen explained in a letter that he wanted his tales to be read on two levels, offering something for the minds of adults as well as appealing to children. Three examples of such adult tales, "The Snow Queen," "The Shadow," and "The Nightingale," demonstrate how, as Andersen said, in writing from his own breast instead of retelling old tales he had now found out how to write fairy tales.

Composed of seven stories, "The Snow Queen" begins with a mirror into which people can look and see the good become small and mean and the bad appear at its very worst. Andersen could remember, in later years, that his father had maintained that "There is no other devil than the one we have in our hearts"; this provides a clue to the plot and theme of "The Snow Queen." Only when the demon's followers confront heaven with the mirror does it shatter into fragments, but unfortunately those fragments enter the hearts of many people.

The second story introduces Little Kay and Gerda who love each other and the summer's flowers until a fragment of the evil mirror lodges in Little Kay's eye and another pierces his heart. Having formerly declared that if the Snow Queen visited he would melt her on the stove, Kay now views snowflakes through a magnifying glass and pronounces them more beautiful than flowers. He protests against the grandmother's tales with a *but* for the logic of each one, and, apparently arrived at adolescence, transfers loyalty from the innocent Gerda to the knowing Snow Queen. He follows the visiting Queen out of town and into the snowy expanses of the distant sky.

The journey from adolescence to maturity becomes for Gerda her quest for the missing Kay, her true love and future mate. Fearing the river has taken Kay, she offers it her new red shoes; but a boat she steps into drifts away from shore and, riding the river's current, she travels far before being pulled ashore and detained by a woman "learned in magic." Gerda here forgets her search for Kay until the sight of a rose reminds her. In one of the story's most abstract passages, she then asks the tiger lilies, convolvulus, snowdrop, hyacinth, buttercup, and narcissus where he might be, but each tells a highly fanciful tale concerned with its own identity. The narcissus, for example, alludes to the Echo and Narcissus myth in saying "I can see myself" and fails to aid Gerda. Barefoot, Gerda runs out of the garden and finds that autumn has arrived.

A crow believes he has seen Kay and contrives a visit with the Prince and Princess, who forgive the invasion of their palatial privacy and then outfit Gerda to continue her search. All her newly acquired equipage attracts a "little robber girl," a perplexing mixture of amorality and good intentions, who threatens Gerda with her knife but provides a reindeer to carry Gerda to Spitsbergen, where the wood pigeons have reported having seen Kay. At one stop, the reindeer begs a Finnish wise woman to give Gerda the strength to conquer all, but the woman points out the great power that Gerda has already evidenced and adds, "We must not tell her what power she has. It is in her heart, because she is such a sweet innocent child." She sends Gerda and the reindeer on their way, with Gerda riding without boots or mittens. Eventually the reindeer deposits her by a redberry bush in freezing icebound Denmark, from which she walks to the Snow Queen's palace.

Here she finds a second mirror, a frozen lake broken into fragments but actually the throne of the Snow Queen which the Queen calls "The Mirror of Reason." Little Kay works diligently to form the fragments into the word "Eternity," for which accomplishment the Snow Queen has said he can be his own master and have the whole world and a new pair of skates. Gerda's love, when she sheds tears of joy at finding Kay, melts the ice in his heart and the mirror within his breast; Kay, himself bursting into tears at recovering Gerda and her love, finds that the fragments magically form themselves into the word "Eternity." The two young people find many changes on their return journey, but much the same at home, where they now realize they are grown up. The grandmother's Bible verse tells them about the kingdom of heaven for those with hearts of children, and they now understand the meaning of the hymn, "Where roses deck the flowery vale,/There Infant Jesus, thee we hail!" The flowers of love, not the mirror of reason, make Kay and Gerda inheritors of the kingdom of heaven, the Snow Queen's elusive eternity.

Only the style makes such stories children's stories, for "The Snow Queen," with devices such as the snowflakes seen under a microscope, obviously attacks empiricism; at the same time, the story offers the symbol of the foot, important to folklore; and the journey of Gerda through obstacles and a final illumination compose a "journey of the hero" as delineated by the mythologist Joseph Campbell. So also Andersen's "The Shadow" presents an alter-ego with psychic dimensions well beyond the ken of children.

The setting with which "The Shadow" begins reflects Andersen's diary entries from his trip to Naples in June, 1846, when he found the sun too hot for venturing out of doors and began writing the story. With the hot sun directly overhead, the shadow disappears, except in morning and evening, and begins to assume a life of its own. Its activities, closely observed by its owner, the "learned man from a cold country," leads him to joke about its going into the house opposite to learn the identity of a lovely maiden. The shadow fails to return, but the learned man soon grows a new shadow. Many years later, once more at home, the original shadow visits him but has now become so corporeal that it has acquired flesh and clothes. Further, it divulges, it has become wealthy and plans to marry. Its three-week visit in the house opposite, it now reveals, placed it close to the lovely maiden Poetry, in whose anteroom the shadow read all the poetry and prose ever written. If the learned man had been there, he would not have remained a human being, but it was there that the shadow became one. Emerging thence he went about under the cover of a pastry cook's gown for some time before growing into his present affluence.

Later, the learned man's writing of the good, the true, and the beautiful fails to provide him an income; only after he has suffered long and become so thin that people tell him he looks like a shadow does he accede to the shadow's request that he become a traveling companion. Shadow and master have now exchanged places, but the king's daughter notices that the new master cannot cast a shadow. To this accusation he replies that the person who is always at his side is his shadow. When the new master cannot answer her scientific inquiries, he defers to the shadow, whose knowledge impresses the princess. Clearly, she reasons, to have such a learned servant the master must be the most learned man on earth.

Against the upcoming marriage of princess and shadow, the learned man protests and threatens to reveal the truth. "Not a soul would believe you," says the shadow, and with his new status as fiancé he has the learned man cast into prison. The princess agrees that it would be a charity to deliver the learned man from his delusions and has him promptly executed.

That Poetry would make a human being divine or "more than human" gives Poetry the identity of Psyche, whose statue by Thorvaldsen Andersen had admired in 1833 in the Danish sculptor's studio. (Also, Andersen in 1861 wrote a story called "The Psyche.") In "The Shadow," the human qualities with which Poetry's presence infuses the shadow function for him as a soul. Thereafter, his incubation under the pastry cook's gown provides him a proper maturation from which, still as shadow, he looks into people's lives, spies on their evils and their intimacies, and acquires power over them. This phase of his existence explains the acquisition of wealth, but as the shadow grows human and powerful the learned man declines.

The shadow, the other self of the learned man, reflects the psychic stress Andersen suffered in his relationship with Edvard Collin. What Andersen desired between himself and Collin has been recognized by scholars as the *Blütbruderschaft* that D. H. Lawrence wrote about–a close relationship with another male. Collin persisted, however, in fending off all Andersen's attempts at informality, even in regard to the use of language; in the story, the shadow is obviously Collin, whose separate identity thrives at the expense of the learned man's–Andersen's–psyche. Writing in his diary of the distress and illness brought on by a letter from Edvard Collin, Andersen contemplated suicide and pleaded "he must use the language of a friend" (1834); so also the story's shadow rejects such language and commits the learned man to prison and to death. The problem of language appears twice in the story, although various translations diminish its effect. The shadow's newly acquired affluence, on his first visit to his former master, provides him with the daring to suggest that the learned man speak "less familiarly," and to say "sir," or–in other translations–to replace "you" with "thee" and "thou." Frequently argued between Andersen and Collin as the question of *"Du"* versus *"De,"* the problem reappears in the story when the learned man asks the shadow, because of their childhood together, to pledge themselves to address each other as *"Du."* (In some translations, this reads merely "to drink to our good fellowship" and "call each other by our names.") In the shadow's reply, Andersen improved upon Collin's objection by having the shadow cite the feel of gray paper or the scraping of a nail on a pane of glass as similar to the sound of *"Du"* spoken by the learned man.

Such touches of individuality made Andersen's writing succeed, as evidenced by a tale he borrowed from a Spanish source, the tale of "The Emperor's New Clothes," which he said he read in a German translation from Prince don Juan Manuel (1282-c. 1349). Andersen's version improved upon the original in several respects, including his theme of pretense of understanding as well as ridicule of snobbery and his ending with the objection of the child—an ending which Andersen added after the original manuscript had been sent to the publisher.

Andersen's talent for universalizing the appeal of a story and for capitalizing on personal experiences appears time and again throughout his many tales. Because of his grotesque appearance, which interfered with his longed-for stage career, Andersen knew personally the anguish of "The Ugly Duckling," but his success as a writer made him a beautiful swan. His extreme sensitivity he wrote into "The Princess and the Pea," detailing the adventures of a princess who could feel a pea through twenty mattresses. Andersen in this story borrowed from a folktale in which the little girl understands the test she is being put to because a dog or cat aids her by relaying the information, but Andersen contrived that her sensitivity alone would suffice. Nevertheless some translators could not accept the idea of her feeling a single pea and changed the text to read three peas and the title to read "The Real Princess."

Andersen's stories thus objectify psychic conditions, and among these his frequent association with nobility enabled him to depict with humor the qualities of egotism, arrogance, and subservience found at court. In "The Snow Queen" the crow describes court ladies and attendants standing around, and the nearer to the door they stand the greater is their haughtiness; the footman's boy is too proud to be looked at. The princess is so clever she has read all the newspapers in the world and forgotten them again.

One of Andersen's best depictions of court life and, at the same time, one of his best satires is "The Nightingale," which he wrote in honor of Jenny Lind, the singer known as the Swedish Nightingale. The story's theme contrasts the artificial manners and preferences of the court with the natural song of the nightingale and the ways of simple folk. Far from the palace of the Emperor of China where bells on the flowers in the garden tinkle to attract attention to the flowers, the nightingale sings in the woods by the deep sea, so that a poor fisherman listens to it each day and travelers returning home write about it. The Emperor discovers this nightingale from reading about it in a book, but his gentleman-in-waiting knows nothing about it because it has never been presented at court. Inquiring throughout the court, he finds only a little girl in the kitchen who has heard it and who helps him find it. Brought to the court, it must sing on a golden perch, and, when acclaimed successful, it has its own cage and can walk out twice a day and once in the night with twelve footmen, each one holding a ribbon tied around its leg.

When the Emperor of Japan sends as a gift an artificial nightingale studded with diamonds, rubies, and sapphires, the two birds cannot sing together and the real nightingale flies away in chagrin. The court throng honors the mechanical bird with jewels and gold as gifts, and the Master of Music writes twenty-five volumes about it. The mechanical bird earns the title of Chief Imperial Singer-of-the-Bed-Chamber, and in rank it stands number one on the left side, for even an Emperor's heart is on the left side.

Eventually the mechanical bird breaks down, and the watchmaker cannot assure repair with the same admirable tune. Five years later the Emperor becomes ill, and his successor is proclaimed. Then, with Death sitting on his chest and wearing his golden crown, he calls upon the mechanical bird to sing. While it sits mute, the nightingale appears at the window and sings Death away and brings new life to the Emperor. With the generosity of a true heroine, it advises the king not to destroy the mechanical bird, which did all the good it could; however, it reminds the Emperor, a little singing bird sings to the fisherman and the peasant and must continue to go and to return. Although it loves the Emperor's heart more than his crown, the crown has an odor of sanctity also. The nightingale will return, but the Emperor must keep its secret that a little bird tells him everything.

Andersen's comment comparing the heart and the crown of the emperor may be his finest on the attraction of the great, an attraction which he felt all his life. Early in 1874, after visiting a count in South Zealand, he wrote to Mrs. Melchior that no fairy tales occurred to him any more. If he walks in the garden, he said, Thumbelina has ended her journey on the water lily; the wind and the Old Oak Tree have already told him their tales and have nothing more to tell him. It is, he wrote, as if he had filled out the entire circle with fairy-tale radii close to one another. On his seventieth birthday, April 2, 1875, the royal carriage was sent to fetch him to the castle, and the king bestowed another decoration. It was his last birthday celebration, for in a few months Andersen had filled out the circle of his life.

Other major works

NOVELS: *Improvisatoren*, 1835 (2 volumes; *The Improvisatore*, 1845); *O. T.*, 1836 (English translation, 1845); *Kun en Spillemand*, 1837 (*Only a Fiddler*, 1845); *De To Baronesser*, 1848 (*The Two Baronesses*, 1848); *At være eller ikke være*, 1857 (*To Be or Not to Be*, 1857); *Lykke-Peer*, 1870.

PLAYS: *Kjærlighed paa Nicolai Taarn: Elle, Hvad siger Parterret*, 1829; *Agnete og havmanden*, 1833; *Mulatten*, 1840.

POETRY: *Digte*, 1830.

NONFICTION: *Skyggebilleder af en reise til Harzen, det sachiske Schweitz,* 1831 *(Rambles in the Romantic Regions of the Hartz Mountains, Saxon Switzerland etc.,* 1848); *Billebog uden billeder,* 1840 *(Tales the Moon Can Tell,* 1855); *En digters bazar,* 1842 *(A Poet's Bazaar,* 1846); *Mit Livs Eventyr,* 1847 *(The Story of My Life,* 1852); *I Sverrig,* 1851 *(In Sweden,* 1852); *The Fairy Tale of My Life,* 1855; *I Spanien,* 1863 *(In Spain,* 1864); *Et besøg i Portugal,* 1866 *(A Visit to Portugal,* 1870); *Levnedsbogen, 1805-1831,* 1926 *(Diaries of Hans Christian Andersen,* 1990). MISCELLANEOUS: *Fodreise fra Holmens Canal til Østpynten af Amager,* 1829; *The Collected Works of Hans Christian Andersen,* 1870-1884 (10 volumes).

Bibliography

Book, Frederik. *Hans Christian Andersen.* Norman: University of Oklahoma Press, 1962. This biography studies Andersen's personal and literary history. It considers how psychiatry, folklore, and the history of religion affected Andersen's life. Andersen's autobiographies are examined in the light of what was real and what was the fairy tale he was creating about his life. Contains illustrations of his fairy tales and photographs.

Bresdorff, Elias. *Hans Christian Andersen: The Story of His Life and Work, 1805-1875.* London: Phaidon Press, 1975, repr. 1994. This book is divided in two sections: the first part is a biographical study of Andersen's complex personality; the second is a critical study of his most famous fairy tales and stories.

Conroy, Patricia L., and Sven H. Rossel, eds. *The Diaries of Hans Christian Andersen.* Seattle: University of Washington Press, 1990. A wide selection of excerpts from Andersen's diaries written from as early as when he was a schoolboy and throughout the artist's life. Complete diaries from two trips to England are translated in entirety. Includes illustration of his drawings and paper cuttings, plus a useful bibliography.

Greene, Carol. *Hans Christian Andersen, Teller of Tales.* Chicago, Ill.: Childrens Press, 1986. A good choice for juveniles grades four through seven. It is part of the "People of Distinction Series."

Spink, Reginald. *Hans Christian Andersen and His World.* New York: G. P. Putnam's Sons, 1972. An excellent overview of Andersen's life. Emphasizes how his background and childhood affected his art. Extensively illustrated with photographs, drawings, and reprints of the illustrated fairy tales in several foreign-language editions.

Toksvig, Signe. *The Life of Hans Christian Andersen.* New York: Harcourt, Brace, 1934. An in-depth biography that provides valuable information in spite of its early publication date. Illustrated.

Grace Eckley
(Revised by *Leslie A. Pearl*)

SHERWOOD ANDERSON

Born: Camden, Ohio; September 13, 1876
Died: Colón, Panama Canal Zone; March 8, 1941

Principal short fiction · *Winesburg, Ohio,* 1919 · *The Triumph of the Egg,* 1921 · *Horses and Men,* 1923 · *Death in the Woods and Other Stories,* 1933 · *The Sherwood Anderson Reader,* 1947

Other literary forms · Sherwood Anderson published seven novels, collections of essays, memoirs, poetry, and dramatizations of *Winesburg, Ohio,* as well as other stories. He was a prolific article writer and for a time owned and edited both the Republican and Democratic newspapers in Marion, Virginia. In 1921, he received a two-thousand-dollar literary prize from *The Dial* magazine. While employed as a copywriter, Anderson wrote many successful advertisements.

Courtesy of the Library of Congress

25

Achievements · Sherwood Anderson, a protomodernist, is generally accepted as an innovator in the field of the short story despite having produced only one masterpiece, *Winesburg, Ohio.* In his work, he not only revolutionized the structure of short fiction by resisting the literary slickness of the contrived plot, but also he encouraged a simple and direct prose style, one which reflects the spare poetry of ordinary American speech. Anderson's thematic concerns were also innovative. He was one of the first writers to dramatize the artistic repudiation of the business world and to give the craft of the short story a decided push toward presenting a slice of life as a significant moment. His concern with the "grotesques" in society—the neurotics and eccentrics—is also innovative as is the straightforward attention he pays to his characters' sexuality. Anderson's contemporaries Ernest Hemingway, William Faulkner, and John Steinbeck were influenced by his work, as were several later writers: Carson McCullers, Flannery O'Connor, Saul Bellow, Bobbie Ann Mason, and Raymond Carver.

Biography · Sherwood Anderson was the third of seven children of a father who was an itinerant harness maker and house painter and a mother of either German or Italian descent. His father was a Civil War veteran (a Southerner who fought with the Union), locally famed as a storyteller. His elder brother, Karl, became a prominent painter who later introduced Sherwood to Chicago's bohemia, which gained him access to the literary world. Declining fortunes caused the family to move repeatedly until they settled in Clyde, Ohio (the model for Winesburg), a village just south of Lake Erie. The young Anderson experienced a desultory schooling and worked at several jobs: as a newsboy, a housepainter, a stableboy, a farmhand, and a laborer in a bicycle factory.

After serving in Cuba during the Spanish-American War (he saw no combat), he acquired a further year of schooling at Wittenberg Academy in Springfield, Ohio, but remained undereducated throughout his life. Jobs as an advertising copywriter gave him a first taste of writing, and he went on to a successful business career. In 1912, the central psychological event of his life occurred; he suffered a nervous breakdown, which led him to walk out of his paint factory in Elyria, Ohio. He moved to Chicago, where he began to meet writers such as Floyd Dell, Carl Sandburg, and Ben Hecht, a group collectively known as the Chicago Renaissance. A significant nonliterary contact was Dr. Trigant Burrow of Baltimore, who operated a Freudian therapeutic camp in Lake Chateaugay, New York, during the summers of 1915 and 1916. It should be noted, however, that Anderson ultimately rejected scientific probing of the psyche, for he typically believed that the human mind is static and incapable of meaningful change for the better. Publication of *Winesburg, Ohio* catapulted him into first prominence, and he traveled to Europe in 1921, where he became acquainted with Gertrude Stein, Ernest Hemingway, and James Joyce. In 1923, while living in New Orleans, he shared an apartment with William Faulkner.

Anderson married and divorced four times. He and his first wife had three children. His second wife, Tennessee Mitchell, had been a lover to Edgar Lee Masters, author of the *Spoon River Anthology* (1915). His last wife, Eleanor Copenhaver, had an interest in the Southern labor movement which drew Anderson somewhat out of his social primitivism, and, for a time in the 1930's, he became a favorite of communists and socialists. His death, in Colón, Panama Canal Zone, while on a voyage to South America, was notable for its unique circumstances: he died of peritonitis caused by a toothpick accidentally swallowed while eating hors d'œuvres.

Analysis · Sherwood Anderson's best-known and most important work is the American classic, *Winesburg, Ohio.* It is a collection of associated short stories set in the mythical town of Winesburg in the latter part of the nineteenth century. The stories catalog Anderson's negative reaction to the transformation of Ohio from a largely agricultural to an industrial society which culminated about the time he was growing up in the village of Clyde in the 1880's. Its twenty-five stories are vignettes of the town doctor; the voluble baseball coach; the still attractive but aging-with-loneliness high school teacher; the prosperous and harsh farmer-turned-religious fanatic; the dirt laborer; the hotel keeper, the banker's daughter, and her adolescent suitors; the Presbyterian minister struggling with temptation; the town drunk; the town rough; the town homosexual; and the town "half-wit." The comparison to Edgar Lee Masters' *Spoon River Anthology* is obvious: both works purport to reveal the secret lives of small-town Americans living in the Middle West, and ironically both owe their popular success to the elegiac recording of this era, which most Americans insist upon viewing idyllically. Anderson's work, however, differs by more directly relating sexuality to the bizarre behavior of many of his characters and by employing a coherent theme.

That theme is an exploration of psychological "grotesques"–the casualties of economic progress–and how these grotesques participate in the maturing of George Willard, the teenage reporter for the *Winesburg Eagle*, who at the end of the book departs for a bigger city to become a journalist. By then his sometimes callous ambition to get ahead has been tempered by a sense of what Anderson chooses to call "sophistication," the title of the penultimate story. The achievement of George's sophistication gives

Winesburg, Ohio its artistic movement but makes it problematic for many critics and thoughtful Americans.

The prefacing story defines grotesques. A dying old writer hires a carpenter to build up his bed so that he can observe the trees outside without getting out of it (while living in Chicago in 1915 Anderson had his own bed similarly raised so that he could observe the Loop). After the carpenter leaves, the writer returns to his project—the writing of "The Book of the Grotesque," which grieves over the notion that in the beginning of the world there were a great many thoughts but no such thing as a "truth." Men turned these thoughts into many beautiful truths such as the truth of passion, wealth, poverty, profligacy, carelessness, and others; a person could then appropriate a single one of these truths and try to live by it. It was thus that he or she would become a grotesque—a personality dominated by an overriding concern which in time squeezed out other facets of life.

This epistemological fable, which involves a triple-reduction, raises at least two invalidating questions: first, can there be "thoughts" without the truth to establish the self-differentiating process which generates thought, and second, if universals are denied and all truths have equal value (they are *all* beautiful), then why should a person be condemned for choosing only one of these pluralistic "truths"? Needless to say, these questions are not answered in *Winesburg, Ohio* (or anywhere else in Anderson's works), and it does not ever occur to Anderson to raise them. The stories in *Winesburg, Ohio* nevertheless do grapple with Anderson's intended theme, and a story such as "Hands" clearly illustrates what he means by a grotesque. The hands belong to Wing Biddlebaum, formerly Adolph Myers, a teacher in a Pennsylvania village who was beaten and run out of town for caressing boys. Anderson is delicately oblique about Wing's homosexuality, for the thrust of the story demonstrates how a single traumatic event can forever after rule a person's life—Wing is now a fretful recluse whose only human contact occurs when George Willard visits him occasionally. Even so George puzzles over Wing's expressive hands, but never fathoms the reason for his suffering diffidence. "Hands," besides giving first flesh to the word grotesque, makes the reader understand that a character's volition is not necessarily the factor which traps him into such an ideological straightjacket; sympathy can therefore be more readily extended.

"The Philosopher" provides a more subtle illustration of a grotesque and introduces the idea that a grotesque need not be pitiable or tragic; in fact, he can be wildly humorous as demonstrated at the beginning of the story with the philosopher's description:

Doctor Parcival, the philosopher, was a large man with a drooping mouth covered by a yellow moustache . . . he wore a dirty white waistcoat out of whose pocket protruded a number of black cigars . . . there was something strange about his eyes: the lid of his left eye twitched; it fell down and it snapped up; it was exactly as though the lid of the eye were a window shade and someone stood inside playing with the cord.

It is George Willard's misfortune that Dr. Parcival likes him and uses him as a sounding board for his wacky pomposity. He wishes to convince the boy of the advisability of adopting a line of conduct that he himself is unable to define but amply illustrates with many "parables" which add up to the belief (as George begins to suspect) that all men are despicable. He tells George that his father died in an insane asylum, and then he continues on about a Dr. Cronin from Chicago who may have been murdered by several men, one of whom could have been Dr. Parcival. He announces that he actually arrived in Winesburg to write a book. About to launch on the subject of the book, he is sidetracked into the story of his brother who worked for the railroad as part of a roving paint crew (which painted everything orange), and on payday the brother would place his money on the kitchen table—daring any member of the family to touch it. The brother, while drunk, is run over by the rail car housing the other members of his crew.

One day George drops into Dr. Parcival's office for his customary morning visit and discovers him quaking with fear. Earlier a little girl had been thrown from her buggy, and the doctor had inexplicably refused to heed a passerby's call (perhaps because he is not a medical doctor). Other doctors, however, arrived on the scene, and no one noticed Dr. Parcival's absence. Not realizing this, the doctor shouts to George that he knows human nature and that soon a hanging party will be formed to hang him from a lamppost as punishment for his callous refusal to attend to the dying child. When his certainty dissipates, he whimpers to George, "If not now, sometime." He begs George to take him seriously and asks him to finish his book if something should happen to him; to this end he informs George of the subject of the book, which is that everyone in the world is Christ and they are all crucified.

Many critics have singled out one or another story as the best in *Winesburg, Ohio*; frequently mentioned are "The Untold Lie," "Hands," and "Sophistication." Aside from the fact that this may be an unfair exercise because the stories in *Winesburg, Ohio* were written to stand together, these choices bring out the accusation that much of Anderson's work has a "setup" quality—a facile solemnity which makes his fictions manifest. "The

Philosopher" may be the best story because Dr. Parcival's grotesqueness eludes overt labeling; its finely timed humor reveals Anderson's ability to spoof his literary weaknesses, and the story captures one of those character types who, like Joe Welling of "A Man of Ideas," is readily observable and remembered, but proves irritatingly elusive when set down.

Anderson exhibits a particular interest in the distorting effect that religious mania has upon the personality, and several stories in *Winesburg, Ohio* attack or ridicule examples of conspicuous religiosity. "Godliness," a tetralogy with a gothic flavor, follows the life of Jesse Bentley, a wealthy, progressive farmer who poisons the life of several generations of his relatives with his relentless harshness until he becomes inflamed by Old Testament stories and conceives the idea of replicating an act of animal sacrifice. Because of this behavior, he succeeds in terrifying his fifteen-year-old grandson, the only person he loves, who flees from him never to be heard from again, thus breaking the grandfather's spirit.

Two stories, "The Strength of God" and "The Teacher," are juxtaposed to mock cleverly a less extravagent example of piety. The Reverend Curtis Hartman espies Kate Swift, the worldly high school teacher, reading in bed and smoking a cigarette. The sight affronts and preoccupies him severely and plunges him into a prolonged moral struggle which is resolved when one night he observes her kneeling naked by her bed praying. He smashes the window through which he has been watching her and runs into George Willard's office shouting that Kate Swift is an instrument of God bearing a message of truth. Kate remains entirely oblivious of the Reverend, for she is preoccupied with George, in whom she has detected a spark of literary genius worthy of her cultivation. Her praying episode–an act of desperation which the Reverend mistook for a return to faith–was the result of her realization, while in George's arms, that her altruism had turned physical.

It is exposure to these disparate egoisms, the death of his mother and a poignant evening with Helen White, the banker's daughter, which are gathered into the components of George's "sophistication," the achievement of which causes him to leave town. George's departure, however, has a decidedly ambivalent meaning. Anderson as well as other writers before and after him have shown that American small-town life can be less than idyllic, but *Winesburg, Ohio* is problematic because it is not simply another example of "the revolt from the village." In the story "Paper Pills," the narrator states that apples picked from Winesburg orchards will be eaten in city apartments that are filled with books, magazines, furniture, and people. A few rejected apples, however, which have gathered all their sweetness in one corner and are delicious to eat, remain on the trees and are eaten by those who are not discouraged by their lack of cosmetic appeal. Thus the neuroses of Anderson's grotesques are sentimentalized and become part of his increasingly strident polemic against rationality, the idea of progress, mechanization, scientific innovation, urban culture, and other expressions of social potency. Anderson never wonders why pastorals are not written by pastors but rather by metropolitans whose consciousnesses are heightened by the advantages of urban life; his own version of a pastoral, *Winesburg, Ohio,* was itself written in Chicago.

Anderson published three other collections of short stories in his lifetime, and other stories which had appeared in various magazines were posthumously gathered by Paul Rosenfeld in *The Sherwood Anderson Reader.* These are anthologies with no common theme or recurring characters, although some, such as *Horses and Men,* portray a particular milieu such as the racing world or rustic life. Many of the stories, and nearly all of those singled out by the critics for their high quality, are first-person narratives. They are told in a rambling, reminiscent vein and are often preferred to those in *Winesburg, Ohio* because they lack a staged gravity. The grotesques are there, but less as syndromes than as atmospheric effects. The gothic nature of the later stories becomes more pronounced, and violence, desolation, and decay gain ascendancy in his best story, "Death in the Woods," from the collection of the same name. This work also has another dimension: it is considered "to be among that wide and interesting mass of creative literature written about literature," for as the narrator tells the story of the elderly drudge who freezes to death while taking a shortcut through the snowy woods, he explains that as a young man he worked on the farm of a German who kept a bound servant like the young Mrs. Grimes. He recalls the circular track that her dogs made about her body while growing bold enough to get at her bag of meat when he himself has an encounter with dogs on a moonlit winter night. When the woman's body is found and identified, the townspeople turn against her ruffian husband and son and force them out of town, and their dwelling is visited by the narrator after it becomes an abandoned and vandalized hulk.

Because Mrs. Grimes is such an unobtrusive and inarticulate character, the narrator is forced to tell her story, as well as how he gained each aspect of the story, until the reader's interest is awakened by the uncovering of the narrator's mental operations. This process leads the narrator to ponder further how literature itself is written and guides him to the final expansion: consciousness of his own creative processes. The transfer of interest from the uncanny circumstances of Mrs. Grimes's death to this awareness of human creativity lends some credibility to Sherwood Anderson's epitaph, "Life, Not Death, Is the Great Adventure."

"The Man Who Became a Woman," from *Horses and Men,* is another critic's choice. A young horse groom is sneaking a drink at a bar and imagines that his image on the counter mirror is that of a young girl. He becomes involved in an appalling barroom brawl (its horror contradicts the popular image of brawls in Westerns), and later, while sleeping nude on top of a pile of horse blankets, he is nearly raped by two drunken black grooms who mistake him for a slim young woman. The several strong foci in this long story tend to cancel one another out, and its built-in narrative devices for explaining the reason for the telling of the story succeed only in giving it a disconnected feel, although it is the equal of "Death in the Woods" in gothic details.

"I Am a Fool," also from *Horses and Men*, is Anderson's most popular story. Here a young horse groom describes a humiliation caused less by his own gaucheness with the opposite sex than by the gulf of social class and education which separates him from the girl. The story re-creates the universe of adolescent romance so well presented in *Winesburg, Ohio* and brings a knowing smile from all manner of readers.

In "The Egg" (from *The Triumph of the Egg*), a husband-and-wife team of entrepreneurs try their hand at chicken-raising and running a restaurant. They fail at both, and the cause in both instances is an egg. This is a mildly humorous spoof on the American penchant for quick-success schemes, which nevertheless does not explain the praise the story has been given.

"The Corn Planting" (from *The Sherwood Anderson Reader*) is Anderson without histrionics. An elderly farm couple are told that their city-dwelling son has been killed in an automobile accident. In response, the pair rig a planting machine and set about planting corn in the middle of the night while still in their nightgowns. While this conclusion evokes varying responses, it does bring to mind that Anderson's favorite appellation (and the title of one of his short stories) was An Ohio Pagan.

Other major works

NOVELS: *Windy McPherson's Son*, 1916; *Marching Men*, 1917; *Poor White*, 1920; *Many Marriages*, 1923; *Dark Laughter*, 1925; *Beyond Desire*, 1932; *Kit Brandon*, 1936.

PLAYS: *Plays: Winesburg and Others*, 1937.

POETRY: *Mid-American Chants*, 1918; *A New Testament*, 1927.

NONFICTION: *A Story Teller's Story*, 1924; *The Modern Writer*, 1925; *Tar: A Midwest Childhood*, 1926; *Sherwood Anderson's Notebook*, 1926; *Hello Towns!*, 1929; *Perhaps Women*, 1931; *No Swank*, 1934; *Puzzled America*, 1935; *Home Town*, 1940; *Sherwood Anderson's Memoirs*, 1942; *The Letters of Sherwood Anderson*, 1953; *Sherwood Anderson: Selected Letters*, 1984; *Letters to Bab: Sherwood Anderson to Marietta D. Finley, 1916-1933*, 1985.

Bibliography

Anderson, David D. *Sherwood Anderson: An Introduction and Interpretation.* New York: Holt, Rinehart and Winston, 1967. This critical biography argues that all Anderson's work, not only *Winesburg, Ohio,* must be considered when attempting to understand Anderson's career and his place in the literary canon.

Appel, Paul P. *Homage to Sherwood Anderson: 1876-1941.* Mamaroneck, N.Y.: Paul P. Appel, 1970. A collection of essays originally published in homage to Anderson after his death in 1941. Among the contributors are Theodore Dreiser, Gertrude Stein, Thomas Wolfe, Henry Miller, and William Saroyan. Also includes Anderson's previously unpublished letters and his essay "The Modern Writer," which had been issued as a limited edition in 1925.

Campbell, Hilbert H., and Charles E. Modlin, eds. *Sherwood Anderson: Centennial Studies.* Troy, N. Y.: Whitston, 1976. Written for Anderson's centenary, these eleven previously unpublished essays were solicited by the editors. Some of the essays explore Anderson's relationship with other artists, including Edgar Lee Masters, Henry Adams, Alfred Stieglitz, and J. J. Lankes.

Howe, Irving. *Sherwood Anderson.* Toronto: William Sloane Associates, 1951. This highly biographical work explores why Anderson, a writer with only one crucial book, remains an outstanding artist in American literature. The chapters on *Winesburg, Ohio* and the short stories are noteworthy; both were later published in collections of essays on Anderson. Includes a useful bibliography.

Papinchak, Robert Allen. *Sherwood Anderson: A Study of the Short Fiction.* New York: Twayne Publishers, 1992.

Townsend, Kim. *Sherwood Anderson.* Boston: Houghton Mifflin, 1987. In this biography of Sherwood Anderson, Townsend focuses, in part, on how Anderson's life appears in his writing. Supplemented by twenty-six photographs and a useful bibliography of Anderson's work.

Williams, Kenny J. *A Storyteller and a City: Sherwood Anderson's Chicago.* DeKalb, Ill.: Northern Illinois University Press, 1988. Investigates Anderson's sense of place.

Julian Grajewski
(Revised by *Cassandra Kircher*)

ISAAC BABEL

Born: Odessa, Ukraine, Russia; July 13, 1894
Died: Siberia, Soviet Union; March 17, 1941

Principal short fiction · *Rasskazy*, 1925 · *Istoriia moei golubiatni*, 1926 · *Konarmiia*, 1926 (*Red Cavalry*, 1929) · *Odesskie rasskazy*, 1931 (*Tales of Odessa*, 1955) · *Benya Krik, the Gangster and Other Stories*, 1948 · *The Collected Stories*, 1955 · *Izbrannoe*, 1957, 1966 · *Lyubka the Cossack and Other Stories*, 1963 · *The Lonely Years, 1925-1939* · *Unpublished Stories and Private Correspondence*, 1964 · *You Must Know Everything: Stories, 1915-1937*, 1969

Other literary forms · Although Isaac Babel spent most of his career writing short stories, he tried his hand at other genres without making significant contributions to them. He wrote two plays: *Zakat* (1928; *Sunset*, 1960) and *Mariia* (1935; *Maria*, 1966). He also wrote several screenplays, most of which remain unpublished. Babel was known to have worked on several novels, but only a few fragments have been published. If he ever completed them, either he destroyed them or they were confiscated by police when he was arrested in 1939, never to be seen in public again. Because of their fragmentary nature, the tendency among critics is to treat them as short fiction. He also wrote a brief autobiography, a diary, reminiscences, and newspaper articles.

Achievements · Babel's greatest achievement lies in short fiction. From the outset, he established himself as a premier short-story writer not only in Russian but in world literature as well. He achieved this reputation not only through his innovative approach to the subject matter—the civil war in Russia, for example, or the Jewish world of his ancestry—but also through his stylistic excellence. His mastery of style earned for him, early in his career, a reputation of an avant-garde writer, a model to be emulated, but at the same time, he was very difficult to emulate. He elevated the Russian short story to a new level and attracted the attention of foreign writers such as Ernest Hemingway, who read him in Paris. At the same time, it would be unjust to attribute his greatness only to the uniqueness of his subject matter or to his avant-garde style. Rather, it is the combination of these and other qualities that contributed to his indisputably high reputation among both critics and readers, a respect that seems to grow with time.

Biography · Isaac Emmanuilovich Babel was born in Odessa on July 13, 1894, into a Jewish family that had lived in southern Russia for generations. Soon after his birth, the family moved from this thriving port on the Black Sea to the nearby small town of Nikolayev, where Babel spent the first ten years of his life. His childhood was typical of a child growing up in a colorful Jewish environment and, at the same time, in a Russian society replete with prejudices against Jews. In his stories, Babel describes the difficult lessons of survival that he had to learn from childhood on, which enabled him not only to survive but also to keep striving for excellence against all odds. He was a studious child who read under all conditions, even on his way home, and his imagination was always on fire, as he said in one of his stories. Among many other subjects, he studied Hebrew and French vigorously, becoming more proficient in them than in Russian.

After finishing high school in Odessa—which was difficult for a Jewish child to enter and complete—Babel could not attend the university, again because of the Jewish quota. He enrolled in a business school in Kiev instead. It was at this time that he began to write stories, in French, imitating his favorite writers, François Rabelais, Gustave Flaubert, and Guy de Maupassant. In 1915, he went to St. Petersburg, already thinking seriously of a writing career. He had no success with editors, however, until he met Maxim Gorky, a leading Russian writer of the older generation, who published two of his stories and took him under his wing. This great friendship lasted until Gorky's death in 1936. Gorky had encouraged Babel to write and had protected him but had published no more of his stories, and one day Gorky told Babel to go out into the world and learn about real life. Babel heeded his advice in 1917, setting off on a journey lasting several years, during which he volunteered for the army, took part in the revolution and civil war, married, worked for the secret police, was a war correspondent, and finally served in the famous cavalry division of Semyon Mikhaylovich Budenny in the war against the Poles. Out of these dramatic experiences, Babel was able to publish two books of short stories, which immediately thrust him into the forefront of the young Soviet literature. The period from 1921 to 1925 was the most productive and successful of his entire career.

By the end of the 1920's, however, the political climate in the Soviet Union had begun to change, forcing Babel to conform to the new demands on writers to serve the state, which he could not do, no matter how he tried. His attempts at writing a novel about collectivization never materialized. His inability (or, more likely, unwillingness) to change marks the beginning of a decade-long silent struggle between him and the state. Refusing to follow his family into emigration, he tried to survive by writing film scenarios, unable to publish anything else. In May, 1939, he was arrested and sent to a concentration camp. In 1954, it was revealed that he had died on March 17, 1941, but neither the location nor the exact circumstances of his death were specified. His confiscated manuscripts—a large crate of them—were never found.

Analysis · Isaac Babel's short stories fall into three basic groups: autobiographical stories, tales about Jews in Odessa, and stories about the Russian Revolution and Civil War. Even though the stories were written and published at different times, in retrospect they can be conveniently, if arbitrarily, classified into these three categories. A small number of stories do not fall into any of these groups, but they are exceptions and do not figure significantly in Babel's opus.

While it is true that many of Babel's stories are autobiographical, even if indirectly, a number of them are openly so. Several refer to his childhood spent in Nikolayev and Odessa. In one of his earliest stories, "Detstvo: U babushki" ("Childhood: At Grandmother's"), Babel pays his emotional due to his kind grandmother, who kept quiet vigil over his studying for hours on end, giving him her bits of wisdom every now and then: "You must know everything. The whole world will fall at your feet and grovel before you. . . . Do not trust people. Do not have friends. Do not lend them money. Do not give them your heart!" Babel loved his childhood because, he said, "I grew up in it, was happy, sad, and dreamed my dreams—fervent dreams that will never return." This early wistful realization of the inevitable transience of all things echoes through much of his writings. The mixture of happiness and sadness is reflected in one of his best stories, "Istoriia moei golubiatni" ("The Story of My Dovecote"), where a child's dream of owning a dovecote is realized during a pogrom, but the dove, which his father had promised him if he was accepted to high school, is squashed against his face. The trickling of the dove's entrails down his face symbolizes the boy's loss of innocence and a premature farewell to childhood.

Babel's discovery of love as a most potent feeling of humankind came to him rather early. As he describes in "Pervaia liubov" ("First Love"), he was ten years old when he fell in love with the wife of an officer, perhaps out of gratitude for her protection of Babel's family during the pogrom in Nikolayev. The puppy love, however, soon gave way to fear and prolonged hiccuping—an early indication of the author's rather sensitive nervous system that accompanied him all his life. This innocent, if incongruous, setting points to a sophisticated sense of humor and to irony, the two devices used by Babel in most of his works. It also foreshadows his unabashed approach to erotica in his later stories, for which they are well known.

As mentioned already, Babel lived as a child in a world of books, dreams, and rampant imagination. In addition, like many Jewish children, he had to take music lessons, for which he had no inclination at all. He had little time for play and fun and, as a consequence, did not develop fully physically. He was aware of this anomaly and tried to break out of it. During one such attempt, as he describes it in "Probuzhdenie" ("Awakening"), he ran away from a music lesson to the beach, only to discover that "the waves refused to support" him. Nevertheless, this experience made him realize that he had to develop "a feel for nature" if he wanted to become a writer. Another experience of "breaking out" concerns Babel's awareness of his social status, as depicted in the story "V podvale" ("In the Basement"). In this story, he visits the luxurious home of the top student in his class and has to use his power of imagination to convince the rich boy that socially he is on equal footing with him. When the boy visits the apartment of Babel's family, "in the basement," however, the truth becomes obvious, and the little Isaac tries to drown himself in a barrel of water. This realization of the discrepancy between reality and the world of dreams and the need and desire to break out of various imposed confines were constant sources of aggravation in Babel's life. Other autobiographical stories, as well as many other stories seemingly detached from the author's personal life, attest to this perennial struggle.

The stories about the life of Jews, in the collection *Tales of Odessa*, demonstrate Babel's attachment to his ethnic background as well as his efforts to be objective about it. In addition to being an economic and cultural center, Odessa had a strong underground world of criminals consisting mostly of Jews, which fueled the imagination of growing Isaac; later, he used his reminiscences about the Jewish mafia in some of his best stories. He immortalized one of the leaders, Benya Krik, alias the King, in "Korol" ("The King"). Benya's daring and resourcefulness are shown during the wedding of his elderly sister, whose husband he had purchased. When the police plan to arrest Benya's gang during the wedding celebration, he simply arranges for the police station to be set on fire. He himself married the daughter of a man he had blackmailed in one of his operations.

An old man who saw in Babel a boy with "the spectacles on the nose and the autumn in the heart" told him the story of Benya's rise to fame in "Kak eto delalos v Odesse" ("How It Was Done in Odessa"). Here, Benya orders the liquidation of a man who did not give in to blackmail, but Benya's executor kills the wrong man, a poor clerk who had very little joy in life. Benya orders a magnificent funeral for the unfortunate clerk and a lifelong financial support for his mother, thus showing his true nature and revealing that it is not crime that attracted him to the underground life but rather a subconscious desire to right the wrongs and help the downtrodden. Through such characters and their motives, Babel is able to lend his stories a redeeming grace, neutralizing the mayhem saturating them.

Loyalty is another quality that binds these lawbreakers, as illustrated in the story "Otec" ("The Father"), where Benya helps an old gangster, who had given him his start, to marry off his daughter to the son of a man who had rejected the marriage. They are assisted by another legendary figure, Lyubka, known also from the story "Liubka Kazak" ("Lyubka the Cossack"). Lyubka, a middle-aged shop and whore-house keeper, reigns supreme in her dealings with customers, who, in turn, help her wean her baby from breast-feeding. This interdependency in a life fraught with danger and risks gives Babel's characters a human face and his stories a patina of real drama.

Not all stories about Jews in Odessa deal with the underground world, as "Di Grasso," a colorful tale about theater life in Odessa shows. Di Grasso, a Sicilian tragedian, and his troupe flop the first night of the show. After a favorable newspaper review praising Di Grasso as "the most remarkable actor of the century," the second night the theater is full, and the spectators are so enthralled that the wife of the theater "mogul," to whom the fourteen-year-old Isaac had pawned his father's watch, makes the husband return the watch, sparing Isaac much trouble. Babel's uncanny ability to intertwine high aspirations and small concerns, pathos with bathos, turns seemingly insignificant events into genuine human dramas. This is even more evident in the story "Konets bogadel'ni" ("The End of the Old Folks' Home"), where the inmates of a poorhouse near the Jewish cemetery make a living by using the same coffins again and again, until one day the authorities refuse to allow a used coffin for the burial of a revolutionary hero. The ensuing rebellion by the inmates leads to their dispersal and to the end of their life-sustaining scheme. Thus, what began as a clever business proposition turns into tragedy, making Babel's story a timeless statement of the human condition.

Babel uses a similar technique in the collection *Red Cavalry*. Although the stories here are based on Babel's real-life experiences in the war between the Russian revolutionaries and the Poles, their real significance lies beyond the factual presentation of a historical event, as the author endows every gesture, almost every word, with a potential deeper meaning. It is not coincidental that the entire campaign is seen through the eyes of, and told by, a baggage-train officer named Liutov (a persona standing for Babel), not by a frontline participant. Readers learn about the general nature of the conflict, recognize the place names, and even follow the course of the battles, but they cannot piece together the exact history of the conflict simply because that was not the author's intention. Babel gives readers single episodes in miniature form instead, like individual pieces of a mosaic; only after finishing the book are readers able to take in the complete picture.

The first story, "Perekhod cherez Zbruch" ("Crossing into Poland"), sets the tone for the entire collection. The opening lines reveal that a military objective has been taken, but Liutov's baggage train that follows sinks into a hazy, dreamy, impressionistic atmosphere, as if having nothing to do with the campaign:

> Fields flowered around us, crimson with poppies; a noontide breeze played in the yellowing rye; on the horizon virginal buckwheat rose like the wall of a distant monastery. The Volyn's peaceful stream moved away from us in sinuous curves and was lost in the pearly haze of the birch groves; crawling between flowery slopes, it wound weary arms through a wilderness of hops. . . .

This passage shows a poetic proclivity of Babel, but it is also his deliberate attempt to take his readers away from the factual course of events and move them to what he considers to be more important—the human perception of the events. Many of the stories in the collection bear the same trademark.

Although many stories deserve detailed comment, several stand out for their "message" or meaning that can be culled from the story. Nowhere is the brutal nature of the civil war depicted more poignantly than in "Pis'mo" ("A Letter"). A young, illiterate cossack, Vasily, dictates to Liutov a letter to his mother. He inquires about his beloved foal back home, and only after giving detailed advice about handling him does he tell how his father, who is on the other side, killed one of his sons and was then killed in return by another. This most tragic piece of news is relayed matter-of-factly, as if to underscore the degree of desensitization to which all the participants have fallen prey through endless killing.

The cruelty of the civil war is brought into sharp focus by an old Jewish shopkeeper in "Gedali." Gedali reasons like a legitimate humanitarian and libertarian: "The Revolution—we will say 'yes' to it, but are we to say 'no' to the Sabbath? . . . I cry yes to [the Revolution], but it hides its face from Gedali and sends out on front naught but shooting." He understands when the Poles commit atrocities, but he is perplexed when the Reds do the same in the name of the revolution. "You shoot because you are the Revolution. But surely the Revolution means joy. . . . The Revolution is the good deed of good men. But good men do not kill." Gedali says that all he wants is an International of good people. Liutov's answer that the International "is eaten with gunpowder," though realistic, falls short of satisfying the old man's yearning for justice, which, after all, was the primary driving force of the revolution. It is interesting that, by presenting the case in such uncompromising terms, Babel himself is questioning the rationale behind the revolution and the justification of all the sacrifices and suffering.

A similar moral issue is brought to a climactic head in perhaps the best story in *Red Cavalry*, "Smert' Dolgushova" ("The Death of Dolgushov"). Dolgushov is wounded beyond repair and is left behind the fighting line to die. He is begging Liutov to finish him off because he is afraid that the Poles, if they caught him alive, would mutilate his body. Liutov refuses. The commander gallops by, evaluates the situation, and shoots Dolgushov in the mouth. Before galloping away, the commander threatens to kill Liutov, too, screaming, "You guys in specks have about as much pity for chaps like us as a cat has for a mouse." Aside from the revolutionaries' mistrust of Liutov (alias Babel) and the age-old question of euthanasia, the story poses a weighty moral question: has a human being the right to kill another human being? Even though Babel seems to allow for this possibility, he himself cannot make that step, making it appear that he is shirking his responsibility (after all, he is fighting alongside the revolutionaries). More likely, he is hoping that there should be at least someone to say no to the incessant killing, thus saving the face of the revolution (as if answering Gedali's mournful plea). More important, this hope hints at Babel's real attitude toward the revolution. For such "misunderstanding" of the revolution he was criticized severely, and it is most likely that through such attitudes he sowed the seeds of his own destruction two decades later.

Not all stories in *Red Cavalry* are weighed down with ultimate moral questions. There are stories of pure human interest, colorful slices of the war, and even some genuinely humorous ones. In "Moi pervyi gus'" ("My First Goose"), Liutov is faced with the problem of gaining the respect of the illiterate cossacks in his unit. As a bespectacled intellectual ("a four-eyed devil," as they called him), and a Jew at that, he knows that the only way to win them over is by committing an act of bravery. He thinks of raping a woman, but he sees only an old woman around. He finally kills a goose with his saber, thereby gaining the respect of his "peers." Only then are they willing to let him read to them Vladimir Ilich Lenin's latest pronouncements. With this mixture of mocking seriousness and irony, Babel attempts to put the revolution in a proper perspective. His difficulties at adjusting to military life are evident also in the story "Argamak," where he ruins a good horse by not knowing how to handle it.

The Jews are frequently mentioned in these stories because the war was taking place in an area heavily populated by them. Babel uses these opportunities to stress their perennial role as sufferers and martyrs, but also to gauge his own Jewish identification. In "Rabbi" ("The Rabbi"), he visits, with Gedali, an old rabbi, who asks him where he came from, what he has been studying, and what he was seeking—typical identification questions. Later, they and the rabbi's son, "the cursed son, the last son, the unruly son," sit amid the wilderness of war, in silence and prayers, as if to underscore the isolation of people threatened by an alien war. In "Berestechko," a cossack is shown cutting the throat of an old Jewish "spy," being careful not to stain himself with blood. This one detail completes the picture of a Jew as an ultimate victim.

Many characters are etched out in these miniature stories. There is Sandy the Christ in the story by the same title ("Sashka Khristov"), a meek herdsman who at the age of fourteen caught "an evil disease" while carousing with his stepfather and who later joined the Reds and became a good fighter. There is Pan Apolek ("Pan Apolek"), an itinerant artist who painted church icons in the images not of the saints but of local people. There is Afonka Bida ("Afonka Bida"), the commander who almost shot Liutov because of Dolgushov, who loses his horse Stepan and disappears hunting for another. After several weeks, he reappears with a gray stallion, but the loss of Stepan still makes him want to destroy the whole world. In "So" ("Salt"), a woman carrying a bundled baby uses him to gain sympathy and hitch a train ride. It turns out that the bundle is nothing but a two-pound sack of salt; she is thrown out of the moving train and then shot from a distance. The man who killed her pronounces solemnly, "We will deal mercilessly with all the traitors that are dragging us to the dogs and want to turn everything upside down and cover Russia with nothing but corpses and dead grass," which is exactly what he has just done. Finally, in one of the best stories in the book, "Vdova" ("The Widow"), a lover of the dying commander is bequeathed all of his belongings, with the request that she send some of them to his mother. When the widow shows signs of not following the will of the deceased, she is beaten, and, if she forgets the second time, she will be reminded again in the same fashion. These stories are perfect illustrations of Babel's ability to create unforgettable but credible characters, to set up dramatic scenes, and to conjure a proper atmosphere, while endowing his creations with a truly human pathos—qualities that characterize most of his stories but especially those in *Red Cavalry*.

Among the stories outside the three groups, several are worth mentioning. An early story, "Mama, Rimma i Alla" ("Mama, Rimma, and Alla"), resembles a Chekhov story in that the domestic problems in a family (a mother finds it difficult to cope with her daughters in the absence of her husband) are not solved and the story dissolves in hopelessness. "Iisusov grekh" ("The Sin of Jesus") is a colorful tale of a woman whose husband is away at war and who goes to Jesus for advice about loneliness. When Jesus sends her an angel, she accidentally smothers him to death in sleep. She goes again to Jesus, but now he damns her as a slut, which she resents, for it is not her fault that she lusts, that people drink vodka, and that he has created "a woman's soul, stupid and lonely." When finally Jesus admits his error and asks for forgiveness, she refuses to give it, saying, "There is no forgiveness for you and never will be." The story displays Babel's exquisite sense of humor along with a keen understanding of human nature and the complexities of life. A variant, "Skazka pro babu" ("The Tale of a Woman"), another Chekhovian story, again depicts the plight of a widow who, in her loneliness, asks a friend to find her a husband. When she does, he mistreats her and walks out on her, which causes her to lose her job. Finally, "Ulitsa Dante" ("Dante Street") is a Paris story in the Maupassant tradition, showing Babel's versatility and imagination.

Babel's stylistic excellence has been often praised by critics. Among the outstanding features of his style, several are worth mentioning. First and foremost, there is a miniature form linked with a spartan economy of words. He is known to have worked on a story for ten or more years and to revise it by deleting until no single word could be omitted any more. Babel pays a religious attention to detail, especially to line and color, often resulting in fine etchings. There is a pronounced poetic bent in his stories, whether they are located in a city milieu or in the countryside. This poetic proclivity is reinforced by a prolific use of images and metaphors in the style of the following passages, quoted at random: "A dead man's fingers were picking at the frozen entrails of Petersburg. . . . The gentleman had drooping jowls, like the sacks of an old-clothes man, and wounded cats prowled in his reddish eyes." One finds in Babel also a surprising amount of humor, as if to offset the cruelty and gruesome injustice of his world.

Babel's artfulness is especially noticeable in his treatment of irony as his strongest device. He refuses to accept reality as one perceives it. He also plays games with the reader's perceptions, as he says openly, "I set myself a reader who is intelligent, well educated, with sensible and severe standards of taste. . . . Then I try to think how I can deceive and stun the reader." This cool intellectual approach, coupled with a strong emotional charge of his stories, gives his stories an aura of not only skillfully executed works of art but also pristine innocence of divine creation.

Other major works

PLAYS: *Zakat,* 1928 (*Sunset,* 1960); *Mariia,* 1935 (*Maria,* 1966).

SCREENPLAYS: *Benia Krik: Kinopovest',* 1926 (*Benia Krik: A Film Novel,* 1935); *Bluzhdaiushchie zvezdy: Kinostsenarii,* 1926.

Bibliography

Carden, Patricia. *The Art of Isaac Babel.* Ithaca, N.Y.: Cornell University Press, 1972. In this discerning study of Babel's art, Carden combines biography and analysis of his main works and themes, especially his search for style and form, and philosophical, religious, and aesthetic connotations. The meticulous scholarship is accompanied by keen insight and empathy, making the book anything but cut-and-dry. Includes a select bibliography.

Ehre, Milton. "Babel's *Red Cavalry*: Epic and Pathos, History and Culture." *Slavic Review* 40 (1981): 228-240. A stimulating study of Babel's chief work, incorporating its literary, historical, and cultural aspects. No attention to detail, but rather a sweeping overview.

_____. *Isaac Babel.* Boston: Twayne Publishers, 1986. A basic text for the general reader by a reliable scholar.

Falen, James E. *Isaac Babel, Russian Master of the Short Story.* Knoxville: University of Tennessee Press, 1974. Falen's appraisal of Babel is the best overall. Following the main stages of Babel's life, Falen analyzes in minute detail his works, emphasizing the short stories. Lucidly written and provided with the complete scholarly apparatus, the study offers an exhaustive bibliography as well.

Hyman, Stanley Edgar. "Identities of Isaac Babel." *The Hudson Review* 8 (1956): 620-627. Hyman sees as one of the major themes in Babel's stories changes of identity through ritual of rebirth. Their true dichotomy is that of culture and nature, of art and the life of action, of necessity and freedom. For Hyman, the Jews are the heirs of all world cultures. A thought-provoking essay.

Mann, Robert. *The Dionysian Art of Isaac Babel.* Oakland, Calif.: Barbary Coast Books, 1994. Provides a good critical view.

Mendelsohn, Danuta. *Metaphor in Babel's Short Stories.* Ann Arbor, Mich.: Ardis, 1982.

Pirozhkova, A. N. *At His Side: The Last Years of Isaac Babel.* South Royalton, Vt.: Steerforth Press, 1996. Anne Frydman and Robert L. Busch, translators.

Poggioli, Renato. "Isaac Babel in Retrospect." In *The Phoenix and the Spider.* Cambridge, Mass.: Harvard University Press, 1957. Poggioli discusses the three curses of Babel's life: race, poverty, and the calling of an artist.

He also comments on Babel's attitude toward war and his inferiority complex, resulting in his admiration for the cossacks as men of action.

Sicher, Ephraim. *Style and Structure in the Prose of Isaak Babel.* Columbus, Ohio: Slavica Publishers, 1986.

Terras, Victor. "Line and Color: The Structure of I. Babel's Short Stories in *Red Cavalry." Studies in Short Fiction* 3, no. 2 (Winter, 1966): 141-156. In one of the best treatments of a particular aspect of Babel's stories, Terras discusses his style in terms of line and color and of his poetic inclination.

Trilling, Lionel. Introduction to *The Collected Stories.* Cleveland: World Publishing, 1955. Trilling stresses the difference between the cossacks and the Jews as one of the backbones of *Red Cavalry* and Babel's relationship to them in terms of test and initiation. A good general introduction to Babel's works.

Vasa D. Mihailovich

DONALD BARTHELME

Born: Philadelphia, Pennsylvania; April 7, 1931
Died: Houston, Texas; July 23, 1989

Principal short fiction · *Come Back, Dr. Caligari,* 1964 · *Unspeakable Practices, Unnatural Acts,* 1968 · *City Life,* 1970 · *Sadness,* 1972 · *Guilty Pleasures,* 1974 · *Amateurs,* 1976 · *Great Days,* 1979 · *Sixty Stories,* 1981 · *Overnight to Many Distant Cities,* 1983 · *Forty Stories,* 1987

Other literary forms · In addition to his one hundred and fifty or so short stories, Donald Barthelme published four novels, a children's volume that won a National Book Award, a number of film reviews and unsigned "Comment" pieces for *The New Yorker,* a small but interesting body of art criticism, and a handful of book reviews and literary essays, two of which deserve special notice: "After Joyce" and "Not Knowing."

Achievements · For nearly three decades, Barthelme served as American literature's most imitated and imitative yet inimitable writer. One of a small but influential group of innovative American fictionists that included maximalists John Barth, Robert Coover, and Thomas Pynchon, Barthelme evidenced an even greater affinity to the international minimalists Samuel Beckett and Jorge Luis Borges. What distinguishes Barthelme's fiction is not only his unique "zero degree" writing style but also, thanks to his long association with the mass-circulation magazine *The New Yorker,* his reaching a larger and more diversified audience than most of the experimentalists, whose readership has chiefly been limited to the ranks of college professors and their students. For all the oddity of a fiction based largely upon "the odd linguistic trip, stutter, and fall" (*Snow White,* 1967), Barthelme may well come to be seen as the Anthony Trollope of his age. Although antirealistic in form, his fictions are in fact densely packed time capsules—not the "slices of life" of nineteenth century realists such as Émile Zola but "the thin edge of the wedge" of postmodernism's version of Charles Dickens' hard times and Charles Chaplin's modern ones. For all their seeming sameness, his stories cover a remarkable range of styles, subjects, linguistic idioms, and historical periods (often in the same work, sometimes in the same sentence). For all their referential density, Barthelme's stories do not attempt to reproduce mimetically external reality but instead offer a playful medita-tion on it (or alternately the materials for such a meditation). Such an art

Bill Wittliff/courtesy of Harper & Row

makes Barthelme in many respects the most representative American writer of the 1960's and of the two decades that followed: postmodern, postmodernist, post-Freudian, poststructuralist, postindustrial, even (to borrow Jerome Klinkowitz's apt term) postcontemporary.

Biography · Often praised and sometimes disparaged as one of *The New Yorker* writers, a narrative innovator, and a moral relativist whose only advice (John Gardner claimed) is that it is better to be disillusioned than deluded, Barthelme was born in Philadelphia on April 7, 1931, and moved to Houston two years later. He grew up in Texas, attended Catholic diocesan schools, and began his writing career as a journalist in Ernest Hemingway's footsteps. His father, an architect who favored the modernist style of Ludwig Mies Van Der Rohe and Le Corbusier, taught at the University of Houston and designed the family's house, which became as much an object of surprise and wonder on the flat Texas landscape as his son's oddly shaped fictions were to become on the equally flat narrative landscape of postwar American fiction. While majoring in journalism, Barthelme wrote for the university newspaper as well as the *Houston Post.* He was drafted in 1953 and arrived in Korea on the day the truce was signed—the kind of coincidence one comes to expect in Barthelme's stories of strange juxtapositions and incongruous couplings. After his military service, during which he also edited an Army newspaper, he returned to Houston, where he worked in the university's public relations department ("writing poppycock for the President," as he put it in one story), and where he founded *Forum,* a literary and intellectual quarterly that published early works by Walker Percy, William H. Gass, Alain Robbe-Grillet, Leslie Fiedler, and others. He published his first story in 1961, the same year that he became director of the Contemporary Arts Museum of Houston. The following year, Thomas Hess and Harold Rosenberg offered him the position of managing editor of their new arts journal, *Location.* The journal was short-lived (only two issues ever appeared), but Barthelme's move to New York was not. Taking up residence in Greenwich Village, he published his first story in *The New Yorker* in 1963, his first collection of stories, *Come Back, Dr. Caligari,* in 1964, and his first novel, *Snow White* (among other things an updating of the Grimm Brothers' fairy tale and the Walt Disney feature-length animated cartoon), in 1967. Although he left occasionally for brief periods abroad or to teach writing at Buffalo, Houston, and elsewhere, Barthelme spent the rest of his life chiefly in Greenwich Village, with his fourth wife, Marion Knox. He lived as a writer, registering and remaking the "exquisite mysterious muck" of contemporary urban American existence, as witnessed from his corner of the global (Greenwich) village.

Analysis · Barthelme's fiction exhausts and ultimately defeats conventional approaches (including character, plot, setting, theme—"the enemies of the novel" as fellow writer John Hawkes once called them) and defeats too all attempts at generic classification. His stories are not conventional, nor are they Borgesian *ficciones* or Beckettian "texts for nothing." Thematic studies of his writing have proven utterly inadequate, yet purely formalist critiques have seemed almost as unsatisfying. To approach a Barthelme story, the reader must proceed circuitously via various, indeed at times simultaneous, extraliterary forms: collage, caricature, Calder mobile, action painting, jazz, atonality, the chance music of John Cage, architecture, information theory, magazine editing and layout, ventriloquism, even Legos (with all their permutational possibilities, in contrast to the High Moderns' love of cubist jigsaw puzzles). In Barthelme's case, comparisons with twentieth century painters and sculptors seem especially apropos: comical like Jean Dubuffet, whimsical and sad like Amedeo Modigliani, chaste like Piet Mondrian, attenuated like Alberto Giacometti, composite like Kurt Schwitters, improvisational like Jackson Pollock, whimsical like Marc Chagall and Paul Klee. Like theirs, his is an art of surfaces, dense rather than deep, textured rather than symbolic, an intersection of forces rather than a rendered meaning. Adjusting to the shift in perspective that reading Barthelme entails—and adjusting as well to Barthelme's (like the poet John Ashbery's) unwillingness to distinguish between foreground and background, message and noise—is difficult, sometimes impossible, and perhaps always fruitless.

However attenuated and elliptical the stories may be, they commit a kind of "sensory assault" on a frequently distracted reader who experiences immediate gratification in dealing with parts but epistemological frustration in considering the stories as wholes, a frustration which mirrors that of the characters. Not surprisingly, one finds Barthelme's characters and the fictions themselves engaged in a process of scaling back even as they and their readers yearn for that "more" to which Beckett's figures despairingly and clownishly give voice. Entering "the complicated city" and singing their "song of great expectations," they nevertheless—or also—discover that theirs is a world not of romantic possibilities (as in F. Scott Fitzgerald's fiction) but of postmodern permutations, a world of words and indecidability, where "our Song of Songs is the Uncertainty Principle" and where "double-mindedness makes for mixtures." These are stories that, like the red snow in Barthelme's favorite and most Borgesian work, "Paraguay," invite "contemplation" of a mystery that there is "no point solving—an ongoing low-grade mystery." Expressed despondently, the answer to the question "Why do I live this way?"—or Why does Barthelme write this way?—is, as the character Bishop says, "Best I can do." This, however, sums up only one side of Barthelme's double-mindedness; the other is the pleasure, however fleeting, to be taken "in the sweet of the here and the now."

Originally published as "The Darling Duckling at School" in 1961, "Me and Miss Mandible" is one of Barthelme's earliest stories and one of his best. Written in the form of twenty-six journal entries (dated September 13 to December 9), the story evidences Barthelme's genius for rendering even the most fantastic, dreamlike events in the most matter-of-fact manner possible. The thirty-five-year-old narrator, Joseph, finds himself sitting in a too-small desk in Miss Mandible's classroom, having been declared "officially a child of eleven," either by mistake or, more likely, as punishment for having himself made a mistake in his former life as claims adjuster (a mistake for justice but against his company's interests). Having spent ten years "amid the debris of our civilization," he has come "to see the world as a vast junkyard" that includes the failure of his marriage and the absurdity of his military duty. At once a biblical Joseph in a foreign land and a Swiftian Gulliver among the Lilliputians, he will spend his time observing others and especially observing the widening gap between word and world, signifier and signified, the ideals expressed in teachers' manuals and the passions of a class of prepubescents fueled by film magazine stories about the Eddie Fisher/Debbie Reynolds/Elizabeth Taylor love triangle. Unlike his biblical namesake, Joseph will fail at reeducation as he has failed at marriage and other forms of social adjustment, caught by a jealous classmate making love to the freakishly named Miss Mandible.

The coming together of unlike possibilities and the seeming affirmation of failure (maladjustment) takes a slightly different and more varied form in "A Shower of Gold." The former claims adjuster, Joseph, becomes the impoverished artist, Peterson, who specializes in large junk sculptures that no one buys and that even his dealer will not display. Desperate for money, he volunteers to appear on *Who Am I?*, the odd offspring of the game show craze on American television and of existentialism transformed into pop culture commodity. (There is also *veal engagé* and a barber who doubles as an analyst and triples as the author of four books all titled *The Decision to Be.*) Peterson convinces the show's Miss Arbor that he is both interesting enough and sufficiently de trop to appear on *Who Am I?*, only to feel guilty about selling out for two hundred dollars. Watching the other panelists be subjected to a humiliating barrage of questions designed to expose their bad faith, Peterson, accepting his position as a minor artist, short-circuits the host's existential script by out-absurding the absurd (his mother, he says, was a royal virgin and his father, a shower of gold). Peterson's situation parallels Barthelme's, or indeed any American writing at a time when, as Philip Roth pointed out in 1961, American reality had begun to outstrip the writer's imagination, offering a steady diet of actual people and events far more fantastic than any that the writer could hope to offer. What, Roth wondered, was left for the writer to do? "A Shower of Gold" offers one possibility.

"The Indian Uprising" and "The Balloon" represent another possibility, in which in two quite different ways Barthelme directs the reader away from story and toward the act of interpretation itself (interpretation as story). As Brian McHale and Moshe Ron have demonstrated, "The Indian Uprising" comprises three overlapping yet divergent and even internally inconsistent narratives: an attack by Comanche on an unidentified but clearly modern American city; the narrator's (one of the city's defender's) unsatisfying love life; and the conflict between modern and postmodern sensibilities manifesting itself in a variety of allusions to modernist texts, including T. S. Eliot's *The Waste Land* (1922). Near the end of his poem, Eliot writes, "These fragments I have shored against my ruins." "The Indian Uprising" presents a very different approach, transforming Eliot's shoring up of high culture into a "barricade" that recycles Eliot and Thomas Mann along with ashtrays, doors, bottles of Fad #6 sherry, "and other items." Behind Eliot's poem lies the possibility of psychic, spiritual, and sociocultural wholeness implied by Eliot's use of the "mythic method." Behind Barthelme's story one finds recycling rather than redemption and instead of the mythic method what Ronald Sukenick has called "the Mosaic Law," or "the law of mosaics, a way of dealing with parts in the absence of wholes." Short but beyond summary, filled with non sequiturs, ill-logic, self-doubts, and anti-explanations, "The Indian Uprising" rises against readers in their efforts to know it by reducing the story to some manageable whole. At once inviting and frustrating the reader's interpretive maneuvers, "The Indian Uprising" follows the "plan" outlined in "Paraguay" insofar as it proves "a way of allowing a very wide range of tendencies to interact."

Attacking and defending are two operant principles at play here, but just who is attacking and what is being defended are never made clear. Sides change, shapes shift in a story in which American Westerns, the Civil Rights movement, and American involvement in Vietnam all seem to have their parts to play, but never to the point where any one can be said to dominate the others. Small but indomitable, the story resists the linearity of an interpretive domino theory in favor of a semiotic quagmire (more evidence of Barthelme's interest in current affairs–Vietnam, in this case–and "mysterious muck"). In "The Indian Uprising," there is no final authority to come like the cavalry to the rescue and so no release from the anxiety evident in this and so many other Barthelme stories. While there may be no permanent release, however, there is some temporary relief to be had in the "aesthetic excitement" of "the hard, brown, nutlike word" and in the fact that "Strings of language extend in every direction to bind the world into a rushing ribald whole."

"The Balloon" is a more compact exploration and a more relentless exploitation of interpretation as a semiotic process rather than a narrowly coded act. Covering only a few pages (or alternately an area forty-five city blocks long by up to six blocks wide), "The Balloon" is Barthelme's American tall-tale version of the short French film *The Red Balloon* and an *hommage* to Frederick Law Olmsted (who designed New York's Central Park) and environmental artist Cristo (one of his huge sculptural wrappings). Analogies such as these help readers situate themselves in relation to the inexplicable but unavoidable oddity of "The Balloon" in much the same way that the viewers in the story attempt to situate themselves in relation to the sudden appearance of a balloon which, even if it cannot be understood ("We had learned not to insist on meanings"), can at least be used (for graffiti, for example) and appreciated despite, or perhaps because, of its apparent uselessness. Ultimately the narrator will explain the balloon, thus adding his interpretive graffiti to its blank surface. The balloon, he says, was "a spontaneous autobiographical disclosure" occasioned by his lover's departure; when, after twenty-two days, she returns, he deflates the balloon, folds it, and ships it to West Virginia to be stored for future use. His explanation is doubly deflating, for while the balloon's "apparent purposelessness" may be vexing, in a world of "complex machinery," "specialized training," and pseudoscientific theories that make people marginal and passive, it has come to exist as the "prototype" or "rough draft" of the kind of solution to which people will increasingly turn, to what the Balloon Man calls his best balloon, the Balloon of Perhaps. Until the narrator's closing comments, the balloon is not a scripted text but a blank page, not an object but an event, not a ready-made product, a prefab, but a performance that invites response and participation. It is a performance that the narrator's explanation concludes, assigning both an origin (cause) and destination (result, function, use, addressee). Yet even as the explanation brings a measure of relief, it also adds a new level of anxiety insofar as the reader perceives its inadequacy and feels perhaps a twinge of guilty pleasure over having made so much of so little. In a way, however, the balloon was always doomed to extinction, for it exists in a consumer culture in which even the most remarkable objects (including "The Balloon") quickly become all too familiar, and it exists too in a therapeutic society in thrall to the illusion of authoritative explanations.

Appearing only two months before the real Robert F. Kennedy's assassination, "Robert Kennedy Saved from Drowning" explores epistemological uncertainty by exploiting the contemporary media's and its audience's claiming to know public figures, whether politicians or celebrities (a distinction that began to blur during the eponymous Kennedy years). The story exists at the intersection of two narrative styles. One is journalistic: twenty-four sections of what appear to be notes, each with its own subject heading and for the most part arranged in random order (the last section being a conspicuous exception), presumably to be used in the writing of a profile or essay "about" Kennedy. The other is Kafkaesque fantasy and is evoked solely by means of the reporter's use of journalistic shorthand, the initial "K," which "refers" to Kennedy but alludes to the main characters of the enigmatic (and unfinished) novels *Der Prozess* (1925; *The Trial*, 1937) and *Das Schloss* (1926; *The Castle*, 1930) and ultimately to their equally enigmatic author, Franz Kafka himself. The narrator of "See the Moon?" claims that fragments are the only forms he trusts; in "Robert Kennedy Saved from Drowning," fragments are the only forms the reader gets. The conflicting mass of seemingly raw material–quotes, impressions, even fragments of orders to waiters–saves Kennedy from drowning in a media-produced narcissistic image that turns even the most inane remarks into orphic sayings. Kennedy cannot drown; he can only float on the postmodern surface. Instead of the Kennedy image, Barthelme turns Kennedy into a series of images, the last being the most ludicrous and yet also the most revealing: Kennedy as Zorro, masked and floundering in the sea, his hat, cape, and sword safely on the beach. Saved from drowning (by the narrator), Kennedy is unmasked as a masked image, a free-floating signifier, a chameleon in super-hero's clothing who proves most revealing when most chameleon-like, offering a summary of Georges Poulet's analysis of the eighteenth century writer Pierre Marivaux. Only here, at this third or even fourth remove, will many readers feel that they have gotten close to the "real" Kennedy:

> The Marivaudian being is, according to Poulet, a pastless, futureless man, born anew at every instant. The instants are points which organize themselves into a line, but what is important is the instant, not the line. The Marivaudian being has in a sense no history. Nothing follows from what has gone before. He is constantly surprised. He cannot predict his own reaction to events. He is constantly being *overtaken* by events. A condition of breathlessness and dazzlement surrounds him. In consequence he exists in a certain freshness which seems, if I may say so, very desirable. This freshness Poulet, quoting Marivaux, describes very well.

"Views of My Father Weeping" combines epistemological uncertainty with typically postmodern problematizing of the relationship between past and present (hinted at in the above quotation). Several days after his father has died under the wheels of an aristocrat's carriage, the narrator sets out to investigate whether the death was accidental, as the police reported, or an example of the aristocracy's (and the police's) indifference to the poor. Spurred on less by a desire for truth and justice than a vague sense of filial obligation and even more by the slight possibility of financial gain, but fearful that he may be beaten for making inquiries, perhaps (like his father) even killed, the narrator-son proceeds, more hesitant than Hamlet. Hamlet of course had his father's ghost appear to remind him of his duty to avenge a murder most foul. Barthelme's story also has a ghost (of sorts), a weeping father who sits on his son's bed acting in decidedly untragic fashion like a spoiled, sulky child whose very identity as father the son quietly questions. Complicating matters still further, this father seems to appear in a second story within "Views of My Father Weeping," which takes place in a more contemporary and clearly, although fantastically, American setting. These important if often blurred differences aside, the two narrators suffer from the same twin diseases that are pandemic in Barthelme's fiction: abulia (loss of the ability to decide or act) and acedia (spiritual torpor). They certainly would benefit from a reading of a slightly later story, "A Manual for Sons," a self-contained part of Barthelme's second novel, *The Dead Father* (1975), which concludes with this advice:

> You must become your father, but a paler, weaker version of him. The enormities go with the job, but close study will allow you to perform the job less well than it previously has been done, thus moving toward a golden age of decency, quite, and calmed fever. Your contribution will not be a small one, but "small" is one of the concepts that you should shoot for. . . . *Fatherhood can be, if not conquered, at least "turned down" in this generation*–by the combined efforts of all of us together.

The extreme brevity of his densely allusive and highly elliptical stories suggests that Barthelme sides with the smallness of sons in their comic struggle with their various fathers (biological, historical, cultural). Against the authoritative word of the All Father, Barthelme offers a range of ventriloquized voices. "Here I differ from Kierkegaard," says one of the characters in "The Leap." "Purity of heart is not," as Kierkegaard claimed, to will one thing; it is, rather, "to will several things, and not know which is the better, truer thing, and to worry about this forever." Barthelme's own double-mindedness and preference for mixtures and the guilty pleasures of the son's uncertainty and anxiety of influence become especially apparent in his collages of verbal and visual materials in which he puts the magazine editor's skills–layout in particular–to the fiction writer's use in order to achieve for fiction the kind of "immediate impact" generally available only to those working in the visual arts. "At the Tolstoy Museum," one of the best of these collages, literalizes, chiefly through visual means, the canonization of Leo Tolstoy as a metaphorical giant of literature, a cultural institution, an object of public veneration. Visitors to the "Tolstoy museum" must gaze at the prescribed distances and times and in the proper attitude of awe and submission. Readers of "At the Tolstoy Museum," on the other hand, find all the rules broken, temporal and spatial boundaries transgressed, and distances subject to a new and fantastic geometry. Against the museum as a repository of cult(ural) memorabilia, the story serves a narrative riposte in the form of a study in perspective. Barthelme whittles Tolstoy down to manageable size by exaggerating his proportions (much as he does with another dead father in his second novel): the thirty thousand photographs, the 640,086 pages of the Jubilee edition of Tolstoy's works, the coat that measures at least twenty feet high, the head so large it has a hall of its own (closed Mondays, Barthelme parenthetically adds), even a pagelong summary of one of Tolstoy's shortest stories, "The Three Hermits." There are also the two huge Soviet-style portraits on facing pages, identical in all but one feature: the tiny figure of Napoleon I (The Little Emperor), from Tolstoy's *Voyna i mir* (1865-1869; *War and Peace*, 1886), playing the part of viewer/reader. Best of all is Barthelme's rendering of The Anna-Vronsky Pavilion devoted to the adulterous pair from *Anna Karenina* (1875-1877; English translation, 1886), a cut-out of a nineteenth century man and woman superimposed on an early (and now adulterated) study in perspective dating from 1603. "At the Tolstoy Museum" does more than merely mix and match, cut and paste. It makes hilariously clear the artifice of art and of what the passive consumer of culture may naïvely assume is both natural and eternal.

"Sentence" makes a similar point, but it does so by exploring the literal in a quite different way. As its title suggests, the story takes the form of a single sentence of approximately twenty-five hundred words and manages to combine the brevity, open-endedness, and formal innovation that together serve as the hallmarks of Barthelme's idiosyncratic art. The subject of "Sentence" is the sentence itself: its progress and process. Beginning with one of Barthelme's favorite words, "or" ("etc." and "amid" are others), it proceeds by means of accretion and ends (if a work without any terminal punctuation can be said to end) as much an "anxious object" as any of those works of modern art to which Harold Rosenberg applied that phrase. Even as it pursues its own meandering, self-regarding, seemingly nonreferential way down the page, "Sentence" remains mindful of its reader, no less susceptible to distraction than the sentence itself and lured on by whatever promise the sentence holds out yet also feeling threatened by the sentence's failure to play by the rules. As the narrator sums up, "Sentence" is "a man-made object, not the one we wanted of course, but still a construction of man, a structure to be treasured for its weakness, as opposed to the strength of stones."

Earlier in "Sentence," Barthelme alludes to the Rosetta Stone that Champollion used to decipher the ancient Egyptian hieroglyphs. Barthelme's fiction, although written in a familiar language, proves more resistant to decoding. Barthelme uses the past as he uses the present, but neither offers anything approaching an interpretive touchstone, only the raw material, the bits and bytes out of which he constructs his oddly shaped but nevertheless aesthetically crafted "archaeological slices." Built upon the cultural ruins of an ancient Norse tale entitled "The Princess and the Glass Hill," "The Glass Mountain" resembles "Sentence" and "The Balloon" more than it does its nominal source in that it too is largely about one's reading of it. "I was trying to climb the glass mountain," the narrator declares in the first of the story's one hundred numbered sections (most only one sentence long). Like the reader, the narrator is "new to the neighborhood," persistent, comically methodical, and methodologically absurd; the plumber's friends he uses to scale the glass mountain at the corner of Thirteenth Street and Eighth Avenue seem no less inappropriate than his by-the-book how-to approach drawn from medieval romance—or the reader's efforts to climb (surmount, master) Barthelme's see-through metafiction by means of equally outdated reading strategies. Once atop the glass mountain the narrator finds exactly what he hoped to, "a beautiful enchanted symbol" to disenchant. Once kissed (like the frog of fairy tales), the symbol proves disenchanting in a quite different sense of the word, changed "into only a beautiful princess" whom the narrator (now himself disenchanted) hurls down in disappointment. Having staked his life on the eternal symbol of medieval romance, the narrator finds the temporary and the merely human (princess) disappointing.

Making a postmodern something, however small and self-consuming, out of the existential nothing became Barthelme's stock-in-trade, most noticeably in "Nothing: A Preliminary Account." His art of the nearly negligible works itself out comically but almost always against a sympathetic understanding for the permanence for which the climber in "The Glass Mountain" and the characters in so many of his other stories, "The New Music" for example, yearn. A fusion of two stories published earlier the same year, one with the same title, the other entitled "Momma," "The New Music" takes the dialogue form that Barthelme often used to new and dizzying heights of nearly musical abstraction, akin to what Philip Roth would accomplish more than a decade later in his novel, *Deception* (1990). The subject here is slight (even for Barthelme), as the story's two unidentified, no-longer-young speakers go through (or are put through) a number of routines analogous to vaudeville comedy and improvisational jazz. After a few opening bars, one speaker suggests that they go to Pool, "the city of

new hope. One of those new towns. Where everyone would be happier."
They then segue into an exchange on, or consideration of, the new music
done as a version of the familiar song "Momma don' 'low." Among the
many things that Momma (now dead) did not allow was the new music.
"The new music burns things together, like a welder," or like the sculptor
Peterson from "A Shower of Gold" or like Barthelme who along with his
two speakers understands that the new music always has been and always
will be: ever changing, ever ephemeral, ever new, and forever beyond
Momma's prohibitions and the reader's explanations.

Other major works

NOVELS: *Snow White*, 1967; *The Dead Father*, 1975; *Paradise*, 1986; *The King*,
1990.

NONFICTION: *Guilty Pleasures*, 1974.

CHILDREN'S LITERATURE: *The Slightly Irregular Fire Engine: Or, The Hithering
Thithering Djinn*, 1971.

Bibliography

Couturier, Maurice, and Regis Durand. *Donald Barthelme*. London:
    Methuen, 1982. This brief study focuses on the performance aspect of
    Barthelme's stories and considers them in relation to the multiplicity of
    varied responses that they elicit from readers. Readings are few in
    number but highly suggestive.
Gordon, Lois. *Donald Barthelme*. Boston: Twayne, 1981. This volume, in
    Twayne's United States Authors series, makes up in breadth what it lacks
    in depth. Although the book has no particular point to make about
    Barthelme and his work, it does provide useful and accurate summaries
    of most of his work. A comprehensive introduction for undergraduates
    unfamiliar with the fiction, as is Stanley Trachtenberg's *Understanding
    Donald Barthelme*.
Klinkowitz, Jerome. *Donald Barthelme: An Exhibition*. Durham, N.C.: Duke
    University Press, 1991. Klinkowitz is easily the best informed and most
    judicious scholar and critic of contemporary American fiction in general
    and Barthelme in particular. Building on his Barthelme chapter in
    Literary Disruptions (below), he emphasizes the ways in which Barthelme
    reinvented narrative in the postmodern age and places Barthelme's
    fiction in the larger aesthetic, cultural, and historical contexts. The
    single most important study of Barthelme.
_____. *Literary Disruptions: The Making of a Post-Contemporary Ameri-
    can Fiction*. 2d ed. Urbana: University of Illinois Press, 1980. Informed,
    accurate, and intelligent, Klinkowitz's book is the necessary starting

point for any serious discussion of Barthelme and his work. The emphasis is on Barthelme's interest in structure, his revitalizing of exhausted forms, his words as objects in space rather than mimetic mirrors, and the imagination as a valid way of knowing the world.

McCaffery, Larry. *The Metafictional Muse: The Works of Robert Coover, Donald Barthelme, and William H. Gass.* Pittsburgh: University of Pittsburgh Press, 1982. After situating the three writers in their historical period, McCaffery provides excellent readings of individual works. Views Barthelme as a critic of language whose "metafictional concerns are intimately related to his other thematic interests."

Molesworth, Charles. *Donald Barthelme's Fiction: The Ironist Saved from Drowning.* Columbia: University of Missouri Press, 1982. Objecting to those who emphasize the experimental nature of Barthelme's fiction, Molesworth views Barthelme as essentially a parodist and satirist whose ironic stance saves him from drowning in mere innovation.

Olsen, Lance, ed. *Review of Contemporary Fiction* 11 (Summer, 1991). In addition to the editor's excellent biocritical introduction and Steven Weisenburger's bibliography of works by and about Barthelme, this special issue on Barthelme reprints an early story and offers seven new essays (including especially noteworthy ones by Jerome Klinkowitz on the uses to which Barthelme put his unsigned "Comment" pieces from *The New Yorker* and Brian McHale and Ron Moshe on "The Indian Uprising") and shorter appreciations of and critical commentary on Barthelme from twenty critics and fiction writers.

Robert A. Morace

AMBROSE BIERCE

Born: Meigs County, Ohio; June 24, 1842
Died: Mexico(?); 1914(?)

Principal short fiction · *Cobwebs: Being the Fables of Zambri the Parse*, 1884
· *Tales of Soldiers and Civilians*, 1891 (republished under the title *In the Midst of Life*, 1898) · *Can Such Things Be?*, 1893 · *Fantastic Fables*, 1899 · *The Cynic's Word Book*, 1906 · *My Favourite Murder*, 1916 · *Ghost and Horror Stories of Ambrose Bierce*, 1964

Other literary forms · As a lifelong journalist and commentator, Ambrose Bierce wrote prodigiously. He was fond of vitriolic epigrams and sketches, together with miscellaneous literary criticism, and both prose and verse aphorisms.

Achievement · For many years, Bierce was labeled a misanthrope or pessimist, and his dark short stories of murder and violence were understood as the work of a man who, obsessed with the idea of death, showed himself incapable of compassion. A less moralistic and biographical re-evaluation of Bierce's work, however, reveals his intellectual fascination with the effect of the supernatural on the human imagination. Many of his morally outrageous stories are "tall tales," which certainly cannot be taken at face value. Their black humor, combined with the coolly understated voices of their criminal or psychopathic narrators, reflects a society gone to seed and pokes fun at the murderous dangers of American life in the West during the Gilded Age.

Biography · Ambrose Gwinett Bierce was brought up on the farm in Meigs County, Ohio, where he was born in 1842. Although information about his early life is sparse, the evidence of his stories and the fact that he quarreled with and repudiated his large family with the exception of one brother indicate an unhappy childhood and an abnormal hatred of parental figures. His only formal education consisted of one year at a military academy. He fought with the Indiana infantry in the American Civil War, was wounded at the battle of Kennesaw Mountain, and ended the conflict as a brevet major. After the war, he settled in California, where, following a brief stint as a watchman at the San Francisco mint, he drifted into literary work. He wrote for the San Francisco *Argonaut* and *News Letter* and published his first story, "The Haunted Valley" (1871), in the *Overland Monthly*. He married and, on money received as a gift from his father-in-law, traveled abroad to England in 1872, returning to California in 1876 because of bad health. Upon his return he again became associated with the *Argonaut*. From 1879 to 1881 he took part in the Black Hills gold rush, returning in 1881 to San Francisco, having found no success as a miner. There he began, in association with the San Francisco *Wap*, his famous

column "The Prattler," transferred to William Randolph Hearst's San Francisco *Examiner* upon the *Wasp*'s failure, and continued at the *Examiner* until 1896, when Hearst sent him to Washington as a correspondent for the New York *American.* Much of Bierce's subsequently collected work appeared first in "The Prattler." Divorced in 1904, Bierce resigned from the Hearst organization in 1909 and, in a final quixotic gesture, disappeared into Mexico in the thick of the Mexican Revolution. He was never heard from again.

Analysis · Perhaps the most rewarding way to approach Ambrose Bierce's writing is to note that it was in many respects the product of two intertwined biographical factors, inseparable for purposes of analysis. The first of these reflects Bierce's thorny and irascible personality which made him, on the one hand, quarrel with practically everyone he ever knew, and on the other, a follower of romantic and often impossible causes, the last of which led to his death. The second reflects his lifelong employment as a journalist, more specifically as a writer of short columns, generally aphoristic in nature, for various newspapers. The interaction of these two often contradictory strands explains, as well as any single factor can, both the strengths and weaknesses of Bierce's writing.

Philosophically, Bierce's work is almost completely uncompromising in its iconoclasm; his view of existence is despairing, revealing only the bitterness of life within a totally fallen world promising neither present happiness nor future redemption. This "bitterness," which almost every critic has remarked in Bierce's work, is not completely fortunate. It can, and in Bierce's case often does, lead to that kind of adolescent cynicism which delights in discovering clouds in every silver lining. Too many of the insights which once seemed sterling are now fairly obviously only tinfoil. The definition of "economy" in *The Devil's Dictionary* (1906) is a case in point: "Purchasing the barrel of whiskey that you do not need for the price of the cow that you cannot afford"–an arresting idea, certainly, succinctly expressed, but by no means a profound one. In fact, it is precisely the kind of item one would expect to find on the editorial page of the morning newspaper and perhaps remember long enough to repeat at the office. Indeed, this particular aphorism did first appear in a newspaper, with most of the other contents of *The Devil's Dictionary* and, predictably, did not really survive the transformation into book form. *The Devil's Dictionary*, like much of Bierce's work, is now much more generally read about than actually read. At its best, however, Bierce's cynicism is transformed into often passionate statements of the tragedy of existence in a world in which present joys are unreal and future hopes vain, as a glance at one of Bierce's best-known stories, "An Occurrence at Owl Creek Bridge," will show.

This story, for all its apparent simplicity, has attracted uniform critical admiration and has been complimented not only by being extensively anthologized but also by having been made into an award-winning film. Purporting to be an incident from the American Civil War, the story opens with the execution by hanging of a nameless Confederate civilian. His name, Peyton Farquhar, is revealed later, as is his apparent crime: he was apprehended by Union soldiers in an attempt to destroy the railroad bridge at Owl Creek, from which he is about to be hanged. The hangman's rope breaks, however, precipitating Farquhar into the current below. He frees his bound hands and, by swimming, manages to escape both the fire of the Union riflemen who have been assembled to witness the execution and, more miraculously, the fire of their cannon. Reaching shore, Farquhar sets out for home along an unfamiliar road, and after a nightlong journey in a semidelirious condition arrives at his plantation some thirty miles away. His wife greets him at the entrance, but as he reaches to clasp her in his arms he suffers what is apparently a stroke and loses his senses. He has not, it develops, suffered a stroke; the last sentence of the story tells us what has really happened. The rope had not broken at all: "Peyton Farquhar was dead; his body, with a broken neck, swung gently from side to side beneath the timbers of the Owl Creek bridge."

"An Occurrence at Owl Creek Bridge" sounds, in summary, contrived. What is it, after all, more than a tired descant on the familiar theme of the dying man whose life passes before his eyes, coupled with the familiar trick of the unexpected happy ending put in negative terms? The answer, from the perspective of one who has read the story rather than its summary, is that it is much more. For one thing, the careful reader is not left totally unprepared for the final revelation; he has been alerted to the fact that something may be amiss by Bierce's remark that Farquhar had, before his apparent death, fixed "his last thoughts upon his wife and children." Moreover, Farquhar's journey home is described in terms which become constantly less real. The unreality of the details of his homeward journey not only expresses Farquhar's growing estrangement from the world of reality, his "doom," perhaps, or—for those more at home in modern Freudianism—his "death wish," but also subtly indicates that what *seems* to be happening in the story may not in fact actually *be* happening, at least in the real world. In any event, Bierce's point is clear and reinforced within the story by a consistent movement in grammatical usage from the actual, "he was still sinking" (speaking of Farquhar's fall from the bridge into the water), toward the hypothetical, such as "doubtless," the word Bierce uses to describe Farquhar's apparent return to his plantation.

What, then, makes this story more than the predictable reverse of the typical tricky story with the illogical happy ending? The difference is to be found simply in Bierce's uncompromisingly negative view of the world. We begin in a world where every man is symbolically sentenced to death, from which his reprieve is only temporary, and we wander with him through a field of illusions which become more attractive as they escape the confines of reality. We end, reaching for a beauty and love which we sought but which was unobtainable, dead under Owl Creek Bridge. The symbolism of Owl Creek is not gratuitous: wise old owls discover that every road leads only to death.

The master image of "An Occurrence at Owl Creek Bridge" of a delusory journey leading to an ultimately horrible and horrifying revelation is central to many of Bierce's stories, one more of which is worth brief mention here. "Chickamauga," not as well known as the former story, is equally chilling and equally cunning in its artistry. It tells of a nameless young boy, "aged about six years," who with toy sword in hand wanders away from his home one day into the adjacent woods, where he successfully plays soldier until, unexpectedly frightened by a rabbit, he runs away and becomes lost. He falls asleep, and when he awakens it is nearly dusk. Still lost, his directionless night journey through the forest brings him upon a column of retreating soldiers, all horribly wounded and unable to walk, who are trying to withdraw from a battle (presumably the 1863 Battle of Chickamauga in the American Civil War, although this is never specifically stated) which has been fought in the neighborhood and of which the child, whom we later discover to be both deaf and mute, has been unaware. In a ghastly parody of military splendor, the child takes command of these horribly wounded soldiers and leads them on, waving his wooden sword. As the ghastly cavalcade limps forward, the wood mysteriously begins to brighten. The brightness is not the sun, however, but the light from a burning house, and when the little boy sees the blazing dwelling he deserts his troops and, fascinated by the flames, approaches the conflagration. Suddenly he recognizes the house as his own, and at its doorway he finds the corpse of his mother.

Again, the magic of this story vanishes in paraphrase, in which the masterfully controlled feeling of horror inevitably sounds contrived, the revelation slick rather than profound. The compelling quality of "Chickamauga" is largely a function of Bierce's style, which at once conceals and reveals what is going on. The story of a small boy who wanders off into the woods with a toy sword and who is frightened by a rabbit scarcely seems to be the kind of fictional world in which such uncompromising horrors should logically take place. Yet on a symbolic level, the story has a curiously compelling logic. The first reading of the tale leaves one with a slightly false impression of its meaning. The story does not tell us, as it seems to, and as so many fairy tales do, that it is better not to leave home and venture into the wild wood; the story's meaning is darker than this. In the world of "Chickamauga," safety is to be found neither at home nor abroad. By wandering away into the woods the boy perhaps escaped the fate of those who remained at home, and yet his symbolic journey has only brought him back to a world where death is everywhere supreme. To emphasize this point more strongly, in 1898 Bierce retitled the book of short stories in which both the above tales appeared *In the Midst of Life*. Readers, of course, are expected to complete the quotation themselves: "we are in death."

Although most of Bierce's stories which are widely remembered today deal with military themes, many of his other stories are quite frankly supernatural. By and large these supernatural stories seem less likely to survive than his military ones, if only because Bierce has less sense for the implicit thematic structure of supernatural tales than he does for macabre stories about the military. His ghost stories are avowedly "shockers," without the psychological depth to be found in the works of true masters of the supernatural. They do not have the profundity, for example, of Mary Shelley's *Frankenstein* (1818) or Bram Stoker's *Dracula* (1897). Nevertheless, the best of them do have a certain compelling quality simply because of the bizarre nature of the revelation of what lies at the heart of the super-natural event which Bierce relates.

"The Damned Thing" offers a convenient case in point. This is, quite simply, the story of a man who is hunted down and finally killed by some kind of animal, apparently a wildcat. We never know precisely what kind of animal it is, however, since it has one peculiar quality: it is invisible. The story is told with the last scene first. This last scene, tastelessly entitled "One Does Not Always Eat What Is on the Table," takes place at the coroner's inquest over the body of one Hugh Morgan, who has met a violent death. His friend, William Harker, explains how Morgan had acted inexplicably on a hunting trip, apparently falling into a fit. The coroner's jury agrees, at least to an extent. Their ungrammatical verdict is "We, the jury, do find that the remains come to their death at the hands of a mountain lion, but some of us thinks, all the same, they had fits." In the closing scene of the story, Morgan's diary is introduced as explanation, and in it we read of his growing awareness that he is being stalked by some kind of invisible animal. A pseudoscientific rationale is given for this invisibility. The animal is "actinic," at least according to Morgan. "Actinic" colors, we are informed, are colors that exist at either end of the spectrum and that cannot be perceived by the human eye. We have, in other words, either an infrared or an ultraviolet mountain lion. Neither choice is particularly satisfactory, and the difficulty with our willing suspension of disbelief in the tale is indicated by precisely this: the science is bad, and yet it pretends not to be. The notion of an ultraviolet mountain lion is basically more silly than chilling, and since the story has no fiber to it other than the revelation of what the mountain lion actually consists of, we cannot take it seriously. In fact, the reader feels vaguely victimized and resentful, as though having been set up as the butt of some kind of pointless joke.

Yet even in this story, relatively unsuccessful as it is, we see at work the underlying preoccupations which make some of Bierce's other stories unforgettable. The attempt in a Bierce story is always to shock someone by removing him from a commonplace world and placing him—like the little boy in "Chickamauga"—in another world whose laws are recognizable, though strange. The logic of a Bierce story is often very like the logic of a nightmare, in which the reader is placed in the position of the dreamer. When we are trapped in the toils of nightmare we feel the presence of a certain inexorable logic, even though we may not, at the moment, be able to define exactly how that logic operates or of what precisely it consists. It is the feeling for the presence of this hostile and malevolent order which gives the best of Bierce's stories their perennial fascination.

Other major works

POETRY: *Black Beetles in Amber*, 1892; *How Blind Is He?*, 1896; *Vision of Doom*, 1890; *Shapes of Clay*, 1903.

NONFICTION: *The Fiend's Delight*, 1873; *Nuggets and Dust Panned in California*, 1873; *Cobwebs from an Empty Skull*, 1874; *The Dance of Death*, 1877; *The Dance of Life: An Answer to the Dance of Death*, 1877 (with Mrs. J. Milton Bowers); *The Devil's Dictionary*, 1906; *The Shadow on the Dial and Other Essays*, 1909; *Write It Right: A Little Blacklist of Literary Faults*, 1909; *The Letters of Ambrose Bierce*, 1922; *Twenty-one Letters of Ambrose Bierce*, 1922; *Selections from Prattle*, 1936; *Ambrose Bierce on Richard Realf by Wm. McDevitt*, 1948.

TRANSLATION: *The Monk and the Hangman's Daughter*, 1892 (with Gustav Adolph Danziger; of Richard Voss's novel).

MISCELLANEOUS: *The Collected Works of Ambrose Bierce*, 1909-1912.

Bibliography

Davidson, Cathy N., ed. *Critical Essays on Ambrose Bierce*. Boston: G. K. Hall, 1982. A comprehensive compilation of thirty essays and reviews of Bierce's work, this collection is an essential tool for any serious study of Bierce. Davidson's introduction locates the essays in relation to the ongoing process of reevaluating Bierce's work, and her thoroughly researched bibliography contains more than eighty further critical references.

_____. *The Experimental Fictions of Ambrose Bierce.* Lincoln: University of Nebraska Press, 1984.

De Castro, Alphonse Danziger. *Portrait of Ambrose Bierce.* New York: Century, 1929. De Castro's admiring portrait of his friend has made this text a favorite with some speculative readers, yet his facts have been shown to be rather unreliable. Includes some photographs of Bierce's letters.

Fatout, Paul. *Ambrose Bierce, the Devil's Lexicographer.* Norman: University of Oklahoma Press, 1951. Fatout's impressive collation of painstakingly researched biographical data represents an important landmark in the scholarly study of Bierce's life. Supplemented by illustrations and a bibliography.

Fuentes, Carlos. *Old Gringo.* New York: Farrar, Straus & Giroux, 1985.

Grattan, Clinton Hartley. *Bitter Bierce.* Garden City, N. Y.: Doubleday, 1929. An early critical study of Bierce's work. Grattan's volume is unsympathetic to the point of outright hostility. He accuses Bierce of being an unsystematic and derivative thinker, and a morally reprehensible person.

Grenander, Mary Elizabeth. *Ambrose Bierce.* New York: Twayne, 1971. This volume is well researched, balanced, and readable, and it is perhaps the single most accessible study of Bierce's work and life. Contains a valuable, annotated bibliography and a list of primary sources.

McWilliams, Carey. *Ambrose Bierce: A Biography.* Hamden, Conn.: Archon Books, 1967. A reprint of the 1929 edition, with a new introduction that tells of the book's origin in McWilliams' collaboration with Bierce's surviving daughter Helen. Based on oral interviews of people who knew Bierce, this is the first scholarly study of his life.

O'Connor, Richard. *Ambrose Bierce.* Boston: Little, Brown, 1967. A popular biography by a prolific writer on the American West. Very readable, the book interprets Bierce's work as that of a despairing moralist. Complemented by a select bibliography.

Saunders, Richard. *Ambrose Bierce: The Making of a Misanthrope.* San Francisco: Chronicle Books, 1984.

James K. Folsom
(Revised by *R. C. Lutz*)

GIOVANNI BOCCACCIO

Born: Florence or Certaldo, Italy; June or July, 1313
Died: Certaldo, Italy; December 21, 1375

Principal short fiction · *Decameron: O, Prencipe Galetto*, 1349-1351 (*The Decameron*, 1620)

Other literary forms · Although Giovanni Boccaccio's greatest work is the masterfully framed collection of one hundred Italian short stories known as *The Decameron*, he also left a large and significant corpus of poetry. His earliest poetry, written in Naples, is in Italian and includes the *Rime* (c. 1330-1340; poems), which comprises more than one hundred lyrics, mostly sonnets and not all of sure attribution. These short poems are largely dedicated to the poet's beloved Fiammetta, who is identified in some of Boccaccio's pseudoautobiographical writings as Maria d'Aquino; supposedly, she was the illegitimate daughter of King Robert of Naples, but more probably she was the invention of the poet. Similarly, the longer poem *La caccia di Diana* (c. 1334; Diana's hunt), *Il filostrato* (c. 1335; *The Filostrato*, 1873), *Il filocolo* (c. 1336; *Labor of Love*, 1566), and *Teseida* (1340-1341; *The Book of Theseus*, 1974) are all poems ostensibly inspired by Boccaccio's ardor for Fiammetta, whose name means "little flame." Other poems that were composed in the 1340's also treat the formidable power of love and include the *Commedia delle ninfe*, entitled *Il ninfale d'Ameto* by fifteenth century copyists (1341-1342; the comedy of the nymphs of Florence), *L'amorosa visione* (1342-1343; English translation, 1986), *Elegia di Madonna Fiammetta* (1343-1344; *Amorous Fiammetta*, 1587), and *Il ninfale fiesolano* (1344-1346; *The Nymph of Fiesole*, 1597).

Achievements · Boccaccio created many literary firsts in Italian letters. He is often credited, for example, with the first Italian hunting poem (*La caccia di Diana*), the first Italian verse romance by a nonminstrel (*The Filostrato*), the first Italian prose romance (*Labor of Love*), and the first Italian idyll (*The Nymph of Fiesole*). Many scholars also regard Boccaccio as the greatest narrator Europe has produced. Such high esteem for the Tuscan author assuredly arises from his masterpiece, *The Decameron*, which has provided a model or source material for many notable European and English authors, from Marguerite de Navarre and Lope de Vega Carpio to Gotthold Ephraim Lessing and Alfred, Lord Tennyson. Even if Boccaccio

Courtesy of the Library of Congress

had never composed his magnum opus, however, he would still enjoy significant acclaim in European literary history for his presumedly minor writings. For example, many consider his *Amorous Fiammetta* to be the first modern (that is, postclassical) psychological novel. Certainly his *Il ninfale d'Ameto* anticipates Renaissance bucolic literature. Contemporary medieval authors also looked to Boccaccio for inspiration. In *The Filostrato*, Geoffrey Chaucer found ample material for his *Troilus and Criseyde* (1382), and in *The Book of Theseus* Chaucer discovered the source for "The Knight's Tale." Boccaccio's encyclopedic works in Latin resulted in his being regarded as one of the most prominent Trecento humanists. Indeed, it was as a Latin humanist, rather than as a raconteur of vernacular tales, that Boccaccio was primarily remembered during the first century following his demise.

Biography · The exact place and date of the birth of Giovanni Boccaccio are not known. Until the first half of the twentieth century, it was believed that he was born in Paris of a noble Frenchwoman; scholars now regard that story as another one of the author's fictional tales. Most likely, he was born in Florence or Certaldo, Italy, in June or July, 1313, the natural son of Boccaccio di Chellino and an unidentified Tuscan woman. His father, an agent for a powerful Florentine banking family (the Bardi), recognized Giovanni early as his son; the boy, as a result, passed both his infancy and his childhood in his father's house. Boccaccio's teacher in his youth was Giovanni Mazzuoli da Strada, undoubtedly an admirer of Dante Alighieri, whose *La divina commedia* (c. 1320; *The Divine Comedy*, 1802) greatly influenced Boccaccio's own writings.

In his early teens, sometime between 1325 and 1328, Boccaccio was sent to Naples to learn the merchant trade and banking business as an apprentice to the Neapolitan branch of the Bardi Company. The Bardi family, as the financiers of King Robert of Anjou, exerted a powerful influence at the Angevin court in Naples. The experiences Boccaccio enjoyed with the Neapolitan aristocracy and with the breathtaking countryside and beautiful sea are reflected in many of his early poems. During his sojourn in Naples, Boccaccio also studied canon law, between 1330 or 1331 and 1334. While studying business and law, however, he anxiously sought cultural experiences to broaden his awareness of belles lettres. Largely self-taught in literary matters, he soon began to study the writings of his somewhat older contemporary, Francesco Petrarca, known as Petrarch. Later, the two men became friends and met on a number of occasions (1350 in Florence, 1351 in Padua, 1359 in Milano, 1363 in Venice, and 1368 in Padua again).

Boccaccio left Naples and returned to Florence between 1340 and 1341 because of a financial crisis in the Bardi empire. Although Boccaccio rued having to leave Naples, so often associated in his imagination and writings with love and adventure and poetry, his highly bourgeois Florentine experience added an important and desirable dimension of realism to his work. Unfortunately, very little is documented about Boccaccio's life between 1340 and 1348, although it is known (from one of Petrarch's letters) that he was in Ravenna between 1345 and 1346 and that he sent a letter from Forlì in 1347. He was back in Florence in 1348, where he witnessed at first hand the horrible ravages of the Black Death, or bubonic plague. Between 1349 and 1351, he gave final form to *The Decameron*, which takes as its *mise en scène* Florence and the Tuscan countryside during the plague of 1348.

After his father's death in 1349, Boccaccio assumed many more familial responsibilities and financial burdens. As his fame as an author and scholar burgeoned, his fellow Florentines began to honor him with various ambassadorial duties, starting with his 1350 assignment as ambassador to the lords of Romagna. Such posts, however, did little to alleviate the financial difficulties caused by the collapse of the Bardi Company. Boccaccio longed to return to the pleasant life he had known in Naples, but visits there in 1355 and again in 1362 and 1370 to 1371 were extremely disappointing. Between 1360 and 1362, he studied Greek, the first among the literati of his time to do so seriously; from that time until his death, his home became the center for Italian humanism. Sometime around 1361 or 1362, he left Florence to take up residence in the family home in Certaldo, where he died, on December 21, 1375, the year after the death of his friend and fellow humanist, Petrarch.

Analysis · Giovanni Boccaccio's short fiction, one hundred *novelle*, or tales, is collectively and contemporaneously his longest work of fiction, known as *The Decameron*. That fact must be kept foremost in mind in any serious analysis of the tales. In other words, Boccaccio's individual short stories are best understood when examined as part of a much larger work of fiction which has an elaborate *cornice*, or frame, striking symmetry, and selective and oft-repeated themes.

The word *decameron*, Greek for "ten days," refers to the number of days Boccaccio's fictional characters (three young men and seven young women) dedicate to swapping tales with one another in the tranquil Tuscan countryside away from the plague-infested city of Florence. The work's subtitle, "Prencipe Galeotto" (Prince Galahalt), refers to the panderer Galahalt, who brought Guinevere and Lancelot together, and emphasizes that Boccaccio's book—dedicated to women—is written, not unlike many of his early poems, in the service of love. As the narration of the First Day begins, three men—Panfilo ("all love"), Filostrato ("overcome by love"), and Dioneo ("the lascivious"), alluding to the love goddess Venus, daughter of Dione—come by chance one Tuesday upon seven women, who are between the ages of eighteen and twenty-eight, in the Church of Santa Maria Novella. The year is 1348, and the Black Death is the macabre background for what happens in the course of the telling of the tales. The seven women—Pampinea ("the vigorous"), Fiammetta (whose name echoes that of Boccaccio's beloved), Filomena ("lover of song"), Emilia ("the flatterer"), Lauretta (in homage to Petrarch's beloved Laura), Neifile ("new in love"), and Elissa (another name for Vergil's tragic heroine Dido)–anxiously wish to remove themselves from the diseased and strife-torn city and repair to the healthful and peaceful countryside. The young men agree to accompany the ladies, and the following day (a Wednesday) the group leaves for a villa in nearby and idyllic Fiesole. Better to enjoy what is essentially a fortnight's holiday, Pampinea suggests that they tell stories in the late afternoon when it is too hot to play or go on walks. It is decided that one of them will be chosen as king or queen for each day, and he or she will select a theme for the stories to be told on that day. Only Dioneo, who tells the last tale each day, has the liberty of ignoring the general theme if he so desires. They then proceed to tell ten stories per day over a two-week period, refraining from tale-telling on Fridays and Saturdays out of reverence for Christ's crucifixion and in order to prepare properly for the Sabbath. On a Wednesday, the day following the last day of telling tales and exactly two weeks from the day the group left Florence, they return to their respective homes.

The emphasis on order and propriety, the presentation of the countryside as a *locus amoenus*, the repetition of the number ten (considered a symbol of perfection in the Middle Ages), and even the total number of tales (one hundred, equal to the number of cantos in Dante's *The Divine Comedy*) are all aspects of the work which contrast sharply with the disorder, impropriety, and lack of harmony which characterized Florence during the 1348 plague. The author graphically depicts, in the opening pages of the book, examples of the social chaos caused by the plethora of plague-induced deaths. The pleasant pastime of telling tales in the shade of trees and the skillful ordering of the stories serve, in other words, as an obvious antidote or salutary response to the breakdown of society which resulted from the deadly pestilence which swept Italy and much of Europe in the mid-fourteenth century. Further supporting the notion that *The Decameron* presents an ordered universe as an alternative to the chaos and anarchy created by the plague is Boccaccio's insistence that his storytellers, though they may occasionally tell ribald tales, are uniformly chaste and proper in their behavior toward one another.

The stories told on each of the ten days which make up *The Decameron* explore a predetermined subject or theme. On the First Day, everyone is free to choose a topic–one is the character "Abraam giudeo" ("Abraham the Jew"). On the Second Day, the stories treat those, such as the subject of "Andreuccio da Perugia" ("Andreuccio of Perugia"), who realize unexpected happiness after serious misfortune. Then, on the Third Day, the stories discuss people who have accomplished difficult goals or who have repossessed something once lost, among which is the tale "Alibech" ("Alibech and Rustico"). The next day, the narrators tell love stories which end unhappily (see "Tancredi, Prenze di Salerno" and its English translation). On the Fifth Day, they tell love stories which depict misfortune but end felicitously (see "Nastagio degli Onesti" and the English translation). The stories told on the Sixth Day deal with the role of intelligence in helping one avoid problems—one of the most famous among these is "Cisti fornaio" ("Cisti the Baker"). On the Seventh Day, the stories relate tricks which wives play on husbands (see "Petronella mette un so amante in un doglio," or "Petronella and the Barrel"), and on the Eighth Day, the stories recount tricks men and women play on each other, as in "Calandrino" ("Calandrino and the Heliotrope"). On the Ninth Day, once again everyone is free to choose a topic (one is described in "Le vasi una badessa in fretta ed al buio per trovare una sua monaca a lei accusata" and its translation, "The Abbess and the Nun"). Finally, on the Tenth Day, the narrators tell of men and women who have performed magnanimous deeds and acquired renown in so doing (see "Il Marchese di Saluzzo," or "The Marchese di Saluzzo and Griselda").

In addition to the pronounced framing technique created by the introductions to the various days and by the themes themselves, there seems to be a degree of subtle thematic framing within the stories themselves from first to last. The first story of the First Day, "Ser Cepparello," tells how a most wicked man—clearly a *figura diaboli*, or type of the devil—deceived a friar with a false confession and came to be reputed a saint. On one hand, the tale ridicules gullible priests and credulous common folk, but on the other hand, it presents the undeniable power of human cunning. The tenth story of the Tenth Day recounts the story of how the Marquis of Saluzzo marries the peasant Griselda and subjects her to inhuman trials to ascertain her devotion; for example, he pretends to have their two children killed. His cruelty is ostensibly designed to test her love or respect for him; her extraordinary patience in responding to his bestiality assuredly makes of her a *figura Christi*, or type of Christ. From the comedic devil figure of Cepparello to the tragic Christ figure of Griselda there appears to be in *The Decameron* a revelation of the breadth of the human condition and the wide-ranging possibilities of human experience. Nevertheless, Boccaccio explores a variation on at least one of two themes in almost all of his stories: the power of human intelligence (for good or bad) and the effect of love or human passion (for the well-being or detriment of those involved). At times, these themes are intermingled, as in so many of the stories of the Seventh Day having to do with the ingenious tricks wives play on their (usually cuckolded) spouses.

Often when treating the advantages of human wit, the author provides a Florentine or Tuscan setting to his story. For example, in the Sixth Day, "Cisti the Baker" is set in Florence and illustrates the rise and power of the hardworking and hard-thinking merchant class Boccaccio knew so well in his hometown. Similarly, "Guido Cavalcanti," told on the same day, has Florence as its setting and reveals the barbed wit of one of the city's native sons. There are also tales told of Florentines who are dull-witted; examples would include the various Eighth Day and Ninth Day stories about the simple-minded painter Calandrino, who is constantly being tricked by his supposed friends Bruno and Buffalmacco. Those who outsmart him, however, are fellow Florentines. By contrast, many of the highly adventurous tales are set in cities far away from Florence, often in exotic locations. Not surprisingly, Naples figures prominently in perhaps the most notable of the adventure tales–that is, "Andreuccio of Perugia," the story of a provincial young man who goes to a big city (Naples) to buy horses and ends up suffering a series of misfortunes only to return home with a ruby of great value. In the tale, Naples symbolizes adventure and daring and is undoubtedly meant to recall the city of the author's youth.

Boccaccio's love tales repeatedly, though not exclusively, present realistic women in place of the idealized and angelic women Dante was wont to exalt. In stories scattered throughout *The Decameron*, but especially in those of the Third Day and Fifth Day, the physical and pleasurable union of man and woman is portrayed as the healthy and correct goal of human love. While some interpret such unabashed celebration of humankind's sexuality as a sure indication that *The Decameron* is a Renaissance work, it should be remembered that approximately ninety percent of Boccaccio's tales derive from medieval sources. G. H. McWilliam, in the introduction to his excellent English translation of *The Decameron*, reviews with insight the problem of how to classify the book with regard to historical period. He points out that the harsh judgment leveled against friars and monks, whether they are philanderers or simoniacs, has numerous precedents in the literature of the Middle Ages, including Dante's thoroughly medieval *The Divine Comedy*. This is not to say, however, that *The Decameron* does not look to the future, for it most certainly does. For one thing, when Boccaccio attacks the superstitious religious beliefs and corrupt ecclesiastical practices of his times, he does so with more severity than did his predecessors; for another, he presents the centrality of sexuality to the human condition without recourse to sermons or condemnations of the same. In both ways, he draws closer to the spirit of a new age and distances himself from the Middle Ages. His overriding purpose in the tales, however, is to illuminate the spectrum of humankind's experiences and to point, in a world accustomed to pain and disease, a way to happiness and health. Boccaccio's medium is always the well-worded and exquisitely framed story; his best medicine, more often than not, is laughter or the praise of life.

Other major works

POETRY: *Rime*, c. 1330-1340; *La caccia di Diana*, c. 1334; *Il filostrato*, c. 1335 (*The Filostrato*, 1873); *Il filocolo*, c. 1336 (*Labor of Love*, 1566); *Teseida*, 1340-1341 (*The Book of Theseus*, 1974); *Il ninfale d'Ameto*, 1341-1342 (also known as *Commedia delle ninfe*); *L'amorosa visione*, 1342-1343 (English translation, 1986); *Elegia di Madonna Fiammetta*, 1343-1344 (*Amorous Fiammetta*, 1587); *Il ninfale fiesolano*, 1344-1346 (*The Nymph of Fiesole*, 1597); *Buccolicum carmen*, c. 1351-1366 (*Boccaccio's Olympia*, 1913).

NONFICTION: *Genealogia deorum gentilium*, c. 1350-1375; *Trattatello in laude di Dante*, 1351, 1360, 1373 (*Life of Dante*, 1898); *Corbaccio*, c. 1355 (*The Corbaccio*, 1975); *De casibus virorum illustrium*, 1355-1374 (*The Fall of Princes*, 1431-1438); *De montibus, silvis, fontibus lacubus, fluminubus, stagnis seu paludibus, et de nominbus maris*, c. 1355-1374; *De mulieribus claris*, c. 1361-1375 (*Concerning Famous Women*, 1943); *Esposizioni sopra la Commedia di Dante*, 1373-1374.

Bibliography

Bergin, Thomas G. *Boccaccio*. New York: Viking Press, 1981. An excellent general introduction to Boccaccio. It begins with a historical background to Florentine life in the fourteenth century and proceeds to delineate the life of the author with emphasis on the major influences on his work. The early works are analyzed individually for their own merit and for their relationship to *The Decameron*. Contains lengthy but lucid discussion of *The Decameron* followed by notes and a useful list of works cited.

Branca, Vittore. *Boccaccio: The Man and His Works*. Translated by Richard Monges. New York: New York University Press, 1976. The definitive biography of Boccaccio by an eminent scholar in the field of medieval literature. Branca analyzes Boccaccio from a historical perspective, provides an overview of the Middle Ages, discusses Florentine life during the period of the emerging merchant middle class, and focuses on the episode of the horrendous Black Plague. Branca offers many scholarly insights into Boccaccio's prose production within a readable style that is accessible to the general public.

Cassell, Anthony K., and Victoria Kirkham, eds. and trans. *Diana's Hunt: Boccaccio's First Fiction*. Philadelphia: University of Pennsylvania Press, 1991.

Cottino-Jones, Marga. *An Anatomy of Boccaccio's Style.* Napoli, Italy: Cymba, 1968. While the influence of Boccaccio on prose literature and the novel is of major importance, his linguistic contribution cannot be ignored. Boccaccio's style was to be emulated by the writers of ensuing genera- tions, and in the Renaissance he officially became the model for all Italian prose. Cottino-Jones analyzes the style of Boccaccio, its mixture of Latin and Florentine idioms, and illustrates how a study of its linguistic peculiarities can offer interesting insights into an interpreta- tion of *The Decameron.*

Hollander, Robert. *Boccaccio's Last Fiction, "Il Corbaccio."* Philadelphia: University of Pennsylvania Press, 1988.

_____. *Boccaccio's Two Venuses.* New York: Columbia University Press, 1977. A thorough analysis of all Boccaccio's works except *The Decameron.* The author contrasts classical and Christian influences in Boccaccio's work and concludes that, although the latter predominates in the later works, even in the earlier prose the classical Venus is tempered by the use of irony. Concludes that Boccaccio is a moral philosopher who, unlike Dante, is not concerned with human appetites that lead to a spiritual death but with their negative effects in this world. More than one hundred pages of notes provide a tool for further research.

Serafini-Sauli, Judith. *Giovanni Boccaccio.* Boston: Twayne Publishers, 1982.

Wright, Herbert G. *Boccaccio in England, from Chaucer to Tennyson.* London: Athlone Press, 1957. Boccaccio's fame is not limited to Italy, and it is particularly in England that his works had a major impact. This book analyzes the influence of Boccaccio on well-known authors such as Geoffrey Chaucer, William Shakespeare, and Alfred, Lord Tennyson, with an especially lengthy and perspicacious discussion of the presence of Boccaccio in *The Canterbury Tales.* This volume is also a fine introduc- tion to the comparative study of literatures, and it illustrates how masterpieces of literature in any language belong to the world commu- nity.

Madison V. Sowell
(Revised by *Victor A. Santi*)

JORGE LUIS BORGES

Born: Buenos Aires, Argentina; August 24, 1899
Died: Geneva, Switzerland; June 14, 1986

Principal short fiction · *Historia universal de la infamia*, 1935 (*A Universal History of Infamy*, 1972) · *El jardín de senderos que se bifurcan*, 1941 · *Seis problemas para don Isidro Parodi*, 1942 (with Bioy Casares, under joint pseudonym H. Bustos Domecq; *Six Problems for Don Isidro Parodi*, 1981) · *Ficciones, 1935-1944*, 1944 (English translation, 1962) · *Dos fantasías memorables*, 1946 (with Bioy Casares, under joint pseudonym H. Bustos Domecq) · *El Aleph*, 1949, 1952 (translated in *The Aleph and Other Stories, 1933-1969*, 1970) · *La muerte y la brújula*, 1951 · *La hermana de Eloísa*, 1955 (with Luisa Mercedes Levinson) · *Cuentos*, 1958 · *Crónicas de H. Bustos Domecq*, 1967 (with Bioy Casares; *Chronicles of Bustos Domecq*, 1976) · *El informe de Brodie*, 1970 (*Doctor Brodie's Report*, 1972) · *El matrero*, 1970 · *El congreso*, 1971 (*The Congress*, 1974) · *El libro de arena*, 1975 (*The Book of Sand*, 1977) · *Narraciones*, 1980

Other literary forms · Though most famous for his work in short fiction, Jorge Luis Borges also holds a significant place in Spanish American literature for his work in poetry and the essay. In fact, Borges would be considered a major writer in Spanish American letters for his work in these two genres (the vast majority of which was produced before the Argentine writer branched into short fiction) even had he never written a single short story. Borges' early poetry (that for which he earned his reputation as a poet) is of the ultraist school, an avant-grade brand of poetry influenced by expressionism and Dadaism and

intended by its Spanish American practitioners as a reaction to Spanish American modernism. Borges' essays, as readers familiar with his fiction might expect, are imaginative and witty and usually deal with topics in literature or philosophy. Interestingly, because of the writer's playful imagination, many of his essays read more like fiction than essay, while, because of his propensity both for toying with philosophical concepts and for fusing the fictitious and the real, much of his fiction reads more like essay than fiction. It seems only fitting, however, that for a writer for whom the line between fiction and reality is almost nonexistent the line between fiction and essay should be almost nonexistent as well.

Achievements · It is virtually impossible to overstate the importance of Borges within the context of Spanish American fiction, for he is, quite simply, the single most important writer of short fiction in the history of Spanish American literature. This is true not only because of his stories themselves, and chiefly those published in *Ficciones, 1935-1944* and *El Aleph*, but also, just as important, because of how his stories contributed to the evolution of Spanish American fiction, both short and long, in the latter half of the twentieth century.

Borges was the father of Spanish America's "new narrative," the type of narrative practiced by the likes of Julio Cortázar, Gabriel García Márquez, Carlos Fuentes, Mario Vargas Llosa, and others. Spanish American fiction prior to Borges was chiefly concerned with painting a realistic and detailed picture of external Spanish American reality. Borges' imaginative *ficciones* (or fictions) almost single-handedly changed this, teaching Spanish American writers to be creative, to use their imagination, to treat fiction as fiction, to allow the fictional world to be just that: fictional. Borges' works also taught Spanish American writers to deal with universal themes and to write for an intellectual reader. Without Borges, not only would the literary world be without some superb stories, but also Spanish American narrative in the second half of the twentieth century would have been radically different from what it evolved to be.

Biography · Jorge Luis Borges was born on August 24, 1899, in Buenos Aires, Argentina, the first of two children born to Jorge Guillermo Borges and Leonor Acevedo de Borges. (His sister, Norah, was born in 1901.) Borges' ancestors included prominent Argentine military and historical figures on both sides of his family and an English grandmother on his father's.

"Georgie," as Borges' family called him, began reading very early, first in English, then in Spanish. Tutored first by his English grandmother and later by a private governess, and with access to his father's library (which contained numerous volumes in English), young Borges devoured a wide range of writings, among them those of Robert Louis Stevenson, Rudyard Kipling, and Mark Twain, as well as works of mythology, novels of chivalry, *The Thousand and One Nights* (c. 1450), and Miguel de Cervantes' *Don Quixote de la Mancha* (1605, 1615).

Borges finally entered school at age nine, and at age thirteen he published his first story, a dramatic sketch entitled "El rey de la selva" (the king of the jungle), about his favorite animal, the tiger. Borges and his family traveled to Europe in 1914. World War I broke out while they were visiting Geneva, Switzerland, and they remained there until 1918. During his time in Geneva, Borges began to take an interest in French poetry, particularly that of Victor Hugo and Charles Baudelaire, as well as the poetry of Heinrich Heine and the German expressionists. He also began to read the works of Walt Whitman, Arthur Schopenhauer, and G. K. Chesterton, and he maintained his literary connection to his native Argentina by reading *gauchesca* (gaucho) poetry.

In 1919 Borges and his family moved to Spain, living for various lengths of time in Barcelona, Majorca, Seville, and Madrid. While in Spain, Borges associated with a group of ultraist poets and published some poetry in an ultraist magazine. In 1921, Borges and his family returned to Buenos Aires. His return to his native city after a seven-year absence inspired him to write his first volume of poetry, entitled *Fervor de Buenos Aires* (fervor of Buenos Aires) and published in 1923. During this same period (in 1922), he collaborated on a "billboard review" entitled *Prisma* (prism) and edited the manifesto "Ultraísmo" (ultraism), published in the magazine *Nosotros* (us). He also helped found a short-lived magazine entitled *Proa* (prow). Following a second trip with his family to Europe (1923-1924), Borges continued to write poetry during the 1920's, but he began to branch out into the essay genre as well, publishing three collections of essays during this period: *Inquisiciones* (inquisitions) in 1925, *El tamaño de mi esperanza* (the size of my hope) in 1926, and *El idioma de los argentinos* (the language of the argentines) in 1928. One of his collections of poetry, *Cuaderno San Martín* (San Martín notebook), won for him second prize in the Municipal Literature Competition in 1929. The prize carried an award of three thousand pesos, which Borges used to buy an edition of the *Encyclopædia Britannica*.

Borges continued writing both poetry and essay in the 1930's, but this decade would also bring his first (though unconventional) steps into fiction. He began contributing to the magazine *Sur* (south) in 1931 (through which he met his friend and future literary collaborator Adolfo Bioy Casares); later, in 1933, he became the director of *Crítica* (criticism), a Saturday literary supplement for a Buenos Aires newspaper. As a contributor to the supplement, Borges began to rewrite stories that he took from various sources, adding his own personal touches and reworking them as he saw fit. He finally wrote, under a pen name, a wholly original piece entitled "Hombres de las orillas" (men from the outskirts), which appeared on September 16, 1933, in the supplement. This story and his other *Crítica* pieces were well received and published together in 1935 in a volume entitled *Historia universal de la infamia.*

Borges' foray into fiction writing continued to follow an unconventional path when in 1936 he began writing a book-review page for the magazine *El Hogar* (the home). Each entry carried a brief biography of the author whose work was being reviewed. Once again, Borges could not leave well enough alone. To the author's true biographical facts, Borges began to add his own "facts," even including apocryphal anecdotes from the author's life and supplementing the author's bibliography with false titles. This mix of fact and fiction, with no regard or concern for which was which, would come to be one of the trademarks of Borges' fiction.

Borges took a job as an assistant librarian in a suburban Buenos Aires library in 1937, a position whose work load and setting afforded the writer ample time and resources to read and write. In December of 1938, however, the Argentine writer suffered a near-fatal accident, slipping in a staircase and striking his head while returning to his apartment. The resulting head injury developed into septicemia, and Borges was hospitalized for more than two weeks. While still recovering in early 1939, Borges decided that he would abandon poetry and the essay (though he would later return to these genres) and dedicate his literary efforts to short fiction. Though it is somewhat unclear as to precisely why he made this decision (there are various accounts), it is speculated by some (and Borges' own comments have supported such speculation) that he did so because after his head injury he was not sure that he could write poetry and essays of the quality for which he was known before the accident. Short stories, for which he was virtually unknown at this point, would not allow anyone to compare an old Borges with a new, and potentially inferior, Borges. Again, this is only one suggestion as to why the Argentine writer made the decision he did; what is most important, however, is that he made it, and this decision, and the accident that seems to have caused it, would change the face of Spanish American fiction of the twentieth century.

Almost immediately, Borges began to produce a series of short stories that would make him the most important writer in Spanish American fiction and that would eventually make him famous. The first of these stories was "Pierre Menard, autor del *Quijote*" ("Pierre Menard, Author of the *Quixote*"), which appeared in *Sur* in May of 1939. This story was followed in 1940 by "Tlön, Uqbar, Orbis Tertius" ("Tlön, Uqbar, Orbis Tertius") and the collection *El jardín de senderos que se bifurcan* (the garden of forking paths) in 1941. Six stories were added to the eight collected in *El jardín de senderos que se bifurcan*, and a new collection, entitled *Ficciones, 1935-1944*, the single most important collection of short fiction in Spanish American literature, appeared in 1944. Another landmark collection, *El Aleph*, followed in 1949.

During this time, the height of his literary career up to this point, Borges, who was anti-Peronist, fell into disfavor with the government of Argentine president Juan Perón. He was dismissed from his position at the library in 1944 and appointed inspector of poultry and eggs in the municipal market. He resigned, but he did return to public service in 1955 when, following the fall of Perón, he was named the director of the National Library. Ironically, in the same year, he lost his sight, which had been declining for several years.

Despite the loss of his sight, Borges continued to write (through dictation), though less than before. At the same time, his two collections of stories from the 1940's had made him a household name among Spanish American literati. Worldwide recognition came in 1961, when he shared the Formentor Prize (worth ten thousand dollars) with Samuel Beckett. The fame that this award brought Borges changed his life. That fall, he traveled to the United States to lecture at the University of Texas, and between 1961 and his death, in 1986, he would make numerous trips to the United States and elsewhere around the world, teaching and speaking at colleges and universities, attending literary conferences on his works, collecting literary awards, and otherwise serving as an international ambassador for Spanish American literature.

Borges married for the first time (at age sixty-eight) in 1967, the same year that he accepted an invitation to teach at Harvard University as a Charles Eliot Norton lecturer. The marriage dissolved in 1970, with Borges, according to one popular anecdote, leaving the home he shared with his wife and taking only his prized *Encyclopædia Britannica* with him. Perón returned to the Argentine presidency in 1973, and Borges resigned as director of the National Library. His mother died at age ninety-nine in 1975.

Borges continued to write during the 1970's and until his death, working in short fiction, poetry, and the essay (having returned to these last two genres in the 1950's). The bulk of his fame, however, and particularly that specifically related to short fiction, had come from his two collections of stories from the 1940's. He was nominated repeatedly for the Nobel Prize in Literature but never won it. In 1986, he married his companion María

Kodama and shortly thereafter died of cancer of the liver on June 14, 1986, in Geneva, Switzerland.

Analysis · Jorge Luis Borges is, quite simply, the single most important writer of short fiction in the history of Spanish American literature. The stories he published in his collections *Ficciones, 1935-1944* and *El Aleph,* particularly the former, not only gave Spanish American (and world) literature a body of remarkable stories but also opened the door to a whole new type of fiction in Spanish America, a type of fiction that would be practiced by the likes of Cortázar, García Márquez, Fuentes, and Vargas Llosa, and that, in the hands of these writers and others like them, would put Spanish American fiction on the world literary map in the 1960's.

Prior to Borges, and particularly between 1920 and 1940, Spanish American fiction, as stated previously, was concerned chiefly with painting a realistic and detailed picture of external Spanish American reality. Description frequently ruled over action, environment over character, and types over individuals. Social message, also, was often more important to the writer than was narrative artistry. Spanish American fiction after Borges (that is, after his landmark collections of stories of the 1940's) was decidedly different in that it was no longer documentary in nature, turned its focus toward the inner workings of its fully individualized human characters, presented various interpretations of reality, expressed universal as well as regional and national themes, invited reader participation, and emphasized the importance of artistic—and frequently unconventional—presentation of the story, particularly with respect to narrative voice, language, structure (and the closely related element of time), and characterization. This "new narrative," as it came to be called, would have been impossible without Borges' tradition-breaking fiction.

This is not to say that Borges' stories fully embody each of the characteristics of Spanish America's "new narrative" listed above. Ironically, they do not. For example, Borges' characters are often far more archetypal than individual, his presentation tends to be for the most part quite traditional, and reader participation (at least as compared to that required in the works of other "new narrativists") is frequently not a factor. The major contributions that Borges made to Spanish American narrative through his stories lie, first, in his use of imagination, second, in his focus on universal themes common to all human beings, and third, in the intellectual aspect of his works. In the 1940's, Borges, unlike most who were writing so-called "fiction" in Spanish America at the time, treated fiction as fiction. Rather than use fiction to document everyday reality, Borges used it to invent new realities, to toy with philosophical concepts, and in the process to create truly fictional worlds, governed by their own rules. He also chose to write chiefly about universal human beings rather than exclusively about Spanish Americans. His characters are, for example, European, or Chinese, frequently of no discernible nationality, and only occasionally Spanish American. In most cases, even when a character's nationality is revealed, it is of no real importance, particularly with respect to theme. Almost all Borges' characters are important not because of the country from which they come but because they are human beings, faced not with situations and conflicts particular to their nationality but with situations and conflicts common to all human beings. Finally, unlike his predecessors and many of his contemporaries, Borges did not aim his fiction at the masses. He wrote instead, it seems, more for himself, and, by extension, for the intellectual reader. These three aspects of his fiction—treating fiction as fiction, placing universal characters in universal conflicts, and writing for a more intellectual audience—stand as the Argentine writer's three most important contributions to Spanish American fiction in the latter half of the twentieth century, and to one degree or another, virtually every one of Spanish America's "new narrativists," from Cortázar to García Márquez, followed Borges' lead in these areas.

Given the above, it is no surprise that Borges' *ficciones* (his stories are more aptly called "fictions" than "stories," for while all fit emphatically into the first category, since they contain fictitious elements, many do not fit nearly so well into a traditional definition of the second, since they read more like essays than stories) are sophisticated, compact, even mathematically precise narratives that range in type from what might be called the "traditional" short story (a rarity) to fictionalized essay (neither pure story nor pure essay but instead a unique mix of the two, complete, oddly enough, with both fictitious characters and footnotes, both fictitious and factual) to detective story or spy thriller (though always with an unmistakably Borgesian touch) to fictional illustration of a philosophical concept (this last type being, perhaps, most common). Regardless of the specific category into which each story might fall, almost all, to one degree or another, touch on either what Borges viewed as the labyrinthine nature of the universe, irony (particularly with respect to human destiny), the concept of time, the hubris of those who believe they know all there is to know, or any combination of these elements.

As stated above, most of Borges' fame as a writer of fiction and virtually all of his considerable influence on Spanish American "new narrative" are derived from his two masterpiece collections, *Ficciones, 1935-1944* and *El Aleph.* Of these two, the first stands out as the more important and is, in fact, the single most important collection of short fiction in the history of

Spanish American literature.

Ficciones, 1935-1944 contains fourteen stories (seventeen for editions published after 1956). Seven of the fourteen were written between 1939 and 1941 and, along with an eighth story, were originally collected in *El jardín de senderos que se bifurcan* (the garden of forking paths). The other six stories were added in 1944. Virtually every story in this collection has become a Spanish American classic, and together they reveal the variety of Borges' themes and story types.

"La muerte y la brújula" ("Death and the Compass") is one of the most popular of the stories found in *Ficciones, 1935-1944.* In it, detective Erik Lönnrot is faced with the task of solving three apparent murders that have taken place exactly one month apart at locations that form a geographical equilateral triangle. The overly rational Lönnrot, through elaborate reasoning, divines when and where the next murder is to take place. He goes there to prevent the murder and to capture the murderer, only to find himself captured, having been lured to the scene by his archenemy, Red Scharlach, so that he, Lönnrot, can be killed.

This story is a perfect example of Borges' ability to take a standard subgenre, in this case the detective story, and give it his own personal signature, as the story is replete with Borgesian trademarks. The most prominent of these concerns irony and hubris. Following the first murder and published reports of Lönnrot's line of investigation, Scharlach, who has sworn to kill Lönnrot, constructs the remainder of the murder scenario, knowing that Lönnrot will not rest until he deciphers the apparent patterns and then—believing he knows, by virtue of his reasoning, all there is to know—will blindly show up at the right spot at the right time for Scharlach to capture and kill him. Ironically, Lönnrot's intelligence and his reliance (or over-reliance) on reasoning, accompanied in no small measure by his self-assurance and intellectual vanity, which blind him to any potential danger, bring him to his death. Other trademark Borgesian elements in the story include the totally non-Spanish American content (from characters to setting), numerous references to Jews and things Jewish (a talmudic congress, rabbis, and Cabalistic studies, to name only a few), and an intellectual content and ambience throughout not typical of the traditional detective story. (Lönnrot figures out, for example, that the four points that indicate the four apparent murders—there are really only three—correspond to the Tetragrammaton, the four Hebrew letters that make up "the ineffable name of God.")

"The Garden of Forking Paths" is another story from *Ficciones, 1935-1944* which in the most general sense (but only in the most general sense) fits comfortably into a traditional category, that of spy thriller, but like

"Death and the Compass," in Borges' hands it is anything but a story typical of its particular subgenre. In this story, Dr. Yu Tsun (once again, a non-Spanish American character), a Chinese professor of English, working in England (a non-Spanish American setting as well) as a spy for the Germans during World War I, has been captured and now dictates his story. Yu tells of how he had needed to transmit vital information to the Germans concerning the name of the town in which the British were massing artillery in preparation for an attack. Yu's superior, however, had been captured, thus severing Yu's normal lines of communication. Identified as a spy and pursued by the British, Yu tells how he had selected, from the phone directory, the only man he believed could help him communicate his message, one Stephen Albert (though the reader at this point is not aware of exactly how Albert could be of help to Yu). Yu tells of how he traveled to Albert's house, hotly pursued by a British agent. Yu had never met Albert, but Albert mistook him for someone else and invited Yu in the house. The two talked for an hour about Chinese astrologer and writer Ts'ui Pêen (who happened to be one of Yu's ancestors) and Ts'ui's labyrinthine book *The Garden of Forking Paths* (which, given its content, gives Borges' story a story-within-a-story element) as Yu stalled for time for the British agent to catch up with him. Yu says that as the agent approached the house, Yu killed Albert and then allowed himself to be captured by the agent. The final paragraph of the story reveals that Yu had chosen to kill Albert and then be arrested so that news of the incident would appear in the newspaper. He knew that his German colleagues would read the small news item and would divine Yu's intended message: that the British had been massing artillery near the French town of Albert—thus Yu's reason for having chosen Stephen Albert.

"Las ruinas circulares" ("The Circular Ruins") is one of a number of examples in *Ficciones, 1935-1944* of Borges' frequent practice of using a story to illustrate (or at least toy with) philosophical concepts, in this particular case, most notably, the Gnostic concept of one creator behind another creator. In this story, a mysterious man travels to an equally mysterious place with the intention of creating another person by dreaming him. The man experiences great difficulty in this at first, but eventually he is successful. The man instructs his creation and then sends him off. Before he does, however, the man erases his creation's knowledge of how he came to be, for the man does not wish him to know that he exists only as the dream of another. Soon after the man's creation has left, fire breaks out and surrounds the man. He prepares for death, but as the flames begin to engulf him, he cannot feel them. He realizes then that he too, ironically, is but an illusion, not real at all but simply the dream of another.

"Pierre Menard, autor del *Quijote*" ("Pierre Menard, Author of the *Quixote*"), also from *Ficciones, 1935-1944*, is one of Borges' most famous stories that may be classified as a fictionalized essay, for it is clearly not a story: a fiction, yes, but a story (at least by any traditional definition of the term), no. In it, a pompous first-person narrator, a literary critic, in what is presented as an essay of literary criticism, tells of the writer Pierre Menard (fictional in the real world but completely real in Borges' fictive universe). After considerable discussion of Menard's bibliography (complete with titles and publication dates, all fictional, of course, but with titles of real literary journals—once again, an example of Borges' practice of fusing the fictive and the real), as well as other facts about the author, the critic discusses Menard's attempt to compose a contemporary version of Cervantes' *Don Quixote de la Mancha*. Menard accomplishes this not by writing a new *Don Quixote de la Mancha* but simply by copying Cervantes' original text word for word. The critic even examines identical passages from the two versions and declares that Menard's version, though identical to Cervantes', is actually richer. The critic pursues the reasons and ramifications of this fact further. The result is, among other things, a tongue-in-cheek send-up of scholars and literary critics and the snobbish and often ridiculous criticism that they publish.

Finally, "El Sur" ("The South"), from *Ficciones, 1935-1944* as well, is a classic Borges story that demonstrates the author's ability to mix reality (at best a relative term in Borges' world and in Spanish American "new narrative" as a whole) with fantasy and, more important, to show that the line between the two is not only very subtle but also of no real importance, for fantasy is just as much a part of the universe as so-called reality. This story, which Borges once said he considered his best, concerns Johannes Dahlmann, a librarian in Buenos Aires. Dahlmann, the reader is told, has several heroic, military ancestors, and though he himself is a city-dwelling intellectual, he prefers to identify himself with his more romantic ancestors. In that spirit, Dahlmann even maintains a family ranch in the "South" (capitalized here and roughly the Argentine equivalent, in history and image, to North America's "Old West"). He is, however, an absentee landowner, spending all of his time in Buenos Aires, keeping the ranch only to maintain a connection, although a chiefly symbolic one, with his family's more exciting past. Entering his apartment one night, Dahlmann accidentally runs into a doorway (an accident very similar to that which Borges suffered in 1938). The resulting head injury develops into septicemia (as was the case with Borges as well), and he is sent off to a sanatorium. Finally, he recovers well enough to travel, at his doctor's suggestion, to his ranch in the South to convalesce. His train trip to the South is vague to him at best, as he slips in and out of sleep. Unfamiliar with the region, he disembarks one stop too early and waits in a general store for transportation. While there, he is harassed by a group of ruffians. He accepts the challenge of one among them, and as the story ends, he is about to step outside for a knife fight he knows he cannot win.

If that were all there were to "The South," the story would be interesting, perhaps, but certainly nothing spectacular, and it would probably fit fairly comfortably into the type of Spanish American narrative popular before Borges. There is more, however, and it is this "more" that places the story firmly within the parameters of Spanish American "new narrative." The story is, in fact, the literary equivalent of an optical illusion. For those who can perceive only one angle, the story is essentially that described above. For those who can make out the other angle, however, the story is completely different. There are numerous subtle though undeniably present hints throughout the second half of the story, after Dahlmann supposedly leaves the sanatorium, that suggest that the protagonist does not step out to fight at the end of the story. In fact, he never even leaves the sanatorium at all but instead dies there. His trip to the South, his encounter with the ruffians, and his acceptance of their challenge, which will lead to certain death, are all nothing but a dream, dreamt, it seems, in the sanatorium, for death in a knife fight is the death that he, Dahlmann–the librarian who likes to identify himself with his heroic and romantic ancestors–would have preferred compared to that of the sanatorium. This added dimension as well as the rather subtle manner in which it is suggested (an attentive reader is required) separates both the story and its author from the type of fiction and fiction writer that characterized Spanish American fiction before Borges. It is this type of added dimension that makes Borges' fiction "new" and makes him a truly fascinating writer to read.

Borges continued to write short fiction after *Ficciones, 1935-1944* and *El Aleph,* but the stories produced during this period never approached the popularity among readers nor the acclaim among critics associated with the two earlier collections. This is attributable in part to the fact that most of the stories the Argentine writer published in the 1960's, as well as the 1970's and 1980's, lack much of what makes Borges Borges. Most are decidedly more realistic, often more Argentine in focus, and in general less complex–all in all, less Borgesian and, according to critics, less impressive. Some of this, particularly the change in complexity, has been explained as attributable to the fact that because of his loss of sight, Borges turned to dictation, which made reediting and polishing more difficult. Regardless of the reason, most of Borges' fiction after his two landmark collections of the 1940's is largely ignored. In fact, when one thinks of Borges' fiction, with very rare exception, one immediately thinks of those stories included in *Ficciones, 1935-1944* and *El Aleph*, but these two collections, particularly the former, are enough to make Borges the single most important writer of short fiction in the history of Spanish American literature.

Other major works

NOVEL: *Un modelo para la muerte*, 1946 (with Adolfo Bioy Casares, under joint pseudonym B. Suárez Lynch).

SCREENPLAYS: *Los orilleros y El paraíso de los creyentes*, 1955 (with Bioy Casares); *Les Autres*, 1974 (with Bioy Casares and Hugo Santiago).

POETRY: *Fervor de Buenos Aires*, 1923, 1969; *Luna de enfrente*, 1925; *Cuaderno San Martín*, 1929; *Poemas, 1923-1943*, 1943; *Poemas, 1923-1953*, 1954; *Obra poética, 1923-1958*, 1958; *Obra poética, 1923-1964*, 1964; *Seis poemas escandinavos*, 1966; *Siete poemas*, 1967; *El otro, el mismo*, 1969; *Elogio de la sombra*, 1969 (*In Praise of Darkness*, 1974); *El oro de los tigres*, 1972 (translated in *The Gold of Tigers: Selected Later Poems*, 1977); *La rosa profunda*, 1975 (translated in *The Gold of Tigers); La moneda de hierro*, 1976; *Historia de la noche*, 1977; *La cifra*, 1981; *Los conjurados*, 1986.

NONFICTION: *Inquisiciones*, 1925; *El tamaño de mi esperanza*, 1926; *El idioma de los argentinos*, 1928; *Evaristo Carriego*, 1930 (English translation, 1984); *Figari*, 1930; *Discusión*, 1932; *Las Kennigar*, 1933; *Historia de la eternidad*, 1936; *Nueva refutación del tiempo*, 1947; *Aspectos de la literatura gauchesca*, 1950; *Antiguas literaturas germánicas*, 1951 (with Delia Ingenieros; revised as *Literaturas germánicas medievales*, 1966, with Maria Esther Vásquez); *Otras Inquisiciones*, 1952 (*Other Inquisitions*, 1964); *El "Martin Fierro,"* 1953 (with Margarita Guerrero); *Leopoldo Lugones*, 1955 (with Betina Edelberg); *Manual de zoología fantástica*, 1957 (with Guerrero; *The Imaginary Zoo*, 1969, revised as *El libro de los seres imaginarios*, 1967, *The Book of Imaginary Beings*, 1969); *La poesía gauchesca*, 1960; *Introducción a la literatura norteamericana*, 1967 (with Esther Zemborain de Torres; *An Introduction to American Literature*, 1971); *Prólogos*, 1975; *¿Qué es el budismo?*, 1976 (with Alicia Jurado); *Cosmogonías*, 1976; *Libro de sueños*, 1976; *Siete noches*, 1980 (*Seven Nights*, 1984); *Nueve ensayos dantescos*, 1982.

TRANSLATIONS: *Orlando*, 1937 (of Virginia Woolf's novel); *La metamórfosis*, 1938 (of Franz Kafka's novel *Die Verwandlung); Un bárbaro en Asia*, 1941 (of Henri Michaux's travel notes); *Los mejores cuentos policiales*, 1943 (with Bioy Casares, of detective stories by various authors); *Bartleby, el escribiente*, 1943 (of Herman Melville's novella *Bartleby the Scrivener); Los mejores cuentos policiales, segunda serie*, 1951 (with Bioy Casares, of detective stories by various authors); *Cuentos breves y extraordinarios*, 1955, 1973 (with Bioy

Casares, of short stories by various authors; *Extraordinary Tales*, 1973); *Las palmeras salvajes*, 1956 (of William Faulkner's novel *The Wild Palms); Hojas de hierba*, 1969 (of Walt Whitman's *Leaves of Grass*).

EDITED TEXT: *El compadrito: Su destino, sus barrios, su música*, 1945, 1968 (with Silvina Bullrich).

ANTHOLOGIES: *Antología clásica de la literatura argentina*, 1937; *Antología de la literatura fantástica*, 1940 (with Bioy Casares and Silvia Ocampo); *Antología poética argentina*, 1941 (with Bioy Casares and Ocampo); *Poesía gauchesca*, 1955 (2 volumes, with Bioy Casares); *Libro del cielo y del infierno*, 1960, 1975 (with Bioy Casares); *Versos*, by Evaristo Carriego, 1972; *Antología poética*, by Francisco de Quevedo, 1982; *Antología poética*, by Leopoldo Lugones, 1982; *El amigo de la muerte*, by Pedro Antonio de Alarcón, 1984.

MISCELLANEOUS: *Obras completas*, 1953-1967 (10 volumes); *Antología personal*, 1961 (*A Personal Anthology*, 1967); *Labyrinths: Selected Stories and Other Writings*, 1962, 1964; *Nueva antología personal*, 1968; *Selected Poems, 1923-1967*, 1972 (also includes prose); *Adrogue*, 1977; *Obras completas en colaboración*, 1979 (with others); *Borges: A Reader*, 1981; *Atlas*, 1984 (with María Kodama; English translation, 1985).

Bibliography

Bell-Villada, Gene H. *Borges and His Fiction: A Guide to His Mind and Art.* Chapel Hill: University of North Carolina Press, 1981. An excellent introduction to Borges and his works for North American readers. In lengthy sections entitled "Borges's Worlds," "Borges's Fiction," and "Borges's Place in Literature," Bell-Villada provides detailed and very readable commentary concerning Borges' background, his many stories, and his career, all the while downplaying the Argentine writer's role as a philosopher and intellectual and emphasizing his role as a storyteller. A superb study.

Harss, Luis, and Barbara Dohmann. "Jorge Luis Borges: Or, The Consolation by Philosophy." In *Into the Mainstream: Conversations with Latin American Writers.* New York: Harper & Row, 1967. This piece combines and intertwines personal biography, literary biography, critical commentary, and interview to produce a multifaceted look at Borges' life, his works, and his philosophical beliefs, and, most of all, how his philosophical beliefs are reflected in both his poetry and, more so here, his prose. A classic piece of the body of criticism written on Borges in spite of its publication date.

McMurray, George R. *Jorge Luis Borges.* New York: Frederick Ungar, 1980. Intended by the author as "an attempt to decipher the formal and thematic aspects of a man-made universe that rivals reality in its almost overwhelming complexity," namely Borges' universe. A very good and well-organized study of Borges' dominant themes and narrative devices, with many specific references to the Argentine author's stories. Includes an informative introduction on Borges' life and a conclusion that coherently brings together the diverse elements discussed in the book.

Rodríguez Monegal, Emir. *Jorge Luis Borges: A Literary Biography.* New York: E. P. Dutton, 1978. The definitive biography of Borges by one of the Argentine writer's (and contemporary Latin American literature's) most prominent critics. Particularly interesting for its constant blending of facts about Borges' life and literary text by him concerning or related to the events or personalities discussed. Detailed, lengthy, and highly informative. Very useful for anyone seeking a better understanding of Borges the writer.

Sabajanes, Beatriz Sarlo. *Jorge Luis Borges: A Writer on the Edge.* Edited by John King. New York: Verso, 1993.

Stabb, Martin S. *Borges Revisited.* Boston: Twayne, 1991. An update of Stabb's *Jorge Luis Borges,* published in 1970 and listed below. Though Borges' early works, including those from the 1940's and 1950's, are discussed and analyzed here, emphasis is on Borges' post-1970 writings, how the "canonical" (to use Stabb's term) Borges compares to the later Borges, and "a fresh assessment of the Argentine master's position as a major Western literary presence." An excellent study, particularly used in tandem with Stabb's earlier book on Borges.

_____. *Jorge Luis Borges.* New York: Twayne, 1970. An excellent study of Borges intended by its author "to introduce the work of this fascinating and complex writer to North American readers." Includes an opening chapter on Borges' life and career, followed by chapters on the Argentine writer's work in the genres of poetry, essay, and fiction, as well as a concluding chapter entitled "Borges and the Critics." A superb and very readable introduction to all aspects of Borges' literary production through 1968.

Yates, Donald A. *Jorge Luis Borges: Life, Work, and Criticism.* Fredericton, Canada: York Press, 1985. A brief (forty-one-page) sketch of, as the title indicates, Borges' life, work, and criticism. Chapters include "A Biography of Jorge Luis Borges," "A Chronological List of Borges's Major Works," "A Summary of Borges's Principal Writings," "An Evaluation of Borges's Achievements," and "Annotated Bibliography." Far more complete and information-filled than its length would suggest.

Keith H. Brower

ELIZABETH BOWEN

Born: Dublin, Ireland; June 7, 1899
Died: London, England; February 22, 1973

Principal short fiction · *Encounters*, 1923 · *Ann Lee's and Other Stories*, 1926 · *Joining Charles*, 1929 · *The Cat Jumps and Other Stories*, 1934 · *Look at All Those Roses*, 1941 · *The Demon Lover*, 1945 (published in the United States as *Ivy Gripped the Steps and Other Stories*, 1946) · *The Early Stories*, 1951 · *Stories by Elizabeth Bowen*, 1959 · *A Day in the Dark and Other Stories*, 1965 · *Elizabeth Bowen's Irish Stories*, 1978 · *The Collected Stories of Elizabeth Bowen*, 1980

Other literary forms · Elizabeth Bowen is as well known for her ten novels as she is for her short-story collections. She also wrote books of history, travel, literary essays, personal impressions, a play, and a children's book.

Achievements · Bowen's career is distinguished by achievements on two separate, though related, fronts. On the one hand, she was among the most well-known and accomplished British women novelists of her generation, a generation which, in the interwar period, did much to consolidate the distinctive existence of women's fiction. Bowen's work in this area is noteworthy for its psychological acuity, sense of atmosphere, and impassioned fastidiousness of style.

As an Anglo-Irish writer, on the other hand, she maintained more self-consciously than most of her predecessors an understanding of her class's destiny. Themes that are prevalent throughout her work—loss of innocence, decline of fortune, impoverishment of the will—gain an additional haunting quality from her sensitivity to the Irish context. Her awareness of the apparent historical irrelevance of the Anglo-Irish also gives her short stories in particular an important cultural resonance.

Biography · Elizabeth Dorothea Cole Bowen received her formal education at Downe House in Kent and at the London County Council School of Art. In 1923 she married Alan Charles Cameron and lived with him in Northampton and Old Headington, Oxford. In 1935 she and her husband moved to Regent's Park, London, where Bowen became a member of the Bloomsbury group. During World War II she stayed in London, where she worked for the Ministry of Information and as an air-raid warden. In 1948 she was made a Commander of the British Empire. She was awarded an honorary Doctor of Letters by Trinity College, Dublin, in 1949. After the death of her husband in 1952, Bowen returned to live at Bowen's Court in Ireland, her family estate. In 1957 she was awarded an honorary Doctor of Letters by the University of Oxford. In 1960 she sold Bowen's Court and returned to Old Headington, Oxford. After a final trip to Ireland, Elizabeth Bowen died in London on February 22, 1973.

Analysis · Elizabeth Bowen's stories are set in the first half of the twentieth century in England and Ireland. Often the action takes place against a background of war. Taken together, her stories provide a chronicle of the social, political, and psychic life of England from the beginning of the century through World War II. Her characters are mainly drawn from the middle class, although upper- and lower-class characters appear as well. Although Bowen's protagonist is usually a woman, men also play important roles. By selecting significant detail and by utilizing mythic parallels, Bowen constructs stories whose settings, actions, and characters are simultaneously realistic and symbolic.

Bowen's characters exist in a world which has lost contact with meaning; traditional forms and ideas have lost meaning and vitality. Both identity and a sense of belonging are lost; "Who am I?" and "Where am I?" are typical questions asked by Bowen protagonists. Some characters merely go through the motions and rituals of daily life, experiencing pattern without meaning. Others have a vague consciousness that something is wrong; unfulfilled, they suffer from boredom, apathy, and confusion. Sometimes, such characters are driven to seek alternatives in their lives. In "Summer Night," while the Major, an example of the first type of character, goes about his evening routine, shutting up the house for the night, his wife, Emma, pretending to visit friends, leaves her traditional family for an assignation with Robinson, a man she hardly knows. He represents another type: the man who adapts to meaninglessness by utilizing power amorally to manipulate and control. Emma is disillusioned in her search for vitality and love when she discovers that Robinson wants sex and nothing else. Other characters, such as Justin, are fully conscious of the situation; they know that they "don't live" and conceive the need for a "new form" but are impotent to break through to achieve one.

Although Bowen's stories focus on those characters who seek meaning or who are in the process of breaking through, they also represent a final type—one whose thinking and feeling are unified and in harmony with existence. An example from "Summer Night" is Justin's deaf sister, Queenie. While Robinson is left alone in his house, while Emma leans drunk and crying against a telegraph pole, and while Justin goes to mail an angry letter to Robinson, Queenie lies in bed remembering a time when she sat with a young man beside the lake below the ruin of the castle now on Robinson's land: "while her hand brushed the ferns in the cracks of the stone seat emanations of kindness passed from him to her. The subtle deaf girl had made the transposition of this nothing or everything into an everything." Queenie imagines: "Tonight it was Robinson who, guided by Queenie down leaf tunnels, took the place on the stone seat by the lake." It is Queenie's memory and imagination that creates, at least for herself, a world of love, unrealized, but realizable, by the others. Memory recalls the lost estate of man, represented here by the castle, its grounds, and its garden, as well as man's lost identity. Queenie *is* a queen. All human beings are rightfully queens and kings in Bowen's fiction. Queenie's memory reaches back to the archetypal roots of being, in harmony with life; her imagination projects this condition in the here and now and as a possibility for the future. Queenie's thinking is the true thinking Justin calls for, thinking that breaks through to a "new form," which is composed of archetypal truth transformed to suit the conditions of modern life. Throughout Bowen's fiction this kind of thought takes the form of fantasy, hallucination, and dream. Bowen's fiction itself, the expression of *her* imagination, also exemplifies this thinking.

Toward the end of "Summer Night" it occurs to Justin that possibly Emma should have come to him rather than Robinson. In "Her Table Spread" Bowen brings together two characters much like Emma and Justin. Valeria Cuff, heiress and owner of a castle in Ireland, situated on an estuary where English ships are allowed to anchor, invites Mr. Alban, a cynical and disillusioned young man from London, to a dinner party. These characters represent opposites which concern Bowen throughout her fiction: male and female, darkness and light, thought and feeling, physical and spiritual, rational and irrational. The separation or conflict of these opposites creates a world of war; their unification creates a world of love.

Valeria's orientation is romantic, "irrational," and optimistic: "her mind was made up: she was a princess." She invites Alban to her castle, "excited" at the thought of marrying him. Alban is realistic, rational, and pessimistic: "He had failed to love. . . . He knew some spring had dried up at the root of the world." Alban is disconcerted by Valeria's erratic, impulsive behavior and by her apparent vulgarity. He has heard "she was abnormal–at twenty-five, of statuesque development, still detained in childhood." Ironically, as Alban realizes "his presence must constitute an occasion," he is "put out of" Valeria's mind when a destroyer anchors in the estuary. Valeria believes it is the same destroyer that had anchored there the previous spring at Easter when two officers, Mr. Graves and Mr. Garrett, came ashore and were entertained by friends. Valeria's expectation that the officers will come to dinner initially separates her from Alban. When the officers fail to arrive, she runs outside to signal them with a lantern. Old Mr. Rossiter, uncle to Mrs. Treye, Valeria's aunt, leads Alban to the boathouse to prevent Valeria from rowing out to the destroyer. When a bat flies against Alban's ear, he flees, and, ascending the steps back toward the castle, he hears Valeria sobbing in the dark. When he calls to her, expressing concern and sympathy, she mistakes him for Mr. Garrett. Her fantasy of love is realized as she and Alban stand together, unified in a field of light shining from the castle.

Symbolic details and analogies with pagan and Christian myth universalize the meaning of the story. Alban is associated with the destroyer, with Graves and Garrett, and with their emblems, statues of Mars and Mercury. Like the destroyer, Alban is "fixed in the dark rain, by an indifferent shore." The officers represent aspects of Alban. The name Graves suggests death, and the statue associated with Graves is Mars, god of war. Garrett is a pun on *garret*, which derives from a word meaning to defend or protect. Garrett's statue is Mercury, a god associated by the Romans with peace. Alban's link with the destroyer, with death and war, threatens the destruction of Valeria's dreams of love and peace. The Garrett aspect of Alban, however, linked with protection and peace, offers the possibility of the realization of Valeria's dreams.

Valeria is associated with two symbolic items. Among the gifts she has to offer is a leopard skin, suggesting the animal and the sensual, and a statue of Venus, goddess of love. Valeria thus offers love in both its physical and spiritual aspects. Contained in her fantasies is the expectation that love will put an end to war. She thinks: "Invasions from the water would henceforth be social, perhaps amorous," and she imagines marrying Garrett and inviting "all the Navy up the estuary" for tea: "The Navy would be unable to tear itself away." As Valeria attempts to signal the destroyer with the lantern, she thinks that Graves and Garrett will have to fight for her; instead, the battle takes place within Alban.

The pagan symbolism in "Her Table Spread" is overlaid and transformed by Christian symbolism. Valeria's castle and its grounds, like the ruins of the castle in "Summer Night," represent a lost Eden. Valeria *is* an heiress and a princess; she is an incarnation of Eve seeking her rightful role and place in a paradise of love and peace. Symbolically, she calls to Adam (Alban) to reclaim *his* inheritance–to join her in re-creating the garden. The way is expressed in Bowen's use of the second major Christian myth.

Alban must undergo the experience of Christ, the second Adam, to redeem his "fallen" self; he must reject temptation and undergo crucifixion—sacrifice his ego. The trip to the boathouse is Alban's descent into hell. There he is tempted by Old Mr. Rossiter, the Devil. Rossiter offers Alban whiskey, which he refuses, and tempts him with Valeria: "She's a girl you could shape. She's got a nice income." Alban's rejection of this temptation, his refusal to *listen* to the Devil, is signified by his flight from the boathouse when a bat flies against his ear.

As Alban ascends the steps, he recognizes where he is: "Hell." This recognition is the precondition for discovering where he belongs. At this point he undergoes a symbolic crucifixion. Hearing Valeria "sobbing" in "absolute desperation," Alban clings "to a creaking tree." The sympathy Alban feels for Valeria signifies the death of Graves within him and the resurrection of Garrett. Valeria has also experienced crucifixion. Graves and Garrett have not arrived and her lantern has gone out; she, too, is in hell. Humbled and in darkness, the two meet. Alban speaks with tenderness: "Quietly, my dear girl." Valeria speaks with concern. "Don't you remember the way?" The year before the destroyer had anchored "at Easter." Now Valeria is present at and participates in resurrection: "*Mr. Garrett has landed.*" She laughs "like a princess, and magnificently justified." Standing with Valeria in the glow of light from the castle, observed by the two female guests, Alban experiences love: "such a strong tenderness reached him that, standing there in full manhood, he was for a moment not exiled. For the moment, without moving or speaking, he stood, in the dark, in a flame, as though all three said: 'My darling. . . .'"

A world of love is achieved, if only momentarily, in "Her Table Spread." In "The Demon Lover" Bowen creates a story of love denied or repressed, and its power transformed into the demonic. The stories complement each other. The first takes place at a castle in Ireland in the spring and recalls the previous Easter; the second is set in an abandoned London flat in autumn during the bombing of London in World War II and recalls a previous autumn during World War I. The action of "Her Table Spread" concludes with the coming of night. The protagonists of the first story are a young woman in search of love and a young man associated with war; those of the second are a forty-year-old married woman who has denied love and her fiancé of twenty years before, a solider lost in action during World War I. Both female characters are "abnormal": Valeria of "Her Table Spread" caught up in fantasy, Kathleen of "The Demon Lover" subject to hallucination. Bowen utilizes elements of the Eden myth to universalize the meaning of both stories.

In "The Demon Lover" Mrs. Kathleen Drover returns to her abandoned

London flat to pick up some things she had left behind when her family moved to the country to escape the bombing. In the dark flat where everything is covered with a dustlike film, she opens a door, and reflected light reveals an unstamped letter recently placed on a hall table. Since the caretaker is away and the house has been locked, there is no logical explanation for the appearance of the letter. Unnerved, Mrs. Drover takes it upstairs to her bedroom, where she reads it. The letter reminds her that today is the anniversary of the day years before when she made a promise of fidelity to a young soldier on leave from France during World War I—and that they had agreed to meet on this day "at an hour arranged." Although her "fiancé was reported missing, presumed killed," he has apparently survived and awaits the meeting. When Kathleen hears the church clock strike six, she becomes terrified, but maintains enough control to gather the items she came for and to formulate a plan to leave the house, hire a taxi, and bring the driver back with her to pick up the bundles. Meanwhile, in the basement "a door or window was being opened by someone who chose this moment to leave the house."

This statement provides a realistic solution to the problem of the letter's appearance, but a psychological interpretation offers an alternative conclusion. The London flat symbolizes Kathleen's life as Mrs. Drover, and the shock of finding the letter reveals to Kathleen the meaninglessness of this life and the falseness of her identity as Mrs. Drover. By marrying Drover, Kathleen has been "unfaithful" not only to the soldier but also to herself. It is this self which emerges as a result of the "crisis"—actually the crisis of World War II—and which has unconsciously motivated Mrs. Drover's return to the house. The fact that the letter is signed K., Kathleen's initial, suggests that she wrote the letter, which is a sign of the reemergence of her lost self. The house represents not only Kathleen's life as Mrs. Drover but also the repressed-Kathleen aspect of her identity. The person in the basement who leaves the house at the same moment Mrs. Drover lets herself out the front door is a projection of this repressed self, the self Mrs. Drover now unknowingly goes to face.

Overlying the psychological meaning of the story are two additional levels of meaning, one allegorical, the other archetypal. The young Kathleen represents England, defended and protected by the soldier, who represents the generation of those who fought for the country during the first war. Kathleen's loveless and meaningless marriage to Drover represents England's betrayal of the values the war was fought to defend—a betrayal which has contributed to the creation of World War II. The letter writer asserts: "In view of the fact that nothing has changed, I shall rely upon you to keep your promise." Because Kathleen and England have betrayed themselves, because love has failed, war continues, and both the individual and the country must suffer destructive consequences.

On the archetypal level, Kathleen and the soldier are incarnations of Eve and Adam, although the soldier is an Adam transformed by war into a devil who coerces Eve to "fall," forces her to make the "sinister truth." The soldier's uniform is the sign of his transformation. His true nature, his Adamic self, is covered and denied by the clothes of war. Kathleen is unable to touch the true self of the soldier, and he is unable to reach out to her. The scene takes place at night in a garden beneath a tree. Intimidated by not being kissed, Kathleen imagines "spectral glitters in the place" of the soldier's eyes. To "verify his presence," she puts out a hand, which he takes and presses "painfully, onto one of the breast buttons of his uniform." In this way he forces her to make a vow of fidelity—a pact with the Devil. He says, "I shall be with you . . . sooner or later. You won't forget that. You need do nothing but wait." Kathleen suffers the fate of Eve, feels that unnatural promise drive down between her and the rest of all humankind. When the soldier, her "fiancé," is reported "missing, presumed killed," she experiences "a complete dislocation from everything."

Compelled now to confront her fate, she gets into a taxi, which seems to be awaiting her. When the driver turns in the direction of her house without being told where to drive, Kathleen leans "forward to scratch at the glass panel that divided the driver's head from her own . . . driver and passenger, not six inches between them, remained for an eternity eye to eye." Reunited with her demon lover, Kathleen screams "freely" as the taxi accelerates "without mercy" into the "hinterland of deserted streets." The failure of love condemns Kathleen—and by implication humankind—to insanity and damnation in the modern wasteland.

In spite of the pessimistic conclusion of "The Demon Lover," Bowen's short fiction is ultimately affirmative. In a 1970 *McCall's* essay she lamented that many people, especially the young, are "adrift, psychologically . . . homeless, lost in a void." She expresses her desire to "do something that would arrest the drift, fill up the vacuum, convey the sense that there is, after all, SOMETHING. . . . (For I know that there is.)" Bowen's fiction conveys the existence of this something, which some would call God, others simply the source of being. Whatever it is called, it exists within each individual and in the natural world. Its primary nature is love, expressed in acts of kindness, sympathy, understanding, and tolerance. It is the potential for unity among people and harmony with the world. This potential is mirrored in the unity and harmony of Bowen's stories. The lyric descriptive passages, the coherence of matter and form, the intense visual images, and the emotional force of her stories demonstrate Bowen's mastery of the short-story form. Her stories deserve to be recognized as among the best written in the twentieth century.

Other major works

NOVELS: *The Hotel,* 1927; *The Last September,* 1929; *Friends and Relations,* 1931; *To the North,* 1932; *The House in Paris,* 1935; *The Death of the Heart,* 1938; *The Heat of the Day,* 1949; *A World of Love,* 1955; *The Little Girls,* 1964; *Eva Trout,* 1968.

PLAY: *Castle Anna,* 1948 (with John Perry).

NONFICTION: *Bowen's Court,* 1942; *Seven Winters,* 1942; *English Novelists,* 1942; *Collected Impressions,* 1950; *The Shelbourne: A Center of Dublin Life for More than a Century,* 1951; *A Time in Rome,* 1960; *Afterthought: Pieces About Writing,* 1962; *Pictures and Conversations,* 1975; *The Mulberry Tree: Writings of Elizabeth Bowen,* 1986.

CHILDREN'S LITERATURE: *The Good Tiger,* 1965.

Bibliography

Bloom, Harold, ed. *Elizabeth Bowen: Modern Critical Views.* New York: Chelsea House, 1987. A collection of eleven essays, surveying the range of Bowen criticism. Excerpts from the main book-length critical works on Bowen are included. The volume also contains some comparatively inaccessible articles on Bowen's short fiction, and essays on her work by the poets Mona Van Duyn and Alfred Corn. Supplemented by an extensive bibliography.

Craig, Patricia. *Elizabeth Bowen.* Harmondsworth, Middlesex, England: Penguin Books, 1986. A short biographical study. Indebted to Victoria Glendinning's work (below), though drawing on later research, particularly on Bowen's Irish connections. The work also contains perceptive readings of Bowen's stories and novels. Includes a useful chronology.

Glendinning, Victoria. *Elizabeth Bowen.* New York: Alfred A. Knopf, 1977. A comprehensive biography. The author is well versed in the complexities of Bowen's Irish context and details them informatively. Bowen's standing as an eminent English novelist of the 1930's is also established and assessed. Full use is made of Bowen's numerous autobiographical essays, and her private life is also candidly discussed.

Hoogland, Renee C. *Elizabeth Bowen: A Reputation in Writing.* New York: New York University Press, 1994.

Kenney, Edward J. *Elizabeth Bowen.* Lewisburg, Pa.: Bucknell University Press, 1977. A brief survey of Bowen's life and works. Drawing on Bowen's autobiographical writings, this study opens with a sketch of her background. This leads to a discussion of the theme of identity problems

in her fiction. The study's main concern is then developed. This concern
is with Bowen's use of the illusory, its nature, its necessity, and its frailty.
Lee, Hermione. *Elizabeth Bowen: An Estimation.* London: Vision Press,
1981. A comprehensive and sophisticated study. Large claims are made
for Bowen's work. She is said to be both the equal of her Bloomsbury
contemporaries and an important exponent of the European modernism deriving from Gustave Flaubert and Henry James. Bowen's concentration on the intersection of the cultural and the psychological is also
incisively analyzed.

James L. Green
(Revised by *George O'Brien*)

KAY BOYLE

Born: St. Paul, Minnesota; February 19, 1902
Died: Mill Valley, California; December 27, 1992

Principal short fiction · *Short Stories,* 1929 · *Wedding Day and Other Stories,* 1930 · *The First Lover and Other Stories,* 1933 · *The White Horses of Vienna and Other Stories,* 1936 · *The Crazy Hunter and Other Stories,* 1940 · *Thirty Stories,* 1946 · *The Smoking Mountain: Stories of Postwar Germany,* 1951 · *Three Short Novels,* 1958 · *Nothing Ever Breaks Except the Heart,* 1966 · *Fifty Stories,* 1980 · *Life Being the Best and Other Stories,* 1988

Other literary forms · In addition to her short stories, Kay Boyle published several novels, volumes of poetry, children's books, essay collections, and a book of memoirs. *Breaking the Silence* (1962) is her personal account, written for adolescents, of Europe during the Nazi regime. Boyle also ghostwrote, translated, and edited many other books. Hundreds of her stories, poems, and articles have appeared in periodicals ranging from the "little magazines" published in Paris in the 1920's to *The Saturday Evening Post* and *The New Yorker,* for which she was a correspondent from 1946 to 1953.

Achievements · Both prolific and versatile, Boyle has been respected during her long career for her exquisite technical style and her ardent political activism. She was very much a part of the expatriate group of writers living in Paris in the 1920's, and her work appeared in the avant-garde magazines alongside that of James Joyce, Gertrude Stein, Ernest Hemingway, and others. Her work is in many ways typical of the period, stylistically terse, carefully crafted, displaying keen psychological insight through the use of stream of consciousness and complex interior monologues. That her work was highly regarded is evidenced by her many awards: two Guggenheim Fellowships; O. Henry Awards in both 1935 and 1961; an honorary doctorate from Columbia College, Chicago; and membership in the National Institute of Arts and Letters. She taught at San Francisco State University and Eastern Washington University.

Biography · Born into an affluent family in St. Paul, Minnesota, in 1902, Kay Boyle moved and traveled frequently and extensively with her family during her childhood. After studying architecture for two years in Cincinnati, Boyle married Robert Brault, whose family never accepted her or the marriage. What was to have been a summer trip to France in 1923 became an eighteen-year expatriation, during which Boyle continued to write poetry and fiction. Boyle left her husband to live with editor Ernest Walsh until his death from tuberculosis in 1926. Boyle later returned to Brault with Walsh's child. They divorced in 1932, when she married Laurence Vail, a fellow American expatriate. After her marriage to Vail also ended in divorce, Boyle married Joseph von Franckenstein, an Austrian baron who had been forced out of his homeland during the Nazi invasion. She lived much of the time in Europe and was a correspondent for *The New Yorker*. She returned to the United States in 1953; Franckenstein died in 1963. Boyle taught at San Francisco State University from 1963 to 1979 and at Eastern Washington University in 1982. Her arrest and imprisonment following an anti-Vietnam War demonstration is the basis of her novel *The Underground Woman* (1975). She would remain actively involved in movements protesting social injustices and violations of human rights.

Analysis · In a 1963 article Kay Boyle defines what she saw as the role of the serious writer: to be "the spokesman for those who remain inarticulate . . . an aeolian harp whose sensitive strings respond to the whispers of the concerned people of his time." The short-story writer, she believed, is "a moralist in the highest sense of the word"; the role of the short-story writer has always been "to speak briefly and clearly of the dignity and integrity of [the] individual." Perhaps it is through this definition that the reader may distinguish the central threads that run through the variegated fabric of Boyle's fiction and bind it into a single piece.

In the 1920's, when the young expatriate artists she knew in Paris were struggling to cast off the yokes of literary convention, Boyle championed the bold and experimental in language, and her own early stories are intensely individual explorations of private experiences. Yet when the pressures of the social world came to bear so heavily on private lives in the twentieth century that they could not be ignored, Boyle began to expand the scope of her vision and vibrate to the note of the *new* times to affirm on a broader scale the same basic values—the "dignity and integrity" of the individual. Beginning in the 1930's, her subject matter encompassed the rise of Nazism, the French resistance, the Allied occupation of postwar Germany, and the civil rights and anti-Vietnam War movements in the United States, yet she never lost sight of the individual dramas acted out against these panoramic backdrops.

In the same article Boyle also quotes Albert Camus' statement that "a man's work is nothing but a long journey to recover through the detours

of art, the two or three simple and great images which first gained access
to his heart." In Boyle's journey of more than fifty years, a few central
themes remained constant: a belief in the absolute essentiality of love to
human well-being—whether on a personal or a global level; an awareness
of the many obstacles to its attainment; and a tragic sense of loss when it
fails and the gulfs between human beings stand unbridged.

"Wedding Day," the title story of her first widely circulated volume of
short stories, published in 1930, is typical of her early works. It is an
intense exploration of a unique private experience written in an experimental style. The action is primarily psychological, and outward events are
described as they reflect states of consciousness. Yet it is representative of
Boyle's best work for decades to come, both in its central concern with the
failure of love and in its bold and brilliant use of language.

"The red carpet that was to spurt like a hemorrhage from pillar to post
was stacked in the corner," the story begins. From the first sentence the
reader senses that things are out of joint. The wedding cake is ignored as
it is carried into the pantry "with its beard lying white as hoarfrost on its
bosom." "This was the last lunch," Boyle writes, and the brother and sister
"came in with their buttonholes drooping with violets and sat sadly down,
sat down to eat." To the funereal atmosphere of this wedding day, Boyle
injects tension and bitterness. The son and mother argue as to whether the
daughter will be given the family's prized copper saucepans, and he mocks
the decorum his mother cherishes when he commands her not to cry,
pointing his finger directly at her nose "so that when she looked at him
with dignity her eyes wavered and crossed" and "she sat looking proudly
at him, erect as a needle staring through its one open eye." As the mother
and son bicker over who wanted the wedding in the first place, the
bride-to-be is conspicuously silent. Finally, as the son snatches away each
slice of roast beef his mother carves until she whimpers her fear of getting
none herself, he and his sister burst into laughter. He tosses his napkin over
the chandelier, and she follows him out of the room, leaving their mother
alone "praying that this occasion at least pass off with dignity, with her
heart not in her mouth but beating away in peace in its own bosom."

With the tension between children and mother clearly delineated and
the exclusive camaraderie between brother and sister suggested, Boyle
shifts both mood and scene and describes in almost incantatory prose the
pair's idyllic jaunt through the spring afternoon in the hours remaining
before the wedding:

> The sun was an imposition, an imposition, for they were another race
> stamping an easy trail through the wilderness of Paris, possessed of the

same people, but of themselves like another race. No one else could by lifting of the head only be starting life over again, and it was a wonder the whole city of Paris did not hold its breath for them, for if anyone could have begun a new race, it was these two.

The incestuous overtones are strong. "It isn't too late yet, you know," the brother repeatedly insists as they stride through the streets, take a train into the *bois*, and row to the middle of a pond. "Over them was the sky set like a tomb," and as tears flow down their cheeks, the slow rain begins to fall. There is perfect correspondence between landscape and emotion, external objects mirroring the characters' internal states. The rain underscores the pair's frustration and despair as they realize the intensity of their love and the impossibility of its fulfillment:

> Everywhere, everywhere there were other countries to go to. And how were they to get from the boat with the chains that were on them, how uproot the willowing trees from their hearts, how strike the irons of spring that shackled them? What shame and shame that scorched a burning pathway to their dressing rooms! Their hearts were mourning for every Paris night and its half-hours before lunch when two straws crossed on the round table top on the marble anywhere meant I had a drink here and went on.

The inevitable wedding itself forms the final segment of the story, and the lyrical spell binding the pair is broken the instant they set foot in the house again to find their mother "tying white satin bows under the chins of the potted plants." The boy kicks down the hall the silver tray that will collect the guests' calling cards, and his mother is wearily certain "that this outburst presaged a thousand mishaps that were yet to come." The irony of the story lies not only in the reversal of expectations the title may have aroused in the reader but also in the discrepancy between different characters' perceptions of the same situation. The self-pitying matron worries only about the thousand little mishaps possible when a major disaster—the wedding itself—is imminent; but the guests arrive "in peace" and the brother delivers his sister to the altar. Boyle captures magnificently the enormous gulf between the placid surface appearance and the tumultuous inner reality of the situation as she takes the reader inside the bride's consciousness:

> This was the end, the end, they thought. She turned her face to her brother and suddenly their hearts fled together and sobbed like ringdoves in their bosoms. This was the end, the end, the end, this was the end.

Down the room their feet fled in various ways, seeking an escape. To
the edge of the carpet fled her feet, returned and followed reluctantly
upon her brother's heels. Every piped note of the organ insisted that
she go on. It isn't too late, he said. Too late, too late. The ring was given,
the book was closed. The desolate, the barren sky continued to fling
down dripping handfuls of fresh rain.

The mindless repetition of the phrase "the end" and the blind panic of the
bride's imaginary flight have an intense psychological authenticity, and the
recurrence of the brother's phrase "It isn't too late" and its perversion in
"Too late, too late," along with the continuing rain, are evidence of the skill
with which Boyle has woven motifs into the fabric of her story.

"Wedding Day" ends with dancing, but in an ironic counterpoint to the
flight she had imagined at the altar, the bride's feet "were fleeing in a
hundred ways throughout the rooms, fluttering from the punch bowl to her
bedroom and back again." Through repetition and transformation of the
image, Boyle underscores the fact that her path is now circumscribed.
While the brother, limbered by the punch, dances about scattering calling
cards, the mother, "in triumph on the arm of the General, danced lightly
by" rejoicing that "no glass had yet been broken." "What a real success,
what a *real* success," is her only thought as her feet float "Over the oriental
prayer rugs, through the Persian forests of hemp, away and away" in
another absurdly circumscribed "escape" that is yet another mockery of
the escape to "other countries" that the pair had dreamed of that afternoon
on the lake.

Ironies and incongruities are hallmarks of Kay Boyle's fiction. For
Boyle, reality depends on perception, and the fact that different perceptions of the same situation result in disparate and often conflicting "realities" creates a disturbing world in which individuals badly in need of
contact and connection collide and bounce off one another like atoms. In
"Wedding Day" Boyle juxtaposes a *real* loss of love with the surface gaiety
of a wedding that celebrates no love at all, but which the mother terms "a
real success." She exposes the painful isolation of each individual and the
tragedy that the only remedy—a bonding through love—is so often thwarted
or destroyed.

The barriers to love are many, both natural and man-made. In some of
Boyle's stories those who would love are severed by death. Sometimes, as
in the case of the brother and sister in "Wedding Day," love's fulfillment is
simply made impossible by the facts of life in this imperfect world, and
although readers can mourn for what has been lost, they can hardly argue
about the obstacle itself—the incest taboo is nearly universal. Yet in many

of her works Boyle presents a more assailable villain. In "Wedding Day" she treats unsympathetically the mother, who stands for all the petty proprieties that so often separate people. Boyle finds many barriers to human contact to be as arbitrary and immoral as the social conventions which cause Huck Finn's "conscience" to torment him as he helps his friend Jim to escape slavery, and in her fiction she quietly unleashes her fury against them. An obstacle she attacks repeatedly is a narrow-mindedness which blinds individuals to the inherent dignity and integrity of others, an egotism which in the plural becomes bigotry and chauvinism.

While Boyle and her family were living in Austria in the 1930's, she was an eyewitness as the social world began to impose itself on private lives, and she began to widen the scope of her artistic vision; yet her "political" stories have as their central concern the ways in which external events affect the individual. In one of her best-known stories, "The White Horses of Vienna," which won the O. Henry Award for best story of 1935, Boyle exposes the artificial barricades to human understanding and connection. The story explores the relationship between a Tyrolean doctor, who has injured his leg coming down a mountain after lighting a swastika fire in rebellion against the current government, and Dr. Heine, the young assistant sent from Vienna to take over his patients while he recovers. The Tyrolean doctor and his wife see immediately that Dr. Heine is a Jew.

The Tyrolean doctor is a clean-living, respected man. He had been a prisoner of war in Siberia and had studied abroad, but the many places in which he had been "had never left an evil mark." Boyle writes: "His face was as strong as rock, but it had seen so much of suffering that it had the look of being scarred, it seemed to be split in two, with one side of it given to resolve and the other to compassion." In his personal dealings it is the compassionate side that dominates. When his wife asks in a desperate whisper what they will do with "*him,*" the Tyrolean doctor replies simply that they will send for his bag at the station and give him some *Apfelsaft* if he is thirsty. "It's harder on him than us," he tells her. Neither has the wife's own humanity been extinguished entirely by institutionalized bigotry, for when Dr. Heine's coat catches fire from a sterilizing lamp on the table, she wraps a piece of rug around him immediately and holds him tightly to smother the flames. Almost instinctively, she offers to try patching the burned-out place, but then she suddenly bites her lip and stands back "as if she had remembered the evil thing that stood between them."

The situation of the Tyrolean doctor, described as a "great, golden, wounded bird," is counterpointed in a story Dr. Heine tells at dinner one evening about the famous Lipizzaner horses of the Spanish Riding School in Vienna, still royal, "without any royalty left to bow their heads to, still shouldering into the arena with spirits a man would give his soul for, bending their knees in homage to the empty, canopied loge where royalty no longer sat." He tells of a particular horse that the government, badly in need of money, had sold to an Indian maharaja. When the time had come for the horse to be taken away, a wound was discovered cut in his leg. After it had healed and it was again time for the horse to leave, another wound was found on its other leg. Finally the horse's blood was so poisoned that it had to be destroyed. No one knew who had caused the wounds until the horse's devoted little groom committed suicide that same day. When the after-dinner conversation is interrupted by the knocking of Heimwehr troops at the door, "men brought in from other parts of the country, billeted there to subdue the native people," the identification between the doctor and the steed is underscored. He cannot guide the troops up the mountain in search of those who have lit that evening's swastika fires because of his wounded leg.

Dr. Heine is relieved that the rest of the evening will be spent with family and friends watching one of the Tyrolean doctor's locally renowned marionette shows. After staring out the window at the burning swastikas, the "marvelously living flowers of fire springing out of the arid darkness," the "inexplicable signals given from one mountain to another in some secret gathering of power that cast him and his people out, forever out upon the waters of despair," Dr. Heine turns back, suddenly angry, and proclaims that the whole country is being ruined by politics, that it is impossible to have friends or even casual conversations on any other basis these days. "You're much wiser to make your puppets, *Herr Doktor*," he says.

Even the marionette show is political. The characters are a clown who explains he is carrying artificial flowers because he is on his way to his own funeral and wants them to be fresh when he gets there, and a handsome grasshopper, "a great, gleaming beauty" who prances about the stage with delicacy and wit to the music of Mozart. "It's really marvellous! He's as graceful as the white horses at Vienna, *Herr Doktor*," Dr. Heine calls out in delight. As the conversation continues between the clown, for some reason called "Chancellor," and the grasshopper, inexplicably addressed as "The Leader," Dr. Heine is not laughing so loudly. The Chancellor has a "ludicrous faith in the power of the Church" to support him; the Leader proclaims that the cities are full of churches, but "the country is full of God." The Leader speaks with "a wild and stirring power that sent the cold of wonder up and down one's spine," and he seems "ready to waltz away at any moment with the power of stallion life that was leaping in his limbs." As the Chancellor proclaims, "I believe in the independence of the individual," he promptly trips over his own sword and falls flat among the daisies.

At the story's conclusion, Dr. Heine is standing alone on the cold mountainside, longing to be "indoors, with the warmth of his own people, and the intellect speaking." When he sees "a small necklace of men coming to him" up the mountain, the lights they bear "coming like little beacons of hope carried to him," Dr. Heine thinks, "Come to me . . . come to me. I am a young man alone on a mountain. I am a young man alone, as my race is alone, lost here amongst them all." Yet ironically, what Dr. Heine views as "beacons of hope" are carried by the Heimwehr troops, the Tyrolean doctor's enemies. As in "Wedding Day," Boyle presents a single situation and plays off the characters' reactions to it against one another to illustrate the gaps between individuals and the relativity of truth and reality in the world.

His personal loyalties transcending his politics, Dr. Heine rushes to warn the family of the Heimwehr's approach. When the troops arrive they announce that the Austrian chancellor, Dollfuss, had been assassinated in Vienna that afternoon. They have come to arrest the doctor, whose rebel sympathies are known. "Ah, politics, politics again!" cries Dr. Heine, wringing his hands "like a woman about to cry." He runs outdoors and takes the doctor's hand as he is being carried away on a stretcher, asking what he can do to help. "You can throw me peaches and chocolate from the street," replies the Tyrolean doctor, smiling, "his cheeks scarred with the marks of laughter in the light from the hurricane lamps that the men were carrying down." His wife is not a good shot, he adds, and he missed all the oranges she had thrown him after the February slaughter. At this image of the Tyrolean doctor caged like an animal but still noble, with his spirit still unbroken, Dr. Heine is left "thinking in anguish of the snow-white horses, the Lipizzaners, the relics of pride, the still unbroken vestiges of beauty bending their knees to the empty loge of royalty where there was no royalty any more."

In "The White Horses of Vienna," Boyle expresses hope, if not faith, that even in the face of divisive social forces, the basic connections of compassion between individuals might survive. In a work that is a testament to her humanity, she presents the Tyrolean doctor's plight with such sensitivity that readers, like the Jewish assistant, are forced to view with understanding and empathy this proud man's search for a cause that will redeem the dignity and honor of his wounded people while at the same time abhorring the cause itself. Boyle sees and presents in all its human complexity what at first glance seems a black-and-white political issue. Boyle, however, was no Pollyanna. As the social conflict that motivates this story snowballed into world war and mass genocide, she saw with a cold, realistic eye how little survived of the goodwill among human beings for which she had hoped. In many of her stories written in the 1940's to the present day, she has examined unflinchingly and sometimes bitterly the individual tragedies played out in the shadow of the global one.

In "Winter Night," published in 1946, she draws a delicate portrait of a little girl named Felicia and a woman sent by a "sitting parent" agency to spend the evening with her in a New York apartment. The woman, in her strange accent, tells Felicia that today is an anniversary, that three years ago that night she had begun to care for another little girl who also studied ballet and whose mother, like Felicia's, had had to go away. The difference was that the other girl's mother had been sent away on a train car in which there were no seats, and she never came back, but she was able to write a short letter on a smuggled scrap of paper and slip it through the cracks on the floor of the moving train in the hope that some kind stranger would send it to its destination. The woman can only comfort herself with the thought that "They must be quietly asleep somewhere, and not crying all night because they are hungry and because they are cold."

"There is a time of apprehension which begins with the beginning of darkness, and to which only the speech of love can lend security," the story begins, as Boyle describes the dying light of a January afternoon in New York City. Felicia and the "sitting parent," both left alone, have found that security in each other. When, after midnight, Felicia's mother tiptoes in the front door, slipping the three blue foxskins from her shoulder and dropping the velvet bag on a chair, she hears only the sound of breathing in the dark living room, and no one speaks to her in greeting as she crosses to the bedroom: "And then, as startling as a slap across her delicately tinted face, she saw the woman lying sleeping on the divan, and Felicia, in her school dress still, asleep within the woman's arms." The story is not baldly didactic, but Boyle *is* moralizing. By juxtaposing the cases of the two little girls left alone by their mothers and cared for by a stranger, she shows that the failure of love is a tragic loss on an individual as well as on a global scale. Again, personal concerns merge with political and social ones, and readers find the failure of love on any level to be the fundamental tragedy of life.

Some of the stories Boyle has written about the war and its aftermath are less subtle, "artistic" explorations of individual struggles as they are frankly moralistic adventure stories written for commercial magazines, and they were more popular with the public than with the critics. Yet one of her finest works was also a product of her war experiences. *The Smoking Mountain: Stories of Postwar Germany* (1951) consists of eleven stories, several originally published by *The New Yorker*, which had employed Boyle as a correspondent for the express purpose of sending "fiction out of Germany." It is prefaced by a seventy-seven-page nonfiction account of a denazification trial Boyle witnessed in Frankfurt in 1948, which reveals her immense skill as a reporter as well. The book presents a painful vision. Any hope that a renewed understanding among peoples might result from the catastrophic "lesson" of the war is dashed, for the point of many of the stories and certainly of the introduction is how little difference the war has made in the fundamental attitudes of the defeated but silently defiant Germans who can still say of 1943 and 1944–"the years when the gas chambers burned the brightest"–"Those were the good years for everyone."

In 1929, Boyle, with writers Hart Crane, Vail, and others, signed Eugene Jolas' manifesto, "Revolution of the Word," condemning literary pretentiousness and outdated literary conventions. The goal, then, was to make literature at once fresh and experimental and at the same time accessible to the reader. Boyle would remain politically involved and productive as a writer, publishing collections of poetry, short stories, and essays in the 1980's. She would continue in her work to test the individual against events of historical significance, such as the threat of Nazism or the war in Vietnam. Although critics have accused her later works of selling out to popular taste, and her style of losing its innovative edge, Boyle remained steadfast in defining her artistic purpose as a moral responsibility to defend the integrity of the individual and human rights. To do so, Boyle argued, she must be accessible to the public.

Other major works

NOVELS: *Plagued by the Nightingale*, 1931; *Year Before Last*, 1932; *Gentlemen, I Address You Privately*, 1933; *My Next Bride*, 1934; *Death of a Man*, 1936; *Monday Night*, 1938; *Primer for Combat*, 1942; *Avalanche*, 1944; *A Frenchman Must Die*, 1946; *1939*, 1948; *His Human Majesty*, 1949; *The Seagull on the Step*, 1955; *Generation Without Farewell*, 1960; *The Underground Woman*, 1975.

POETRY: *A Glad Day*, 1938; *American Citizen Naturalized in Leadville, Colorado*, 1944; *Collected Poems*, 1962; *Testament for My Students and Other Poems*, 1970; *This Is Not a Letter and Other Poems*, 1985.

NONFICTION: *365 Days*, 1936 (edited with others); *Breaking the Silence: Why a Mother Tells Her Son About the Nazi Era*, 1962; *The Autobiography of Emanuel Carnevali*, 1967; *Being Geniuses Together, 1920-1930*, 1968 (with Robert McAlmon); *The Long Walk at San Francisco State and Other Essays*, 1970; *Enough of Dying! An Anthology of Peace Writings*, 1972; *Words That Must Somehow Be Said: The Selected Essays of Kay Boyle, 1927-1984*, 1985.

CHILDREN'S LITERATURE: *The Youngest Camel,* 1939, 1959; *Pinky, the Cat Who Liked to Sleep,* 1966; *Pinky in Persia,* 1968.

Bibliography

Bell, Elizabeth S. *Kay Boyle: A Study of the Short Fiction.* New York: Twayne Publishers, 1992.

Boyle, Kay. "Kay Boyle: An Eightieth Birthday Interview." Interview by David R. Mesher. *The Malahat Review* 65 (July, 1983): 82-95. As the title suggests, this interview with Boyle was conducted on the occasion of her eightieth birthday. In it, she discusses her life and her work.

Carpenter, Richard C. "Kay Boyle." *English Journal* 42 (November, 1953): 425-430. This volume provides a helpful and general look at Boyle's early novels and short fiction.

_____. "Kay Boyle: The Figure in the Carpet." *Critique: Studies in Modern Fiction* 7 (Winter, 1964-1965): 65-78. Carpenter rejects the common complaint that Boyle is a mere "stylist," discussing her thematic depth, particularly in "The Bridegroom's Body" and "The Crazy Hunter."

Mellen, Joan. *Kay Boyle: Author of Herself.* New York: Farrar, Straus & Giroux, 1994.

Moore, Harry T. "Kay Boyle's Fiction." In *The Age of the Modern and Other Literary Essays.* Carbondale: Southern Illinois University Press, 1971. Moore attributes Boyle's lack of success, despite her supreme talent, to timing. He examines *Generation Without Farewell,* arguing that it far surpasses other contemporary novels about postwar Germany.

Porter, Katherine Anne. "Kay Boyle: Example to the Young." In *The Critic as Artist: Essays on Books, 1920-1970,* edited by Gilbert A. Harrison. New York: Liveright, 1972. This essay examines Boyle as she fits in the literary movement of her time. Focuses on some of her stories, as well as on the novel *Plagued by the Nightingale.*

Spanier, Sandra Whipple. *Kay Boyle: Artist and Activist.* Carbondale: Southern Illinois University Press, 1986. Heavily annotated, thorough, and the first critical biography and major work on Boyle. Supplemented by select but extensive primary and secondary bibliographies. Illustrated.

Twentieth-Century Literature 34 (Fall, 1988). A special issue on Kay Boyle, with personal reminiscences by Malcolm Cowley, Jessica Mitford, Howard Nemerov, and Studs Terkel, among others. Also contains several critical essays on Boyle's work.

Sandra Whipple Spanier
(Revised by *Lou Thompson*)

RAY BRADBURY

Born: Waukegan, Illinois; August 22, 1920

Principal short fiction · *Dark Carnival,* 1947 · *The Martian Chronicles,* 1950 · *The Illustrated Man,* 1951 · *The Golden Apples of the Sun,* 1953 · *The October Country,* 1955 · *A Medicine for Melancholy,* 1959 · *The Machineries of Joy,* 1964 · *I Sing the Body Electric!,* 1969 · *Long After Midnight,* 1976 · *The Stories of Ray Bradbury,* 1980 · *The Toynbee Convector,* 1988

Other literary forms · Although Ray Bradbury has described himself as essentially a short-story writer, his contributions to a wide variety of other genres have been substantial. Indeed, he has intentionally sought to compose successfully in virtually every literary form. His best-known novels are *Fahrenheit 451* (1953), *Dandelion Wine* (1957), and *Something Wicked This Way Comes* (1962), the last being his favorite of all of his works. Among his screenplays, the most successful have been *Moby Dick* (1956), written in collaboration with John Huston, and *Icarus Montgolfier Wright* (1961), which was nominated for an Academy Award. Bradbury has had his stage plays produced in Los Angeles and New York City, and several of them have been published, representative samples of which are *The Anthem Sprinters and Other Antics* (1963) and *The Pedestrian* (1966). He has also written many plays for radio and television. Some of the most important of the several volumes of poetry that he has published were collected in *The Complete Poems of Ray Bradbury* (1982). He has also written books for children and adolescents, compiled anthologies of fantasy and science-fiction stories, and published nonfiction works dealing with his interests in creativity and the future.

Achievements · Despite Bradbury's being named the United States' best-known science-fiction writer in a poll and despite the claim made on paperback editions of his works that he is "the world's greatest living science fiction writer," his actual literary accomplishments are based on an oeuvre whose vast variety and deeply humanistic themes transcend science fiction as it is commonly understood. His many stories, from gothic horror to social criticism, from playful fantasies to nostalgic accounts of midwestern American life, have been anthologized in several hundred collections, in English as well as many foreign languages, and several of the stories that he published early in his career now occupy a distinguished niche in twentieth century American literature.

©Thomas Victor/courtesy of Alfred A. Knopf

Some of his early tales were recognized with O. Henry Awards in 1947 and 1948, and in 1949 he was voted "best author" by the National Fantasy Fan Federation. Bradbury's "Sun and Shadow" won the Benjamin Franklin Magazine Award as the best story of 1953-1954, and in 1954 he received a National Institute of Arts and Letters Award in Literature. His novel *Fahrenheit 451* won a gold medal from the Commonwealth Club of California, and his book *Switch on the Night* (1955) was honored with a Boy's Club of America Junior Book Award in 1956. He received the Mrs. Ann Radcliffe Award of the Count Dracula Society in 1965 and 1971, the Writers'

Guild of America West Valentine Davies Award in 1974, and the World Fantasy Award for Life Achievement in 1977. Whittier College gave him an honorary doctor of literature degree in 1979. PEN, an international writer's organization of poets, playwrights, editors, essayists, and novelists, gave Bradbury its Body of Work Award in 1985. These and other awards have recognized Bradbury's best works, which are often wrenching indictments of the dangers of unrestrained scientific and technical progress, though his work also encourages the hope that humanity will deal creatively with the new worlds it seems driven to make.

Biography · Ray Bradbury has often made use of his own life in his writings, and he insisted that he had total recall of the myriad experiences of his life through his photographic—some would say eidetic—memory. He has stated that he has vivid recollections of the day of his birth, August 22, 1920, in Waukegan, Illinois, and of his circumcision on the fourth day after his birth. Leonard Spaulding Bradbury, his father, was a lineman with the Bureau of Power and Light (his distant ancestor Mary Bradbury was among those tried for witchcraft in Salem, Massachusetts); Esther Marie (née Moberg) Bradbury, his mother, had emigrated from Sweden to the United States when she was very young. A child with an exceptionally vivid imagination, Ray Bradbury amused himself with his fantasies but experienced anguish from his nightmares. His mother took him to his first film, *The Hunchback of Notre Dame* (1923), when he was three years old, and he was both frightened and entranced by Lon Chaney's performance. This experience originated his lifelong love affair with motion pictures, and he has written that he can remember the scenes and plots of all the films that he has ever attended.

As he grew up, Bradbury passed through a series of passions that included circuses, dinosaurs, and Mars (the latter via the writings of Edgar Rice Burroughs). Neva Bradbury, an aunt, assisted his maturation as a person and writer by introducing him to the joys of fairy tales, L. Frank Baum's Oz books, live theater, and the stories of Edgar Allan Poe. In Bradbury's own view, the most important event in his childhood occurred in 1932 when a carnival came to town. He attended the performance of a magician, Mr. Electrico, whose spellbinding act involved electrifying himself to such an extent that sparks jumped between his teeth, and every white hair on his head stood erect. Bradbury and the magician became friends, and their walks and talks along the Lake Michigan shore behind the carnival so energized his imagination that, a few weeks after this encounter, he began to compose stories for several hours a day. One of his first efforts was a sequel to a Martian novel of Burroughs.

During the Depression, Bradbury's father had difficulty finding work, and in 1932 the family moved to Arizona, where they had previously spent some time in the middle 1920's. Still in search of steady work, his father moved the family to Los Angeles, which was where Ray Bradbury attended high school and which became the permanent site of his life and work. His formal education ended with his graduation from Los Angeles High School, but his education as a writer continued through his extensive reading and his participation in theater groups (one of which was sponsored by the actress Laraine Day). To support his writing, he worked as a newsboy in downtown Los Angeles for several years.

In World War II, Bradbury's poor eyesight prevented him from serving in the army, but this disappointment gave him the freedom to pursue his career as a writer, and his stories began to be published in such pulp magazines as *Weird Tales* and Hugo Gernsback's *Amazing Stories*. The high quality of Bradbury's stories was quickly recognized, and he was able to get his new stories published in such mass-circulation magazines as *Collier's, The Saturday Evening Post, Harper's Magazine*, and *Mademoiselle*. Because of his success as a writer, he had the financial security to marry Marguerite Susan McClure in 1947 (they had met when she, a book clerk, had waited on him). The marriage produced four daughters.

By the early 1950's, Bradbury, now recognized as an accomplished science-fiction and fantasy writer, began his involvement with Hollywood through an original screenplay that would eventually be released as *It Came from Outer Space* (1952). In the mid-1950's, he traveled to Ireland in connection with a screenplay of *Moby Dick* that he wrote with John Huston (he later drew on his experiences with the Irish for several stories and plays that took his work in a new direction). Upon his return to the United States, Bradbury composed a large number of television scripts for such shows as *Alfred Hitchcock Presents, Suspense*, and *The Twilight Zone*.

During the late 1950's and early 1960's, Bradbury moved away from science fiction, and his stories and novels increasingly focused on humanistic themes and his midwestern childhood. In the late 1960's and throughout the 1970's and 1980's, Bradbury's output of short and long fiction decreased, and his ideas found outlets in such literary forms as poems, plays, and essays. He also participated in a number of projects, such as "A Journey Through United States History," the exhibit that occupied the upper floor of the United States Pavilion for the New York World's Fair in 1964. Because of this display's success, the Walt Disney organization hired him to help develop the exhibit Spaceship Earth for the Epcot Center at Disney World in Florida. He continued to diversify his activities during the 1980's by collaborating on projects to turn his novel *Fahrenheit 451* into an opera and his novel *Dandelion Wine* into a musical. In the late 1980's and early 1990's, he returned to some of the subjects and themes that had earlier established his reputation with the publication of a short-story collection, *The Toynbee Convector*, and a novel, *A Graveyard for Lunatics: Another Tale of Two Cities* (1990).

Analysis · Ray Bradbury once said that he had not so much thought his way through life as he had done things and discovered what those things meant and who he was after the doing. This metamorphosis of experience under the aegis of memory also characterizes many of his stories, which are often transmogrifications of his personal experiences. He therefore used his stories as ways of hiding and finding himself, a self whose constant changes interested, amused, and sometimes frightened him. He believed that human beings are composed of time, and in many of his science-fiction stories, a frequent theme is the dialectic between the past and the future. For example, in several of his Martian stories, the invaders of the Red Planet have to come to terms with their transformation into Martians, since survival in an alien world necessitates the invader's union with the invaded. Aggression and submission might represent the initial dialectic, but survival or death becomes the most determinative.

Even in stories where Bradbury's characters and settings seem ordinary, this theme of metamorphosis is nevertheless present, because these stories often show ordinary people being transformed by extraordinary, sometimes bizarre situations. Sometimes Bradbury's purpose is to point out the enlightening power of the abnormal; sometimes he wants to reveal the limitations of the everyday and ordinary. His characters are, of course, changed by their experiences, particularly when they encounter great evil beneath the surface of seemingly normal life, but in other stories Bradbury gives the reader a window through which to see the positive meaning of life (these stories, usually sentimental, are life-affirming, permitting readers to believe that human dreams can be fulfilled). By helping readers to imagine the unimaginable, he helps them to think about the unthinkable. He speaks of his tales as "idea fiction," and he prefers to call himself a magic realist. He casts magic spells through his poetic words and highly imaginative visions, and because of this aura of enchantment, some critics have seen his chief subject as childhood or the child hidden in the adult unconscious.

A danger exists, however, in treating Bradbury as a writer of fantasy suitable only for adolescents. This may be true for some of his works, but many of his stories exhibit emotional depths and logical complexities that call for a sophisticated dialectic between the adult and his buried childhood. The difference between fantasy and reality is not strongly developed in the child, whose experience of the world is minimal. Bradbury often plays with this tension between fantasy and reality in dealing with his principal themes—the power of the past, the freedom of the present, and the temptations and traps of the future. In the world of Bradbury's stories, fantasy becomes essential for a person existing in an increasingly technological era or with experiences that, like an iceberg, are nine-tenths buried below the surface. In these cases, the ability to fantasize various alternatives or futures, and to choose the best among them, becomes necessary for survival.

Because of Bradbury's woefully inadequate knowledge of science and the lack of verisimilitude in the technological gadgetry of his science-fiction stories, many aficionados of the genre do not consider him a genuine science-fiction writer. This assessment does not seem to bother him, as he sees his stories, science fiction and others, as myths, not prophecies, which convey moral, not technical, lessons. Like Isaac Asimov, Bradbury believes that science fiction's value lies in helping human beings to visualize and solve future problems before they actually occur, but unlike Asimov, he has a deep suspicion of the machine and a great faith in the human heart's capacity to perceive, do good, and create beauty. Because of this attitude, many critics view Bradbury as essentially a romantic. Since F. L. Lucas once counted 11,396 definitions of "romanticism," however, perhaps Bradbury's brand of romanticism should be more fully articulated. He has expressed an attraction for spontaneity of thought and action, and he actively cultivates his own unconscious. He believes deeply in the power of the imagination, and he accepts Blaise Pascal's sentiment that the heart has reasons about which the reason knows nothing. Many of these characteristics, along with his penchant for the grotesque and macabre, can be seen in his first collection of stories, *Dark Carnival.*

August Derleth, a Wisconsin writer who had established Arkham House to publish stories of fantasy and horror for a limited audience, had read Bradbury's stories in the pulp magazine *Weird Tales*, recognized their quality, and suggested that Bradbury collect them into a book. *Dark Carnival* was very successful with its specialized market, and its three thousand copies were quickly sold and soon became collector's items. The book's title was aptly chosen, since the stories often deal with the dark and strange. Several stories make use, although in highly altered forms, of emotions and events in Bradbury's own life. For example, "The Small Assassin" depicts an infant, terrified at finding himself in a hostile world, taking revenge on his parents. Bradbury uses this metamorphosis of a supposedly innocent newborn into an assassin to explore some of the feelings he had as a very young child.

Death is a motif that appears often in these tales, but unlike Poe, whom he admired, Bradbury uses the morbid not for its macabre fascination but to shift readers onto a different level from which they can see reality in a new and enlightening way. In most of these tales, more happens in the imaginations of Bradbury's characters than happens in their lives. He has the ability to reach down into the labyrinthine unconscious of his characters and pulling out odd desires, strange dreams, and horrendous fears. For example, in "The Next in Line," a story that grew out of his own experience on a trip to Guanajuato, northwest of Mexico City, a young American wife is simultaneously frightened and fascinated by the rows of propped-up mummified bodies in a Guanajuato catacomb. After her traumatic ordeal, she finds herself increasingly immobilized by her alienation from the death-haunted Mexican society and by her fear that her own body is a potential mummy. Another story, "Skeleton," has a similar theme. A man is obsessed by the horrible bones that he carries within him, but when a strange creature crawls down his throat and consumes the bones that were the source of his obsession, he is transformed into a human jellyfish. These and other fantasies and horrors serve as exorcisms through which the devils of one's unconscious are expelled. The best of these stories leave the reader cleansed and transformed, with an expanded consciousness and control of the fears that can make people prisoners of their own hidden emotions.

Some critics see the twenty-six stories collected in *The Martian Chronicles* as the beginning of the most prolific and productive phase of Bradbury's career. Like *Dark Carnival,* this collection resulted from the suggestion of an editor, but in this case Bradbury added passages to link together his stories about Mars. These bridge passages help to interrelate the stories but they do not make them into a unified novel. This places *The Martian Chronicles* into a peculiar literary category—less than a novel but more than a collection of short stories. Despite difficulties in categorizing this book, it is commonly recognized as Bradbury's most outstanding work. When it was first published, it was widely reviewed and read by people who did not ordinarily read science fiction. The poet Christopher Isherwood, for example, praised the book for its poetic language and its penetrating analysis of human beings forced to function on the frontier of an alien world. Within twenty years of its publication, *The Martian Chronicles* sold more than three million copies and was translated into more than thirty foreign languages.

The Martian Chronicles is not totally unrelated to *Dark Carnival,* since Bradbury's Mars is a fantasy world, a creation not of a highly trained scientific imagination but of a mythmaker and an explorer of the unconscious. Within the time frame of 1999 to 2026, Bradbury orders his stories to give the reader a sense of the coherent evolution of the settling of Mars by "Earthlings." The early stories deal with the difficulties the emigrants from Earth have in establishing successful colonies on Mars. The fifteen stories of the middle section explore the rise and fall of these colonies. The stories in the final section are concerned with the possible renovation of the human race on Mars after an annihilative nuclear war on Earth.

In several of the stories in *The Martian Chronicles*, Bradbury is once again fascinated by the subject of death. Earthlings who make the mistake of trying to duplicate Earth's culture on Mars meet difficulties and death. This theme is particularly clear in "The Third Expedition," a story that was originally titled "Mars Is Heaven" and that deeply impressed the critic and writer Jorge Luis Borges. In "The Third Expedition," Captain John Black and his crew constitute a third attempt by Earthlings to create a successful settlement on Mars, this time in a town that bears a striking resemblance to traditional midwestern American towns of the 1920's. It turns out that the Martians have deceived the Earthlings by using telepathic powers to manufacture this counterfeit town in their receptive imaginations. Captain Black and his crew have such a deep desire to believe in what they think they see that they delude themselves into seeing what the Martians want them to see. This mass hypnosis produced by the Martians capitalizes on the crew's self-delusion and on its members' need to re-create their past. When each Earthling is securely locked within what he believes is his home, he is murdered by the Martians. Trapped by their past and unable to resist, they are destroyed. Illusion and reality, time and identity, change and stability are the themes that intertwine in Bradbury's treatment of this story (one can understand why Borges liked it so much, since his own work dwells on the theme of the Other as an inextricable element in one's own identity).

Soon after *The Martian Chronicles* appeared, Bradbury published another book of interlinked stories, *The Illustrated Man.* Most of its eighteen stories had been published in various magazines between 1947 and 1951, but some had been written specifically for this book. The framing device, which is neither as consistent nor as unifying as the bridge passages in *The Martian Chronicles*, derives from tattoos that completely cover the skin of a running character. The tattoos, however, do not grow out of the personality of this character, as would be expected for a real tattooed man whose likes and dislikes would be represented in the permanent images he chose to decorate his body. Instead, each tattoo embodies a Bradburian idea that comes alive in a particular story. The otherwise unrelated stories fall into several categories—tales of robots and space travel as well as stories of

Mexicans and Martians. Four of the stories are set on Bradbury's Mars, and two of these are closely related to *The Martian Chronicles.* Some of the stories have themes related to those initially developed in *Dark Carnival.* For example, like "The Small Assassin," "The Veldt" concerns the revenge of children against their parents, this time in a futuristic setting. The children, who are obsessed with a room-filling television device that can depict scenes with three-dimensional realism, choose to watch an African veldt inhabited by lions gorging themselves on carcasses. The parents, who try to get their children to control their television addiction, end up as food for the lions. In this story, Bradbury makes use of a favorite theme—the blurred distinction between illusion and reality. Other stories in *The Illustrated Man* are animated by such social concerns as racism and with ethical and religious dilemmas derived from modern science and technology. For example, "The Fire Balloons" focuses on a religious missionary's discovery that the only surviving Martians have metamorphosed from human forms to floating balls of blue flame (reminiscent of the fire balloons in Earth's Fourth of July celebrations). After undergoing this transformation, these Martian flames are no longer capable of sin. Bradbury implies that a new planet means a new theology, and the fall is reversible and a state of innocence can be regained.

Bradbury's fourth collection, *The Golden Apples of the Sun*, used neither linking passages nor a frame narrative to interrelate the twenty-two stories. Instead, this book initiated the Bradburian potpourri of stories that would characterize most of his later collections: nostalgic, satiric, and humorous stories whose settings could be Mars, Mexico, or the Midwest and whose genre could be fantasy, science fiction, crime, or horror. He would use this variety of approach, setting, and genre to cast a revelatory light on aspects of modern life that conventional fiction was avoiding. Although the critical reception of *The Golden Apples of the Sun* was largely favorable, some critics found several of the stories disappointing and noted a falling-off from the high level of quality of *The Martian Chronicles* and *The Illustrated Man.* Despite the divided opinions, general agreement existed on the success of several of the stories, for example, "Sun and Shadow," which was set in Mexico and which won both praise and awards. Another story, "The Fog Horn," became the basis of a film, *The Beast from Twenty Thousand Fathoms* (1953). It is about a lonely dinosaur who is attracted by the sound of a fog horn, interpreting it as the mating call of a potential companion (he dies of a broken heart when he swims to shore and discovers his error). The story "A Sound of Thunder" develops a favorite Bradburian theme of the profound effect of the past on the future. It depicts what happens when a time traveler steps on a butterfly in the past and inadvertently changes the future (this will remind modern readers of the "butterfly effect" in chaos theory, in which the beating of a butterfly's wings in a Brazilian rain forest may cause a tornado in Kansas via a long chain of cause and effect).

The October Country, a collection that has as its core the stories of *Dark Carnival* along with four new stories, appeared appropriately in October of 1955. Bradbury described the country of the title as a place "whose people are autumn people, thinking only autumn thoughts" and whose steps "at night on the empty walks sound like rain." In the light of the earlier success of *Dark Carnival*, it is surprising that several critics were not as kind to this collection as they had been to Bradbury's earlier ones. For example, Carlos Baker, Ernest Hemingway's biographer, predicted in his review that the only route that Bradbury's writings could follow if he continued in the direction that he had chosen was down. Some critics did see him trying, in this and later collections, to develop new subjects, themes, and approaches. For them, his imagination was still nimble, his mind adventurous, and his heart sensitive. They also noticed his increased emphasis on social issues and his desire to treat the joyous side of human nature. For most critics, however, Bradbury's later collections of stories were repetitive mixes of ideas, themes, and treatments that he had used many times before. The problems sensed by these critics can be seen in the collection of twenty-two stories titled *A Medicine for Melancholy*.

In addition to the expected stories of fantasy and science fiction, *A Medicine for Melancholy* includes tales from the lives of the Irish, Mexicans, and Mexican Americans. The title story explores the awakening womanhood of an eighteenth century London girl who is cured of melancholia by the visit of what she interprets as Saint Bosco but who is in reality a dustman. Two of the stories in this collection, "Icarus Montgolfier Wright" and "In a Season of Calm Weather," led to films, and others, "A Fever Dream" for example, are reminiscent of films. In "A Fever Dream," aliens invade Earth not externally but by taking over the minds and hearts of their Earth victims (the film analogue is, of course, *The Invasion of the Body Snatchers*, 1956). Derivative, too, seems the story "All Summer in a Day," about a group of children on cloud-enshrouded Venus who get to see the sun only once every seven years (the analogue here is Asimov's classic story "Nightfall").

In the 1960's and 1970's, Bradbury's career entered a new phase characterized by a decreasing output of short stories and novels and an increasing output of plays and poetry. When he did bring out short-story collections, the majority of critics saw little suggesting artistic growth, though a minority actually preferred his new stories, interpreting them as examples of a mature writer whose stories had acquired humanity, depth, and polish. These latter critics are also the ones who were not attracted to his tales about corpses, vampires, and cemeteries and who preferred his new optimism and his emphasis on civil rights, religion, and morality. Many of the stories in *The Machineries of Joy* provide good examples of these new tendencies. There are still stories characteristic of the earlier Bradbury—a science fiction tale in which the explorers of a new planet find themselves possessed by a resident intelligence, and a horror story in which raising giant mushrooms gets out of hand. Many of the stories, however, contain the epiphanic appearance of human warmth in unexpected situations. For example, in "Almost the End of the World," when sunspots destroy television reception, a world addicted to this opiate of the mind and heart is forced to rediscover the forgotten joys of interpersonal communication.

Bradbury's next collection, *I Sing the Body Electric!* also met with a mixed critical response. Academic critics and readers who had formed their taste for Bradbury on his early works found this potpourri of seventeen stories pretentious and a decline form his best science-fiction, fantasy, and horror stories. Some stories are slight—indeed, little more than anecdotes: In "The Women," for example, a man experiences the sea as a woman and his wife as her rival. On the other hand, some critics found Bradbury's new stories enthralling and insightful, with the unexpected—a robot Abraham Lincoln, Ernest Hemingway's spirit, and an automated Martian city—confronting the reader at every turn of the page. The stories of *I Sing the Body Electric!* certainly contain some of Bradbury's favorite themes—the dialectic between past and future, reality and illusion. For example, the title story concerns a robot grandmother ideally programmed to meet the needs of the children of a recently motherless family. This electrical grandmother embodies the past (she has all the sentiment humans conventionally associate with this figure) and the future (she is a rechargeable AC-DC Mark V model and can never die). Another story that deals with the presentness of the past is "Night Call, Collect." In this tale, an old man alone on a deserted Mars receives a telephone call from himself when he was much younger (he has forgotten that he devised this plan many years before in order to assuage the loneliness of his old age). His young self battles with his old self, and as the old man dies, past, present, and future commingle in an odd but somehow enlightening amalgam.

Long After Midnight contained twenty-two stories, several of which had been written in the late 1940's and early 1950's but never anthologized. Some critics found the new stories aimless, uninspired, and self-indulgent, but others felt that many of them were poignant, sensitive, and touching. These latter critics thought that several of these stories represented Bradbury's new grasp of the power of love to overcome evil and to make permanent valued moments from the past. A few of the stories broke new ground in terms of subject matter: "The Better Part of Wisdom" is a compassionate and restrained treatment of homosexuality and "Have I Got a Chocolate Bar for You!" deals gracefully with a relationship between a priest and penitent.

In 1980, Bradbury selected a hundred stories from three decades of his work in *The Stories of Ray Bradbury*. Many reviewers treated this book's publication as an opportunity to analyze Bradbury's lifetime achievement as a short-story writer. Some found much to praise, comparing his body of work to Poe's, O. Henry's, and Guy de Maupassant's. Thomas M. Disch, however, in an influential essay in *The New York Times Book Review*, denigrated Bradbury's stories as "schmaltzy" and "more often meretricious than not." Unlike those critics who praised Bradbury's early work and saw a decline in the quality of his later stories, Disch stated that early and late are "meaningless distinctions" in Bradbury's output. He criticized Bradbury condescendingly as a child manqué, attributing his success to the fact that "like Peter Pan, he won't grow up." This attack on Bradbury's short fiction en masse certainly hurt his feelings. He has also confessed that he has been bothered that such publications as *The New York Review of Books*, *The New Yorker*, and *The Atlantic Monthly* have largely ignored his work. It is obvious that many in the literary establishment still regard him as a hack writer in the despised genres of fantasy and science fiction. To those who thought, however, that Bradbury was using *The Stories of Ray Bradbury* to bid farewell to the form that had been his home for most of his life as a writer, another collection, *The Toynbee Convector*, showed that they were mistaken. As with his other late collections, this, too, contained the familiar blend of science fiction and gothic horror as well as sentimental tales of Ireland and Middle America, but it broke little new ground.

Despite their mixed critical reception, Bradbury's short stories have been phenomenally successful not only in the United States but also in many other countries. This constitutes evidence that he has something to say that appeals to a wide variety of human beings. His stories have also had a variety of notable devotees, including Nelson Algren, Ingmar Bergman, Graham Greene, Gilbert Highet, Aldous Huxley, Christopher Isherwood, Bertrand Russell, and Angus Wilson. These influential men, with their experience of, and insight into, good ideas and adept communication, have praised Bradbury as a stylist, social thinker, and prophet. His early collections made him the only science-fiction writer to charm a significant portion of the literary establishment, but the receptions that his later collections received revealed that the establishment's earlier estimate of his virtues had soured. With his lack of a university education, he neither views himself nor is viewed by others as an academic or even a literary writer. He has said in interviews that he considers this an advantage, since it left him free to plumb the depths of his unconscious. This openness to his unconscious was responsible for the success of his early horror and fantasy stories in which the unutterable and unthinkable achieve chilling embodiment in his poetic words.

In making an assessment of Bradbury's contribution to modern American literature, one must come to terms with the role he played in popularizing science fiction and making it critically respectable. Bradbury himself once stated that, for him, science fiction is "the most important literature in the history of the world," since it tells the story of "civilization birthing itself." He has also said that he considers himself not a science-fiction writer but an "idea writer," someone who loves ideas and enjoys playing with them. Many of his science-fiction critics would concur in this characterization, since they have had problems categorizing this man who knows so little about science as a traditional science-fiction writer. When asked whether the Mariner mission's revelations about the inhospitability of Mars to humankind had invalidated his stories about the planet, Bradbury responded that these discoveries in no way affected them, because he had been composing poetic myths, not scientific forecasts.

In addition to their lack of scientific verisimilitude, his stories have other weaknesses. Few of his characters are memorable, and most are simply vehicles for his ideas. He has frankly said that he devises characters to personify his ideas and that all of his characters—youths, astronauts, and grotesques—are, in some way, variations on himself. Other critics have noticed failures in Bradbury's imaginative powers, particularly in his later stories. The settings and images that seemed fresh when first used in the early stories became stale as they continued to be used in the later ones. Disch complained that Bradbury's sentimental attachment to his past themes "have made him nearly oblivious to new data from any source."

Despite these criticisms, some of which have bite, Bradbury's stories possess great strengths. If his characters are made negligible by the burden of the ideas that they are forced to carry, these same ideas can open readers to his enchanting sense of wonder. These readers can be inspired by his enthusiasm for new experiences and new worlds. They may also be uplifted by the underlying optimism present even in his most pessimistic work and come to share his belief that human beings will overcome materialism, avarice, and obsession with power to achieve the expansion of what is best in the human spirit that has been his principal theme.

Other major works

NOVELS: *Fahrenheit 451*, 1953; *Dandelion Wine*, 1957; *Something Wicked This Way Comes*, 1962; *Death Is a Lonely Business*, 1985; *A Graveyard for Lunatics: Another Tale of Two Cities*, 1990; *Green Shadows, White Whale*, 1992.

PLAYS: *The Anthem Sprinters and Other Antics*, 1963; *The World of Ray Bradbury: Three Fables of the Future*, 1964; *The Day It Rained Forever*, 1966; *The Pedestrian*, 1966; *The Wonderful Ice Cream Suit and Other Plays*, 1972; *Madrigals for the Space Age*, 1972; *Pillar of Fire and Other Plays for Today, Tomorrow, and Beyond Tomorrow*, 1975; *That Ghost, That Bride of Time: Excerpts from a Play-in-Progress*, 1976; *The Martian Chronicles*, 1977; *Fahrenheit 451* (musical), 1979; *A Device Out of Time*, 1986.

SCREENPLAYS: *It Came from Outer Space*, 1952 (with David Schwartz); *Moby Dick*, 1956 (with John Huston); *Icarus Montgolfier Wright*, 1961 (with George C. Johnson); *That Picasso Summer*, 1967 (with Edwin Boyd).

POETRY: *Old Ahab's Friend, and Friend to Noah, Speaks His Piece: A Celebration*, 1971; *When Elephants Last in the Dooryard Bloomed: Celebrations for Almost Any Day in the Year*, 1973; *Where Robot Mice and Robot Men Run Round in Robot Towns: New Poems, Both Light and Dark*, 1977; *Twin Hieroglyphs That Swim the River Dust*, 1978; *The Bike Repairman*, 1978; *The Haunted Computer and the Android Pope*, 1981; *The Complete Poems of Ray Bradbury*, 1982.

NONFICTION: *Zen in the Art of Writing: Essays on Creativity*, 1989.

CHILDREN'S LITERATURE: *Switch on the Night*, 1955; *R Is for Rocket*, 1962; *S Is for Space*, 1966; *The Halloween Tree*, 1972; *Fever Dream*, 1987.

ANTHOLOGIES: *Timeless Stories for Today and Tomorrow*, 1952; *The Circus of Dr. Lao and Other Improbable Stories*, 1956.

Bibliography

Eller, Jon R. "The Stories of Ray Bradbury: An Annotated Finding List (1938-1991)," *Bulletin of Bibliography* 49 (May, 1992).

Greenberg, Martin Henry, and Joseph D. Olander, eds. *Ray Bradbury*. New York: Taplinger, 1980. This anthology of Bradbury criticism is part of the Writers of the Twenty-first Century series. Some of the articles defend Bradbury against the charge that he is not really a science-fiction writer but an opponent of science and technology; other articles defend him against the charge that he is mawkish. Includes an extensive Bradbury bibliography compiled by Marshall B. Tymn and an index.

Johnson, Wayne L. *Ray Bradbury*. New York: Frederick Ungar, 1980. Although this volume is the work of a fan rather than a critic, it provides a good general introduction to Bradbury's stories of fantasy and science fiction. Johnson's approach is thematic rather than chronological (he uses the categories of magic, monsters, and machines to facilitate his

discussion of Bradbury's principal approaches, ideas, and themes).
Index.

McNelly, Willis E. "Ray Bradbury: Past, Present and Future." In *Voices for the Future: Essays on Major Science Fiction Writers*, edited by Thomas D. Clareson. Vol. 1. Bowling Green, Ohio: Bowling Green University Popular Press, 1976. McNelly's article argues that Bradbury's themes place him in the mainstream of American letters. It should be read in conjunction with the article by A. James Stupple, "The Past, the Future, and Ray Bradbury," which interprets Bradbury's work as responding sensitively to the complexities of the evolution of personal lives and the development of world history.

Mogen, David. *Ray Bradbury*. Boston: Twayne, 1986. This brief introduction to Bradbury's career centers on analyses of the literary influences that shaped the development of his style and the themes whose successful embodiment in his short stories and novels shaped his reputation. The detailed notes at the end of the book contain many useful references. Bibliography and index.

Nolan, William F. *The Ray Bradbury Companion: A Life and Career History, Photolog, and Comprehensive Checklist of Writings with Facsimiles from Ray Bradbury's Unpublished and Uncollected Work in All Media*. Detroit: Gale Research, 1975. The ample subtitle gives a good idea of this book's contents. After its publication, its information on Bradbury has been updated by Donn Albright, in "The Ray Bradbury Index," in several issues of *Xenophile* (May, 1975; September, 1976; and November, 1977).

Slusser, George Edgar. *The Bradbury Chronicles*. San Bernardino, Calif.: Borgo Press, 1977. This booklet is part of a series, Popular Writers of Today. Intended for young students and general audiences, this brief work discusses summarily some of Bradbury's most important writings. Bibliography.

Touponce, William F. *Ray Bradbury*. Mercer Island, Wash.: Starmont House, 1989. Offers a broad analysis of Bradbury's fiction.

Robert J. Paradowski

RAYMOND CARVER

Born: Clatskanie, Oregon; May 25, 1938
Died: Port Angeles, Washington; August 2, 1988

Principal short fiction · *Put Yourself in My Shoes*, 1974 · *Will You Please Be Quiet, Please?*, 1976 · *Furious Seasons and Other Stories*, 1977 · *What We Talk About When We Talk About Love*, 1981 · *Cathedral*, 1983 · *Where I'm Calling From*, 1988

Other literary forms · Raymond Carver distinguished himself as a short-story writer and poet, and he wrote in both forms until his death. His poetry has been published in the following collections: *Near Klamath* (1968), *Winter Insomnia* (1970), *At Night the Salmon Move* (1976), *Two Poems* (1982), *Fires: Essays, Poems, Stories* (1983), *If It Please You* (1984), *This Water* (1985), *Where Water Comes Together with Other Water* (1985), *Ultramarine* (1986), and *A New Path to the Waterfall* (1989).

Achievements · Carver's greatest achievement was overcoming his economically and culturally disadvantaged background to become an author of world renown. He made the short story a viable literary form; since Carver, short-story collections have again become a marketable commodity in the book trade. Both as a model and as a teacher, he had such an influence on younger fiction writers that author Jay McInerney could truthfully say (alluding to a famous statement that Fyodor Dostoevski made about Nikolai Gogol) that there is hardly a single American short-story writer younger than Carver who did not "come out of Carver's overcoat."

With only a bachelor's degree and mediocre grades, Carver was invited to teach at distinguished universities and became a professor of English at Syracuse University in 1980. He received many honors during his lifetime, including a Strauss Living Award, which guaranteed him an annual stipend of thirty-five thousand dollars and enabled him to devote full time to writing during the last years of his life. Just before his death, he received a doctorate of letters from the University of Hartford.

Biography · Raymond Carver grew up in a sparsely populated corner of the Pacific Northwest. This rustic environment had an indelible effect upon his character and writing. Like Ernest Hemingway, one of the writers who influenced him, he loved the purity and freedom of the American wilderness, and he also respected the simplicity, honesty, and directness of the men and women who earned meager and precarious livelihoods in that primitive setting. He married young and had two children to support by the time he was twenty. He had wanted to be a writer from the time he was in the third grade, but the responsibilities of parenthood made it extremely difficult for him to find time to write. His limited education forced him to take menial jobs for which he was temperamentally unsuited. He was unable to consider tackling anything as ambitious as a full-length novel, so he spent his odd free hours writing short stories and poetry. He managed to get some of his work published in little magazines, but these publications paid little or nothing for his work, so he was haunted by financial problems for much of his life.

One of the most important influences in Carver's life was John Gardner, who taught creative writing at California State University at Chico and said, "You cannot be a great writer unless you feel greatly." The idealistic Gardner introduced his students to the literary magazines that represented the cutting edge in contemporary American fiction and poetry, and he urged them to write honestly about what they knew, as opposed to turning out formula fiction in an attempt to make money. This is exactly what Carver did, and ironically, he found that the hardships and distractions that were preventing him from writing were the very things that provided him with material to write about. This may account for the characteristic stoical humor to be found in many of his stories.

Another profound influence in his life was alcohol. One of Carver's distinguishing traits as a writer is his astonishing candor, and anyone who reads a dozen of his short stories will get a good idea of what his life was like for nearly two decades. His drinking caused serious domestic and financial problems, which led to feelings of guilt and more drinking. Amazingly, his strong constitution and unwavering motivation enabled him to continue producing stories and poems.

With the publication of *What We Talk About When We Talk About Love* in 1981, Carver achieved critical and popular fame. His financial problems were ameliorated because he was receiving valuable grants and teaching assignments and was also selling his work to high-paying slick magazines such as *Esquire, Harper's Bazaar, Playgirl,* and *The New Yorker.* Collections of his short stories sold well. He was earning money teaching creative writing courses and appearing as a featured attraction at many workshops and seminars.

By the late 1970's, Carver had separated from his first wife and was living with the poet and teacher Tess Gallagher. She helped him cope with his drinking problem and provided a much-needed stabilizing influence.

Carver, always a heavy cigarette smoker, died of lung cancer in 1988. By that time, his works had been published all over the world in more than twenty languages.

Analysis · Nearly everything written about Raymond Carver begins with two observations: He is a minimalist, and he writes about working-class people. Even when the critic is sympathetic, this dual categorization tends to stigmatize Carver as a minor artist writing little stories about little people. Although it is true that most of Carver's characters belong to the working class, their problems are universal. Carver writes about divorce, infidelity, spiritual alienation, alcoholism, bankruptcy, rootlessness, and existential dread; none of these afflictions is peculiar to the working class, and in fact, all were once more common to members of the higher social classes.

Carver was a minimalist by preference and by necessity. His lifelong experience had been with working-class people. It would have been inappropriate to write about simple people in an ornate style, and furthermore, his limited education would have made it impossible for him to do so effectively. The spare, objective style that he admired in some of Hemingway's short stories, such as "The Killers" and "Hills Like White Elephants," was perfectly suited to Carver's needs.

The advantage and appeal of minimalism in literature is that it draws readers into the story by forcing them to conceptualize missing details. One drawback is that it allows insecure writers to imply that they know more than they know and mean more than they are actually saying. This was true of the early stories that Carver collected in *Will You Please Be Quiet, Please?* A good example of Carver's strengths and weaknesses is a short story in that volume titled "Fat."

As the title suggests, "Fat" is about a fat man. It is little more than a character sketch; nothing happens in the story. Throughout his career, Carver based stories and poems on people or incidents that he observed or scraps of conversation that he overheard; these things seemed to serve as living metaphors or symbols with broader implications. Carver frames his story by setting it in a restaurant and by describing the fat man from the point of view of a waitress. She says that she has never seen such a fat person in her life and is somewhat awestruck by his appearance, by his gracious manners, and by the amount of food that he can consume at one sitting. After she goes home at night, she is still thinking about him. She says that she herself feels "terrifically fat"; she feels depressed, and finally ends by saying, "My life is going to change. I feel it."

The reader can feel it too but might be hard pressed to say what "it" is. The story leaves a strong impression but an ambiguous one. No two readers would agree on what the story means, if anything. It demonstrates Carver's talent for characterization through dialogue and action, which was his greatest asset. Both the waitress and her fat customer come alive as people, partially through the deliberate contrast between them. His treatment of the humble, kindly waitress demonstrates his sensitivity to the feelings of women. His ex-wife, Maryann Carver, said of him, "Ray loved and understood women, and women loved him."

"Fat" also shows Carver's unique sense of humor, which was another trait that set him apart from other writers. Carver was so constituted that he could not help seeing the humorous side of the tragic or the grotesque. His early, experimental short stories most closely resemble the early short stories of William Saroyan reprinted in *The Daring Young Man on the Flying Trapeze and Other Stories* (1934) and subsequent collections of his stories that appeared in the 1930's. Saroyan is perhaps best remembered for his novel *The Human Comedy* (1943), and it might be said that the human comedy was Carver's theme and thesis throughout his career. Like the early stories of Saroyan, Carver's stories are the tentative vignettes of a novice who knows very well that he wants to be a writer but still does not know exactly what he wants to say.

Will You Please Be Quiet, Please? includes the tragicomic "Neighbors," the first of Carver's stories to appear in a slick magazine with a large circulation. Gordon Lish, editor of the venerable men's magazine *Esquire*, recognized Carver's talent early but did not immediately accept any of his submissions. Lish's welcome encouragement, painful rejections, and eventual acceptance represented major influences in Carver's career. "Neighbors" deals with ordinary people but has a surrealistic humor, which was to become a Carver trademark.

Bill and Arlene Miller, a couple in their thirties, have agreed to feed their neighbors' cat and water the plants while they are away. The Stones' apartment holds a mysterious fascination, and they both find excuses to enter it more often than necessary. Bill helps himself to the Chivas Regal, eats food out of their refrigerator, and goes through their closets and dresser drawers. He tries on some of Jim Stone's clothes and lies on their bed masturbating. Then he goes so far as to try on Harriet Stone's brassiere and panties and then a skirt and blouse. Bill's wife also disappears into the neighbors' apartment on her own mysterious errands. They fantasize that they have assumed the identities of their neighbors, whom they regard as happier people leading fuller lives. The shared guilty adventure arouses both Bill and Arlene sexually, and they have better lovemaking than they have experienced in a long while. Then disaster strikes: Arlene discovers that she has inadvertently locked the Stones' key inside the apartment. The cat may starve; the plants may wither; the Stones may find evidence that they have been rummaging through their possessions. The story ends with the frightened Millers clinging to each other outside their lost garden of Eden.

This early story displays some of Carver's strengths: his sense of humor, his powers of description, and his ability to characterize people through what they do and say. It also has the two main qualities that editors look for: timeliness and universality. It is therefore easy to understand why Lish bought this piece after rejecting so many others. "Neighbors" portrays the alienated condition of many contemporary Americans of all social classes.

"Neighbors," however, has certain characteristics that have allowed hostile critics to damn Carver's stories as "vignettes," "anecdotes," "sketches," and "slices-of-life." For one thing, readers realize that the terror they briefly share with the Millers is unnecessary: they can go to the building manager for a passkey or call a locksmith. It is hard to understand how two people who are so bold about violating their neighbors' apartment should suddenly feel so helpless in the face of an everyday mishap. The point of the story is blunted by the unsatisfactory ending.

The publication of the collection titled *What We Talk About When We Talk About Love* made Carver famous. These short, rather ambiguous stories also got him permanently saddled with the term "minimalist." Carver never accepted that label and claimed that he did not even understand what it meant. He had a healthy mistrust of critics who attempted to categorize writers with such epithets: it was as if he sensed their antagonism and felt that they themselves were trying to "minimize" him as an author. A friend of Carver said that he thought a minimalist was a "taker-out" rather than a "putter-in." In that sense, Carver was a minimalist. It was his practice to go over and over his stories trying to delete all superfluous words and even superfluous punctuation marks. He said that he knew he was finished with a story when he found himself putting back punctuation marks that he had previously deleted. It would be more accurate to call Carver a perfectionist rather than a minimalist.

One of the best short stories reprinted in *What We Talk About When We Talk About Love* is "Why Don't You Dance?" It is one of the most representative, the most "Carveresque" of all Carver's short stories. A man who is never given a name has placed all of his furniture and personal possessions outside on the front lawn and has whimsically arranged them as if they were still indoors. He has run an extension cord from the house and hooked up lamps, a television, and a record player. He is sitting outside drinking whiskey, totally indifferent to the amazement and curiosity of his neighbors. One feels as if the worst is over for him: He is the survivor of some great catastrophe, like a marooned sailor who has managed to salvage some flotsam and jetsam.

A young couple, referred to throughout the story as "the boy" and "the girl," drive by and assume that the man is holding a yard sale. They stop and inquire about prices. The man offers them drinks. The boy and girl get into a party spirit. They put old records on the turntable and start dancing in the driveway. The man is anxious to get rid of his possessions and accepts whatever they are willing to offer. He even makes them presents of things that they do not really want. Weeks later, the girl is still talking about the man, but she cannot find the words to express what she really feels about the incident. Perhaps she and her young friends will understand the incident much better after they have worked and worried and bickered and moved from one place to another for ten or twenty years.

"Why Don't You Dance?" is a humorous treatment of a serious subject, in characteristic Carver fashion. The man's tragedy is never spelled out, but the reader can piece the story together quite easily from the clues. Evidently there has been a divorce or separation. Evidently there were financial problems, which are so often associated with divorce, and the man has been evicted. Judging from the fact that he is doing so much drinking, alcoholism is either the cause or the effect of his other problems. The man has given up all hope and now sees hope only in other people, represented by this young couple just starting out in life and trying to collect a few pieces of furniture for their rented apartment.

Divorce, infidelity, domestic strife, financial worry, bankruptcy, alcoholism, rootlessness, consumerism as a substitute for intimacy, and disillusionment with the American Dream are common themes throughout Carver's stories. The symbol of a man sitting outside on his front lawn drinking whiskey, with all of his worldly possessions placed around him but soon to be scattered to the four winds, is a striking symbol of modern human beings. It is easy to acquire possessions but nearly impossible to keep a real home.

Carver did not actually witness such an event but had a similar episode described to him by a friend and eventually used it in this story. A glance at the titles of some of Carver's stories shows his penchant for finding in his mundane environment external symbols of subjective states: "Fat," "Gazebo," "Vitamins," "Feathers," "Cathedral," "Boxes," "Menudo." The same tendency is even more striking in the titles of his poems, for example, "The Car," "Jean's TV," "NyQuil," "My Dad's Wallet," "The Phone Booth," "Heels."

In his famous essay "The Philosophy of Composition," Edgar Allan Poe wrote that he wanted an image that would be "emblematical of Mournful and Never-ending Remembrance," so he created his famous raven perched on the bust of Pallas Athena and croaking the refrain "nevermore." To highlight the difference in Carver's method, Carver might have seen a real raven perched on a real statue, and it would have suggested mournful and never-ending remembrance. This kind of "reverse symbolism" seems characteristic of modern American minimalists in general, and Carver's influence on their movement is paramount.

Poe states that he originally thought of using a parrot in his famous poem but rejected that notion because it did not seem sufficiently poetic and might have produced a comical effect; if Carver had been faced with such a choice, he probably would have chosen the parrot. What distinguishes Carver from most minimalists is a sense of humor that is impervious to catastrophe: like the man on the front lawn, Carver had been so far down that everyplace else looked better. He would have concurred heartily with William Shakespeare's often-quoted lines in *As You Like It* (1599-1600):

> Sweet are the uses of adversity,
> Which, like a toad, ugly and venomous,
> Wears yet a precious jewel in his head

On a different level, "Why Don't You Dance?" reflects Carver's maturation as a person and an author. The responsibilities of parenthood as well as the experience of teaching young students were bringing home to him the fact that his personal problems could hold instructional utility for others. As a teacher of creative writing, placed more and more in the limelight, interacting with writers, editors, professors, and interviewers, he was being forced to formulate his own artistic credo. The older man in the story sees himself in his young yard sale customers and wants to help them along in life; this is evidently a reflection of the author's own attitude. Consequently, the story itself is not merely an autobiographical protest or lament like some of Carver's earlier works but is designed to deliver a message—perhaps a warning—for the profit of others. The melancholy wisdom of Carver's protagonist reflects Carver's own mellowing as he began to appreciate the universally tragic nature of human existence.

"Where I'm Calling From" is a great American short story. It originally appeared in the prestigious *The New Yorker*, was reprinted in the collection titled *Cathedral*, and appears once again as the title story in the best and most comprehensive collection of Carver's stories, *Where I'm Calling From*. The story is narrated by an alcoholic staying at a "drying-out facility," an unpretentious boardinghouse where plain meals are served family style and there is nothing to do but read, watch television, or talk. The bucolic atmosphere is strongly reminiscent of the training-camp scenes in one of Hemingway's most brilliant short stories, "Fifty Grand."

The narrator in Carver's story tells about his drinking problems and interweaves his own biography with that of a friend he has made at the drying-out facility, a man he refers to as J. P. The only thing unusual about their stories is that J. P. is a chimney sweep and is married to a chimney sweep. Both J. P. and the narrator ruined their marriages through their compulsive drinking and are now terrified that they will be unable to control their craving once they get out of the facility. They have made vows of abstinence often enough before and have not kept them. They have dried out before and gone right back to the bottle.

Carver manages to convey all the feelings of guilt, remorse, terror, and helplessness experienced by people who are in the ultimate stages of alcoholism. It is noteworthy that, whereas his alcoholic protagonists of earlier stories were often isolated individuals, the protagonist-narrator of "Where I'm Calling From" not only is actively seeking help but also is surrounded by others with the same problem. This feature indicates that Carver had come to realize that the way to give his stories the point or meaning that they had previously often lacked was to suggest the existence of large-scale social problems of which his characters are victims. He had made what author Joan Didion called "the quantum leap" of realizing that his personal problems were actually social problems. The curse of alcoholism affects all social classes; even people who never touch a drop can have their lives ruined by it.

"The Bridle" first appeared in *The New Yorker* and was reprinted in *Cathedral*. It is an example of Carver's mature period, a highly artistic story fraught with social significance. The story is told from the point of view of one of Carver's *faux-naïf* narrators. Readers immediately feel that they know this good-natured soul, a woman named Marge who manages an apartment building in Arizona and "does hair" as a sideline. She tells about one of the many families who stayed a short while and then moved on as tumbleweeds being blown across the desert. Although Carver typically writes about Northern California and the Pacific Northwest, this part of Arizona is also "Carver Country," a world of freeways, fast-food restaurants, Laundromats, mindless television entertainment, and transient living accommodations, a homogenized world of strangers with minimum-wage jobs and tabloid mentalities.

Mr. Holits pays the rent in cash every month, suggesting that he recently went bankrupt and has neither a bank account nor credit cards. Carver, like minimalists in general, loves such subtle clues. Mrs. Holits confides to Marge that they had owned a farm in Minnesota. Her husband, who "knows everything there is about horses," still keeps one of his bridles, evidently symbolizing his hope that he may escape from "Carver Country." Mrs. Holits proves more adaptable: she gets a job as a waitress, a favorite occupation among Carver characters. Her husband, however, cannot adjust to the service industry jobs, which are all that are available to a man his age with his limited experience. He handles the money, the two boys are his sons by a former marriage, and he has been accustomed to making the decisions, yet he finds that his wife is taking over the family leadership in this brave new post-industrial world.

Like many other Carver males, Holits becomes a heavy drinker. He eventually injures himself while trying to show off his strength at the swimming pool. One day the Holits with their young sons pack and drive off down the long, straight highway without a word of explanation. When Marge trudges upstairs to clean the empty apartment, she finds that Holits has left his bridle behind.

The naïve narrator does not understand the significance of the bridle, but the reader feels its poignancy as a symbol. The bridle is one of those useless objects that everyone carts around and is reluctant to part with because it represents a memory, a hope, or a dream. It is an especially appropriate symbol because it is so utterly out of place in one of those two-story, frame-stucco, look-alike apartment buildings that disfigure the landscape and are the dominant features of "Carver Country." Gigantic economic forces beyond the comprehension of the narrator have driven this farm family from their home and turned them into the modern equivalent of the Joad family in John Steinbeck's classic novel *The Grapes of Wrath* (1939).

There is, however, a big difference between Carver and Steinbeck. Steinbeck believed in and prescribed the panacea of socialism; Carver has no prescriptions to offer. He seems to have no faith either in politicians or in preachers. His characters are more likely to go to church to play bingo than to say prayers or sing hymns. Like many of his contemporary minimalists, he seems to have gone beyond alienation, beyond existentialism, beyond despair. God is dead; so what else is new?

Carver's working-class characters are far more complicated than Steinbeck's Joad family. Americans have become more sophisticated in the past fifty years as a result of the influence of radio, motion pictures, television, more abundant educational opportunities, improved automobiles and highways, cheap air transportation, alcohol and drugs, more leisure time, and the fact that their work is less enervating because of the proliferation of labor-saving machinery. Many Americans have also lost their religious faith, their work ethic, their class consciousness, their family loyalty, their integrity, and their dreams. Steinbeck saw it happening and showed how the Joad family was splitting apart after being uprooted from the soil; Carver's people are the Joad family a half-century down the road. Oddly enough, Carver's mature stories do not seem nihilistic or despairing because they contain the redeeming qualities of humor, compassion, and honesty.

Where I'm Calling From is the most useful volume of Carver's short stories because it contains some of the best stories that had been reprinted in earlier books plus a generous selection of his later and best efforts. One of the new stories reprinted in *Where I'm Calling From* is "Boxes," which first appeared in *The New Yorker*. When Carver's stories began to be regularly accepted by *The New Yorker*, it was an indication that he had found the style of self-expression that he had been searching for since the beginning of his career. It was also a sign that his themes were evoking sympathetic chords in the hearts and minds of *The New Yorker*'s middle and upper-class readership, the people at whom that magazine's sophisticated advertisements for diamonds, furs, highrise condominiums, and luxury vacation cruises are aimed.

"Boxes" is written in Carver's characteristic tragicomic tone. It is a story in which the *faux-naïf* narrator, a favorite with Carver, complains about the eccentric behavior of his widowed mother who, for one specious reason or another, is always changing her place of residence. She moves so frequently that she usually seems to have the bulk of her worldly possessions packed in boxes scattered about on the floor. One of her complaints is the attitude of her landlord, whom she calls "King Larry." Larry Hadlock is a widower and a relatively affluent property owner. It is evident through Carver's unerring dialogue that what she is really bitter about is Larry's indifference to her own fading charms. In the end, she returns to California but telephones to complain about the traffic, the faulty air-conditioning unit in her apartment, and the indifference of management. Her son vaguely understands that what his mother really wants, though she may not realize it herself, is love and a real home, and that she can never have these things again in her lifetime no matter where she moves.

What makes the story significant is its universality: It reflects the macrocosm in a microcosm. In "Boxes," the problem touched on is not only the rootlessness and anonymity of modern life but also the plight of millions of aging people, who are considered by some to be useless in their old age and a burden to their children. It was typical of Raymond Carver to find a metaphor for this important social phenomenon in a bunch of cardboard boxes.

Carver uses working-class people as his models, but he is not writing solely about the working class. It is simply the fact that all Americans can see themselves in his little, inarticulate, bewildered characters that makes Carver an important writer in the dominant tradition of American realism, a worthy successor to Mark Twain, Stephen Crane, Sherwood Anderson, Theodore Dreiser, Willa Cather, John Steinbeck, and William Faulkner, all of whom wrote about humble people. Someday it may be generally appreciated that, despite the odds against him and despite the antipathy of certain mandarins, Raymond Carver managed to become the most important American fiction writer in the second half of the twentieth century.

Other major works

SCREENPLAY: *Dostoevsky*, 1985.

POETRY: *Near Klamath*, 1968; *Winter Insomnia*, 1970; *At Night the Salmon Move*, 1976; *Two Poems*, 1982; *Fires: Essays, Poems, Stories*, 1983; *If It Please You*, 1984; *This Water*, 1985; *Where Water Comes Together with Other Water*, 1985; *Ultramarine*, 1986; *A New Path to the Waterfall*, 1989.

ANTHOLOGY: *American Short Story Pieces*, 1987 (with Tom Jenks).

Bibliography

Adelman, Bob, and Tess Gallagher. *Carver Country: The World of Raymond Carver*. Introduction by Tess Gallagher. New York: Charles Scribner's Sons, 1990. Produced in the spirit of a photographic essay, this book contains excellent photographs of Carver, his relatives, people who served as inspirations for characters in his stories, and places that were important in his life and work. The photographs are accompanied by excerpts from Carver's stories and poems.

Barth, John. "A Few Words about Minimalism." *The New York Times Book Review*, December 28, 1986, 2. A prominent American writer who is considered a leading exponent of the maximalist style of fiction writing defines minimalism in art and concludes that there is a place for both maximalism and minimalism in literature. He regards Carver as the prime shaper of "the new American Short Story."

Bugeja, Michael. "Tarnish and Silver: An Analysis of Carver's Cathedral." *South Dakota Review* 24 no. 3 (1986): 73-87. Discusses the revision of an early Carver story, "The Bath," which was reprinted in *Cathedral* as "A Small Good Thing." The changes made throughout the story, and especially the somewhat more positive resolution, reflect Carver's evolution as a writer.

Campbell, Ewing. *Raymond Carver: A Study of the Short Fiction*. New York: Twayne Publishers, 1992.

Carver, Raymond. "A Storyteller's Shoptalk." *The New York Times Book*

Review, February 15, 1981, 9. In this interesting article, Carver describes his artistic credo, evaluates the work of some of his contemporaries, and offers excellent advice to aspiring young writers. The article reveals his perfectionism and dedication to his craft.

Halpert, Sam, ed. *When We Talk About Raymond Carver*. Layton, Utah: Gibbs Smith, 1991. A collection of transcripts of interviews with ten writers who knew Carver on a personal basis, including a fascinating interview with Carver's first wife, Maryann, who provides a fresh perspective on the incidents on which many of Carver's stories were based.

Nesset, Kirk. *The Stories of Raymond Carver: A Critical Study*. Athens: Ohio University Press, 1995.

Runyon, Randolph. *Reading Raymond Carver*. Syracuse, N.Y.: Syracuse University Press, 1992.

Saltzman, Arthur M. *Understanding Raymond Carver*. Columbia: University of South Carolina Press, 1988. A short overview of Carver's life and work with the emphasis on Carver's short stories and one chapter devoted to his poetry. Contains a valuable bibliography of works by and about Carver.

Stull, William L. "Raymond Carver." In *Dictionary of Literary Biography Year-book: 1984*, edited by Jean W. Ross. Detroit: Gale Research, 1985. This article covers Carver's life and work up until shortly before his death and attempts to analyze his poetry and fiction techniques. It contains a fairly comprehensive list of Carver's books and miscellaneous publications as well as a list of articles about Carver.

Wolff, Tobias. "Raymond Carver Had His Cake and Ate It Too." *Esquire* 112 (September, 1989): 240-248. A friend and fellow author and teacher relates a series of anecdotes about Carver in his wild drinking days. The essay highlights Carver's zest for life, his kindly interest in people, and his unconcealed delight with the recognition that he received toward the end of his life.

Bill Delaney

WILLA CATHER

Born: Back Creek Valley, near Gore, Virginia; December 7, 1873
Died: New York, New York; April 24, 1947

Principal short fiction · *The Troll Garden,* 1905 · *Youth and the Bright Medusa,* 1920 · *Obscure Destinies,* 1932 · *The Old Beauty and Others,* 1948 · *Willa Cather's Collected Short Fiction: 1892-1912,* 1965 · *Uncle Valentine and Other Stories: Willa Cather's Collected Short Fiction, 1915-1929,* 1973

Other literary forms · Willa Cather is best known as a novelist, but she wrote prolifically in other forms, especially as a young woman; she had been publishing short stories for more than twenty years before she published her first novel. Although her fame rests largely on her twelve novels and a few short stories, she has a collection of poetry, several collections of essays, and hundreds of newspaper columns and magazine pieces to her credit. Only one of her books, *A Lost Lady* (1923), was filmed in Hollywood; after that one experience, Cather would not allow any of her work to be filmed again.

Courtesy of the Library of Congress

Achievements · Cather was one of America's first modern writers to make the prairie immigrant experience an important and continuing subject for high-quality fiction. Although her setting is often the American western frontier, she masterfully locates the universal through the specific, and her literary reputation transcends the limitations of regional or gender affiliation. In her exploration of the human spirit, Cather characteristically defends artistic values in an increasingly materialistic world, and she is known for her graceful rendering of place and character.

Praised in the 1920's as one of the most successful novelists of her time, Cather was sometimes criticized in the next decade for neglecting contemporary social issues. Later, however, and especially since her death, she was recognized as a great artist and one of the most important American writers of the twentieth century. In 1923, she was awarded the Pulitzer Prize for the novel *One of Ours* (1922). She also received the Howells Medal for fiction from the Academy of the National Institute of Arts and Letters in 1930, the Prix Fémina Américain for *Shadows on the Rock* (1931) in 1933, and the gold medal from the National Institute of Arts and Letters in 1944. With time, interest in Cather's fiction continued to increase, rather than diminish, and she enjoys appreciative audiences abroad as well as in her own country.

Biography · Willa Sibert Cather moved with her family from Virginia to Nebraska when she was only nine years old, a move that was to influence her mind and art throughout her life. As a student at the University of Nebraska, she wrote for various college magazines; she also became a regular contributor to the *Nebraska State Journal*, publishing book, theater, and concert reviews, as well as commentary on the passing scene. Even after she moved to Pittsburgh to take an editorial job, she continued to send columns home to the *Nebraska State Journal*. Later she also began contributing to the Lincoln *Courier*. She taught English in Pittsburgh (an experience that became the source for one of her most famous short stories, "Paul's Case") and then moved to New York to take a position with *McClure's Magazine*. After the publication of her first novel, *Alexander's Bridge*, in 1912, she left *McClure's Magazine* to devote full time to her creative work.

Analysis · Willa Cather was always conscious of a double urge in herself, toward art and toward the land. As long as her parents were living, she found herself torn between the Western prairie and the cultural centers of the East and Europe. That basic polarity appears again and again in her stories, some of which deal with the artist's struggle against debilitating influences, and some with both the pleasant and the difficult aspects of the prairie experience. Perhaps only in her work did Cather achieve a comfortable reconciliation of these polarities, by making the prairie experience the subject of her art.

All of Cather's work is consistently value-centered. She believed in characters who are good, artists who are true to their callings, people who can appreciate and use what is valuable from the past, and individuals who have a special relationship with the land. Her chief agony lay in what she saw as a general sellout to materialism—in the realm of art, in the prairie and desert, in the small town, in the city.

The struggle of the artist to maintain integrity against an unsympathetic environment and the forces of an exploitive materialism is explored in three stories that are particularly important in the Cather canon. Two of them, "The Sculptor's Funeral" and "Paul's Case," have been widely anthologized and are well known. The third, "Uncle Valentine," is an important later story.

"The Sculptor's Funeral" is about the return in death of a world-renowned sculptor to the pinched little prairie town from which he somehow miraculously sprang. Harvey Merrick's body arrives by train in the dead of winter, accompanied by one of his former students. There to meet the coffin are several prominent townsmen, among them a brusque, red-bearded lawyer named Jim Laird. Only he can appreciate the magnitude of Harvey Merrick's achievement. The watchers around the body chuckle and snort over poor Harvey's uselessness as a farm hand, over his inability to "make it" in the only things that count for them—money-making ventures in Sand City. Jim Laird, in a storm of self-hatred for having become the scheming lawyer these harpies wanted him to be, enters the room and blasts them mercilessly. He reminds the town elders of the young men they have ruined by drumming "nothing but money and knavery into their ears from the time they wore knickerbockers." They hated Harvey, Laird says, because he left them and rose above them, achieving in a world they were not fit to enter. He reminds them that Harvey "wouldn't have given one sunset over your marshes" for all of their material properties and possessions. Laird is too drunk the next day to attend the funeral, and it is learned that he dies some years later from a cold he caught while "driving across the Colorado mountains to defend one of Phelps's sons who had got into trouble there by cutting government timber."

Harvey Merrick is not the tragic figure of the story, for he, thanks to a timid father who sensed something special about this one son, managed to escape destruction. He became the artist he was destined to be, in spite of his unlikely beginnings. The money-grubbing first citizens of Sand City can wag their tongues feebly over his corpse, but they cannot touch him or detract from his accomplishment. If there is a tragic element in the story, it is the life of Jim Laird. Like Harvey, he went away to school full of idealistic fire; like Harvey, he wanted to be a great man and make the hometown people proud of him. Instead, he says, "I came back here to practice, and I found you didn't in the least want me to be a great man. You wanted me to be a shrewd lawyer." He became that shrewd lawyer and lost his soul in the process. The dead artist, imposing and serene in his coffin, serves as a perfect foil for Jim Laird, and the story stands as one of

Cather's most powerful treatments of the conflict between artistic ideals and materialistic value systems.

"Paul's Case" presents a somewhat different view of that conflict. Paul, a high school youngster, is not a practicing artist, but he has an artistic temperament. He loves to hang around art galleries and concert halls and theaters, talking with the performers and basking in their reflected glory. It is glitter, excitement, and escape from the dripping taps in his home on Pittsburgh's Cordelia Street that Paul craves. A hopeless "case," Paul is finally taken out of high school by his widowed father because his mind is never on his studies. Forced from his usher's job at the concert hall and forbidden to associate with the actors at the theater, he loses the only things he had lived for and cared about. When he is denied those vital outlets for his aesthetic needs and sent to do dull work for a dull company, he carries out a desperate plan. One evening, instead of depositing his firm's receipts in the bank, he catches a train for New York. With swift determination, he buys elegant clothes and installs himself in a luxurious hotel suite, there to live for a few brief days the life he had always felt himself suited for. Those days are lovely and perfect, but the inevitable reckoning draws near: he learns from a newspaper that his father is en route to New York to retrieve him. Very deliberately Paul plots his course, even buying carnations for his buttonhole. Traveling to the outskirts of town, he walks to an embankment above the Pennsylvania tracks. There he carefully buries the carnations in the snow, and when the appropriate moment comes, he leaps into the path of an oncoming train.

A sensitive youngster with limited opportunity, Paul is not an artist in the usual sense. His distinction is that he responds to art, almost any art, with an unusual fervor. To him, anything associated with the world of art is beautiful and inspiring, while anything associated with lower-middle-class America is ugly and common. He is wrong about both worlds. With eyes only for the artificial surface glitter that spangles the world of art, he never sees the realities of hard work and struggle that define the life of every artist. Clearly, Cordelia Street is not as bad as Paul imagines it to be; it is, in fact, a moderately nice neighborhood where working people live and rear their families. Cordelia Street, however, has inadvertently taught him that money is the answer to all desires, that it can buy all the trappings that grace the world of art. Cordelia Street's legendary heroes are the Kings of Wall Street.

In spite of his blindness, Paul captures the reader's sympathies because he feels trapped in an aesthetic wasteland to which he cannot and will not return; the reader realizes at the end that perhaps Paul's only escape lies in his final choice. The Waldorf, after all, provided temporary breathing space at best. His only real home is, as Cather tells us, in the "immense design of things."

Valentine Ramsay, the title character in "Uncle Valentine," is like Paul in many ways: he is sensitive, charming, flighty, unpredictable, temperamental, and intolerant of commonness. Unlike Paul, however, Valentine is a true artist, a gifted composer; it is not the artificial shell of art that he values, but the very heart of it. After several years abroad, he decides to return to Greenacre, his family home in the lush Pennsylvania countryside. He feels that perhaps at Greenacre he can shut out the world and find the peace he needs to write music.

He and the neighbors next door, with whom he shares a special affection, both artistic and social, have a magnificent year together, a "golden year." They roam the fields and woods, they share music, and they increase in aesthetic understanding. Casting a tragic shadow over this happy group, however, is the figure of Valentine's uncle, who haunts the premises like a grieving ghost. A child prodigy, he had left home to pursue his art; but for reasons never disclosed, he gave up his music and returned, burying himself in the ashes of his ruined life.

As a young man, Valentine had made a bad marriage to a rich woman whose materialistic coarseness became a constant affront to him; her very presence beside him in a concert hall was enough to shatter his nerves and obliterate the music he came to hear. Valentine has escaped from her, but she is destined to destroy his peace once again. He and his neighbors discover that she has purchased the large piece of property next to theirs, the property they had loved and tramped through for endless days. She intends to move in soon, bringing her fortune, her brash assertiveness, and Valentine's only son. She, along with the encroaching factory smoke downriver, spells the end of the blessed life the little group of art fanciers has known at Greenacre. Valentine is forced to flee again, and we learn that he is killed while crossing a street in France.

Cather's message is clear. The important things in life—art and the sharing of its pleasures, friendships, a feeling for land and place, a reverence for the past—are too often destroyed in the name of progress. When economic concerns are given top priority, whether on the prairie or in Pennsylvania, the human spirit suffers. Happily, in a much-loved story called "Neighbor Rosicky," Cather affirms that material temptations can be successfully resisted. Valentine is defeated, but Rosicky and his values prevail.

Anton Rosicky, recognizable as another rendering of Ántonia's husband in Cather's best-known novel *My Ántonia* (1918), has instinctively established a value system that puts life and the land above every narrow-minded material concern. For example, when his entire corn crop is destroyed in the searing heat one July day, he organizes a little picnic so that the family can enjoy the few things they have left. Instead of despairing with his neighbors, Rosicky plays with his children. It is no surprise that he and his wife Mary agree without discussion as to what things they can let go. They refuse to skim the cream off their milk and sell it for butter because Mary would "rather put some colour into my children's faces than put money into the bank." Doctor Ed, who detects serious heart trouble in Rosicky, observes that "people as generous and warm-hearted and affectionate as the Rosickys never got ahead much; maybe you couldn't enjoy your life and put it into the bank, too."

"Neighbor Rosicky" is one of Cather's finest tributes to life on the Nebraska prairie, to a value system that grows out of human caring and love for the land. Rosicky had lived in cities for many years, had known hard times and good times there, but it occurred to him one lonely day in the city that he had to get to the land. He realized that "the trouble with big cities" was that "they built you in from the earth itself, cemented you away from any contact with the ground," so he made his decision and went West.

The only thing that disturbs his sleep now is the discontentment of his oldest son. Rudolph is married to a town girl, Polly, and he wants to leave the farm and seek work in the city. Rosicky understands Rudolph's restlessness and Polly's lonesomeness and looks for every opportunity to help the young couple find some recreation time in town. In spite of his efforts, however, Polly continues to dislike farm life and to find the Rosickys strange and "foreign." Then one day Rosicky suffers a heart attack near Rudolph's place. No one is there to care for him but Polly, and that day something lovely happens between the two of them: she has a revelation of his goodness that is "like an awakening to her." His warm brown hand somehow brings "her to herself," teaches her more about life than she has ever known before, offers her "some direct and untranslatable message." With this revelation comes the assurance that at last all will be well with Rudolph and Polly. They will remain on the land and Rosicky's spirit will abide with them, for Polly has caught the old man's vision. It is fitting that Rosicky's death a few months later is calmly accepted as a natural thing, and that he is buried in the earth he loved. That way there will be no strangeness, no jarring separation.

Rosicky is Cather's embodiment of all that is finest in the human character. He had been a city man, a lover of opera and the other cultural advantages of city life, but he found his peace in the simple life of a Nebraska farm. By contrast, Harvey Merrick, the sculptor, had been a country boy, a lover of the prairie landscape, but he found his peace in the art capitals of the world. Nevertheless, Merrick and Rosicky would have understood each other perfectly. One's talent lay in molding clay, the other's in molding lives.

Cather is sometimes accused of nostalgia, of denying the present and yearning for the past. What seems clear in her work, however, is not that she wants to live in the past, but that she deplores a total rejection of the values of the past. She fears a materialistic takeover of the human heart, or a shriveled view of human life. She is convinced that the desire for money and the things money can buy corrupts character, cheapens life, destroys the landscape, and enervates art. In her exploration of the conflicts engendered by a destructive materialism, in her celebration of art and the land, Willa Cather's devotion to an enduring system that spans time and space to embrace the good, the beautiful, and the true is made evident.

Other major works

NOVELS: *Alexander's Bridge,* 1912; *O Pioneers!,* 1913; *The Song of the Lark,* 1915; *My Ántonia,* 1918; *One of Ours,* 1922; *A Lost Lady,* 1923; *The Professor's House,* 1925; *My Mortal Enemy,* 1926; *Death Comes for the Archbishop,* 1927; *Shadows on the Rock,* 1931; *Lucy Gayheart,* 1935; *Sapphira and the Slave Girl,* 1940.

POETRY: *April Twilights,* 1903.

NONFICTION: *Not Under Forty,* 1936; *Willa Cather on Writing,* 1949; *Willa Cather in Europe,* 1956; *The Kingdom of Art: Willa Cather's First Principles and Critical Statements, 1893-1896,* 1966; *The World and the Parish: Willa Cather's Articles and Reviews, 1893-1902,* 1970 (2 volumes).

MISCELLANEOUS: *Writings from Willa Cather's Campus Years,* 1950.

Bibliography

Arnold, Marilyn. *Willa Cather's Short Fiction.* Athens: Ohio University Press, 1984. In this indexed volume, Arnold discusses all Cather's known short fiction chronologically. The detailed investigations will be helpful both for readers new to Cather's stories and those who are more familiar with them. Discussions of stories which have received little critical attention are especially useful. Includes a selected bibliography.

Gerber, Philip L. *Willa Cather.* Boston: Twayne, 1975, 1995. Part of Twayne's United States Authors series, this volume presents biographical material and traces the development of Cather's fiction thematically. Includes chapters on Cather's views about art and the critical response to her fiction. An accessible volume that includes a chronology and a select bibliography of primary and secondary sources. The volume was revised in 1995.

March, John. *A Reader's Companion to the Fiction of Willa Cather.* Westport, Conn.: Greenwood Press, 1993.

Murphy, John J., ed. *Critical Essays on Willa Cather.* Boston: G. K. Hall, 1984. Among the thirty-five essays in this substantial collection are reprinted reviews and articles by Eudora Welty, Katherine Anne Porter, Leon Edel, Blanche H. Gelfant, and Bernice Slote. It also includes original essays by David Stouck, James Leslie Woodress, Paul Cameau, and John J. Murphy. The introduction offers a history of Cather scholarship.

Rosowski, Susan J. *The Voyage Perilous: Willa Cather's Romanticism.* Lincoln: University of Nebraska Press, 1986. This thematic study interprets Cather's writing within the literary tradition of Romanticism. Although the main focus is on her novels (with a chapter devoted to each), the volume also investigates the stories in *The Troll Garden* and includes a chapter on *Obscure Destinies.* See also *Cather Studies,* a forum for scholarship and criticism, which is edited by Rosowski and published biennially by the University of Nebraska Press.

Thomas, Susie. *Willa Cather.* Savage, Md.: Barnes & Noble Books, 1990. This feminist study, which draws extensively on Cather's unpublished letters, focuses on the particular contributions Cather made as a woman writing about America and analyzes how her cultural awareness influenced the development of her style. The volume includes a short biography and chapters on Cather's major novels and works of short fiction.

Wagenknecht, Edward. *Willa Cather.* New York: Continuum, 1994.

Wasserman, Loretta. *Willa Cather: A Study of the Short Fiction.* Boston: Twayne, 1991. Part of Twayne's Studies in Short Fiction series, this volume focuses on selected short stories that Wasserman believes are the most challenging and lend themselves to different critical approaches. Includes interviews with Cather, one of Cather's essays on the craft of writing, samples of current criticism, a chronology, and a select bibliography.

Woodress, James. *Willa Cather: A Literary Life.* Lincoln: University of Nebraska Press, 1990. This definitive biography extends previous studies of Cather, including Woodress' own earlier work (*Willa Cather: Her Life and Art,* 1970), with fuller accounts of Cather's life and includes new and expanded critical responses to her work, taking feminist criticism into account. In preparing the volume, Woodress was able to use the papers of Cather scholar Bernice Slote. Scholars and students will appreciate the extensively documented sources. Includes photographs of Cather, as well as of people and places important to her.

Marilyn Arnold
(Revised by *Jean C. Fulton*)

GEOFFREY CHAUCER

Born: London(?), England; c. 1343
Died: London, England; October 25(?), 1400

Principal short fiction · *Book of the Duchess,* c. 1370 · *Romaunt of the Rose,* c. 1370 (translation, possibly not by Chaucer) · *Hous of Fame,* 1372-1380 · *The Legends of St. Cecilia,* 1372-1380 (later used as "The Second Nun's Tale") · *Tragedies of Fortune,* 1372-1380 (later used as "The Monk's Tale") · *Anelida and Arcite,* c. 1380 · *Parlement of Foules,* 1380 · *Palamon and Ersyte,* 1380-1386 (later used as "The Knight's Tale") · *Legend of Good Women,* 1380-1386 · *Troilus and Criseyde,* 1382 · *The Canterbury Tales,* 1387-1400

Other literary forms · In addition to the works listed above, Geoffrey Chaucer composed *Boece* (c. 1380), a translation of Boethius' *The Consolation of Philosophy* (523), which Boethius wrote while in prison. Chaucer also wrote an astrological study, *A Treatise on the Astrolabe* (1387-1392), and a miscellaneous volume entitled *Works* (1957).

Achievements · Chaucer is generally agreed to be the most important writer in English literature before William Shakespeare. Recognized internationally in his own time as the greatest of English poets and dubbed "the father of English poetry" by John Dryden as early as 1700, his central position in the development of English literature and even of the English language is perhaps more secure today than it has ever been. One of the keys to Chaucer's continued critical success is the scope and diversity of his work, which extends from romance to tragedy, from sermon to dream vision, from pious saints' lives to bawdy *fabliaux.* Readers from every century have found something new in Chaucer and learned something about themselves.

Biography · Household records seem to indicate that as a boy, Geoffrey Chaucer served as a page for the Countess of Ulster, wife of Edward III's son Lionel, Duke of Clarence. Chaucer undoubtedly learned French and Latin as a youth, to which languages he later added Italian. Well versed in both science and pseudoscience, Chaucer was familiar with physics, medicine, astronomy, and alchemy. Spending most of his life in government service, he made many trips abroad on diplomatic missions and served at home in such important capacities as Comptroller of Customs for the Port of London, Justice of the Peace for the County of Kent, and Clerk of the King's Works, a position that made him responsible for the maintenance of certain public structures. He married Philippa de Roet, probably in 1367, and he may have had two daughters and two sons, although there is speculation concerning the paternity of some of those children believed to have been Chaucer's. Since Chaucer's career was his service to the monarchy, his poetry was evidently an avocation which did not afford him a living.

Courtesy of the Library of Congress

Analysis · Geoffrey Chaucer's best-known works are *Troilus and Criseyde* and the unfinished *The Canterbury Tales*, with the *Book of the Duchess*, the *Hous of Fame*, the *Parlement of Foules*, and the *Legend of Good Women* positioned in the second rank. In addition to these works and to *Boece* (c. 1380; translation of Boethius' *The Consolation of Philosophy*) and the *Romaunt of the Rose*, there exist a number of shorter and lesser-known poems, some of which merit brief attention.

These lesser-known poems demonstrate Chaucer's abilities in diverse but typically medieval forms. Perhaps the earliest extant example of Chaucer's work is "An ABC to the Virgin"; this poem, primarily a translation from a thirteenth century French source, is a traditional series of prayers in praise of Mary, the stanzas of which are arranged in alphabetical order according to the first letter of each stanza. Another traditional form Chaucer used is the "complaint," or formal lament. "A Complaint to His Lady" is significant in literary history as the first appearance in English of Dante's terza rima, and "The Complaint unto Pity" is one of the earliest examples of rime royal; this latter poem contains an unusual analogy which represents the personified Pity as being buried in a heart. "The Complaint of Mars" illustrates Chaucer's individuality in treating traditional themes and conventions; although the poem purports to be a Valentine poem, and akin to an aubade, its ironic examination of love's intrinsic variability seems to make it an anti-Valentine poem. Chaucer similarly plays with theme and form in *To Rosemounde*, a ballade in which the conventions of courtly love are exaggerated to the point of grotesquerie; the narrator says, for example, that he is as immersed in love as a fish smothered in pickle sauce. Finally, Chaucer's poem "Gentilesse" is worthy of note for its presentation of a theme, developed in "The Wife of Bath's Tale" and in "The Clerk's Tale," which posits that "gentilesse" depends not on inheritance or social position but on character. In sum, these poems, for most of which dates of composition cannot be assigned, represent a variety of themes and forms with which Chaucer may have been experimenting; they indicate not only his solid grounding in poetic conventions but also his innovative spirit in using new forms and ideas and in treating old forms and ideas in new ways.

Of those poems in the second rank, the *Book of the Duchess* was probably the earliest written and is believed to have been composed as a *consolatio* or commemoration of the death of Blanche, Duchess of Lancaster and wife of John of Gaunt, with whom Chaucer was associated. The poem uses the technique of the dream vision and the device of the fictional narrator as two means of objectifying the subject matter, of presenting the consolation at a remove from the narrator and in the person of the bereaved knight himself. The poem thus seems to imply that true consolation can come only from within; the narrator's human sympathy and nature's reassurance can assist in the necessary process of acceptance of and recovery from the loss of a loved one, but that movement from the stasis of deprivation to the action of catharsis and healing can occur only within the mourner's own breast.

The poem is told by a lovesick narrator who battles his insomnia by reading the story of Ceyx and Alcyone. Finally falling asleep, he dreams that he awakens in the morning to the sounds of the hunt and, following a dog, comes upon a distinguished young knight dressed in black who laments his lost love. In response to the dreamer's naïve and persistent questions, the knight is eventually prodded into telling of his loss; he describes his lady in love-filled superlatives, reveals that her outer beauty was symbolic of her inner nobility, and acknowledges the great happiness they enjoyed in their mutual love. At the end of this lengthy discourse, when the narrator inquires as to the lady's whereabouts, the knight states simply that she is dead, to which the narrator replies, "Be God, hyt ys routhe!"

The poem thus blends the mythological world, the natural world, and the realm of human sympathy to create a context within which the mourner can come to accept his loss. The dreamer's lovesickness causes him to have a natural affinity with the knight, and, by posing as stupid, naïve, and slow-witted, the dreamer obliges the knight to speak and to admit his loss, a reality he must acknowledge if he is to move beyond the paralysis caused by his grief to a position where he is accessible to the consolation that can restore him. This restoration is in part accomplished by the dreamer's "naïve" questions which encourage the knight to remember the joys he experienced with his lady and the love which they shared. The knight is then able to be consoled and comforted by the corrective and curative powers of his own memories.

The poem thus offers a psychologically realistic and sophisticated presentation of the grief process, a process in which the dreamer-narrator plays a crucial role, since it is the dreamer who, through his seemingly obtuse questioning, propels the knight out of the stasis to which his grief has made him succumb; the cathartic act of speaking to the dreamer about his lost love renders the knight open to the healing powers available in human sympathy and the natural world. The poem, even as it is elegiac in its tribute to the lost lover, is in the genre of the *consolatio* as it records the knight's conversion from unconsolable grief to quiet acceptance and assuagement. In establishing the persona of the apparently naïve and bumbling narrator, Chaucer initiates a tradition which not only has come to be recognized as typical of his works but also has been used repeatedly throughout literature. Probably the earliest English writer to use such a narrative device, Chaucer thereby discovered the rich possibilities for structural irony implicit in the distance between the author and his naïve narrator.

In contrast to the well-executed whole that is the *Book of the Duchess*, the *Hous of Fame*, believed to have been composed between 1372 and 1380, is an unfinished work; its true nature and Chaucer's intent in the poem continue to elude critics. Beyond the problems posed by any unfinished work is the question of this particular poem's unity, since the connections between the three parts of the poem which Chaucer actually finished are tenuous. In the first book of the poem, the narrator dreams of the Temple of Venus, where he learns of Dido and Aeneas. The second book details the narrator's journey, in the talons of a golden eagle, to the House of Fame, and the contrast between the eagle's chatty friendliness and volubil-

ity and the obviously terrified narrator's monosyllabic responses as they
swoop through the air provides much amusement. The third book, describing the House of Fame and its presiding goddess, demonstrates the total
irrationality of fame, which the goddess awards according to caprice rather
than merit. After visiting the House of Rumor, the narrator notices everyone running to see a man of great authority, at which point the poem
breaks off.

Critical opinion differs considerably as to the poem's meaning. Some
believe it attempts to assess the worth of fame or perhaps even the life of
the poet, in view of the mutability of human existence; others believe the
poem intends to consider the validity of recorded history as opposed to
true experience; yet other critics believe the poem attempts to ascertain
the nature of poetry and its relationship to love. Although scholars have
certainly not as yet settled on the poem's meaning, there is agreement that
the flight of the eagle and the narrator in book 2 is one of literature's most
finely comic passages. Beyond this, it is perhaps wisest to view the poem
as an experiment with various themes which even Chaucer himself was
apparently disinterested in unifying.

In contrast to the *Hous of Fame*, the *Parlement of Foules*, composed around
1380, is a finely crafted and complete work in which Chaucer combines
several popular conventions, such as the dream vision, the parliament of
beasts, and the *demande d'amour* to demonstrate three particular manifestations of love: divine love, erotic love, and procreative or natural love. The
fictional narrator is here a person who lacks love, who knows of it only
through books, and whose very dreams even prove emotionally unsatisfying. The narrator recounts his reading of Scipio Africanus the Younger,
who dreamed that his ancestor came to him, told him of divine justice and
the life hereafter, and urged him to work to the common profit. Having
learned of the nature of divine love, the narrator dreams that Scipio comes
to him as he sleeps to take him to a park where there are two gardens, one
the garden of Venus and the other the garden of Nature. The garden of
Venus is clearly the place of erotic or carnal love; it is located away from
the sun and consequently is dark, and it has an illicit and corrupt atmosphere. In addition to such figures as Cupid, Lust, Courtesy, and Jealousy,
the narrator sees Venus herself, reclining half-naked in an atmosphere that
is close and oppressive.

In contrast, the garden of Nature is in sunlight; it is Valentine's Day and
the birds have congregated to choose their mates. In addition to the natural
surroundings, the presence of Nature herself, presiding over the debate,
helps to create an atmosphere of fertility and creativity. The choice of
mates is, however, impeded by a quarrel among three male eagles who

love a formel. Each eagle has a different claim to press: the first asserts that he has loved her long in silence, the second stresses the length of his devotion, and the third emphasizes his devotion's intensity, pointing out that it is the quality rather than the length of love that matters. Since the lower orders of birds cannot choose mates until the eagles have settled their quarrel, the lesser birds enter the debate, aligning themselves variously either for or against the issues of courtly love which are involved. When the various birds' contributions deteriorate into invective without any positive result, Nature intervenes to settle the matter, but the formel insists upon making her own choice in her own time, that is, at the end of a year. The other birds, their mates chosen, sing a joyful song which ends the dream vision. When the narrator awakes he continues to read, hoping to dream better.

The poem, then, presents love in its divine, erotic, and procreative forms. Although the narrator sees these various manifestations of love, he is unable to experience them since all are unavailable to him. He is, in some ways, thus akin to the eagles and in contrast to the lower orders of birds who obviously fare well, since at the end of the parliament they are paired with their mates and blissfully depart. The eagles and the formel, however, because of the formel's need to deliberate upon and choose among her courtly lovers, are in a kind of emotional limbo for a year; in effect, they are all denied for a relatively long period love's natural expression. Thus, even as the system of courtliness raises and ennobles love, the system also provides an impediment to the ultimate realization of love in mating. Although there seems to be a movement in the debate from the artificiality of courtly love to the naturalness of pairing off, this movement does not affect the eagles, who remain constrained, in large part because of their commitment to the courtly code. The poem examines, then, not merely the various faces of love but the nature of courtly love in particular and its seemingly undesirable effects upon its adherents.

Like the *Hous of Fame*, the *Legend of Good Women* is unfinished; although the poem was intended to contain a prologue and a series of nineteen or twenty stories telling of true women and false men, the extant material consists of two versions of the prologue and only nine legends. The poem purports to be a penance for the poet's offenses against the God of Love in writing of the false Criseyde and in translating the antifeminine *Romaunt of the Rose*.

In the prologues, Chaucer uses the techniques of the dream vision and the court of love to establish a context for his series of tales, which are much akin to saints' lives. In fact, the poem seems to parody the idea of a religion of love; the poet, although he worships the daisy as the God of

Love's symbol, commits by his work heresy against the deity and must therefore repent and do penance by writing of women who were saints and martyrs in love's service. The two prologues differ in the degree to which they use Christian conventions to describe the conduct of love; the "G" prologue, believed to be later than the "F" prologue, has lessened the strength of the analogy to Christian worship. The legends, however, are very much in the hagiographic tradition, even to the extent of canonizing women not customarily regarded as "good," such as Cleopatra and Medea. Evidently wearying of his task, however, Chaucer did not complete the poem, perhaps because of the boredom inherent in the limited perspective.

Of Chaucer's completed work, *Troilus and Criseyde* is without question his supreme accomplishment. Justly considered by many to be the first psychological novel, the poem places against the epic background of the Trojan War the tragedy and the romance of Troilus, son of Priam, and Criseyde, daughter of Calchas the soothsayer. Entwined with their lives is that of Pandarus, friend of Troilus and uncle of Criseyde, who brings the lovers together and who, in consequence, earns lasting disapprobation as the first panderer. In analyzing the conjunction of these three characters' lives, the poem considers the relationship of the individual to the society in which he or she lives and examines the extent to which events in one's life are influenced by external circumstances and by internal character. At a deeper level, the poem assesses the ultimate worth of human life, human love, and human values. Yet the poem does not permit reductive or simplistic interpretation; its many thematic strands and its ambiguities of characterization and narrative voice combine to present a multidimensional poem which defies definitive analysis.

The poem's thematic complexity depends upon a relatively simple plot. When callow Troilus is stricken with love for Criseyde, he follows all the courtly rules: he suffers physically, loves her from a distance, and rises to great heights of heroism on the battlefield so as to be worthy of her. When Troilus admits to Pandarus that his misery can only be cured by Criseyde's love, Pandarus is only too happy to exercise his influence over his niece. By means of a subtle mix of avuncular affection, psychological manipulation, and veiled threats, Pandarus leads Criseyde to fall in love with Troilus. The climax of Pandarus' machinations occurs when he arranges for Troilus and Criseyde to consummate their love affair, ostensibly against the stated will of Criseyde and in spite of Troilus' extremely enfeebled condition. Until this point the poem, reflecting largely the conventions of *fabliau*, has been in the control of Pandarus; he generates the action and manipulates the characters much as a rather bawdy and perhaps slightly prurient stage manager. With the love scene, however, the poem's form shifts from that of *fabliau* to that of romance; Pandarus becomes a minor figure and the love between Troilus and Criseyde achieves much greater spiritual significance than either had anticipated.

Although the tenets of courtly love demand that the lovers keep their affair secret, they enjoy for three years a satisfying and enriching relationship which serves greatly to ennoble Troilus; the poem's shape then shifts again, this time from romance to tragedy. Calchas, having foreseen the Trojan defeat and having therefore defected to the Greeks, requests that a captured Trojan be exchanged for his daughter. The distraught lovers discover that the constraints placed upon them by their commitments to various standards and codes of behavior combine with the constraints imposed upon them by society to preclude their preventing the exchange, but Criseyde promises within ten days to steal away from the Greek camp and return to Troilus. Once in the Greek camp, however, Criseyde finds it difficult to escape; moreover, believing that the Greek Diomede has fallen in love with her, she decides to remain in the Greek encampment until the grief-stricken Troilus eventually has to admit that she has, indeed, betrayed him.

At the end of the poem, having been killed by Achilles, Troilus gazes from the eighth sphere upon the fullness of the universe and laughs at those mortals who indulge in earthly endeavor. In his bitter wisdom he condemns all things of the earth, particularly earthly love, which is so inadequate in comparison to heavenly love. This section of the poem, erroneously called by some "the epilogue," has been viewed as Chaucer's retraction of his poem and a nullification of what has gone before. Chaucer's poetic vision, however, is much more complex than this interpretation supposes; throughout the poem he has been preparing the reader to accept several paradoxes. One is that even as human beings must celebrate and strive for secular love, which is the nearest thing they have to divine love, they must nevertheless and simultaneously concentrate on the hereafter, since secular love and human connections are, indeed, vastly inferior to divine love. A second paradox is that humans should affirm the worth of human life and human values while at the same time recognizing their mutability and their inferiority to Christian values. The poem also presents courtly love as a paradox since, on the one hand, it is the system which inspires Troilus to strive for and achieve a vastly ennobled character even though, on the other, the system is proven unworthy of his devotion. Criseyde is similarly paradoxical in that the narrator portrays her as deserving of Troilus' love, even though she proves faithless to him.

These paradoxes are presented against a classical background which contributes to the poet's juxtaposition of several oppositions. The world of the classical epic provides the setting for a medieval courtly romance so that, although the characters exist in a pagan environment, they are viewed from the Christian medieval perspective which informs the poem. The poem's epic setting and its romance form, then, like its pagan plot and its Christian point of view, seem thus to be temporally misaligned; this misalignment does not, however, lead to dissonance but instead contributes to the poem's thematic elusion and ambiguity.

The characters, of course, also contribute significantly to the poem's ambiguity. Criseyde, particularly, resists classification and categorization. The ambivalent narrator encourages the reader to see Criseyde in a variety of contradictory postures: as a victim, but also as a survivor, one who takes the main chance; as a weak and socially vulnerable person, but also as a woman who is self-confident and strong; as an idealistic and romantic lover, but also as a careful pragmatist; as a greatly self-deceived character, but also as a self-aware character who at times admits painful truths about herself.

Also ambiguous, but to a lesser degree, is Pandarus, whose characterization vacillates between that of the icily unsentimental cynic and that of the sensitive human being who bemoans his failures to achieve happiness in love and who worries about what history will do to his reputation. He seems to see courtly love as a game and to disbelieve in the total melding of two lives, but he betrays his own sentimentality when he indicates that he longs to find such love for himself.

Although his mentor seems not to take courtly love seriously, to Troilus it is the center of his life, his very reality. His virtue lies in large part in his absolute commitment to courtly ideals and to Criseyde. The solidity of that commitment, however, prevents Troilus from taking any active steps to stop the exchange, since such action would reveal their love affair, soil Criseyde's reputation, and violate the courtly love code. In this sense, Troilus is trapped by his own nobility and by his idealism, so that his course of action is restrained not only by external forces but also by his own character.

In fact, the poem seems to show that both Troilus and Criseyde are ultimately responsible for what happens to them; the role of fate in their lives is relatively insignificant because their very characters are their fate. As Troilus is governed by his dedication to heroic and courtly ideals, Criseyde is governed by the fact that she is "slydynge of corage." It is her nature to take the easiest way, and because of her nature she is untrue to Troilus.

From the poet's point of view, however, Criseyde's faithlessness does not invalidate for Troilus the experience of her love. Because of his own limited perspective, Troilus is himself unable to assess the worth of his life, his love affair, and the values to which he subscribed; the parameters of his vision permit him to see only the inadequacy and imperfection of earthly experience in comparison to the experience of the divine. The poet's perspective, however, is the one which informs the poem, and that perspective is broader, clearer, and more complex, capable of encompassing the poem's various paradoxes and oppositions. In consequence, even though Troilus at the end discounts his earthly experience, the poem has proven its worth to an incontrovertible degree; human life, even though inferior to the afterlife, nevertheless affords the opportunity for experiences which, paradoxically, can transcend their earthly limitations. Ultimately, then, the poem affirms the worth of human life, human love, and human idealism.

Although Chaucer never completed *The Canterbury Tales*, it is his most important work and the one for which he is best known. In its conceptual richness, in its grace and precision of execution, and in its broad presentation of humanity, *The Canterbury Tales* is unequaled. The poem occupied Chaucer for the last one and a half decades of his life, although several of the stories date from an earlier period; it was not until sometime in the middle 1380's, when he conceived the idea of using a framing device within which his stories could be placed, that the work began to assume shape. That shape is the form of a springtime pilgrimage to Canterbury to see the shrine of Thomas à Becket. The fictional party consists of some thirty pilgrims, along with the narrator and the host from the Tabard Inn; each pilgrim was to tell two stories en route to Canterbury and two on the return trip, making an approximate total of 120 tales. There are extant, however, only the prologue and twenty-four tales, not all of which are completed; moreover, the sources of these extant tales (more than eighty manuscript fragments) contain considerable textual variations and arrange the tales in many differing orders. Thus, it is impossible for critics to determine the order which Chaucer envisioned for the tales.

The notion of using the pilgrimage as a frame device was a stroke of narrative brilliance, since the device provides infinite possibilities for dramatic action while it simultaneously unifies a collection of widely disparate stories. In response to the host's request for stories of "mirth" or "doctryne," the pilgrims present an eclectic collection of tales, including romances, *fabliaux*, beast-fables, saints' lives, tragedies, sermons, and exempla. The frame of the pilgrimage also permits the poet to represent a cross section of society, since the members of the party range across the social spectrum from the aristocratic knight to the bourgeois guild members to the honest plowman. Moreover, since the tales are connected by passages of dialogue among the pilgrims as they ride along on their journey, the pilgrimage frame also permits the characters of the storytellers to be developed and additional dramatic action to occur from the pilgrims' interaction. These "links" between the tales thus serve to define a constant fictional world, the pilgrimage, which is in juxtaposition to and seemingly in control of the multiple fictional worlds created in the tales themselves; the fictional world of the pilgrims on their pilgrimage thereby acquires a heightened degree of verisimilitude, especially because the pilgrims' interchanges with one another often help to place them at various recognizable points on the road to Canterbury.

The pilgrimage frame also permits the creation of an exquisitely ironic tension between the fictional narrator and the poet himself. The narrator is Chaucer's usual persona, naïve, rather thick-witted, and easily and wrongly impressed by outward show. This narrator's gullible responses to the various pilgrims are contrasted to the attitude of the poet himself; such use of the fictional narrator permits the poet not only to present two points of view on any and all action but also to play upon the tension deriving from the collision of those two perspectives. The device of the pilgrimage frame, in sum, allows the poet virtually unlimited freedom in regard to form, content, and tone.

The context of the pilgrimage is established in the poem's prologue, which begins by indicating that concerns both sacred and secular prompt people to go on pilgrimage. Those people are described in a formal series of portraits which reveals that the group is truly composed of "sondry folk" and is a veritable cross section of medieval society. Yet, the skill of the poet is evident in the fact that even as the pilgrims are "types"–that is, they are representative of a body of others like themselves–they are also individuals who are distinguished not simply by the realistic details describing their external appearances but more crucially by the sharply searching analysis which penetrates their external façades to expose the actualities of character that lie beneath.

The tales begin with a group which has come to be seen as Chaucer's variations on the theme of the love-triangle and which consists of "The Knight's Tale," "The Miller's Tale," and "The Reeve's Tale." Like *Troilus and Criseyde,* "The Knight's Tale" superimposes a romance against the background of the classical world as it tells of Palamon and Arcite, knights of Thebes who are captured by Theseus during his battle with Creon and sentenced to life imprisonment in Athens. While imprisoned they fall in love with Emily, over whom they quarrel; since Palamon, who saw and loved her first, thought she was a goddess, Arcite, who saw her second but who loved her as a woman, insists that his is the better claim. Several years later, Arcite having been freed and Palamon having escaped from prison, the knights meet and again quarrel, agreeing to settle the matter with a duel. When Theseus comes upon them he stops the duel and decrees that they must instead meet a year later with their troops to decide the matter in a tournament.

For this tournament Theseus erects a magnificent stadium with temples to Venus, Mars, and Diana. When the stadium is completed and the time for the tournament has arrived, the three members of the love-triangle pray for the assistance of their particular gods: Palamon asks Venus for Emily or for death; Arcite asks Mars for victory; and Emily asks Diana to permit her to remain a virgin or, failing that, to be wedded to the one who most loves her. These various petitions cause a quarrel between Venus and Mars which Saturn resolves by announcing that Palamon shall have his lady even though Mars assists Arcite to victory. Arcite, in consequence, wins the tournament, but in the midst of his victory parade, his horse rears, and he is mortally injured. From his deathbed Arcite summons both Palamon and Emily and commends them to each other, but they continue to grieve during the next several years. Finally, Theseus summons Palamon and Emily to him and tells them that since grief should end and life go on, they are to marry and thus make joy from sorrows.

The poem's plot, then, concerns the resolution of the love-triangle typical of romance. This plot, however, is in the service of a more serious conflict, that between order and chaos. Theseus serves as the civilizing instrument, the means by which order is imposed on the anarchy of human passion. In actuality, by assuming control over the hostility between Palamon and Arcite, Theseus reshapes their primitive emotional conflict into a clearly defined ritual; by distancing it as well in time and space, Theseus forces that conflict into a shape and an expression which is socially acceptable and which poses no threat to the culture's peaceful continuance. Theseus thus makes order and art out of raw emotion and violent instincts.

The love conflict which in "The Knight's Tale" serves to develop this cosmic theme is in "The Miller's Tale" acted out on the smaller scale and in the more limited space of the sheerly natural world and thus serves no such serious or noble end. Again there is a triangle, but the romantic discord among the aristocratic Palamon, Arcite, and Emily becomes in "The Miller's Tale" the bawdy comedy of the *fabliau* as it arises from the interaction of the young clerk Nicholas and the effeminate dandy Absolon, both of whom desire Alison, the young wife of John, an old and jealous carpenter. At the same time that the amorous Absolon serenades her nightly and sends her gifts in an effort to win her, Alison agrees to give her love to Nicholas as soon as he can create the opportunity. In fact, however, no elaborate stratagem is needed to make possible the encounter Alison and Nicholas both desire. Since Alison's husband is away all day working, and since Nicholas (a student who boards with the couple) is at home with Alison all day, there really are no obstacles preventing the lovers from acting on their passions immediately. Alison's insistence, then, that Nicholas devise a plan whereby they can give rein to their passions, reflects an important stylistic and thematic connection between the tale and "The Knight's Tale." In the latter tale, Theseus controls the passions of Palamon and Arcite by postponing their encounter and dictating its arena; the distancing in time and space results in a civilized, restrained expression of their passions. In "The Miller's Tale," by contrast, the distancing Alison demands parodies the conventions of romance and courtly love. This distance in actuality simply ennobles base instincts, for Alison and Nicholas inhabit not a courtly world but a natural one, and their intellectual, spiritual, and romantic pretensions constitute only a thin veneer covering their healthy animalism. By using distance as a means of ennobling base instincts, "The Miller's Tale" parodies not only the world and the theme of "The Knight's Tale" but also its poetic treatment.

Nicholas' seduction plan plays upon both the strengths and the weaknesses of the carpenter's character. Telling John that another flood is coming, Nicholas convinces the carpenter that he must hang three barrels from the rafters in which Nicholas, John, and Alison can remain until the waters rise, then they will cut themselves free to float away. The carpenter's pretensions to spiritual and theological superiority cause him to accept this prophecy unquestioningly, but at the same time his genuine love for his wife causes his first reaction to be fear for her life. When all three on the appointed night have ostensibly entered their barrels, Nicholas and Alison sneak down to spend a night in amorous play.

At this point the plot is entered by Absolon, who comes to Alison's window to serenade her; pleading for a kiss, he finds himself presented with Alison's backside. Bent then on avenging his misdirected kiss, he brings a hot colter and asks for another kiss; presented this time with the backside of Nicholas, Absolon smacks it smartly with the red-hot colter, causing Nicholas to cry out "Water!" which in turn causes the carpenter to cut the rope on his barrel and crash to the ground, injuring both his person and his dignity. Whereas in "The Knight's Tale" the three major characters ultimately obtain what they desire most—Arcite, victory; Palamon, Emily; and Emily, the man who loves her most—"The Miller's Tale" reverses this idea; John, the jealous carpenter, is cuckolded and humiliated in front of the entire town, the fastidious Absolon has kissed Alison's "nether ye," and Nicholas has lost a hand's-breadth of skin from his backside. Only Alison remains unscathed, but then, she must spend her life being married to John.

The poem thus parodies the romance tradition, the idealistic notion that civilized or courtly processes can elevate and ennoble fundamental human passions. Even as it transfers various themes, mechanisms, and perspectives from "The Knight's Tale," "The Miller's Tale" transforms these and reflects them negatively. The generic differences between the two poems, however, demand that content and tone differ. "The Knight's Tale," combining epic and romance, deals seriously with serious considerations, whereas "The Miller's Tale," by virtue of its being a *fabliau*, has as one of its purposes the humorous depiction of human shortcomings.

"The Knight's Tale" and "The Miller's Tale" are different tales which have structural similarities; "The Reeve's Tale," which completes the poem's first thematic grouping, shares with "The Miller's Tale" the *fabliau* form but the two differ considerably in tone. The Reeve's story results from his outrage at the Miller's story, which has belittled carpenters; in angry retaliation the Reeve relates the popular *fabliau* concerning the two students who, cheated by a dishonest miller, exact revenge by sleeping with both his wife and his daughter. The plot, which hangs in part upon the device of the misplaced cradle, has as its end the unsophisticated students' triumph over the social-climbing miller. The tone of "The Reeve's Tale," therefore, is bitter and vindictive, told, the Reeve acknowledges, solely to repay the Miller.

Chaucer uses the romance and the *fabliau*, these two forms with which he begins his series of tales, again and again in the course of the poem. Other romances are the unfinished "The Squire's Tale," which has an Oriental setting; "The Man of Law's Tale," which blends romance and a saint's life in the story of the unfortunate Constance; and "The Wife of Bath's Tale," "The Clerk's Tale," and "The Franklin's Tale," which will be discussed together as "the marriage group." The genre of the *fabliau* is also further represented in "The Shipman's Tale" of the debt repaid by the adulterous monk to his lender's wife, and in "The Friar's Tale" and "The Summoner's Tale," stories which are attacks on each other's professions and which are told to be mutually insulting.

Another popular genre Chaucer employs in his collection is that of the saints' lives, a type used in "The Second Nun's Tale" of St. Cecilia and in "The Prioress's Tale" of the martyred Christian boy slain by Jews. While both tales conventionally concern "miracles of the virgin," the tale of the Prioress is of particular interest because of the nature of the storyteller. Although she is supposed to be a spiritual being, a guardian of other spiritual beings, she is described in the same manner as the heroine of a courtly romance; moreover, although her description points to sensitivity and charity, her moral sensibility is clearly faulty. She worries over a little mouse but tells a violent tale of religious intolerance. Moreover, the ironies

implicit in the engraving on her brooch—"Amor vincit omnia"—are extensive, as are the ironies deriving from the conflicting perspectives of the
narrator, who naïvely admires her for all the wrong reasons, and the poet,
who clearly sees her as possessed of many shortcomings.

Another popular genre in the Middle Ages was the beast-fable, a form
which Chaucer uses brilliantly in "The Nun's Priest's Tale." The story
concerns Chauntecleer and Pertelote, a cock and hen owned by a poor
widow. When Chauntecleer one night dreams of a fox, he and Pertelote
have an extended discussion on the validity of dreams. Believing that
dreams are caused by bile or overeating, Pertelote advises the use of a
laxative; Chauntecleer, however, holding a different opinion, tells a story
wherein a dream is proven prophetic. At this point the fox appears, to
whom the Nun's Priest likens to such other traitors as Simon and Judas
Iscariot. Even as he insists that his antifeminine statements are not his own
but the cock's, the Nun's Priest clearly believes that woman's counsel often
brings misfortune and points with relish to the fox's sudden appearance as
proof of this belief.

The encounter between the fox and the cock reveals the weaknesses of
both. Relying hugely on flattery, the fox persuades Chauntecleer to relax
his guard, close his eyes, and stretch his neck, providing the perfect
opportunity to seize Chauntecleer and race off. As the widow and her
household set chase, Chauntecleer advises the fox to tell the pursuers to
turn back because he will soon be eating Chauntecleer in spite of them;
when the fox opens his mouth to do this, Chauntecleer of course escapes.
Although the fox tries to persuade Chauntecleer to come down out of the
tree, Chauntecleer wisely declares that he will not again be fooled by
flattery and that no one should prosper who closes his eyes when he should
watch. The fox, as one might expect, disagrees, declaring that no one
should prosper who talks when he should hold his peace.

The poem thus uses the beast-fable's technique of personifying animals
to the end of revealing human truths; it also uses the conventions and the
rhetoric of epic and courtly romance to talk about the lives of chickens,
thus creating a parody of the epic form and a burlesque of the courtly
attitude. The poem is also, to a degree, homiletic in treating the dangers
inherent in succumbing to flattery; each character suffers as a result of this
weakness, the cock by having foolishly permitted himself to be captured,
and the fox by having gullibly permitted himself to be hoodwinked by one
pretending affinity.

Having begun the discussion of *The Canterbury Tales* with an analysis of
the group of tales concerned with the love-triangle, it seems fitting to end
the discussion with an analysis of those tales referred to as "the marriage

group." "The Wife of Bath's Tale," "The Clerk's Tale," "The Merchant's Tale," and "The Franklin's Tale" bring to that group several perspectives on women and the relation between the sexes. The Wife of Bath, in complete opposition to the traditional view of women, presents one extreme point of view which advocates sensuality and female authority. An excellent example of what she advocates, the wife is strong and lusty and insists on dominance in her marriages. In her lengthy prologue to her story she takes issue with patristic doctrine concerning chastity and female inferiority and uses Scriptural allusions to buttress her opinions. Her prologue thus provides a defense of women and of sensuality.

Her tale, an exemplum illustrating the argument contained in her prologue, concerns a knight who must, in order to save his life, find out what women desire most. Despairing over his inability to get a consensus of opinion, he one day comes upon a "loathly lady" who offers to give him the answer if he in turn will do what she requests. Gratefully agreeing, he learns that women most want "sovereynetee" and "maistrie" over their husbands; he is less pleased, however, to learn that her request is that he marry her. Having kept his promise, the knight on their wedding night is understandably distant from his new wife; when pressed for an explanation, he notes that she is ugly, old, and lowly born. She in turn explains that nobility comes not from wealth or birth, that poverty is virtuous, and that her age and ugliness ensure her chastity. She gives the knight a choice: he can have her ugly and old but faithful, or young and pretty but untrue. The knight chooses, however, to transfer this decision and consequently the control of the marriage to her, whereupon she announces that she will be not only young and pretty but also faithful, thus illustrating the good that comes when women are in control.

The Wife's tale, and the wife herself, with her heretical opinions concerning marriage and sexual relations, outrage the Clerk, who tells a tale to counter the Wife's; his tale reinforces the doctrine that male dominance on earth conforms to the order of the divine hierarchy. His story treats the patient Griselda, who promises her husband, Walter, to do everything he wishes and never to complain or in any way indicate disagreement. When a daughter is born to them, Walter, who is an Italian marquis, tells Griselda that since the people are complaining about her low birth, he must have the child killed, to which Griselda meekly agrees; Walter, however, sends the child secretly to a relative to be reared. When a son is born, Walter again does the same thing, again to test her obedience, and again Griselda is perfectly submissive. Twelve years later Walter secretly sends for the two children and tells Griselda that since he is divorcing her in order to marry someone else, she must return to her father. Moreover, he insists that she return to her father just as she had left him, that is, naked, since Walter had provided her with clothes. Griselda, with great dignity, requests at least a shift as recompense for the virginity which she had brought to him but which she cannot take away with her. When asked later to come and make arrangements for Walter's new bride, Griselda cheerfully complies, although she does, at this point, give some indication of the great price she has paid for her obedience and her faithfulness to her vow; she asks Walter not to torment his new wife as he tormented her, the bride-to-be having been tenderly reared and therefore not so well able to withstand such adversity. Walter, finally satisfied as to Griselda's steadfastness, restores her as his wife and reunites her with her children. The Clerk concludes by noting that it is hard to find women like Griselda nowadays.

The tale is one with which critics have long grappled, since it presents seemingly insurmountable interpretive problems. The story can hardly be taken as realistic, even though the Clerk, through his efforts to give Walter psychological motivation, attempts to provide verisimilitude. Although the poem may be intended as allegory, to illustrate that one must be content in adversity, it seems also to have a tropological level of meaning, to illustrate the proper attitude for wives. The narrator's own uncertainty as to whether he tells a tale of real people, a saint's life, or an allegory, contributes to the difficulty one has in assessing the poem's nature and purpose. It is obvious, though, that the Clerk's intended corrective to "The Wife of Bath's Tale" is perfectly accomplished through his tale of the impossibly patient Griselda.

At the end of his tale the Clerk appears to switch directions; he advises that no husband should try what Walter did, and that furthermore wives should be fierce to their husbands, should provoke their jealousy, and should make them weep and wail. The Merchant picks up this notion and echoes the line in the first sentence of his own remarks, which are intended to counter the Clerk's presentation of the saintly wife. The Merchant's own unhappy marriage experience adds a painfully personal coloration to his tale of the old husband and the young wife.

His story of May, Januarie, and the pear tree is well known in the history of the *fabliau*. Immediately after wedding the sixty-year-old Januarie, whose lovemaking she considers not "worth a bene," May meets and falls in love with Damian, who loves her in return. When Januarie becomes temporarily blind, the lovers plot to consummate their love in the pear tree above Januarie's head. Pluto and Proserpina, debating how men and women betray each other, decide to restore Januarie's sight but to give May a facile tongue. Consequently, when Januarie's sight returns and he sees May and Damian making love in the pear tree, May explains that her struggling in a tree with a man was an effort to restore his sight, which is obviously as yet imperfect. Placated, Januarie accepts her explanation, and they are reconciled.

The three tales thus present varying views of woman as lascivious termagant, as obedient saint, and as clever deceiver; marriage, accordingly, is seen as a struggle for power and freedom between combatants who are natural adversaries. It remains for Chaucer in "The Franklin's Tale" to attempt a more balanced view, to try to achieve a reconciliation of the oppositions posed in the tales of the wife of Bath, the clerk, and the merchant.

"The Franklin's Tale" is a particular kind of romance called a Breton lai, which conventionally is concentrated, imaginative, and exaggeratedly romantic. While the tale is interesting in its depiction of an integrity which rests upon absolute commitment to the pledged word, the intricacies of the poem's moral issues are ultimately resolved, in a rather disappointing fashion, by something akin to a *deus ex machina*. The tale, nevertheless, has been seen traditionally to function as the reconciliation of the marriage group because of the more balanced relationship portrayed between Arveragus, a knight, and Dorigen, his wife. The couple agree that he will show no sovereignty except for that semblance of it which may be necessary for his dignity, and that their effort will be for freedom, harmony, and mutual respect in marriage, rather than for mastery. In this regard, they represent an ideal example of marriage which is totally antithetical to those of the preceding marriage tales; in Dorigen and Arveragus, Chaucer seems to be exploring the possibility that chivalric ideals and middle-class virtues can be compatible in marriage. Whether the poet really believes this is possible, however, is placed in question by the tale's romance form and by its contrived ending.

While Arveragus is away on knightly endeavors, Dorigen mourns and grieves, worrying particularly about the black rocks which make the coastline hazardous. When Aurelius, who has loved her long, pleads for her attentions, she explains that she will never be unfaithful to her husband but adds, in jest, that if he will remove the rocks she will love him. Two years after Arveragus has come home, Aurelius, made ill by his long-frustrated passion, finds a magician who, for a large fee, creates the illusion that the rocks have vanished. Asked then to fulfill her end of the bargain, the horrified Dorigen contemplates suicide to avoid this dishonor, but her miserably unhappy husband, declaring that "Trouthe is the hyeste thyng that man may kepe," sends Dorigen to fulfill her promise. Pitying them, Aurelius releases her from her promise and is in turn released from his debt by the magician; the tale ends by asking who was the most generous.

Although Dorigen and Arveragus have a marriage based on respect, honesty, and love, and although they share a moral sensibility and agree on the importance of honor to them individually and to their marriage, the artificial resolution of the plot by totally unexpected elements—the decisions of both Aurelius and the magician not to press their just claims—would seem to suggest that the poet himself dared not treat in a realistic fashion the unpleasant and probably disastrous results of the plot which he had created. In effect, he established an ideal marriage situation, set up a test of that marriage's strength, but then decided not to go through with the test. In placing his attempted solution of the marriage problem in the form of a Breton lai, in failing to pursue to the end the very questions he himself raises, and in providing a typical romance ending, the poet seems to indicate that any real solution to the problems pertaining to women and to marriage are not going to be so easily attained.

The Canterbury Tales, then, represents one of the earliest collections of short stories of almost every conceivable type. In addition to being a generic compendium, the poem is also a compendium of characters, since the pilgrims who tell the stories and the people who inhabit the stories together constitute the widest possible representation of character types. In framing his collection of tales with the pilgrimage, Chaucer permitted himself an eclecticism in form, content, and treatment which was unprecedented in English literature. There are those who would eagerly affirm that the grace of vision which permeates *The Canterbury Tales* makes the work not only one which was unprecedented but also one which has not since been equaled.

Other major works

NONFICTION: *Boece*, c. 1380 (translation of Boethius' *The Consolation of Philosophy*); *A Treatise on the Astrolabe*, 1387-1392.

MISCELLANEOUS: *Works*, 1957 (second edition, F. N. Robinson, editor).

Bibliography

Bowden, Muriel. *A Commentary on the General Prologue to "The Canterbury Tales."* 2d ed. New York: Macmillan, 1967. Restricted in scope to the general prologue, the most widely read (and taught) of Chaucer's writings. Provides a detailed explication that explores the prologue virtually line by line, collecting and arranging all significant discussions of the text. A valuable reference for the specialist, while remaining clear enough to be accessible to the general reader.

Howard, Donald R. *Chaucer*. New York: E. P. Dutton, 1987. The most comprehensive and authoritative biography, by a renowned critic, valuable for both the novice and the advanced student. Combines biographical and historical material with insightful commentary on the poetry. A thorough yet readable introduction to Chaucer, his work, and his world.

Mann, Jill. *Geoffrey Chaucer.* New York: Harvester Wheatsheaf, 1991.

Muscatine, Charles. *Chaucer and the French Tradition: A Study in Style and Meaning.* Berkeley: University of California Press, 1957. Explores the combined influences on Chaucer's poetry of two disparate stylistic traditions from medieval French poetry: the courtly romance and the realistic *fabliau.* Chaucer manipulates the two traditions through juxtaposing and parodying them, producing an ironic tension between the ideal and the everyday. The most influential study of Chaucer's style.

Payne, Robert O. *Geoffrey Chaucer.* 2d ed. Boston: Twayne, 1986. A concise introduction to Chaucer and his period for the beginning student by one of the leading scholars in the field. Addressed to readers who have no previous background in medieval literature or cultural studies.

Pearsall, D. *The Life of Geoffrey Chaucer: A Critical Biography.* Cambridge, Mass.: Blackwell, 1992.

Robertson, D. W., Jr. *A Preface to Chaucer.* Princeton, N.J.: Princeton University Press, 1962. Seeks to reconstruct the intellectual perspectives of Chaucer's original audience, arguing that medieval readers would have seen all Chaucer's stories as allegories of the conflict between true Christian love and worldly love. Includes 118 useful black-and-white illustrations of medieval art.

Rowland, Beryl, ed. *Companion to Chaucer Studies.* Rev. ed. New York: Oxford University Press, 1979. Especially valuable for the student or teacher with little ready access to a research library. Contains twenty-two essays, each followed by an extensive bibliography, by major authorities in the field. Surveys the history of Chaucer criticism in a wide range of topics, beginning with Chaucer's biography and influences on his style. Contains six chapters on *The Canterbury Tales* and individual chapters on the more important minor poems.

Schoeck, Richard, and Jerome Taylor, eds. *Chaucer Criticism.* 2 vols. Notre Dame, Ind.: University of Notre Dame Press, 1960-1961. Volume 1, *The Canterbury Tales,* assembles some of the most important early studies of Chaucer's masterpiece, including John Matthews Manly's "Chaucer and the Rhetoricians" and George Lyman Kittredge's seminal "Chaucer's Discussion of Marriage." A valuable introduction to major critics and approaches. Volume 2 contains an introduction to "The System of Courtly Love" by William George Dodd, followed by twelve essays on *Troilus and Criseyde.* Also includes essays on individual shorter poems.

Evelyn Newlyn (Revised by *William Nelles*)

JOHN CHEEVER

Born: Quincy, Massachusetts; May 27, 1912
Died: Ossining, New York; June 18, 1982

Principal short fiction · *The Way Some People Live*, 1943 · *The Enormous Radio and Other Stories*, 1953 · *The Housebreaker of Shady Hill and Other Stories*, 1958 · *Some People, Places, and Things That Will Not Appear in My Next Novel*, 1961 · *The Brigadier and the Golf Widow*, 1964 · *The World of Apples*, 1973 · *The Stories of John Cheever*, 1978

Other literary forms · Believing that "fiction is our most intimate and acute means of communication, at a profound level, about our deepest apprehension and intuitions on the meaning of life and death," John Cheever devoted himself to the writing of stories and novels. Although he kept voluminous journals, he wrote only a handful of essays and even fewer reviews, and only one television screenplay, *The Shady Hill Kidnapping*, which aired January 12, 1982, on the Public Broadcasting Service (PBS). A number of Cheever's works have also been adapted by other writers, including several early short stories such as "The Town House" (play, 1948), "The Swimmer" (film, 1968), "Goodbye, My Brother" as *Children* (play, 1976), and "O Youth and Beauty," "The Five-Forty-Eight," and "The Sorrows of Gin" (teleplays, 1979). Benjamin Cheever has edited selections of his father's correspondence, *The Letters of John Cheever* (1988), and journals, *The Journals of John Cheever* (1991).

Achievements · A major twentieth century novelist, Cheever has achieved even greater fame as a short-story writer. He published his first story, "Expelled," in *The New Republic* when he was only eighteen. Reviewers of his first collection, *The Way Some People Live*, judged Cheever to be a promising young writer. Numerous awards and honors followed: two Guggenheim grants (1951, 1961), a Benjamin Franklin award for "The Five-Forty-Eight" (1955), an O. Henry Award for "The Country Husband" (1956), election to the National Institute of Arts and Letters in 1957, elevation to the American Academy in 1973, a National Book Award in 1958 for *The Wapshot Chronicle* (1957), the Howells Medal in 1965 for *The Wapshot Scandal* (1964), cover stories in *Time* (1964) and *Newsweek* (1977), the Edward MacDowell Medal in 1979, a Pulitzer Prize and a National Book Critics Circle award (both in 1978), an American Book Award (1979)

for *The Stories of John Cheever*,
and the National Medal for
Literature (1982). Cheever's
achievements, however,
cannot be measured only in
terms of the awards and
honors that he has received
(including the honorary
doctorate bestowed on this
high school dropout), for his
most significant accom-
plishment was to create,
with the publication of *The
Stories of John Cheever*, a resurgence of interest in, and
a new respect for, the short
story on the part of public
and publishers alike.

Biography · The loss of his
father's job in 1930, followed by the loss of the fam-

©1981 Nancy Crampton

ily home and the strained marital situation caused, John Cheever believed,
by his mother's growing financial and emotional dependence, all had a
lifelong effect on Cheever. When he was expelled from Thayer Academy
at the age of seventeen, Cheever was already committed to a writing career.
His career, however, would do little to assuage his sense of emotional and
economic insecurity. Although he liked to claim that "fiction is not crypto-
autobiography," from the beginning, his stories were drawn from his
personal experiences. They have even followed him geographically: from
New England, to New York City, through his military service, to the
suburbs (first Scarborough, then Ossining), with side trips to Italy (1956-
1957), the Soviet Union (on three government-sponsored trips), and Sing
Sing prison, where he taught writing (1971-1972). The stories have more
importantly followed Cheever over hazardous emotional terrain, transforming personal obsessions into published fictions: alcoholism, bisexual-
ity, self-doubts, strained marital relations, and the sense of "otherness." The
stories also evidence the longing for stability and home that manifested
itself in three of the most enduring relationships of his fifty-year career:
with the Yaddo writers colony in Saratoga Springs, New York (beginning
in 1934); with *The New Yorker* (which began publishing his work in 1935);

and with his wife Mary Winternitz Cheever (whom he met in 1939 and married two years later, and with whom he bickered over the next forty years).

Cheever did not become free of his various fears and dependencies—including his nearly suicidal addiction to alcohol—until the mid-1970's. After undergoing treatment for alcoholism at Smithers Rehabilitation Center, he transformed what might well have become his darkest novel into his most affirmative. *Falconer* (1977) was both a critical and commercial success. Like its main character, Cheever seemed for the first time in his life free, willing at least to begin talking about the private life that he had so successfully guarded, even mythified before, when he had played the part of country squire. The triumph was, however, short-lived: two neurological seizures in 1980, a kidney operation and the discovery of cancer in 1981, and, shortly after the publication of his fifth novel, the aptly and perhaps whimsically titled *Oh What a Paradise It Seems* (1982), his death on June 18, 1982.

Analysis · John Cheever has been called both "the Chekhov of the exurbs" and "Ovid in Ossining"—which suggests both the variety and the complexity of the man and his fiction. Accused by some of being a literary lightweight—a writer merely of short stories and an apologist for middle-class life—he has been more often, and more justly, praised as a master chronicler of a way of life that he both celebrates and satirizes in stories that seem at once conventional and innovative, realistic and fantastic. His stories read effortlessly, yet their seeming simplicity masks a complexity that deserves and repays close attention. The line "The light from the cottage, shining into the fog, gave the illusion of substance, and it seems as if I might stumble on a beam of light," for example, only appears simple and straightforward. It begins with a conventional image, light penetrating darkness, thus illuminating the way to truth, but the next five words undermine the "illusion" first by calling attention to it, then by paradoxically literalizing the metaphor, making this substantive light a stumbling block rather than a source of spiritual and/or philosophical truth.

Nothing in Cheever's fiction of stark contrasts—light and dark, male and female, city and country—ever exists independent of its opposite. His stories proceed incrementally and contrapuntally, at times in curiously indirect ways. In "A Miscellany of Characters That Will Not Appear in My Next Novel," for example, Cheever's narrator banishes seven kinds of characters and situations from his fiction, including alcoholics, homosexuals, and "scornful descriptions of American landscapes." However, not only did his next novel, as well as much of the rest of his fiction, include all three; the very act of listing them in this "miscellany" confirms their power, giving them a prominence that far outweighs their hypothetical banishment from any later work. This play of voices and positions within individual works also exists between stories. The same narrative situations will appear in various Cheever stories, handled comically in some, tragically in others. In effect, the stories offer a series of brilliant variations on a number of basic, almost obsessive themes, of which the most general and the most recurrent as well as the most important is the essential conflict between his characters' spiritual longings and social and psychological (especially sexual) nature. "What I wanted to do," one of his narrator-protagonists says, is "to grant my dreams, in so incoherent a world, their legitimacy," "to celebrate," as another claims, "a world that lies spread out around us like a bewildering and stupendous dream." Their longings are tempered not only by the incoherence of their world but also by a doubt concerning whether what they long for actually exists or is rather only an illusion conjured out of nothing more substantial than their own ardent hopes for something or some place or someone other than who, what, and where they presently are. Even when expressed in the most ludicrous terms possible, the characters' longings seem just as profound as they are ridiculous, as in the case of "Artemis the Honest Well Digger" searching "for a girl as pure and fresh as the girl on the oleomargarine package." The line seems both to affirm and to qualify the yearning of a character who may confuse kitsch with Kant, advertising copy with lyrical longings, but who nevertheless seems as much a holy fool as a deluded consumer.

Whether treated comically or tragically, Cheever's characters share a number of traits. Most are male, married, and white-collar workers. All—despite their Sutton Place apartments or, more often, comfortable homes in affluent Westchester communities—feel confused, dispossessed, lost; they all seem to be what the characters in Cheever's Italian stories actually are: expatriates and exiles. Physical ailments are rare, emotional ones epidemic. Instead of disease, there is the "dis-ease" of "spiritual nomadism." They are as restless as any of Cheever's most wayward plots and in need of "building a bridge" between the events of their lives as well as between those lives and their longings. Trapped in routines as restricting as any prison cell and often in marriages that seem little more than sexual battlefields, where even the hair curlers appear "bellicose," his characters appear poised between escaping into the past in a futile effort to repeat what they believe they have lost and aspiring to a lyrical future that can be affirmed, even "sung," though never quite attained. Even the latter can be dangerous. "Dominated by anticipation" (a number of Cheever's characters hope excessively), they are locked in a state of perpetual adolescence, unwilling to grow up, take responsibility, and face death in any form.

Although their world may lie spread out like a bewildering and stupendous dream, they find it nevertheless confining, inhospitable, even haunted by fears of emotional and economic insecurity and a sense of personal inadequacy and inconsequentiality, their sole inheritance, it seems, from the many fathers who figure so prominently in the stories, often by virtue of their absence from the lives of their now middle-aged sons. Adrift in an incoherent world and alone in the midst of suburbs zoned for felicity, they suffer frequent blows to their already fragile sense of self-esteem, seeing through yet wanting the protection of the veneer of social decorum and ceremoniousness that is the outward and visible sign of American middle-class aspiration and which Cheever's characters do not so much court as covet.

The thinness of that veneer is especially apparent in "The Enormous Radio," a work that shows little trace of the Hemingway style that marks many of Cheever's earlier stories. The story begins realistically enough. Jim and Irene Westcott, in their mid-thirties, are an average couple in all respects but one: their above-average interest in classical music (and, one assumes, in the harmony and decorum that such music represents). When their old radio breaks down, Jim generously buys an expensive new one to which Irene takes an instant dislike. Like their interest in music, which they indulge as if a secret but harmless vice, this small disruption in their harmonious married life seems a minor affair, at least at first. The radio, however, appearing "like an aggressive intruder," shedding a "malevolent green light," and possessing a "mistaken sensitivity to discord," soon becomes a divisive, even diabolical presence, but the evil in this story, as in Nathaniel Hawthorne's "Young Goodman Brown," to which it has often been compared, comes from within the characters, not from without (the radio). When the radio begins to broadcast the Westcotts' neighbors' quarrels, lusts, fears, and crimes, Irene becomes dismayed, perversely entertained, and finally apprehensive; if she can eavesdrop on her neighbors' most intimate conversations, she thinks that perhaps they can listen in on hers. Hearing their tales of woe, she demands that her husband affirm their happiness. Far from easing her apprehensiveness, his words only exacerbate it as he first voices his own previously well-guarded frustrations over money, job prospects, and growing old, and as he eventually exposes his wife's own evil nature. As frustration explodes into accusation, the illusion of marital happiness that the Westcotts had so carefully cultivated shatters.

As with so many Cheever stories, "The Enormous Radio" has its origin in biographical fact: while writing in the basement of a Sutton Place apartment house, Cheever would hear the elevator going up and down and would imagine that the wires could carry his neighbors' conversations down to him. "Goodbye, My Brother" derives from another and far more pervasive biographical fact, Cheever's relationship with his elder brother, Fred, the father figure to whom he developed too close an attachment. Fred turned to business and for a time supported Cheever's writing but, like Cheever, eventually became an alcoholic. Beginning with "The Brothers" and culminating in the fratricide in *Falconer*, relations between brothers figure nearly as prominently in Cheever's fiction as those between spouses. Just as stories such as "The Enormous Radio" are not simply about marital spats, "Goodbye, My Brother" is not only about sibling rivalry. Just as the relationship between Irene and the malevolent radio is actually about a condition within the marriage and more especially within Irene herself, the external relationship between the story's narrator and his brother Lawrence is actually about the narrator's own Dr. Jekyll and Mr. Hyde personality—in psychological terms, a matter of split personality and projection. The narrator objectifies in Lawrence his own fears, frustrations, and self-loathing. Lawrence and the narrator are two of the Pommeroys who have gathered on Laud's Head in August for their annual family vacation. Like his sister, just back after her divorce, and their widowed mother, who drinks too much while trying to keep up the family's uppercrust pretensions, the narrator needs these few weeks of respite from the grind of his dead-end teaching job. Together they swim, play cards and tennis, drink, and go to costume dances, where in an almost Jungian freak of chance, all the men come dressed as football players and all the women as brides, as eloquent a statement of the sadness of their blighted but still aspiring lives as one can imagine. Lawrence partakes in none of it. A lawyer moving from one city and job to another, he is the only family member with prospects and the only one unable to enjoy or even tolerate the illusion of happiness that the family seeks to maintain. He is also the only one willing, indeed eager, to detect the flaws and fakery in the Pommeroys' summer home, its protective sea wall, and its equally protective forms of play. Gloomy and morose as well as critical, Lawrence is, to borrow the title of another Cheever story, the worm in the Pommeroy apple. He is the messenger bearing the bad news, whom the narrator nearly kills with a blow to the head as the two walk along the beach. He strikes not only to free himself from his brother's morbid presence but also to extirpate the Lawrence side of his own divided self: Cain and Abel, murderer and good Samaritan. Once Lawrence and his sickly looking wife and daughter leave, the narrator turns to the purifying water and the triumphant vision of his mythically named wife and sister, Helen and Diana, rising naked from the sea. The story closes on a lyrically charged note that seems both to affirm all that the Pommeroys have sought and, by virtue of the degree of lyrical intensity, to accentuate the gap between that vision and Lawrence's more factual and pessimistic point of view.

"O Youth and Beauty" makes explicit what virtually all Cheever's stories imply, the end of youth's promise, of that hopeful vision that the ending of "Goodbye, My Brother" sought to affirm. Thus it seems ironically apt that "O Youth and Beauty" should begin with a long (two-hundred-word) Whitmanesque sentence, which, in addition to setting the scene and establishing the narrative situation, subtly evokes that Transcendental vision that Walt Whitman both espoused and, in his distinctive poetic style, sought to embody. Beginning "At the tag end of nearly every long, large Saturday night party in the suburb of Shady Hill," it proceeds through a series of long anaphoric subordinate clauses beginning with the word "when" and ending with "then Trace Bearden would begin to chide Cash Bentley about his age and thinning hair." The reader is thus introduced to what, for the partygoers, has already become something of a suburban ritual: the perfectly named Cash Bentley's hurdling of the furniture as a way of warding off death and reliving the athletic triumphs of the youth that he refuses to relinquish. When Cash, now forty, breaks his leg, the intimations of mortality begin to multiply in his morbid mind. Although he may run his race alone, and although the Lawrentian gloominess that comes in the wake of the accident may make him increasingly isolated from his neighbors and friends, Cash is not at all unique, and his fears are extreme but nevertheless representative of a fear that pervades the entire community and that evidences itself in his wife's trying to appear younger and slimmer than she is and her "cutting out of the current copy of *Life* those scenes of mayhem, disaster, and violent death that she felt might corrupt her children." It is rather ironic that a moment later she should accidentally kill her husband in their own living room with the starter's pistol, as he attempts to recapture the past glories of all those other late Saturday night races against time and self in an attempt always, already doomed, to recapture the past glories of his days as a young track star. The track is in fact an apt symbol for Cash's circular life, in which, instead of progress, one finds only the horror of Nietzschean eternal recurrence.

Upon first reading, "The Five-Forty-Eight" seems to have little in common with the blackly humorous "O Youth and Beauty." A disturbed woman, Miss Dent, follows Blake, whose secretary she had been for three weeks and whose lover she was for one night, some six months earlier. She trails him from his office building to his commuter train. Threatening to shoot him, she gets off at his stop and forces him to kneel and rub his face in the dirt for having seduced and abandoned her six months earlier. One of Cheever's least likable characters, Blake gets what he deserves. Having chosen Miss Dent as he has chosen his other women (including, it seems, his wife) "for their lack of self-esteem," he not only had her fired the day after they made love but also took the afternoon off. Miss Dent fares considerably better, for in choosing not to kill Blake she discovers "some kindness, some saneness" in herself that she believes she can put to use. Blake too undergoes a change insofar as he experiences regret for the first time and comes to understand his own vulnerability, which he has heretofore managed to safeguard by means of his "protective" routines and scrupulous observance of Shady Hill's sumptuary laws. Whether these changes will be lasting remains unclear; he is last seen picking himself up, cleaning himself off, and walking home, alone.

"The Five-Forty-Eight" is quite literally one of Cheever's darkest stories; only the dimmest of lights and the faintest of hopes shine at its end. Although it too ends at night, "The Housebreaker of Shady Hill" is one of Cheever's brightest and most cheerful works, full of the spiritual phototropism so important in *Falconer,* the novel that *Newsweek* hailed as "Cheever's Triumph." The housebreaker is thirty-six-year-old Johnny Hake, kindly and comical, who suddenly finds himself out of work, at risk of losing his house, his circle of friends, and the last shreds of his self-esteem. Desperate for cash, he steals nine hundred dollars from a neighbor, a theft that transforms his vision of the world. Suddenly, he begins to see evil everywhere and, of course, evidence that everyone can see him for what he now is. The "moral bottom" drops out of his world but in decidedly comic fashion: even a birthday gift from his children—an extension ladder—becomes an acknowledgment of his wrongdoing (and nearly cause for divorce). Chance, however, saves Johnny. Walking to his next victim's house, he feels a few drops of rain fall on his head and awakens from his ludicrous nightmare, his vision of the world restored. Opting for life's simple pleasures (he is after all still unemployed), he returns home and has a pleasant dream in which he is seventeen years old. Johnny cannot get his youth back, but he does get his job (and he does return the money he has stolen). The happy endings proliferate as the story slips the yoke of realism and romps in the magical realm of pure fairy tale, where, as Cheever puts it far more sardonically in his third novel, *Bullet Park* (1969), everything is "wonderful wonderful wonderful wonderful."

Comic exaggeration and hyperbolically happy endings characterize many of the stories of the late 1950's and early 1960's. In "The Housebreaker of Shady Hill," it is losing his job that starts Johnny Hake on his comical crime spree; in "The Country Husband," it is nearly losing his life that sends Francis Weed on an ever more absurdly comical quest for love and understanding. Weed has his brush with death when his plane is forced to make an emergency landing in a field outside Philadelphia. The danger over, his vulnerability (like Blake's) and mortality (like Cash Bentley's) established, the real damage begins when Weed can find no one to lend a sympathetic ear—not his friend, Trace Bearden, on the commuter train, not even his wife, Julia (too busy putting dinner on the table), or his children (the youngest are fighting and the oldest is reading *True Romance*). With his very own True Adventure still untold, Weed goes outside, where he hears a neighbor playing "Moonlight Sonata," *rubato*, "like an outpouring of tearful petulance, lonesomeness, and self-pity—of everything it was Beethoven's greatness not to know," and everything it will now be Weed's comic misfortune to experience as he embarks upon his own True Romance with the rather unromantically named Anne Murchison, his children's new teenage baby-sitter.

Playing the part of a lovesick adolescent, the middle-aged Weed acts out his midlife crisis and in doing so jeopardizes his family's social standing and his marriage. The consequences are potentially serious, as are the various characters' fears and troubles (Anne's alcoholic father, Julia's "natural fear of chaos and loneliness," which leads to her obsessive party-going). What is humorous is Cheever's handling of these fears in a story in which solecisms are slapstick, downfalls are pratfalls, and pariahs turn out to be weeds in Cheever's suburban Garden of Eden. When Francis finally decides to overcome his Emersonian self-reliance, to confide in and seek the help of a psychiatrist (who will do what neither friends nor family have thus far been willing to do—that is, listen), the first words Weed tearfully blurts out are, "I'm in love, Dr. Harzog." Since "The Country Husband" is a comedy, Weed is of course cured of his "dis-ease" and able to channel his desires into more socially acceptable ways (conjugal love and, humorously enough, woodworking). The story ends with a typically Cheever-esque affirmation of F. Scott Fitzgerald-like romantic possibilities, no less apparent in Shady Hill than in the *Great Gatsby*'s (1925) West Egg. It is an affirmation, however, tempered once again by the tenuousness of the characters' situation in a "village that hangs, morally and economically, from a thread."

The thread will break—although still comically—in "The Death of Justina." Here, the focus is double, on the parallel plights of the authorial narrator, a fiction writer, and the protagonist-narrator of the story that he writes (like "The Housebreaker of Shady Hill," in oral style), also a writer (of advertising copy). Briefly stated, their shared predicament is this: how (for the one) to write about and (for the other) to live in a world that seems to grow increasingly chaotic and preposterous. As the authorial narrator explains, "Fiction is art and art is the triumph over chaos (no less) and we can accomplish this only by the most vigilant exercise of choice, but in a world that changes more swiftly than we can perceive there is always the danger that our powers of selection will be mistaken and that the vision we serve will come to nothing." The authorial narrator then offers Moses' account of the death of his wife's cousin Justina as "one example of chaos." Ordered by his doctor to stop smoking and drinking and by his boss to write copy for a product called Elixircol (something of a cross between Geritol and the Fountain of Youth), Moses suddenly finds himself at a complete loss when he tries to arrange for Justina's funeral, for Justina has died in his house and his house is an area of Proxmire Manor not zoned for death. No doctor will issue a death certificate, and the mayor refuses to sign an exemption until a quorum of the village council is available, but when Moses threatens to bury Justina in his yard, the mayor relents. Victorious but still shaken, Moses that night has a strange dream set in a vast supermarket where the shoppers stock their carts with unlabeled, shapeless packages, which are then, much to their shame, torn open at the checkout counters by brutish men who first ridicule the selections and then push the shoppers out the doors into what sounds much like Dante's inferno. The scene is amusing but, like the ludicrously comical scenes in Franz Kafka's works, also unsettling. The story does not affirm the shoppers any more than it does the village council that drew up the zoning laws, but it does understand what compels them even as it sympathetically satirizes the inadequacy of their means. As Moses points out, "How can a people who do not mean to understand death hope to understand love, and who will sound the alarm?"

"The Brigadier and the Golf Widow" makes a similar point in a similar way. Here too, the authorial narrator is perplexed, wondering what the nineteenth century writers Charles Dickens, Anton Chekhov, Nikolai Gogol, and William Makepeace Thackeray would have made of a fallout shelter (bizarrely decorated and disguised with gnomes, plaster ducks, and a birdbath). He also understands, however, that fallout shelters are as much a part of his mid-twentieth century landscape as are trees and shrubbery. The shelter in question belongs to Charlie Pastern, the country club general who spends his time calling loudly for nuclear attacks on any and all of his nation's enemies. His world begins to unravel when, by chance, he begins an affair with a neighbor whose own fears and insecurity lead her first to promiscuity and then to demanding the key to the Pasterns' shelter (a key that the local bishop also covets). Apparently the last words of "The Death of Justina," taken verbatim from the Twenty-third Psalm, about walking through the shadow of the valley of death and fearing no evil, no longer apply.

For all the good cheer, hearty advice, biblical quotations, comical predicaments, and lyrical affirmations, there lies at the center of Cheever's fiction the fear of insufficiency and inadequacy—of shelters that will not protect, marriages that will not endure, jobs that will be lost, threads that will not hold. That the thread does not hold in "The Swimmer," Cheever's most painstakingly crafted and horrific work, is especially odd for the story begins as comedy, a lighthearted satire, involving a group of suburban couples sitting around the Westerhazys' pool on a beautiful midsummer Sunday afternoon talking about what and how much they drank the night before. Suddenly Neddy Merrill, yet another of Cheever's middle-aged but youthfully named protagonists, decides to swim home pool to pool. More than a prank, it is for him a celebration of the fineness of the day, a voyage of discovery, a testament to life's romantic possibilities. Neddy's swim will cover eight miles, sixteen pools, in only ten pages (as printed in *The Stories of John Cheever*). Although he encounters some delays and obstacles—drinks graciously offered and politely, even ceremoniously, drunk, a thorny hedge to be gotten over, gravel underfoot—Neddy completes nearly half the journey in only two pages (pages 3-4; pages 1-2 are purely preparatory). The story and its reader move as confidently and rapidly as Neddy, but then there are a few interruptions: a brief rain shower that forces Neddy to seek shelter, a dry pool at one house, and a for-sale sign inexplicably posted at another. Midway through both journey and story, the point of view suddenly and briefly veers away from Neddy, who now looks pitifully exposed and foolishly stranded as he attempts to cross a divided highway. His strength and confidence ebbing, he seems unprepared for whatever lies ahead yet unable to turn back. Like the reader, he is unsure when his little joke turned so deadly serious. At the one public pool on his itinerary, he is assaulted by crowds, shrill sounds, and harsh odors. After being very nearly stalled for two pages, the pace quickens ever so slightly but only to leave Neddy still weaker and more disoriented. Each "breach in the succession" exposes Neddy's inability to bridge the widening gap between his vision of the world and his actual place in it. He is painfully rebuffed by those he had previously been powerful enough to mistreat—a former mistress, a socially inferior couple whose invitations he and his wife routinely discarded. The apparent cause of Neddy's downfall begins to become clear to the reader only as it begins to become clear to Neddy—a sudden and major financial reversal—but Neddy's situation cannot be attributed to merely economic factors, nor is it susceptible to purely rational analysis. Somewhere along Neddy's and the reader's way, everything has changed: the passing of hours becomes the passage of whole seasons, perhaps even years, as realism gives way to fantasy, humor to horror as the swimmer sees his whole life pass before him in a sea of repressed memories. Somehow Neddy has woken into his own worst dream. Looking into his empty house, he comes face to face with the insecurity that nearly all Cheever's characters fear and the inadequacy that they all feel.

The stories (and novels) that Cheever wrote during the last two decades of his life grew increasingly and innovatively disparate in structure. "The Jewels of the Cabots," for example, or "The President of the Argentine" match the intensifying disunity of the author's personal life. Against this narrative waywardness, however, Cheever continued to offer and even to extend an affirmation of the world and his protagonists' place in it in a lyrically charged prose at once serene and expansive ("The World of Apples," *Falconer*). In other words, he continued to do during these last two decades what he had been doing so well for the previous three: writing a fiction of celebration and incoherence.

Other major works

NOVELS: *The Wapshot Chronicle,* 1957; *The Wapshot Scandal,* 1964; *Bullet Park,* 1969; *Falconer,* 1977; *Oh What a Paradise It Seems,* 1982.

SCREENPLAY: *The Shady Hill Kidnapping,* 1982.

NONFICTION: *The Letters of John Cheever,* 1988; *The Journals of John Cheever,* 1991.

Bibliography

Bosha, Francis J., ed. *The Critical Response to John Cheever.* Westport, Conn.: Greenwood Press, 1994.

_____. *John Cheever: A Reference Guide.* Boston: G. K. Hall, 1981. Especially useful for its annotated listing of works about Cheever and for its brief overview of the critical response to Cheever's fiction. For a more complete listing of primary works, see Dennis Coale's checklist in *Bulletin of Bibliography* (volume 36, 1979) and the supplement in Robert G. Collins' book (below). Robert A. Morace's exhaustive assessment of all available biographical, bibliographical, and critical materials appears in *Contemporary Authors: Bibliographical Series: American Authors* (1986) and can be updated by reference to *American Literary Annual* (1985-   ).

Cheever, Susan. *Home Before Dark.* Boston: Houghton Mifflin, 1984. Although superseded by Scott Donaldson's book (below), this memoir by Cheever's daughter provides a detailed and harrowing account of Cheever's fears as they originated in his relations with his parents and brother and as they manifested themselves in his life with his wife and children. The book is not suitable for quick reference: the material is not organized chronologically and contains neither index nor documentation.

Collins, Robert G., ed. *Critical Essays on John Cheever.* Boston: G. K. Hall, 1982. Reprints an excellent sampling of reviews, interviews, and early criticism (including many dubbed "new" that are in fact only slightly reworked older pieces). Of the truly new items, three deserve special mention: Collins' biocritical introduction, Dennis Coale's bibliogaphical supplement, and particularly Samuel Coale's "Cheever and Hawthorne: The American Romancer's Art," arguably one of the most important critical essays on Cheever.

Donaldson, Scott, ed. *Conversations with John Cheever.* Jackson: University Press of Mississippi, 1987. Until his final years a rather reticent man, Cheever granted relatively few interviews. The most important ones are reprinted here, along with the editor's thorough chronology and brief but useful introduction.

_____. *John Cheever: A Biography.* New York: Random House, 1988. Scrupulously researched, interestingly written, and judiciously argued, Donaldson's biography presents Cheever as both author and private man. Donaldson fleshes out most of the previously unknown areas in Cheever's biography and dispels many of the biographical myths that Cheever himself encouraged. The account is sympathetic yet objective.

Hunt, George. *John Cheever: The Hobgoblin in Company of Love.* Grand Rapids, Mich.: Wm. B. Eerdmans, 1983. The two previous book-length studies of Cheever's fiction are both introductory in nature: Samuel Coale's fine *John Cheever* (1977) and Lynne Waldeland's less insightful but more exhaustive volume in Twayne's United States Authors series (1979). Hunt's study is something more. A Jesuit and a professor of religion, Hunt reads Cheever as a writer of Christian sensibility, dialectical intelligence, and poetic style. Discussions of individual novels, particularly their structural integrity, are strong; those of the stories seem almost perfunctory by comparison.

Meanor, Patrick. *John Cheever Revisited.* New York: Twayne Publishers, 1995. An updated introduction for the Twayne U.S. Authors series.

O'Hara, James E. *John Cheever: A Study of the Short Fiction.* Boston: Twayne, 1989. In addition to reprinting five important reviews and critical essays and providing a detailed chronology and annotated selected bibliography, this volume offers a 120-page analysis of Cheever as a writer of short stories that goes well beyond the introductory level. O'Hara's discussion of the early unanthologized stories is especially noteworthy.

Robert A. Morace

CHARLES WADDELL CHESNUTT

Born: Cleveland, Ohio; June 20, 1858
Died: Cleveland, Ohio; November 15, 1932

Principal short fiction · *The Conjure Woman*, 1899 · *The Wife of His Youth and Other Stories of the Color Line*, 1899

Other literary forms · Charles Waddell Chesnutt achieved his literary reputation and stature as a short-story writer. His scholarly bent and indelible concern for human conditions in American society, however, occasionally moved him to experiment in other literary forms. Based on his study of race relations in the American South, he wrote the novel *The Marrow of Tradition* (1901). As a result of the critical acclaim for this novel and for his first, *The House Behind the Cedars* (1900), Chesnutt became known not only as a short-story writer but as a first-rate novelist as well. He wrote two other novels, *The Colonel's Dream* (1905) and "The Quarry," which remains unpublished.

In 1885, Chesnutt published several poems in *The Cleveland Voice*. The acceptance of his essay "What Is a White Man?" by the *Independent* in May of 1889 began his career as an essayist. Illustrating his diverse talent still further and becoming an impassioned voice for human justice, he wrote essays for a major portion of his life. Chesnutt demonstrated his skill as a biographer when he prepared *The Life of Frederick Douglass* (1899) for the Beacon biography series.

Achievements · One of Chesnutt's most significant achievements was his own education. Self-taught in the higher principles of algebra, the intricate details of history, the linguistic dicta of Latin, and the tenets of natural philosophy, he crowned this series of intellectual achievements by passing the Ohio bar examination after teaching himself law for two years.

A man of outstanding social reputation, Chesnutt received an invitation to Mark Twain's seventieth birthday party, an invitation "extended to about one hundred and fifty of America's most distinguished writers of imaginative literature." The party was held on December 5, 1905, at Delmonico's, in New York City. Chesnutt's greatest public honor was being chosen as the recipient of the Joel E. Springarn Medal, an award annually bestowed on an American citizen of African descent for distinguished service.

Biography · Charles Waddell Chesnutt was born in Cleveland, Ohio, on June 20, 1858. He attended Cleveland public schools and the Howard School in Fayetteville, North Carolina. Having distinguished himself academically early in his schooling, Chesnutt was taken into the tutelage of two established educators, Robert Harris of the Howard School and his brother, Cicero Harris, of Charlotte, North Carolina. He later succeeded Cicero Harris as principal of the school in Charlotte in 1877 and followed this venture with an appointment to the Normal School in Fayetteville to train teachers for colored schools.

On June 6, 1878, Chesnutt was married to Susan Perry. Shortly after his marriage, he began his training as a stenographer. Even at this time, however, his interest in writing competed for his energies. He spent his spare time writing essays, poems, short stories, and sketches. His public writing career began in December of 1885 with the printing of the story "Uncle Peter's House" in the *Cleveland News and Herald*. Several years passed and "The Goophered Grapevine" was accepted by *The Atlantic Monthly* and published in 1888. Continuing his dual career as a man of letters and a businessman/attorney for more than a decade after his reception as a literary artist, Chesnutt decided, on September 30, 1899, to devote himself full-time to his literary career. From that moment on he enjoyed a full and productive career as a man of letters.

At the beginning of the twentieth century, Chesnutt became more politically active as a spokesman for racial justice. He toured the South and its educational institutions such as Tuskegee Institute and Atlanta University. He joined forces with black leaders such as Booker T. Washington and W. E. B. Du Bois. In May of 1909, he became a member of the National Negro Committee, which later became the National Association for the Advancement of Colored People (NAACP). The last two decades of Chesnutt's life were less active because his health began to fail him in 1919. He was, however, elected to the Cleveland Chamber of Commerce in 1912. Chesnutt continued to write until his death on November 15, 1932.

Analysis · The short fiction of Charles Waddell Chesnutt embraces traditions characteristic of both formal and folk art. Indeed, the elements of Chesnutt's narrative technique evolved in a fashion that conspicuously parallels the historical shaping of the formal short story itself. The typical Chesnutt narrative, like the classic short story, assumes its heritage from a rich oral tradition immersed in folkways, mannerisms, and beliefs. Holding true to the historical development of the short story as an artistic form, his early imaginative narratives were episodic in nature. The next stage of development in Chesnutt's short fiction was a parody of the fable form with a folkloric variation. Having become proficient at telling a story with a unified effect, Chesnutt achieved the symbolic resonance characteristic of the Romantic tale, yet his awareness of the plight of his people urged him toward an increasingly realistic depiction of social conditions. As a mature writer, Chesnutt achieved depth of characterization, distinguishable thematic features, and a rare skillfulness in creation of mood, while a shrewdly moralizing tone allowed him to achieve his dual goal as artist and social activist.

Chesnutt's journal stories constituted the first phase of his writing career, but when *The Atlantic Monthly* published "The Goophered Grapevine" in 1888, the serious aspects of his artistic skill became apparent. "The Goophered Grapevine" belongs to a tradition in Chesnutt's writings which captures the fable form with a folkloric variation. These stories also unfold with a didactic strain which matures significantly in Chesnutt's later writings. To understand clearly the series of stories in *The Conjure Woman*, of which "The Goophered Grapevine" is one, the reader must comprehend the allegorical features in the principal narrative situation and the thematic intent of the mythic incidents from African-American lore.

The Conjure Woman contains narratives revealed through the accounts of a Northern white person's rendition of the tales of Uncle Julius, a former slave. This storytelling device lays the foundation for Chesnutt's sociological commentary. The real and perceived voices represent the perspectives he wishes to expose, those of the white capitalist and the impoverished, disadvantaged African American. The primary persona is that of the capitalist, while the perceived voice is that of the struggling poor. Chesnutt skillfully melds the two perspectives.

Chesnutt's two volumes of short stories contain pieces which are unified in theme, tone, and mood. Each volume also contains a piece which might be considered the lead story. In *The Conjure Women*, the preeminent story is "The Goophered Grapevine." This story embodies the overriding thematic intent of the narratives in this collection. Chesnutt points out the foibles of the capitalistic quest in the post-Civil War South, a venture pursued at the expense of the newly freed African-American slave. He illustrates this point in "The Goophered Grapevine" by skillfully intertwining Aunt Peggy's gains as a result of her conjurations and Henry's destruction as a result of man's inhumanity to man. Chesnutt discloses his ultimate point when the plantation owner, McAdoo, is deceived by a Yankee horticulturist and his grape vineyard becomes totally unproductive.

Running episodes, such as Aunt Peggy's conjurations to keep the field hands from consuming the grape crop and the seasonal benefit McAdoo gains from selling Henry, serve to illustrate the interplay between a monied white capitalist and his less privileged black human resources. McAdoo used Aunt Peggy to deny his field laborers any benefit from the land they worked, and he sold Henry every spring to increase his cash flow and prepare for the next gardening season.

The central metaphor in "The Goophered Grapevine" is the bewitched vineyard. To illustrate and condemn man's inhumanity to man, Chesnutt contrasts the black conjure woman's protection of the grape vineyard with the white Yankee's destruction of it. McAdoo's exploitation of Henry serves to justify McAdoo's ultimate ruin. Through allegory, Chesnutt is able to draw attention to the immorality of capitalistic gain through a sacrifice of basic humanity to other people.

Following the theme of inhumanity established in "The Goophered Grapevine," "Po' Sandy" highlights the abuse of a former slave laborer. Accordingly, a situation with a folkloric variation is used to convey this message. Sandy, Master Marabo's field hand, is shifted from relative to relative at various points during the year to perform various duties. During the course of these transactions, he is separated from his second common-law wife, Tenie. (His first wife has been sent to work at a distant plantation.) Tenie is a conjurer. She transforms Sandy into a tree, and she changes him back to his original state periodically so that they can be together. With Sandy's apparent disappearance, Master Marabo decides to send Tenie away to nurse his ailing daughter-in-law. There is therefore no one left to watch Sandy, the tree. The dehumanizing effects of industrialization creep into the story line at this point. The "tree" is to be used as lumber for a kitchen at the Marabo home. Tenie returns just in time to try to stop this transformation at the lumber mill, but she is deemed "mad."

Sandy's spirit thereafter haunts the Marabo kitchen, and no one wants to work there. The complaints are so extensive that the kitchen is dismantled and the lumber donated toward the building of a school. This structure is then haunted, too. The point is that industrialization and economic gain diminish essential human concerns and can lead to destruction. The destruction of Sandy's marital relationships in order to increase his usefulness as a field worker justifies this defiant spirit. In his depiction of Sandy as a tree, Chesnutt illustrates an enslaved spirit desperately seeking freedom.

"The Conjurer's Revenge," also contained in *The Conjure Woman*, illustrates Chesnutt's mastery of the exemplum. The allegory in this work conveys a strong message, and Chesnutt's evolving skill in characterization becomes apparent. The characters' actions, rather than the situation, contain the didactic message of the story. Some qualities of the fable unfold as the various dimensions of characters are portrayed. Consequently, "The

Conjurer's Revenge" is a good example of Chesnutt's short imaginative sketch. These qualities are also most characteristic of Chesnutt's early short fiction.

"The Conjurer's Revenge" begins when Primus, a field hand, discovers the conjure man's hog alone in a bush one evening. Concerned for the hog and not knowing to whom the animal belongs, Primus carries it to the plantation where he works. Unfortunately, the conjurer identifies Primus as a thief and transforms Primus into a mule. Chesnutt uses this transformation to reveal Primus' personality. As a mule, Primus displays jealousy when other men show an attraction to his woman, Sally. The mule's reaction is one of shocking violence in instances when Sally is approached by other men. The mule has a tremendous appetite for food and drink, an apparent compensation for his unhappiness. Laying the foundation for his exemplum, Chesnutt brings these human foibles to the forefront and illustrates the consequences of even the mildest appearance of dishonesty.

The conjurer's character is also developed more fully as the story progresses. After attending a religious revival, he becomes ill, confesses his act of vengeance, and repents. During the conjurer's metamorphosis, Chesnutt captures the remorse, grief, and forgiveness in this character. He also reveals the benefits of human compassion and concern for other human beings. A hardened heart undergoes reform and develops an ability to demonstrate sensitivity. Nevertheless, the conjurer suffers the consequences of his evil deed: he is mistakenly given poison by a companion and he dies before he completely restores Primus' human features, a deed he undertakes after repenting. The conjurer dies prematurely, and Primus lives with a clubfoot for the rest of his life.

Features of Chesnutt's more mature writing emerge in the series of narratives which make up *The Wife of His Youth and Other Stories of the Color Line.* The stories in this collection center on the identity crisis experienced by African Americans, portraying their true human qualities in the face of the grotesque distortions wrought by racism. In order to achieve his goal, Chesnutt abandons his earlier imaginative posture and embraces realism as a means to unfold his message. The dimensions of his characters are therefore appropriately self-revealing. The characters respond to the stresses and pressures in their external environment with genuine emotion; Mr. Ryder in "The Wife of His Youth" is no exception.

"The Wife of His Youth" follows the structural pattern which appears to typify the narratives in the collection. This pattern evolves in three phases: crisis, character response, and resolution. The crisis in "The Wife of His Youth" is Mr. Ryder's attempt to reconcile his new and old ways of life. He has moved North from a Southern plantation and entered black middle-class society. Adapting to the customs, traditions, and mores of this stratum of society is a stressful challenge for Mr. Ryder. Tensions exist between his old life and his new life. He fears being unable to appear as if he belongs to this "blue vein" society and exposing his lowly background. This probable eventuality is his constant preoccupation.

The "blue veins" were primarily lighter-skinned blacks who were better educated and more advantaged than their darker counterparts. Relishing their perceived superiority, they segregated themselves from their brothers and sisters. It is within this web of social clamoring and essential self-denial that Mr. Ryder finds himself. The inherent contradictions of this lifestyle present a crisis for him, although a resolution is attained during the course of the narrative.

Mr. Ryder's efforts to fit into this society are thwarted when his slave wife appears at his doorstep on the day before a major social event that he has planned. He is about to introduce the Blue Vein Society to a widow, Mrs. Dixon, upon whom he has set his affections. The appearance of Liza Jane, his slave wife, forces Mr. Ryder to confront his new life. This situation also allows Chesnutt to assume his typically moralizing tone. Mr. Ryder moves from self-denial to self-pride as he decides to present Liza Jane to his society friends instead of Mrs. Dixon. The narrative ends on a note of personal triumph for Mr. Ryder as he proudly introduces the wife of his youth to society.

Chesnutt does not totally relinquish his allegiance to the use of myth in *The Wife of His Youth and Other Stories of the Color Line.* The myth of the ascent journey, or the quest for freedom, is evident in several stories in the collection, among them "The Passing of Grandison" and "Wellington's Wives." Following the structured pattern of crisis, character response, and resolution, "The Passing of Grandison" is a commentary on the newly emerging moral values of the postbellum South. Colonel Owens, a plantation owner, has a son, Dick, who is in love with a belle named Charity Lomax. Charity's human values reflect the principles of human equality and freedom, and the challenge that she presents to Dick Owens becomes the crisis of the narrative.

Dick is scheduled to take a trip North, and his father insists on his being escorted by one of the servants. Grandison is selected to accompany his young master. Charity Lomax challenges Dick to find a way to entice Grandison to remain in the North and receive his well-deserved liberation. Charity's request conflicts with the values held by Dick and Grandison. Dick believes that slave/master relationships are essential to the survival of the South. Grandison holds that servants should be unequivocally loyal to their masters.

In spite of Dick's attempts to connect Grandison unobtrusively with the abolitionist movement in the North, the former slave remains loyal to Dick. Grandison's steadfastness perplexes Dick because his proposed marriage to Charity is at risk if he does not succeed in freeing Grandison. After a series of faulty attempts, Dick succeeds in losing Grandison. Dick then returns home alone and triumphant. Grandison ultimately returns to the plantation. He had previously proven himself so trustworthy that goodwill toward him is restored. To make the characterization of Grandison realistic, however, Chesnutt must have him pursue his freedom.

In a surprise ending typical of Chesnutt, Grandison plans the escape of all of his relatives who remain on the plantation. They succeed, and in the last scene of the narrative, Colonel Owens spots them from a distance on a boat journeying to a new destination. "The Passing of Grandison" successfully achieves the social and artistic goals of *The Wife of His Youth and Other Stories of the Color Line.* Chesnutt creates characters with convincing human qualities and captures their responses to the stresses and pressures of their environment. While so doing, he advocates the quest for human freedom.

"Uncle Wellington's Wives" contains several of the thematic dimensions mentioned above. The story concerns the self-identity of the African American and the freedom quest. Wellington Braboy, a light-skinned mulatto, is determined to move North and seek his freedom. His crisis is the result of a lack of resources, primarily financial, to achieve his goal.

Braboy is portrayed as having a distorted view of loyalty and commitment. He justifies stealing money from his slave wife's life savings by saying that, as her husband, he is entitled to the money. On the other hand, he denies his responsibility to his slave wife once he reaches the North. He denies the legality of a slave marriage in order to marry a white woman.

Chesnutt takes Braboy on a journey of purgation and catharsis as he moves toward resolution. After being subjected to much ridicule and humiliation as a result of his mixed marriage, Braboy must honestly confront himself and come to terms with his true identity. Abandoned by his wife for her former white husband, Braboy returns to the South. This journey is also a symbolic return to himself; his temporary escape from himself has failed.

Milly, Braboy's first wife, does not deny her love for him, in spite of his previous actions. Milly receives and accepts him with a forgiving spirit. Chesnutt capitalizes on the contrast between Braboy's African and Anglo wives. The African wife loves him unconditionally because she has the capacity to know and understand him, regardless of his foibles. Braboy's Anglo wife was frustrated by what she considered to be irreparable inadequacies in his character and abandoned him.

In his character development, Chesnutt repeatedly sought to dispel some of the stereotypical thinking about African Americans. An example of his success in this effort is found in "Cicely's Dream," set in the period of Reconstruction. Cicely Green is depicted as a young woman of considerable ambition. Like most African Americans, she has had very little education and is apparently limited in her capacity to achieve. She does have, however, many dreams.

Cicely's crisis begins when she discovers a wounded man on her way home one day. The man is delirious and has no recollection of who he is. Cicely and her grandmother care for the man until his physical health is restored, but he is still mentally distraught. The tenderness and sensitivity displayed by Cicely keep the stranger reasonably content. Over a period of time, they become close and eventually pledge their love to each other. Chesnutt portrays a caring, giving relationship between the two lovers, one which is not complicated by any caste system which would destroy love through separation of the lovers. This relationship, therefore, provides a poignant contrast to the relationships among blacks during the days of slavery, and Chesnutt thereby exposes an unexplored dimension of the African American.

Typically, however, there is a surprise ending: Martha Chandler, an African-American teacher, enters the picture. She teaches Cicely and other black youths for one school term. During the final program of the term, the teacher reveals her story of lost love. Her lover had been killed in the Civil War. Cicely's lover's memory is jolted by the teacher's story, and he proves to be the teacher's long-lost love. The happy reunion is a celebration of purely committed love. Again, Chesnutt examines qualities in African Americans which had largely been ignored. He emphasizes the innate humanity of the African American in a natural and realistic way, combining great artistic skill with a forceful moral vision.

Other major works

NOVELS: *The House Behind the Cedars,* 1900; *The Marrow of Tradition,* 1901; *The Colonel's Dream,* 1905.

NONFICTION: *The Life of Frederick Douglass,* 1899; *The Journals of Charles W. Chesnutt,* 1993.

Bibliography

Andrews, William. "A Reconsideration of Charles Waddell Chesnutt: Pioneer of the Color Line." *College Language Association Journal* 19 (1975): 136-151. This article reevaluates the status of Chesnutt within the framework of the history of major African-American novelists and indicates that Chesnutt was one of the first African-American novelists to treat the problem of race relations in a manner that was necessary at the time. Andrews also states that Chesnutt was an excellent stylist and a good storyteller.

Brodhead, Richard H., ed. *The Journals of Charles W. Chesnutt.* Durham, N.C.: Duke University Press, 1993. The journals reveal that Chesnutt was less interested in writing as art than in writing as a means of accomplishing social justice; they also reveal the extent of his contact with poor, rural African Americans and what he learned from them and from his family.

Filetti, Jean. "The Goophered Grapevine." *Explicator* 48 (Spring, 1990): 201-203. Discusses the use of master-slave relationships within the context of storytelling and explains how Chesnutt's "The Goophered Grapevine" relates to this tradition. Indicates that one of Chesnutt's concerns was man's inhumanity to man, but the story is told from a humorous perspective with the newly freed slave outwitting the white capitalist.

Heermance, Noel. *Charles Chesnutt: America's First Great Black Novelist.* Hamden, Conn.: Archon Books, 1974. This book is a good introduction to the overall life and themes of Chesnutt. It discusses Chesnutt's short fiction, his novels, and his other writings, and it asserts that Chesnutt was the first great African-American novelist.

Render, Sylvia. *Charles W. Chesnutt.* Boston: Twayne, 1980. A good general introduction to the life and writing of Charles Chesnutt. Render discusses Chesnutt's major concerns with narrative technique, social justice, and the place of the African American in American society.

_____. *The Short Fiction of Charles Chesnutt.* Washington, D.C.: Howard University Press, 1974. Discusses the collected short fiction of Chesnutt and indicates that it came out of the storytelling tradition of African Americans and was written within the conventions of local humor that was popular at the time.

Patricia A. R. Williams
(Revised by *Earl Paulus Murphy*)

G. K. CHESTERTON

Born: London, England; May 29, 1874
Died: Beaconsfield, England; June 14, 1936

Principal short fiction · *The Tremendous Adventures of Major Brown*, 1903 · *The Club of Queer Trades*, 1905 · *The Man Who Was Thursday*, 1908 · *The Innocence of Father Brown*, 1911 · *The Wisdom of Father Brown*, 1914 · *The Perishing of the Pendragons*, 1914 · *The Man Who Knew Too Much and Other Stories*, 1922 · *Tales of the Long Bow*, 1925 · *The Incredulity of Father Brown*, 1926 · *The Secret of Father Brown*, 1927 · *Stories*, 1928 · *The Sword of Wood*, 1928 · *The Moderate Murder and the Honest Quack*, 1929 · *The Poet and the Lunatic: Episodes in the Life of Gabriel Gale*, 1929 · *Four Faultless Felons*, 1930 · *The Ecstatic Thief*, 1930 · *The Floating Admiral*, 1931 (with others) · *The Scandal of Father Brown*, 1935 · *The Paradoxes of Mr. Pond*, 1936 · *The Vampire of the Village*, 1947

Other literary forms · From 1901 until his death in 1936, G. K. Chesterton worked as a journalist in London. He was a prolific essayist and literary critic, and his 1909 book on his close friend George Bernard Shaw is still held in the highest esteem. He wrote several volumes of poetry, foremost of which was his 1911 *The Ballad of the White Horse*. After his conversion to Catholicism in 1922, he became a fervent but tactful apologist for his new faith. His 1925 book *The Everlasting Man* and his 1933 study on Thomas Aquinas reveal the depth of his insights into the essential beliefs of Catholicism. His *Autobiography* was published posthumously in late 1936.

Achievements · Chesterton was a man of letters in the finest sense of the term. He expressed effectively and eloquently his ideas on a wide variety of literary, social, and religious topics. He was a master of paradox and always encouraged his readers to reflect on the subtle differences between appearance and reality. Reading his well-crafted short stories is a stimulating aesthetic experience because he makes readers think about the moral implications of what they are reading.

Although his critical writings on literature and religion reveal the depth of his intellect, Chesterton's major achievement was in the field of detective fiction. Between 1911 and 1935, he published five volumes of short stories in which his amateur sleuth is a Catholic priest named Father Brown. Unlike such famous fictional detectives as Arthur Conan Doyle's

Sherlock Holmes and Edgar Allan Poe's Auguste Dupin, Father Brown relied not on deductive reasoning but rather on intuition in order to solve perplexing crimes. Father Brown made judicious use of his theological training in order to recognize the specious reasoning of criminals and to lead them to confess their guilt. His Father Brown stories explored moral and theological topics not previously treated in detective fiction.

Biography · Gilbert Keith Chesterton was born on May 29, 1874, in London. He was the second of three children born to Edward and Marie Louise Chesterton. Edward Chesterton was a real estate salesman. Gilbert's older sister, Beatrice, died at the age of eight, in 1877, and two years later his brother, Cecil, was born. Everything seems to indicate that Edward and Marie Louise were loving parents.

In 1892, Gilbert was graduated from St. Paul's School in London. For the next three years, he studied at London's Slade Art School, but he finally realized that he would never develop into a truly creative artist. From 1895 until 1900, he worked for a publishing firm. From 1901 until his death, in 1936, he served as a journalist and editor for various London newspapers and magazines.

In 1901, he married Frances Blogg. Gilbert and Frances had no children. Theirs was a good marriage, each helping the other. Frances survived her husband by two years. During the first decade of the twentieth century, Chesterton met the writers Hilaire Belloc and Shaw, who became his lifelong friends. Although Belloc and Shaw seemed to have little in common because Belloc was an apologist for Catholicism and Shaw was an agnostic, Chesterton liked them both very much. Several times, Belloc organized lively but good-natured debates in which Shaw and Chesterton discussed religion and politics. Throughout his adult life, Chesterton supported the Liberal Party in Great Britain, but gradually he became disillusioned with the leadership of the Liberal prime minister David Lloyd George. After the coalition government run by Lloyd George fell apart in 1922, Chesterton lost much interest in politics. During the last fourteen years of his life, his major interests were literature and religion.

Before World War I began, Chesterton was already a well-known English writer, but he had not yet explored profound philosophical and religious themes. Two unexpected events forced Chesterton to think about his mortality and the reasons for his existence. In late 1914, he fell into a coma, which lasted four months. The cause of this coma was never fully explained to the public. After his recovery, he was a changed man. His view of the world became very serious. Then, less than one month after the end of World War I, Chesterton suffered a terrible personal loss when his only brother, Cecil, died from nephritis in a military hospital in France.

After Cecil's death, Chesterton felt a void in his life. His friend Father John O'Connor, who was the apparent inspiration for Father Brown, spoke to him at length about Catholicism, and Chesterton became a Catholic on July 30, 1922. Four years later, his wife Frances joined him in the Catholic church. The last decade of his life was a very productive period. He continued to write his Father Brown stories, but he also found much pleasure in writing and giving speeches on religious topics. Although firmly convinced that Catholicism was essential for his own spiritual growth and salvation, he was always tolerant and respectful of friends such as H. G. Wells and Shaw, who did not share his religious beliefs. Soon after he had completed his *Autobiography* in early 1936, he developed serious heart problems. He died at his home in Beaconsfield, England, on June 14, 1936, at the age of sixty-two.

Analysis · Before he began writing his Father Brown stories, G. K. Chesterton had already published one book of detective fiction. In *The Man Who Was Thursday*, Chesterton created a detective named Gabriel Syme, who infiltrates an anarchist group in which each of the seven members is named for a different day of the week. Syme replaces the man who had been Thursday. At first, this group seems strange to Syme because he does not understand what the anarchists wish to accomplish. This paradox is resolved when Chesterton explains that all seven "anarchists" were, in fact, detectives assigned separately to investigate this nonexistent threat to society. Although *The Man Who Was Thursday* does demonstrate Chesterton's ability to think clearly in order to resolve a problem, the solution to this paradox is so preposterous that many readers have wondered why Chesterton wrote this book, whose ending is so odd. It is hardly credible that all seven members of a secret organization could be police officers. Critics have not been sure how they should interpret this work. Chesterton's own brother, Cecil, thought that it expressed an excessively optimistic view of the world, but other reviewers criticized *The Man Who Was Thursday* for its pessimism. This book lacked a central focus.

In his Father Brown stories, this problem of perspective does not exist because it is the levelheaded Father Brown who always explains the true significance of scenes and events that had mystified readers and other characters as well. The other characters, be they detectives, criminals, suspects, or acquaintances of the victim, always come to the conclusion that Father Brown has correctly solved the case.

In his 1927 short story "The Secret of Father Brown," Chesterton describes the two basic premises of his detective. First, Father Brown is very suspicious of any suspect who utilizes specious reasoning or expresses insincere religious beliefs. Father Brown senses intuitively that a character who reasons incorrectly might well be a criminal. Second, Father Brown strives to "get inside" the mind of "the murderer" so completely that he is "thinking his thoughts, wrestling with his passions." Father Brown needs to understand what drives the guilty party to commit a specific crime before he can determine who the criminal is and how the crime was committed.

Most critics believe that the best Father Brown stories are those that were published in Chesterton's 1911 volume *The Innocence of Father Brown*. Although his later Father Brown stories should not be neglected, his very early stories are ingenious and have remained popular with generations of readers. Several stories in *The Innocence of Father Brown* illustrate nicely how Father Brown intuitively and correctly solves crimes.

In "The Blue Cross," Aristide Valentin (the head of the Paris police) is sent to London to arrest a notorious thief named Flambeau, who is a master of disguises. Valentin knows that Flambeau is well over six feet tall, but he does not know how Flambeau is dressed. As Valentin is walking through London, his attraction is suddenly drawn to two Catholic priests. One is short and the other is tall. The short priest acts strangely so that he would attract attention. He deliberately throws soup on a wall in a restaurant, upsets the apples outside of a grocery store, and breaks a window in another restaurant. This odd behavior disturbs the merchants, who, consequently, ask police officers to follow the priests, who are walking toward the Hampstead Heath. Readers soon learn that the short priest wants to be followed for his own protection. Just as the tall priest, who is, in fact, Flambeau, orders Father Brown, the short priest, to turn over a sapphire cross that he was carrying to a church in Hampstead, Father Brown tells him that "two strong policemen" and Valentin are waiting behind a tree in order to arrest Flambeau. The astonished Flambeau asks Father Brown how he knew that he was not a real priest. Readers learn that Father Brown's suspicion began when, earlier in the story, the tall priest affirmed that only "modern infidels appeal to reason," whereas true Catholics have no use for it. Father Brown tells Flambeau: "You attacked reason. It's bad theology." His intuition told him that his tall companion could not have been a priest, and he was right.

Father Brown is not merely an amateur detective. He is above all a priest whose primary responsibility is to serve as a spiritual guide to upright people and sinners alike. Although he brought about Flambeau's arrest, Flambeau soon turned away from a life of crime. After his release from prison, he became a private detective, and his closest friend became Father

Brown. This transformation can be attributed only to the religious teaching that Flambeau received from his spiritual mentor, Father Brown.

The tenth story in *The Innocence of Father Brown* is entitled "The Eye of Apollo." At the beginning of this short story, Flambeau has just opened his detective agency in a new building located near Westminster Abbey. The other tenants in the building are a religious charlatan named Kalon, who claims to be "the New Priest of Apollo," and two sisters, who are typists. Flambeau and Father Brown instinctively distrust Kalon, who has installed a huge eye of Apollo outside his office. Pauline Stacey, the elder of the two sisters, is attracted to Kalon, whom Joan Stacey dislikes intensely. One afternoon, Pauline falls down an elevator shaft and dies. Flambeau concludes hastily that this was an accident, but Father Brown wants to examine her death more thoroughly. He and Flambeau decide to talk with Kalon before the police officers arrive. Kalon presents the preposterous argument that his "religion" favors life, whereas Christianity is concerned only with death. Father Brown becomes more and more convinced that Kalon is a murderer. To the astonishment of Flambeau, Father Brown proves that Pauline "was murdered while she was alone." Pauline was blind, and Kalon knew it. As Kalon was waiting in the elevator, he called Pauline, but suddenly he moved the elevator, and the blind Pauline fell into the open shaft. Flambeau wonders, however, why Kalon killed her. Readers learn that Pauline had told Kalon that she was going to change her will and leave her fortune of five hundred thousand pounds to him. Kalon did not realize, however, that her pen had run out of ink before she could finish writing her will. When he first hears Kalon speak, Father Brown knows instantly that this hypocrite is a criminal. At the end of the story, he tells Flambeau: "I tell you I knew he [Kalon] had done it even before I knew what he had done." Once again Father Brown's intuition is perfectly correct.

Father Brown has the special ability to recognize the true meaning of seemingly insignificant clues, which other characters see but overlook. In *The Innocence of Father Brown*, there are two other stories, "The Secret Garden" and "The Hammer of God," that illustrate the effectiveness of Father Brown's powers of intuition and that also contain rather unexpected endings. Just like in "The Blue Cross," Valentin and Father Brown are major characters in "The Secret Garden." As the head of the Paris police, Valentin has been so successful in arresting criminals that many men whom he sent to prison have threatened to kill him as soon as they regain their freedom. For his own protection, Valentin has very high walls built around his garden, with the only access to it being through his house. His servants guard the entrance to his house at all times. One evening, Valentin holds a reception, which is attended by Father Brown, a medical doctor, an American philanthropist named Julius Brayne, Commandant O'Brien from the French Foreign Legion, Lord and Lady Galloway, and their adult daughter Lady Margaret. Father Brown learns that Valentin is especially suspicious of all organized religions, especially Catholicism, and Julius Brayne likes to contribute huge sums of money to various religions. During the party, a body with a severed head is found in the garden. All the guests are mystified because the head found next to the body does not belong to any of Valentin's servants or to any of the guests.

After much reflection on this apparent paradox, Father Brown proves that the head and the body belong to different men. The body was that of Julius Brayne, and the head belonged to a murderer named Louis Becker, whom the French police had guillotined earlier that day in the presence of Valentin, who had obtained permission to bring Becker's head back to his house. Valentin killed Brayne because of a rumor that Brayne was about to become a Catholic and donate millions to his new church. His hatred for Christianity drove Valentin mad. Father Brown explains calmly that Valentin "would do anything, *anything*, to break what he calls the superstition of the Cross. He has fought for it and starved for it, and now he has murdered for it." Valentin's butler Ivan could not accept this explanation, but as they all went to question Valentin in his study, they found him "dead in his chair." He had committed suicide by taking an overdose of pills. The ending of this short story is surprising because readers of detective fiction do not suspect that a police commissioner can also be a murderer.

In "The Hammer of God," readers are surprised to learn from Father Brown that the murderer is not a violent madman but rather a very respected member of the community. The Reverend Wilfred Bohun could no longer stand the scandalous behavior of his alcoholic brother Norman, who blasphemed God and humiliated Reverend Bohun in the eyes of his parishioners. Chesterton states that Wilfred and Norman Bohun belong to an old noble family whose descendants are now mostly "drunkards and dandy degenerates." Rumor has it that there has been "a whisper of insanity" in the Bohun family. Although Father Brown empathizes with Reverend Bohun, he nevertheless believes that he should express Christian charity toward his brother. When the body of Norman Bohun is found outside his brother's church, Father Brown begins to examine the case. Father Brown finally comes to the conclusion that Reverend Bohun killed his brother by dropping a hammer on him from the church tower. The murderer tried to frame the village idiot because he knew that the courts would never hold an idiot responsible for murder. At the end of this story, Reverend Bohun and Father Brown have a long conversation, and Father Brown dissuades Reverend Bohun from committing suicide because "that door leads to hell." He persuades him instead to confess his sin to God and admit his guilt to the police. In prison, Reverend Bohun, like Flambeau, may find salvation. In both "The Blue Cross" and "The Hammer of God," Father Brown hates the crime but loves the sinner. Readers are left with the definite impression that Father Brown is absolutely essential for the spiritual growth and eventual salvation of Flambeau and Reverend Bohun.

Several critics have remarked that the character of Father Brown did not change much in the four volumes of detective fiction that Chesterton wrote after *The Innocence of Father Brown*. This stability represents, however, strength and not weakness. It would have been inappropriate for a member of the clergy to have stopped caring about the spiritual life of others. Father Brown knows that evil exists in the world, but he also believes that even sinners and murderers can be reformed in this life and saved in the next. Father Brown is a fascinating fictional detective who uses his own religious beliefs in order to solve crimes and express profound insights into the dignity of every person.

Other major works

NOVELS: *The Napoleon of Notting Hill*, 1904; *The Man Who Was Thursday: A Nightmare*, 1908; *The Ball and the Cross*, 1909; *Manalive*, 1912; *The Flying Inn*, 1914; *The Return of Don Quixote*, 1926.

PLAYS: *Magic: A Fantastic Comedy*, 1913; *The Judgment of Dr. Johnson*, 1927; *The Surprise*, 1953.

POETRY: *Greybeards at Play: Literature and Art for Old Gentlemen—Rhymes and Sketches*, 1900; *The Wild Knight and Other Poems*, 1900, revised 1914; *The Ballad of the White Horse*, 1911; *A Poem*, 1915; *Poems*, 1915; *Wine, Water, and Song*, 1915; *Old King Cole*, 1920; *The Ballad of St. Barbara and Other Verses*, 1922; *Poems*, 1925; *The Queen of Seven Swords*, 1926; *Gloria in Profundis*, 1927; *Ubi Ecclesia*, 1929; *The Grave of Arthur*, 1930.

NONFICTION: *The Defendant*, 1901; *Twelve Types*, 1902 (revised as *Varied Types*, 1903; also as *Simplicity and Tolstoy*); *Thomas Carlyle*, 1902; *Robert Louis Stevenson*, 1902 (with W. Robertson Nicoll); *Leo Tolstoy*, 1903 (with G. H. Perris and Edward Garnett); *Charles Dickens*, 1903 (with F. G. Kitton); *Robert Browning*, 1903; *Tennyson*, 1903 (with Richard Garnett); *Thackeray*, 1903 (with Lewis Melville); *G. F. Watts*, 1904; *Heretics*, 1905; *Charles Dickens: A Critical Study*, 1906; *All Things Considered*, 1908; *Orthodoxy*, 1908; *George Bernard Shaw*, 1909, revised 1935; *Tremendous Trifles*, 1909; *What's Wrong with the World*, 1910; *Alarms and Discursions*, 1910; *William Blake*, 1910; *The Ultimate Lie*, 1910; *Appreciations and Criticisms of the Works of Charles Dickens*, 1911; *A Defence of Nonsense and Other Essays*, 1911; *The Future of Religion: Mr. G. K. Chesterton's Reply to Mr. Bernard Shaw*, 1911; *The Conversion of an*

Anarchist, 1912; *A Miscellany of Men,* 1912; *The Victorian Age in Literature,* 1913; *Thoughts from Chesterton,* 1913; *The Barbarism of Berlin,* 1914; *London,* 1914 (with Alvin Langdon Coburn); *Prussian Versus Belgian Culture,* 1914; *Letters to an Old Garibaldian,* 1915; *The So-Called Belgian Bargain,* 1915; *The Crimes of England,* 1915; *Divorce Versus Democracy,* 1916; *Temperance and the Great Alliance,* 1916; *A Shilling for My Thoughts,* 1916; *Lord Kitchener,* 1917; *A Short History of England,* 1917; *Utopia of Usurers and Other Essays,* 1917; *How to Help Annexation,* 1918; *Irish Impressions,* 1920; *The Superstition of Divorce,* 1920; *Charles Dickens Fifty Years After,* 1920; *The Uses of Diversity,* 1920; *The New Jerusalem,* 1920; *Eugenics and Other Evils,* 1922; *What I Saw in America,* 1922; *Fancies Versus Fads,* 1923; *St. Francis of Assisi,* 1923; *The End of the Roman Road: A Pageant of Wayfarers,* 1924; *The Superstitions of the Sceptic,* 1925; *The Everlasting Man,* 1925; *William Cobbett,* 1925; *The Outline of Sanity,* 1926; *The Catholic Church and Conversion,* 1926; *A Gleaming Cohort, Being from the Words of G. K. Chesterton,* 1926; *Social Reform Versus Birth Control,* 1927; *Culture and the Coming Peril,* 1927; *Robert Louis Stevenson,* 1927; *Generally Speaking,* 1928 (essays); *Do We Agree? A Debate,* 1928 (with George Bernard Shaw); *The Thing,* 1929; *G. K. C. a M. C., Being a Collection of Thirty-seven Introductions,* 1929; *The Resurrection of Rome,* 1930; *Come to Think of It,* 1930; *The Turkey and the Turk,* 1930; *At the Sign of the World's End,* 1930; *Is There a Return to Religion?,* 1931 (with E. Haldeman-Julius); *All Is Grist,* 1931; *Chaucer,* 1932; *Sidelights on New London and Newer York and Other Essays,* 1932; *Christendom in Dublin,* 1932; *All I Survey,* 1933; *St. Thomas Aquinas,* 1933; *G. K. Chesterton,* 1933 (also as *Running After One's Hat and Other Whimsies); Avowals and Denials,* 1934; *The Well and the Shallows,* 1935; *Explaining the English,* 1935; *As I Was Saying,* 1936; *Autobiography,* 1936; *The Man Who Was Chesterton,* 1937; *The End of the Armistice,* 1940; *The Common Man,* 1950; *The Glass Walking-Stick and Other Essays from the "Illustrated London News," 1905-1936,* 1955; *Lunacy and Letters,* 1958; *Where All Roads Lead,* 1961; *The Man Who Was Orthodox: A Selection from the Uncollected Writings of G. K. Chesterton,* 1963; *The Spice of Life and Other Essays,* 1964; *Chesterton on Shakespeare,* 1971.

EDITED TEXTS: *Thackeray,* 1909; *Samuel Johnson,* 1911 (with Alice Meynell); *Essays by Divers Hands 6,* 1926; *G. K.'s,* 1934.

MISCELLANEOUS: *Stories, Essays, and Poems,* 1935; *The Coloured Lands,* 1938.

Bibliography

Clipper, Lawrence J. *G. K. Chesterton.* New York: Twayne, 1974. In this useful introduction to the works of Chesterton, Clipper does a fine job of describing the recurring themes in Chesterton's fictional and nonfictional writings. He analyzes very well Chesterton's poetry and literary criticism. Contains an excellent annotated bibliography.

Conlon, D. J., ed. *Chesterton: A Half Century of Views.* New York: Oxford University Press, 1987. Contains numerous short essays on Chesterton published during the first fifty years after his death. The wide diversity of positive critical reactions shows that not only his popular fiction but also his writings on literature and religion continue to fascinate readers.

Coren, Michael. *Gilbert, the Man Who Was G. K. Chesterton.* London: J. Cape, 1989.

Hollis, Christopher. *The Mind of Chesterton.* Coral Gables, Fla.: University of Miami Press, 1970. This especially thoughtful study explores above all Chesterton's evolution as a writer before his conversion to Catholicism in 1922. In his final chapter, entitled "Chesterton and His Survival," Hollis explains why Chesterton's work continues to fascinate readers who do not share his religious beliefs.

Hunter, Lynette. *G. K. Chesterton: Explorations in Allegory.* London: Macmillan, 1979. Examines with much sensitivity how Chesterton's writings on literature and religion contributed greatly to his intellectual and moral growth. Hunter argues persuasively that Chesterton's detective fiction represents his most creative contribution to literature. A well-annotated book.

Lauer, Quentin. *G. K. Chesterton: Philosopher Without Portfolio.* New York: Fordham University Press, 1988. This volume is a thought-provoking study of Chesterton's philosophical reflections on the uses and limitation of reason, Christian humanism, religious tolerance, and moral values.

Tadie, Andrew A., and Michael H. Macdonald, eds. *Permanent Things: Toward the Recovery of a More Human Scale at the End of the Twentieth Century.* Grand Rapids, Mich.: Wm. B. Eerdmans, 1995.

Ward, Maisie. *Gilbert Keith Chesterton.* New York: Sheed & Ward, 1943. This well-researched book remains the essential biography of Chesterton. Ward had full access to Chesterton's manuscripts and spoke with many people who had known him personally. Reveals much about his evolution as a writer and the importance of friendship in his life.

Edmund J. Campion

KATE CHOPIN

Born: St. Louis, Missouri, February 8, 1851
Died: St. Louis, Missouri, August 22, 1904

Principal short fiction · *Bayou Folk*, 1894 · *A Night in Acadie*, 1897

Other literary forms · In addition to the short stories which brought her some fame as a writer during her own lifetime, Kate Chopin published two novels, *At Fault* (1890) and *The Awakening* (1899), the latter of which was either ignored or condemned because of its theme of adultery and frank depiction of a woman's sexual urges. Chopin also wrote a few reviews and casual essays and a number of undistinguished poems.

Achievements · Chopin's short stories, published in contemporary popular magazines, won her fame as a local colorist with a good ear for dialect and as a writer concerned with women's issues (sexuality, equality, independence). After the publication of *The Awakening* in 1899, however, her popularity waned, in part because of the furor over the open treatment of adultery and sex in the novel. She wrote few stories after 1900, and her work was largely neglected until the rediscovery of *The Awakening* by feminist critics. Criticism of that novel and new biographies have spurred a new interest in her Creole short stories, which have been analyzed in detail in terms of their regionalism and their treatment of gender. Influenced by Guy de Maupassant, she did not exert any literary influence on later short-story writers, at least until the rediscovery of *The Awakening*.

Biography · Kate Chopin was born Katherine O'Flaherty in St. Louis, Missouri, in 1851. Her mother's family was Creole, descended from French settlers, and her father, a successful merchant, was an Irish immigrant. She was educated at the Academy of the Sacred Heart in St. Louis beginning in 1860, five years after her father's accidental death, and was graduated in 1868. In 1870, she married Oscar Chopin, who took her to live in Louisiana, first in New Orleans and later in Natchitoches Parish, the setting for many of her stories. In 1882, Oscar died of swamp fever; Kate Chopin managed her husband's properties for a year and in 1884 returned to St. Louis. The next year her mother died, and in 1888 Chopin began writing out of a need for personal expression and to help support her family financially. Her stories appeared regularly in popular periodicals, and she published a novel, *At Fault*, in 1890. *Bayou Folk*, a collection of stories and sketches, appeared in 1894, the year her widely anthologized "The Story of an Hour" was written. *A Night in Acadie* followed, and she was identified as one of four outstanding literary figures in St. Louis by the *Star-Times.* Her celebrated novel, *The Awakening,* received hostile reviews that upset her, though reports about the book being banned were greatly exaggerated. She did, however, write relatively little after this controversy and died five years later in St. Louis, where she was attending the world's fair.

Analysis · Until recently, Chopin was known best literarily, if at all, as a "local colorist," primarily for her tales of life in New Orleans and rural Louisiana. Chopin manages in these stories (about two-thirds of her total output) to bring to life subtly the settings and personalities of her characters, usually Creoles (descendants of the original French settlers of Louisiana) or Cajuns (or Acadians, the French colonists who were exiled to Louisiana following the British conquest of Nova Scotia). What makes Chopin especially important for modern readers, however, is her insight into human characters and relationships in the context of their societies whether Creole, Cajun, or Anglo-Saxon—and into the social, emotional, and sexual roles of women within those societies.

Chopin's desire and hope for female independence can be seen in two

of her earliest stories, "Wiser Than a God" and "A Point at Issue!" (both 1889). In the first story, the heroine Paula Von Stoltz rejects an offer of marriage in order to begin a successful career as a concert pianist because music is the true sole passion of her life; it is an act which anticipates the actions of Edna Pontellier in *The Awakening.* In the second story, Eleanor Gail and Charles Faraday enter into a marriage based on reason and equality and pursue their individual careers in separate places. This arrangement works very well for some

Missouri Historical Society

time, but finally each of the two succumbs to jealousy; in spite of this blemish in their relationship, Chopin's humorous tone manages to poke fun at traditional attitudes toward marriage as well.

This questioning though humorous attitude is strongly evident in one of Chopin's most anthologized and best-known tales, "The Story of an Hour" (1894). Mrs. Mallard, a woman suffering from a heart condition, is told that her husband has been killed in a train accident. She is at first deeply sorrowful, but soon realizes that even though she had loved and will mourn her husband, his death has set her free: "There would be no powerful will bending hers in that blind persistence with which men and women believe they have a right to impose a private will upon a fellow-creature." As Mrs. Mallard descends the stairs, however, the front door is opened by her husband, who had never been on the train. This time her heart gives out and the cause ironically is given by the doctors as "the joy that kills."

It is in her Louisiana stories, however, that Chopin's sympathy for female and indeed human longings emerges most fully, subtly blended with a distinct and evocative sense of locale and folkways. "La Belle Zoraïde" (1893) is presented in the form of a folktale being told by a black servant, Manna-Loulou, to her mistress, Madame Delisle (these two characters also are central to the story "A Lady of Bayou St. John," 1893). The tale itself is the story of a black slave, Zoraïde, who is forbidden by her mistress to marry another slave with whom she has fallen in love because his skin is too black and her mistress intends her for another, more "gentlemanly" servant. In spite of this, and although the slave she loves is sold away, she bears his child and refuses marriage to the other slave. Her mistress falsely tells Zoraïde that her child has been born dead, and the slave descends into madness. Even when her real daughter is finally brought back to her, Zoraïde rejects her, preferring to cling to the bundle of rags which she has fashioned as a surrogate baby. From then on, "She was never known again as la belle Zoraïde, but ever after as Zoraïde la folle, whom no one ever wanted to marry. . . . She lived to be an old woman, whom some people pitied and others laughed at–always clasping her bundle of rags–her 'piti.'" The indirect narration of this story prevents it from slipping into the melodramatic or the maudlin. Chopin's ending, presenting the conversation of Manna-Loulou and Madame Delisle in the Creole dialect, pointedly avoids a concluding moral judgment, an avoidance typical of Chopin's stories. Instead, the reader is brought back to the frame for the tale and concentrated upon the charm of the Creole dialect even while he or she retains pity and sympathy for Zoraïde.

In spite of their Southern locale, Chopin's stories rarely deal with racial relations between whites and blacks. One important exception is

"Désirée's Baby" (1892). Désirée Valmondé, who was originally a foundling, marries Armand Aubigny, a plantation owner who is proud of his aristocratic heritage but very much in love with Désirée. He is at first delighted when she bears him a son, but soon begins to grow cold and distant. Désirée, puzzled at first, soon realizes with horror that her child has Negro blood. Armand, whose love for Désirée has been killed by "the unconscious injury she had brought upon his home and his name," turns her out of the house, and she disappears with her child into the bayou, never to be seen again. Later, in a surprise ending reminiscent of Maupassant, Armand is having all reminders of Désirée burned when he discovers a letter from his mother to his father which reveals that his mother had had Negro blood. In this story we see the continuation of Chopin's most central theme, the evil that follows when one human being gains power over another and attempts to make that person conform to preset standards or expectations.

As suggested earlier, Chopin finds that power of one person over another is often manifested in the institution of marriage. Yet, as even her earliest stories suggest, she does not always find that marriage necessarily requires that a wife be dominated by her husband, and she demonstrates that both men and women are capable of emotional and spiritual growth. That possibility for growth is perhaps best seen in the story "Athénaïse" (1895). Athénaïse, an emotionally immature young woman, has married the planter Cazeau, but has found that she is not ready for marriage. She runs back to her family, explaining that she does not hate Cazeau himself: "It's jus' being married that I detes' an' despise. . . . I can't stan' to live with a man; to have him always there; his coats and pantaloons hanging in my room; his ugly bare feet—washing them in my tub, befo' my very eyes, ugh!" When Cazeau arrives to bring her back, however, she finds that she has to go with him. As the couple rides home, they pass an oak tree which Cazeau recalls was where his father had once apprehended a runaway slave: "The whole impression was for some reason hideous, and to dispel it Cazeau spurred his horse to a swift gallop."

Despite Cazeau's attempt to make up and live with Athénaïse at least as friends, she remains bitter and unhappy and finally runs away again, aided by her romantic and rather foolish brother Montéclin. Cazeau, a sensitive and proud man, refuses to go after her again as though she too were a runaway slave: "For the companionship of no woman on earth would he again undergo the humiliating sensation of baseness that had overtaken him in passing the old oak-tree in the fallow meadow."

Athénaïse takes refuge in a boarding house in New Orleans where she becomes friendly with Mr. Gouvernail, a newspaper editor. Gouvernail hopes to make Athénaïse his lover, but he refrains from forcing himself on her: "When the time came that she wanted him . . . he felt he would have a right to her. So long as she did not want him, he had no right to her,—no more than her husband had." Gouvernail, though, never gets his chance; Athénaïse has previously been described to us as someone who does not yet know her own mind, and that such knowledge will not come through rational analysis but "as the song to the bird, the perfume and color to the flower." This knowledge does come to her when she discovers that she is pregnant. As she thinks of Cazeau, "the first purely sensuous tremor of her life swept over her. . . . Her whole passionate nature was aroused as if by a miracle." Thus, Athénaïse returns to reconciliation and happiness with her husband.

Chopin's story illustrates that happiness in a relationship can come only with maturity and with mutual respect. Cazeau realizes that he cannot force his wife to love him, and Athénaïse finally knows what she wants when she awakens to an awareness of her own sexuality. If Cazeau has to learn to restrain himself, though, Mr. Gouvernail learns the need to take more initiative as well; not having declared his love for Athénaïse he suffers when she goes back home. The tone of the entire story is subtly balanced between poignancy and humor, allowing us to see the characters' flaws while remaining sympathetic with each of them.

The importance of physical passion and of sexual self-awareness which can be found in "Athénaïse" can also be found in many of Chopin's stories and is one of the characteristics which make her writing so far ahead of its time. It is this theme which, as the title suggests, is central to her novel *The Awakening* and which was partly responsible for the scandal which that novel provoked. Chopin's insistence not merely on the fact of women's sexual desires but also on the propriety and healthiness of those desires in some ways anticipates the writings of D. H. Lawrence, but without Lawrence's insistence on the importance of male dominance.

Sexual fulfillment outside of marriage without moral judgments can be found in "The Storm," written in 1898, just before *The Awakening*, but not published until 1969. The story concerns four characters from an earlier tale, "At the 'Cadian Ball" (1892). In that earlier story, a young woman, Clarisse, rides out in the night to the 'Cadian Ball to declare her love for the planter Alcée Laballière. Alcée is at the ball with an old girlfriend of his, Calixta, a woman of Spanish descent. Clarisse claims Alcée and Calixta agrees to marry Bobinôt, a man who has been in love with her for some time.

"The Storm" is set several years later. Calixta and Bobinôt have had a child, and Alcée and Clarisse have been happily married. One day, while

Bobinôt and his son are out on an errand, a huge storm breaks out. Alcée takes refuge at Calixta's house, and the old passion between the two is rekindled; as the storm breaks about them in mounting intensity, the two make love, Calixta's body "knowing for the first time its birthright." While the storm mirrors the physical passion of the couple, neither it nor the passion itself is destructive. Where one would expect some retribution for this infidelity in a story, the results are only beneficial: Calixta, physically fulfilled, happily welcomes back her returning husband and son; Alcée writes to Clarisse, off visiting relatives, that he does not need her back right away; and Clarisse, enjoying "the first free breath since her marriage," is content to stay where she is for the time. Even today, Chopin's ending seems audacious: "So the storm passed and every one was happy."

Although written about a century ago, Chopin's stories seem very modern in many ways. Her concern with women's place in society and in marriage, her refusal to mix guilt with sexuality, and her narrative stance of sympathetic detachment make her as relevant to modern readers as her marked ability to convey character and setting simply yet completely. In the little more than a decade in which she produced most of her work, her command of her art grows ever stronger as does her willingness to deal with controversial subjects. It is unfortunate that this career was cut so short by the reaction to *The Awakening* and her early death; but it is fortunate that Chopin left us the writing that she did, and that it has been preserved.

Other major works

NOVELS: *At Fault*, 1890; *The Awakening*, 1899.

MISCELLANEOUS: *The Complete Works of Kate Chopin*, 1969 (Per Seyersted, editor, 2 volumes).

Bibliography

Bonner, Thomas. *The Kate Chopin Companion: With Chopin's Translations from French Fiction.* New York: Greenwood Publishing, 1988.

Boren, Lynda S., and Sara deSaussure Davis. *Kate Chopin Reconsidered: Beyond the Bayou.* Baton Rouge: Louisiana State University Press, 1992.

Koloski, Bernard, ed. *Approaches to Teaching Chopin's "The Awakening."* New York: Modern Language Association of America, 1988. Though the book is intended for English teachers, it provides an excellent overview of Chopin's novella. In addition to a bibliographical essay, the volume contains some twenty essays on the story by eminent Chopin scholars. Topics include women's language, mythic patterns, and symbolism and imagery. The latest critical approaches are represented.

Martin, Wendy, ed. *New Essays on "The Awakening."* New York: Cambridge University Press, 1988. While this slender volume includes only five essays, the previously unpublished articles are both lengthy and thought-provoking pieces by eminent scholars, some of whom (Martin and Elaine Showalter) are ardent feminists. Supplemented by an excellent bibliography of recent Chopin scholarship.

Seyersted, Per. *Kate Chopin: A Critical Biography.* Baton Rouge: Louisiana State University Press, 1980. (Originally published in 1969.) Seyersted's biography, besides providing invaluable information about the New Orleans of the 1870's, examines Chopin's life, views, and work. Provides lengthy discussions not only of *The Awakening* but also of her many short stories. Seyersted sees her as a transitional literary figure, a link between George Sand and Simone de Beauvoir.

Seyersted, Per, and Emily Toth, eds. *A Kate Chopin Miscellany.* Natchitoches, Louisiana: Northwestern State University Press, 1979. This volume contains some previously unpublished stories, some poems, two of Chopin's diaries, Chopin's letters and those written to her, and a translation of Cyrille Arnavon's introduction to a 1953 edition of *The Awakening.* Contains also an excellent annotated bibliography, arranged chronologically, of Chopin scholarship from 1890 to 1979, and several photographs of Chopin's family.

Skaggs, Peggy. *Kate Chopin.* Boston: Twayne, 1985. Skaggs reads Chopin's work in terms of the theme of the search for identity, which pervades the two chapters devoted to Chopin's short fiction. Also included in this helpful overview of Chopin's life and work are a biographical chapter, a chronology, and a select bibliography. The book is indispensable for readers of Chopin's short fiction.

Taylor, Helen. *Gender, Race, and Religion in the Writings of Grace King, Ruth McEnery Stuart, and Kate Chopin.* Baton Rouge: Louisiana State University Press, 1989. Taylor divides her chapter on Chopin between the novels and the short stories, some of which are given extensive feminist readings. Taylor focuses on Chopin as a local colorist who uses regional and historical themes to explore gender issues. The book is invaluable in its material on literary influences, particularly Guy de Maupassant, and the intellectual climate of the time.

Toth, Emily. *Kate Chopin.* New York: William Morrow, 1990. Toth's thoroughly documented, exhaustive work is the definitive Chopin biography. She covers not only Chopin's life but also her literary works and mentions many of the short stories in considerable detail. Toth updates Per Seyersted's bibliography of Chopin's work, supplies a helpful chronology of her life, and discusses the alleged banning of *The Awakening.* The starting point for Chopin research.

Donald F. Larsson (Revised by *Thomas L. Erskine*)

WALTER VAN TILBURG CLARK

Born: East Orland, Maine; August 3, 1909
Died: Reno, Nevada; November 10, 1971

Principal short fiction · *The Watchful Gods and Other Stories*, 1950

Other literary forms · In addition to his short stories, Walter Van Tilburg Clark wrote three novels—*The Ox-Bow Incident* (1940), *The City of Trembling Leaves* (1945), and *The Track of the Cat* (1949). The first and last of these were made into motion pictures. *Tim Hazard* (1951) is the enlarged version of *The City of Trembling Leaves*. Clark also produced an early book of poems, *Ten Women in Gale's House and Shorter Poems* (1932).

Achievements · Although Clark is known primarily for his novels, his one volume of stories, as well as his uncollected short stories, have established him as a fine writer of short stories. In fact, his "The Wind and the Snow of Winter" received the O. Henry Award in 1945. In their Western settings, their ambiguous depiction of the American dream, their concern about personal identity and oneness with nature, and their essentially tragic vision, the short stories are of a piece with his three novels. Unlike some "Western" writers, Clark used his landscape as both subject and backdrop for his own philosophical themes. Less concerned with characters—one story virtually omits them, concentrating instead on animals as "characters"—than with ideas, Clark used his characters, many of whom seem stereotypical, to embody and actualize his notions about the possibility of defining self and position in the cosmos.

Biography · Walter Van Tilburg Clark was born on August 3, 1909, in East Orland, Maine, the first child of Walter Ernest and Euphemia Abrams Clark. In 1917, his father, a distinguished economics professor, became president of the University of Nevada at Reno. Therefore, the family had to move when Clark was only eight. In Reno, Clark attended public schools and later received his B.A. and M.A. degrees in English from the University of Nevada. Clark married Barbara Morse in 1933, and they became the parents of two children, Barbara Ann and Robert Morse. The couple settled in Cazenovia, New York, where Clark began a career in high school and college teaching as well as creative writing. In the next several years, Clark continued writing and taught at several schools, including the University of Montana, Reed College, and the University of Nevada, where he resigned after protesting the autocratic tendencies of the administration.

He eventually returned there, however, to teach creative writing. Clark was also director of creative writing at San Francisco State College from 1956 to 1962. He died of cancer on November 10, 1971, at the age of sixty-two.

Analysis · Walter Van Tilburg Clark once wrote that the primary impulse of the arts has been religious and ritualistic—with the central hope of "propitiating or enlisting Nature, the Gods, God, or whatever name one wishes to give the encompassing and still mysterious whole." Certainly Clark's fiction attests to such a view. In a world in which thought is often confused and fragmented, he advocates for humanity a stance of intellectual honesty, an acceptance of instinctive values, and a belief in love. The key is human experience. As Max Westbrook so aptly put it in his study of Clark, "Clark's literary credo, then, is based on the capacity of the unconscious mind to discover and to give shape to objective knowledge about the human experience."

"The Buck in the Hills" may be Clark's clearest reflection in his stories of the literary credo mentioned above. Writing more or less in the terse, almost brittle, style of Ernest Hemingway, Clark opens the story with vividly descriptive passages of mountain scenery. The narrator, whose name the reader never learns, has returned to this setting after five years. It is really more than a return for him; it is a pilgrimage to a sacred place. Like Hemingway's heroes, he feels a deep need to replenish his spirit, to reattach himself to things solid and lasting. The clear sky, the strong mountains, and the cold wind all serve as a natural backdrop for the spiritual ritual of his pilgrimage. As he climbs toward the peak of a mountain, he recalls with pleasure an earlier climb with a dark girl "who knew all the flowers, and who, when I bet her she couldn't find more than thirty kinds, found more than fifty." On that day, as on this, the narrator felt a clear sense of the majesty of the mountains and the "big arch of the world we looked at," and he recalls spending two hours another time watching a hawk, "feeling myself lift magnificently when he swooped up toward me on the current up the col, and then balanced and turned above."

When he returns to his campsite by a shallow snow-water lake, he swims, naked, and as he floats in this cleansing ritual, looking up at the first stars showing above the ridge, he sings out "an operatic sounding something." At this point, just when his spiritual rejuvenation is nearly complete, the ritual is broken by the appearance of Tom Williams, one of the two men whom he had accompanied on this trip to the mountains. The plan had been for Williams and the other man, Chet McKenny, to spend a few days hunting, leaving the narrator alone. As he watches Williams approach, the narrator unhappily expects to see McKenny also, a man he dislikes not because of his stupidity but because of something deeper than that. Williams, however, is alone.

After a while Williams tells the narrator of the experience he has just had with McKenny, whom he calls a "first-rate bastard." During their hunt McKenny had purposely shot a deer in the leg so that he could herd it back to their camp rather than carry it. When they arrived at the camp, he slit the deer's throat, saying, "I never take more than one shot." Sickened by this brutal act, Williams drove off in his car, leaving McKenny to get out of the mountains as best he could. After Williams' story, both men agree that McKenny deserves to be left behind for what he did. In another cleansing ritual, they both take a swim, becoming cheerful later as they sit by their fire drinking beer. The next morning, however, it is snowing, and as they silently head back down the mountain, the narrator feels that there is "something listening behind each tree and rock we passed, and something waiting among the taller trees down slope, blue through the falling snow. They wouldn't stop us, but they didn't like us either. The snow was their ally."

Thus there are two contrasting moods in "The Buck in the Hills": that of harmony and that of dissonance. At the beginning of the story, the narrator has succeeded after five years in reestablishing a right relationship with nature and thus with himself, but at the end, this relationship has been destroyed by the cruel actions of McKenny. The narrator's ritual of acceptance of the primordial in man has been overshadowed by McKenny's ritual of acceptance that man is somehow above nature. Ernest Hemingway's belief that morality is what one feels good after is in one sense reversed here to the idea that immorality is what one feels bad after; certainly the narrator and Williams, on their way down the mountain, feel bad. Man and nature in a right relationship is not a mere romantic notion to Clark. It is reality—indeed, perhaps man's only reality.

In "The Portable Phonograph" Clark ventures, if not into science fiction, at least into a kind of speculative fiction as he sets his story in a world of the future, one marked by the "toothed impress of great tanks" and the "scars of gigantic bombs." It seems a world devoid of human existence; the only visible life is a flock of wild geese flying south to escape the cold of winter. Above the frozen creek in a cave dug into the bank, however, there is human life: four men—survivors of some undescribed Armageddon—huddle before a smoldering peat fire in an image of primitive existence. Clark provides little background of these four almost grotesque men. One, the reader learns, is a doctor, probably of philosophy rather than of medicine. One is a young musician, quite ill with a cough. The other two are middle-aged. All are obviously intelligent. The cave is the doctor's, whose name is Jenkins, and he has invited the others to hear him read from one of his four books–the Bible, *Moby Dick*, *The Divine Comedy*, and William Shakespeare. In selfish satisfaction he explains that when he saw what was happening to the world, "I told myself, 'It is the end. I cannot take much; I will take these.'" His justification is his love for the books and his belief that they represent the "soul of what was good in us here."

When Jenkins finishes his reading from *The Tempest*, the others wait expectantly; and the former finally says grudgingly, "You wish to hear the phonograph." This is obviously the moment for which they have been waiting. Jenkins tenderly and almost lovingly brings out his portable phonograph and places it on the dirt-packed floor where the firelight will fall on it. He comments that he has been using thorns as needles, but that in deference to the musician, he will use one of the three steel needles that he has left. Since Jenkins will play only one record a week, there is some discussion as to what they will hear. The musician selects a Debussy nocturne, and as Jenkins places the record on the phonograph, the others all rise to their knees "in an attitude of worship."

As the piercing and singularly sweet sounds of the nocturne flood the cave, the men are captivated. In all but the musician there occur "sequences of tragically heightened recollection"; the musician, clenching the fingers of one hand over his teeth, hears only the music. At the conclusion of the piece, the three guests leave–the musician by himself, the other two together. Jenkins peers anxiously after them, waiting. When he hears the cough of the musician some distance off, he drops his canvas door and hurries to hide his phonograph in a deep hole in the cave wall. Sealing up the hole, he prays and then gets under the covers of his grass bed, feeling with his hand the "comfortable piece of lead pipe."

Structurally a very simple story, "The Portable Phonograph" is rich in its implications. In a devastated world four men represent what Jenkins refers to as "the doddering remnant of a race of mechanical fools." The books that he has saved symbolize the beauty of man's artistic creativity as opposed to the destructiveness of his mechanical creativity. Again, Clark portrays two sides of man, that which aspires to the heights of human spiritual and moral vision and that which drives him on to his own destruction. The cruel and bitter irony is that essentially man's imagination is at once his glory and his undoing. As the men kneel in expectation before the mechanical wonder of the phonograph, they worship it as a symbol of human ingenuity. The music that comes from the record provides for at least three of the men a temporary escape from their grim reality. Thus, man's drive for mechanical accomplishment–the same drive that has destroyed a world–now has also preserved the beauty of his musical accomplishment. This may well be what the musician understands as he lets his head "fall back in agony" while listening to the music. Man is forever blessed to create and doomed to destroy. That is why the piece of lead pipe is such a protective comfort to Jenkins as he closes "his smoke-smarting eyes." In order to protect what is left of art, he must rely on the very methods that have brought about its demise.

In his excellent novel *The Track of the Cat,* Clark takes the reader into the realm of human unconscious as Curt Bridges, the protagonist, is driven to his own death while tracking both a real and an imagined cougar. In the short story "The Indian Well," set in the desert in 1940, Jim Suttler also seeks to kill a cougar, and although the mythological and psychological implications are not developed as fully as they are in the novel, the story is still powerful in its total effect. In what must be one of the best word pictures of the desert and the creatures that inhabit it, Clark devotes a half-dozen pages to the stark drama of life and death that takes place around a desert well; rattlesnakes, road runners, jackrabbits, hawks, lizards, coyotes, and a cow and her calf all play a part.

The story's only character is Jim Suttler, a grizzled old prospector who, with his mule Jenny, still seeks gold in abandoned and long-forgotten mines. Suttler is a man well-attuned to life in the desert wilderness. Armed with a rifle, an old six-shooter, and primitive mining tools, he is not merely a stereotyped prospector; his red beard and shoulder-length red hair might lead some to see in him a resemblance to Christ, but Suttler is unlike Christ in several ways. Early in the story, Suttler and Jenny arrive at Indian Well. The history of Indian Well is recorded on the walls of the rundown cabin nearby; names and dates go back to the previous century. All had used the well, and all had given vent to some expression, ranging from "God guide us" to "Giv it back to the injuns" to a more familiar libel: "Fifty miles from water, a hundred miles from wood, a million miles from God, and three feet from hell." Before Suttler leaves, he too will leave a message.

Finding some traces of gold in an abandoned mine near the well, Suttler decides to stay for a while to see if he can make it pay off. It is a comfortable time, and both he and Jenny regain some of the weight lost during their recent travels. Two events, however, change the idyllic mood of their stay. The first occurs when Suttler kills a range calf that, along with its mother, has strayed close to the well. While he has some qualms about killing the calf, Suttler, enjoying the sensation of providence, soon puts them out of his mind. Next, a cougar kills Jenny. This event enflames Suttler with the desire for revenge–even if "it takes a year"–so throughout the winter he sits up nights waiting for the cat to return. When he eventually kills it, he skins it and, uncovering Jenny's grave, places the skin over her carcass. His revenge complete, he cleanses himself at the well and leaves as a "starved but revived and volatile spirit." Thus, one more passerby has contributed to the history of Indian Well, and the life around the well goes on.

The basic element in "The Indian Well" is the ironic contrast between the beginning and the ending of the story, just as it is in "The Buck in the Hills." When they come upon Indian Well, Suttler and Jenny enter into a natural world that has its own ordered life and death, and they blend easily into it. Suttler appears to be a man at one with nature, yet at the end of the story, the death that he has inflicted upon the cougar stands as something apart from the ordered world of the well. It is a death that was motivated by the desire for revenge, a very human emotion. The reader might be suspicious when Suttler kills the calf, but he justifies such a killing on the basis of the meat that the calf provides. Killing the cougar, on the other hand, cannot be justified in any external way. The deep satisfaction that it brings to Suttler stands in opposition to any right relationship between man and nature; it is solely a part of Suttler's inner self. When the deed is done, Suttler can blend back into the natural world around him. For that one winter, however, as he lies in wait for the cougar, he exhibits man's all-too-common flaw of putting himself above the natural world. Still, because he knows what he has done and, moreover, accepts it, he is able once more to establish his relationship with the cosmic forces.

In a very real sense, this establishing of a relationship with the cosmic forces is the goal of many of Clark's characters. Caught in the ambiguities of good and evil, of morality and immorality, they struggle to maintain a faith in humanity and to bring moral law into accordance with natural law, for only in that way can man be saved from his own destructive tendencies. Some critics, such as Chester Eisinger, see Clark as being rather pessimistic regarding the success of such a human attempt at unity and attribute to him a desire to retreat from man. If this view is correct, then perhaps the story "Hook" is the best expression of what Clark wants to say. The main character in this story is a hawk who fulfills himself in flight, in battle, and in sex, until he is killed by a dog. His is a life cycle of instinct, and, as he lives it, he can easily enough be seen as an antihuman symbol. If Eisinger's view is wrong however, then it is possible to see Clark as a writer who seeks not a retreat from man, but an explanation of man. For, like the hawks that appear so often in Clark's stories, man is also a part of nature and because he is, it is possible to see his task as one of defining himself in the context of the natural order of things. Whatever the outcome, Clark's characters do make the attempt.

Other major works

NOVELS: *The Ox-Bow Incident,* 1940; *The City of Trembling Leaves,* 1945; *The Track of the Cat,* 1949; *Tim Hazard,* 1951.

POETRY: *Ten Women in Gale's House and Shorter Poems,* 1932.

NONFICTION: *The Journals of Alfred Doten, 1849-1903,* 1973 (3 volumes).

Bibliography

Eisinger, Chester E. *Fiction of the Forties.* Chicago: University of Chicago Press, 1963. Eisinger regards Clark's short stories as similar in theme (search for identity, desire to merge with nature, and rejection by nature) to the novels. While several short stories are mentioned in passing, Eisinger includes lengthy analyses of "The Buck in the Hills," "Hook," and "The Watchful Gods."

Laird, Charlton, ed. *Walter Van Tilburg Clark: Critiques.* Reno: University of Nevada Press, 1983. A collection of eighteen pieces, some by Clark himself, on Clark's life, his major published work, and his literary craftsmanship. The book is most valuable for the essays on "The Watchful Gods" and "The Pretender," essays that portray Clark as a reviser/craftsman, and for the autobiographical information and the detailed chronology provided by his son.

Lee, Lawrence L. *Walter Van Tilburg Clark.* Boise, Idaho: Boise State College Press, 1973. In his monograph, Lee devotes a separate chapter to the short stories, which he believes repeat the themes of the novels but with greater clarity and insight. "The Portable Phonograph" and "The Watchful Gods" are discussed in some detail. Supplemented by a helpful bibliography.

Westbrook, Max. "Walter Van Tilburg Clark and the American Dream." In *A Literary History of the American West,* edited by J. Golden Taylor. Fort Worth: Texas Christian University Press, 1987. Westbrook blends biography with criticism as he analyzes Clark's fiction and defines Clark's place in literary history. Using characters from stories and novels, Westbrook depicts the Clark "hero" as an idealistic dreamer incapable of practical action. As a result, the American dream, or its nightmarish counterpart, becomes a real concern for Clark.

_____. *Walter Van Tilburg Clark.* New York: Twayne, 1969. Westbrook's book remains the best overall assessment of Clark's literary work; in addition to a chronology of Clark's life, a biographical chapter, and a select bibliography, Westbrook includes a chapter on Clark's novella, *The Watchful Gods and Other Stories,* and several paragraph-length discussions of Clark's best short stories.

Wilton Eckley (Revised by *Thomas L. Erskine*)

JOSEPH CONRAD

Jósef Teodor Konrad Nalecz Korzeniowski

Born: Near Berdyczów, Poland (later Ukraine); December 3, 1857
Died: Oswalds, Bishopsbourne, England; August 3, 1924

Principal short fiction · *Tales of Unrest*, 1898 · *Youth: A Narrative, and Two Other Stories*, 1902 · *Heart of Darkness*, 1902 · *Typhoon, and Other Stories*, 1903 · *A Set of Six*, 1908 · *'Twixt Land and Sea*, 1912 · *Within the Tides*, 1915 · *Tales of Hearsay*, 1925 · *The Sisters*, 1928 · *The Complete Stories of Joseph Conrad*, 1933

Other literary forms · Joseph Conrad is best known for his powerful and psychologically penetrating novels, which, like his shorter fiction, are often set in exotic locales, frequently the Far East, at sea, or a combination of the two, as with his most famous work *Lord Jim: A Tale* (1900). Even when using a more conventional setting, such as London in *The Secret Agent: A Simple Tale* (1907), or Geneva, Switzerland, in *Under Western Eyes* (1910), Conrad maintains a sense of otherness because his characters live in a moral shadow world of revolutionaries and adventures.

In addition to three plays based on his stories, Conrad produced three volumes of autobiographical writings, which, however, often conceal more than they explain about his varied and often dramatic personal life. Following his death, several edited collections of Conrad's correspondence were published, and these letters offer some insight into his fiction.

Achievements · Conrad is one of the outstanding writers in English literature and, because of his background and achievements, occupies a unique position. To a great degree, Conrad was the creator of the psychological story and modern spy novel. Because of his genius and insight, Conrad transformed the typical setting of the adventure romance—the mysterious Far East, the shadowy underworld of the secret agent—into an acceptable setting for the serious writer and greatly expanded the range of English literature.

Conrad avoided direct narrative, presenting his plots as a tale told by someone who either recounted the events from memory or passed along a story heard from someone else. The narrator in a Conrad story also gives events obliquely, partially revealing them, speculating on their cause and possible meaning, and then adding new and often essential information, so that the reader must participate in interpreting the unfolding story.

Conrad used this method because he felt that it accurately reflected the manner in which people understand actions in real life but also employed it because of his characters, who cannot be understood quickly, for they are not simple persons. Complicated and often contradictory figures, their actions, like their personalities, must be apprehended gradually and from different angles.

A writer who did not learn English until his twenties, Conrad brought a sense of newness and scrupulous care to the language. He uses an extensive vocabulary, particularly in his descriptive passages of settings, internal as well as external. His style produces in the reader the moral and psychological equivalent to the emotions and inner struggles felt by the characters.

These qualities of plot, character, and style were recognized by the noted American critic H. L. Mencken when he wrote about Conrad that "[t]here was something almost suggesting the vastness of a natural phenomenon. He transcended all the rules."

Biography · Joseph Conrad had one of the most unusual lives of any major writer in English literature. He was born in Berdyczów, Poland, on December 3, 1857, and was christened Jósef Teodor Konrad Nalecz Korzeniowski. His father, Apollo Korzeniowski, was a Polish intellectual and writer whose works included original verse and translations of William Shakespeare. Apollo Korzeniowski was also a fervent Polish patriot, and his activities against Russian repression (Poland was at that time part of the Russian Empire) caused his arrest and exile in 1861. Apollo Korzeniowski, along with his wife, Ewelina Bobrowska, and his young son, Josef, were sent to Vologda, a dismal town northeast of Moscow.

The climate was severe, and living conditions were harsh. Ewelina died in April, 1865, when young Josef was only seven years old. A few years later, after Apollo had been released from exile because of ill health, he too died, and at eleven years old, Josef was placed in the care of his maternal uncle, a kindly man who provided for his education and supported him with funds for many years.

Because of these memories and his own intense patriotism, Josef found life in occupied Poland unbearable, and, when doctors recommended a seaside environment for his own frail health, he left for Marseilles, France, in October, 1874. In Marseilles, he lived on funds from his uncle and engaged in a shadowy enterprise to smuggle weapons to royalist rebels in Spain. In 1877, Josef and some companions bought a ship for that purpose, but their plot was betrayed and their vessel, the *Tremolino*, was deliberately run aground to avoid capture. The spring of the following year, having lost all of his money gambling at Monte Carlo, Josef attempted suicide. The wound was minor, and within a month he was able to sign aboard his first English ship, the *Mavis*. On April 24, 1878, Jósef Korzeniowski, soon known as Joseph Conrad, became an English sailor; he would remain one for the next seventeen years, serving on eighteen different vessels but commanding only one, the *Otago*, in 1888.

During these voyages, Conrad traveled to the settings for his stories. In

Courtesy of the Library of Congress

1883, he was second mate on board the *Palestine,* which caught fire and later sank, leaving the crew to survive in open boats until they reached land. In 1890, Conrad was in the Belgian Congo as part of a trading company, but within a year he left, his health seriously weakened by malaria and his psychological and moral sense severely shaken by the ruthless, amoral exploitation of the natives by Europeans who were avid for ivory.

By this time, Conrad had concluded that his seafaring career was unsuccessful, and he had already started work, in 1889, on his first novel, *Almayer's Folly* (1895), and achieved English citizenship in 1886. In January, 1894, Conrad ended his naval career, determined to become a writer. *Almayer's Folly* gained favorable critical notice, primarily for its exotic setting and characters. Conrad's next work, *An Outcast of the Islands* (1896), seemed to mark him as a talented but perhaps limited author of exotic romances. With the appearance of *The Nigger of the "Narcissus"* (1898), however, the literary world was forced to take note of a new and strikingly original talent.

Dedicated now to writing, Conrad settled at Pent Farm, in Kent, with his wife, Jessie George, to whom he was married on March 24, 1896. The Conrads had two sons, Alfred Borys, born in 1898, and John Alexander, born in 1906.

As an author, Conrad was critically acknowledged but was not very popular for many years. Even such powerful novels as *Lord Jim: A Tale* or *Nostromo: A Tale of the Seaboard* (1904) or *Under Western Eyes,* which today are recognized as classics, had relatively modest sales. To supplement his income, Conrad wrote shorter fiction for popular magazines; these stories were collected in eight volumes during Conrad's lifetime. In 1913 came his first truly popular work, *Chance.* Having achieved financial stability, Conrad moved in 1919 to Oswalds, near Canterbury, where he spent the remaining years of his life. He was offered, but declined, a knighthood in 1924. That same year, after long bouts of frequent bad health, he died of a heart attack on August 3. He was buried at Canterbury.

Analysis · Throughout his career, Joseph Conrad returned to a constellation of central themes that were expressed through the actions of his characters and, more important, through those characters' reactions to events around them. These themes can best be considered when they are grouped into two generally opposing categories. A sense of personal, moral heroism and honor is contrasted to betrayal and guilt. Typically, a Conradian character will discover, in the crucible of a dangerous situation, that he does or does not live up to the inner standards he has hoped to maintain.

This realization may not come immediately, and often the true meanings of a character's actions are revealed only long afterward, through a retelling of his story.

The second grouping contrasts illusion with reality. Illusion is often a belief in "progress" or some grand political scheme. It is unmasked by reality, which, in Conrad, inevitably assumes the form and tone of pessimistic irony. Through the device of a narrator recounting the story, the truth gradually emerges, revealing the tragic difference between what characters believe themselves and the world to be, and what it actually is.

The division between these two groupings is present even in Conrad's early story "An Outpost of Progress." Like many of his fictions, it is set in the tropics, specifically a desolate ivory trading station in the isolated reaches of the Congo. Two hapless Europeans, Kayerts and Carlier, arrive at the station, filled with dreams of riches and slogans of civilization. They quickly disintegrate, their original illusions giving way to true madness. Kayerts shoots his companion, then hangs himself from a cross in the station's unkempt graveyard. The outpost of progress has been overrun by the forces of savagery.

The story is fiercely ironic. Kayerts and Carlier are caricatures, the first fat, the second thin, both incredibly stupid. "Incapable of independent thought," as Conrad describes them, they are lost without society to dictate their thoughts and actions. Although they loudly repeat the hollow slogans of progress, the two white men are obviously greatly inferior to their native helper, who watches their decay with dark satisfaction. Using simple, unsympathetic characters and a violent, even melodramatic plot, Conrad presents his themes in the starkest possible fashion.

In the story "The Lagoon," written at almost the same time as "An Outpost of Progress," Conrad handles the conflict between betrayal and guilt, on the one hand, and guilt versus honor and heroism, on the other, with more subtlety. An unnamed white man spends the night in the house of Arsat, a young Malay, who is tending his dying wife. During the long tropical night, Arsat tells his friend the story of how he and his brother had fled with the woman from their local chief. The three had been pursued and, at the moment of their escape, Arsat's brother had fallen behind and cried out for help. Arsat had not responded, however, fleeing instead to safety with his lover. Now, when she is dead, he speaks of returning for revenge.

In a moment of crisis Arsat made a decision, and for years he has suffered the moral consequences of that action. Although Conrad refrains from judging his character, Arsat clearly believes that he has failed; his only hope is to perform some heroic action, such as seeking vengeance, that will restore his earlier sense of himself as an honorable, loyal person and brother. Implicit in the story, however, is the sense that Arsat cannot undo the past and that his hopes are only illusions. This sense is reinforced powerfully by Conrad's extensive descriptions of the Malaysian jungle, which seems to overwhelm the characters, rendering them incapable of action while mocking their vain hopes.

"Youth," Conrad's first indisputable masterpiece among his shorter fiction, introduces his famous narrator Marlow. In the story, Marlow, forty-two when he tells his tale, recounts events that happened twenty years before when he sailed on the *Judea*, laden with a cargo of coal for Bangkok. An ill-fated ship, the *Judea* is beset by an endless, almost comical series of calamities that climax when the coal catches fire and explodes, leaving the crew to reach land in open boats. The events are drawn largely from Conrad's own experiences as mate on the *Palestine* in 1881.

The contrasts between heroism and cowardice, between reality and illusion run throughout the story, but Conrad blends them in a fashion that reveals that the distinctions between them are not as simple as might be supposed. As Marlow recognizes, his earlier self was full of the illusions of youth, yet it was those very illusions that sustained him and allowed him to achieve the standards by which he wished to live and act. In that sense, illusion made heroism possible. Such a situation is obviously ironic, and throughout his story Marlow comments frequently on the tangled relationship between romanticism and practicality, illusion and reality. Unlike other Conrad tales, however, "Youth" does not treat this division with pessimism but with optimism, no doubt because it is a story of youth and because Marlow, for whatever reason, did uphold his personal standards of integrity and moral courage.

Heart of Darkness, perhaps Conrad's most famous work, is a novella based on his experience as mate on the riverboat *Roi des Belges* in the Congo during 1890. In this story, Conrad once again uses Marlow as his main character and narrator, and the events are a literal and symbolic journey by Marlow into that "immense heart of darkness" that is both the African jungle and the human soul. A powerful, searing work, *Heart of Darkness* is one of the first masterpieces of symbolism in English literature and Conrad's most acutely penetrating psychological study.

The story itself is relatively simple. Marlow signs on with a Belgian company that exports ivory from the Congo; employed as a mate on the company's steamboat, he sails upriver to meet the renowned Kurtz, a trader who has become legendary for the success of his efforts and the force of his character. Marlow has heard, however, that Kurtz is more than an ivory trader and that he has evolved into a powerful force of civilization and progress. When Marlow arrives at Kurtz's station, he finds instead that the man has reverted to savagery, becoming a dreaded, almost supernatural figure to the natives. The site is ringed with posts decorated with human skulls, and Kurtz's presence casts an evil presence over the African jungle. Marlow carries the sick, delirious Kurtz back down the river, but the man dies during the journey as the riverboat narrowly escapes an ambush by the terrified and outraged natives.

The impact of *Heart of Darkness* comes from the nearly devastating effects of what Marlow sees and experiences. A naïve young man in the earlier "Youth," Marlow is still relatively innocent at the start of *Heart of Darkness.* By the end of the story, that innocence has been forever shattered, a loss shared by the attentive reader. The world of the story grows increasingly corrupted and corrupting. The adventures Marlow undergoes become stranger, and the characters whom he meets are increasingly odd, starting with the greedy traders whom Marlow ironically describes as "pilgrims," to an eccentric Russian who wanders in dress clothes through the jungle, to Kurtz himself, that figure of ultimate madness. The native Africans, whether cruelly abused workers, actually slaves, of the trading company or savages in awe of Kurtz, retain a sort of primeval dignity, but they, too, are beyond Marlow's experience and initial comprehension. The Congo of *Heart of Darkness* is a strange and terrifying world, a place where the normal order of civilized life has become not only inverted but also perverted.

To render this complex and disturbing moral vision, Conrad uses an intricate framing structure for his narrative. The story opens with Marlow and four friends talking about their experiences. One of the listeners, who is never named, in turn conveys to the reader the story told by Marlow. This story-within-a-story shuttles back and forth, as Marlow recounts part of his tale, then comments upon it, and then often makes an additional reflection upon his own observations. In a sense, by retelling the events, Marlow comes to understand them, a process that is shared by the reader. Instead of interrupting the flow of the story, Marlow's remarks become an essential part of the plot, and often the reader does not fully understand what has happened until Marlow's explanations reveal the extent and significance of the action.

Heart of Darkness displays some of Conrad's most vivid and powerful writing, made especially telling by his use of symbolism. *Heart of Darkness* gains immensely by Conrad's use of symbolism, because much of the meaning of the story is too terrifying and bleak to be expressed in plain prose; the inhumanity and savagery of the European exploiters, Kurtz in particular, are expressed more powerfully through a symbolic, rather than overt, presentation. Throughout the narrative, clusters of images occur at significant points to underscore the meaning of events as Marlow comes to understand them. Opposites are frequent: brightness is contrasted with gloom, the lush growth of the jungle is juxtaposed to the sterility of the white traders, and the luxuriant, even alarming life of the wild is always connected with death and decomposition. Running throughout the story are images and metaphors of madness, especially the insanity caused by isolation. Of course, the dominant symbol for the entire work is found in its title and final words: all creation is a vast "heart of darkness." Since its publication, *Heart of Darkness* has been recognized as a masterpiece of English literature, and readers have responded to the work on several different levels. An attack on imperialism, a parable of moral and ethical growth and decline, a psychological study—*Heart of Darkness* is all these things and something more.

With the writing of "Typhoon," Conrad suspended his customary moral and psychological complexities to present a fairly straightforward sea story. The *Nan-Shan*, a vessel filled with Chinese coolies returning home from Malaysia, runs headlong into a ferocious typhoon. As the crew struggles above decks to save the ship, an equally dangerous furor erupts below, as the sea's violent motions scatter the passengers' baggage, mixing their hard-earned silver coins in total confusion. The Chinese begin a desperate combat among themselves, each man intent upon regaining his own money. Captain MacWhirr and his first mate, Jukes, must battle these two storms, either of which could wreck the ship.

Captain MacWhirr and Jukes are total opposites. MacWhirr is a stolid, perhaps stupid man, so devoid of imagination that he experiences little self-doubt and few terrors. Even the looming typhoon does not frighten him, since he has never experienced such a storm and cannot comprehend its dangers. Jukes, on the other hand, is a more typical Conradian character, sensitive, anxious to prove worthy of his own inner moral code, and acutely conscious of the dangers that the sea can pose. As with so many other figures in Conrad's fictions, Jukes seems to believe in a sense that these dangers are somehow meant for him personally, as a trial of his own character. MacWhirr, of course, suffers from no such beliefs, since they are beyond his comprehension.

With the onset of the typhoon, the seeming limitations of Captain MacWhirr become strengths, while Jukes's supposedly higher qualities might, if left unchecked, paralyze him at the critical moment. Ironically, MacWhirr is Jukes's salvation. Since the Captain lacks the imagination to realize that he should be afraid, he is therefore not afraid and continues in his plodding but effective fashion. Jukes, in order to live up to his moral code, has no choice but to follow, acting more bravely and coolly than his inner doubts might otherwise allow. Together, the two men lead the crew in heroic efforts that save the *Nan-Shan*.

The only complexity that Conrad employs in "Typhoon" is in his narrative structure. The story shifts from third person to passages of letters from Captain MacWhirr, Jukes, and the ship's engineer to their families. This second layer is overlaid by a third, in which the letters are read, sometimes with commentary, by the families in England. Through this method, Conrad allows the major characters to present the story as they experience and perceive it and adds a further contrast between the men who actually endure the storm and those who only read about it, and so cannot fully grasp its strength and danger.

"The Duel," sometimes titled "The Duellists," is the story of two officers in Napoleon Bonaparte's army, who wage their own private war for sixteen years, while about them all Europe is plunged into a larger, much more deadly combat. Conrad was an avid student of the Napoleonic period, and he based his story on an actual rivalry. More than the story of two men, "The Duel" is Conrad's reflections upon the Napoleonic age.

The two progatonists are Feraud from Gascony in southern France—a region noted for its hot-blooded, impetuous natives—and D'Hubert, a Picard, with the reserved nature characteristic of that northern region. Through an accidental incident, the two become engaged in an affair of honor that can be settled only by a duel. Once begun, the duel is protracted to farcical lengths, extending from Paris to Moscow, from the time of Napoleon's greatest triumphs to his final defeat at Waterloo. Finally, D'Hubert falls in love and marries, finding life more worthwhile than this questionable affair of honor. In the final encounter, he emerges victorious and spares Feraud's life on the promise that the combat will now, finally, end.

The tale is briskly and even comically rendered, with Conrad's typical ironies in this case turned positive. The darker aspects of his vision are reserved for his wider view of the Napoleonic age: what might be seen as humorous when only two men are involved becomes tragic almost beyond comprehension when entire nations are the duelists. Feraud and D'Hubert fight only themselves in their affair, while Napoleon engaged all the countries of Europe. At the end of that wider struggle, Conrad implies, there was no happy resolution, only the desolation that follows the exhausted silence of the battlefield. This bleaker vision, however, is not allowed to overwhelm the essentially humorous basis of the story.

The title of the work may contain a clue to one of its themes, the typical Conrad subject of the "double," the other person who is so like the hero yet somehow different. During the interminable encounters, D'Hubert comes to believe that he is linked, in some mysterious and unbreakable fashion, to Feraud. They are "secret sharers," in one sense literally so, because they cannot reveal that their duel began over a trivial misunderstanding and was prolonged out of fear of embarrassment. They are also "secret sharers" in a wider sense, because their lives have fullest meaning only when joined together. In this way, the "duellists" are indeed "dual," and their relationship is not only one of combat but also, in fact, one of union.

"Gaspar Ruiz" was based upon actual events in the Chilean revolution against Spain of the 1830's. The title character, an immensely strong but rather simpleminded peasant, joins the army of the rebels. Captured during battle, he is forced to join the Loyalist army and is then once again made a prisoner, this time by his former comrades. Condemned as a traitor, Gaspar Ruiz escapes and is sheltered by a Loyalist family whose daughter, Erminia, he later marries. A series of misadventures leads Gaspar to become a general in the Loyalist army, although his political sense is almost nonexistent and he wishes, as much as he can comprehend the matter, to be a Chilean patriot. When Erminia and her daughter are captured by the rebels and held in a mountain fort, Gaspar has a cannon strapped to his huge back so it can batter open the gate and free them. The desperate tactic works, but Gaspar is mortally wounded, and Erminia kills herself, dying with her husband.

The story is told in typical Conrad fashion—that is, long after the events have occurred and by two different narrators. One of them is General Santierra, who, as a lieutenant in the rebel army, knew Gaspar Ruiz and is now the guardian of Gaspar's grown daughter. The second narrator, who opens the story in the third person but who is revealed, at the close, to be a guest of General Santierra, answers questions that Santierra raises. This narrator explains that revolutions are a distillation of human experience and that they bring some human beings to fame who otherwise would be resigned to oblivion. In revolutions, genuine social ideals, such as freedom or equality, may be passionately held in the abstract but are ferociously violated in actuality, just as Gaspar Ruiz, a true if bewildered patriot, was condemned and made a traitor by circumstances and false accusations. In a sense, the unnamed guest is reinforcing a constant Conrad theme, the difference between reality and illusion.

Probably Conrad's most famous short story, "The Secret Sharer" is a deceptively simple tale that carries such deep, perhaps unfathomable moral and psychological undertones that since its publication readers and critics have remained puzzled and fascinated by its elusive, evocative power. In the story, a young captain, new to his first command, is startled to discover a naked man swimming by his ship's side. Once aboard, the swimmer, named Leggatt, confesses that he is fleeing from his own ship, the *Sephora*, because he murdered a fellow sailor. The act was justified, as the young captain quickly realizes, for the *Sephora* was in danger of foundering during a violent storm, and the murdered man, by failing to obey Leggatt's orders, had placed the ship and its crew in immediate danger. Now, however, Leggatt is a hunted man. The captain hides Leggatt in his own cabin, keeping him safely out of sight until he can sail his ship close enough to an island to allow Leggatt to escape.

By pledging and then keeping his word to the mysterious Leggatt, the young captain upholds his own moral code, even though it runs counter to conventional law and morality. In doing so, he proves that he is capable of living up to that "ideal conception of one's personality every man sets up for himself secretly." The fact that morality is established and maintained secretly—in this case, literally so—is a Conradian irony and a central paradox of this tale. Adding to the reader's bewilderment is the fact that the young captain's "ideal conception" is nowhere presented explicitly. The reader is able to see the captain's code in action and perhaps assess its consequences but must deduce from these tantalizing clues what must constitute the standards that the young officer so earnestly desires to uphold.

The captain's code is indeed a puzzling one, for not only does it require him to be faithful to a murderer, but also it causes him to risk his own ship. To give Leggatt the best possible chance to swim to safety, the captain steers dangerously close to shore, risking running aground or perhaps breaking up on the shoals. Naturally, he cannot tell his crew why he orders this difficult, dangerous maneuver, so another secret is layered upon those already present. When the captain is successful in his plan, for the first time he feels a sense of unity and closeness with his vessel, a mystical—and again, secret—bond.

The meanings of "The Secret Sharer" are hidden in its deceptively straightforward narrative. The work is full of ambiguity and possible double meanings, all presented in brisk, even prosaic fashion. Even the title is multiple: since Leggatt is unknown to anyone but the captain, his presence is indeed a secret, but he and the young commander also share common secrets, both Leggatt's presence and the "ideal conception of one's personality," which seems to be their joint moral code. Since these meanings are complementary, rather than contradictory, they add to the resonance of the story.

Other touches add to the story's depth. The young captain and Leggatt are so similar that they seem to be doubles, and Conrad obviously intends this identification to be as much moral as physical. Both men feel themselves to be outcasts, Leggatt actually so, because of his crime; the captain, psychologically, because of his newness to the ship and its crew. In one sense, Leggatt can be seen as an alter ego of the narrator, perhaps even a projection of his darker, maybe criminal, side. It may even be possible, as some critics have suggested, that Leggatt does not actually exist but is only a figment of the young captain's imagination.

Such an unusual, even implausible interpretation indicates the perplexity that "The Secret Sharer" elicits in readers and underscores why this story, so famous in itself, is also emblematic of all Conrad's fiction. Under the guise of a simple sea tale, he has gathered the themes that constantly flowed through his works; the ideal sense of self that must be tested and proved under difficult situations; the conflict between loyalty and betrayal, reality and illusion; and, above all, the innate need for human beings to preserve, even in trying circumstances and against conventional pressures, a moral code whose only reward is a secret that may, perhaps, never be shared.

Other major works

NOVELS: *Almayer's Folly*, 1895; *An Outcast of the Islands*, 1896; *The Children of the Sea: A Tale of the Forecastle*, 1897 (republished as *The Nigger of the "Narcissus": A Tale of the Sea*, 1898); *Lord Jim: A Tale*, 1900; *The Inheritors*, 1901 (with Ford Madox Ford); *Romance*, 1903 (with Ford Madox Ford); *Nostromo: A Tale of the Seaboard*, 1904; *The Secret Agent: A Simple Tale*, 1907; *Under Western Eyes*, 1910; *Chance*, 1913; *Victory: An Island Tale*, 1915; *The Shadow-Line: A Confession*, 1917; *The Arrow of Gold*, 1919; *The Rescue: A Romance of the Shadows*, 1920; *The Rover*, 1923; *The Nature of a Crime*, 1924 (with Ford Madox Ford); *Suspense: A Napoleonic Novel*, 1925 (incomplete).

PLAYS: *One Day More: A Play in One Act*, 1905; *The Secret Agent: A Drama in Four Acts*, 1921; *Laughing Anne: A Play*, 1923.

NONFICTION: *The Mirror of the Sea*, 1906; *Some Reminiscences*, 1912 (pb. in the U.S. as *A Personal Record*); *Notes on Life and Letters*, 1921; *Joseph Conrad's Diary of His Journey Up the Valley of the Congo in 1890*, 1926; *Last Essays*, 1926; *Joseph Conrad: Life and Letters*, 1927 (Gérard Jean-Aubry, editor); *Joseph Conrad's Letters to His Wife*, 1927; *Conrad to a Friend*, 1928 (Richard Curle, editor); *Letters from Joseph Conrad, 1895-1924*, 1928 (Edward Garnett, editor); *Lettres françaises de Joseph Conrad*, 1929 (Gérard Jean-Aubry, editor); *Letters of Joseph Conrad to Marguerite Doradowska*, 1940 (John A. Gee and Paul J. Sturm, editors); *The Collected Letters of Joseph Conrad: Volume I, 1861-1897*, 1983; *The Collected Letters of Joseph Conrad: Volume II, 1898-1902*, 1986; *The Collected Letters of Joseph Conrad: Volume III, 1903-1907*, 1988.

Bibliography

Batchelor, John. *The Life of Joseph Conrad: A Critical Biography.* Oxford, England: Blackwell Publishers, 1994.

Gillon, Adam. *Joseph Conrad.* Boston: Twayne, 1982. A solid introduction to Conrad's life and art, written by a native Pole. Provides relatively brief but insightful analysis of the more significant shorter works.

Graver, Lawrence. *Conrad's Short Fiction.* Berkeley: University of California Press, 1969. This study of Conrad's stories is grouped chronologically and displays the linkages between the shorter fictions and individual stories, and between them as a group and the novels. Since it covers the lesser-known stories as well as the more famous ones, it is essential for placing Conrad's development of themes and styles within a larger artistic context.

Leavis, F. R. *The Great Tradition.* London: Chatto & Windus, 1948. Leavis, one of the most distinguished of modern English literary critics, places Conrad within the scope of the English literary world, showing how he drew from, and added to, that heritage. An invaluable study for those trying to understand what Conrad might have been attempting in his writing and how he could have perceived his place within a wider literary context.

Meyers, Jeffrey. *Joseph Conrad: A Bibliography.* New York: Charles Scribner's Sons, 1991. A briskly moving, no-nonsense biography that surveys the key points and themes of the major works. Very good at placing Conrad within the social and intellectual milieu of his day and offering good insights from other literary figures, such as Ford Madox Ford, who significantly influenced Conrad's literary career.

Najder, Zdzislaw. *Joseph Conrad: A Chronicle.* Translated by Halina Carroll-Najder. Cambridge, England: Cambridge University Press, 1983. A thorough and sympathetic biography of Conrad written by a countryman. The volume stresses the influence of Conrad's Polish heritage on his personality and art. Najder draws many telling and intriguing parallels between Conrad's life and his writing.

Tennant, Roger. *Joseph Conrad: A Biography.* New York: Atheneum, 1987. Not a scholarly work, but a readable study that concentrates on Conrad's sea years and his later struggles with ill health and financial difficulties. Its main weakness is a lack of emphasis on Conrad's early and formative years in Poland, but, when used with Zdzislaw Najder's work (above), it can be helpful.

Watts, Cedric Thomas. *Joseph Conrad: A Literary Life.* New York: St. Martin's Press, 1989.

Michael Witkoski

ROBERT COOVER

Born: Charles City, Iowa; February 4, 1932

Principal short fiction · *Pricksongs & Descants,* 1969 · *Whatever Happened to Gloomy Gus of the Chicago Bears,* 1975 · *Hair o' the Chine,* 1979 · *A Political Fable,* 1980 · *Spanking the Maid,* 1981 · *In the Bed One Night and Other Brief Encounters,* 1983 · *A Night at the Movies,* 1987

Other literary forms · Besides the above-mentioned collections of short fiction and novellas and many uncollected short stories, Robert Coover's production includes several novels; a collection of plays entitled *A Theological Position* (1972), which contains "The Kid," "Love Scene," "Rip Awake," and the title play; several poems, reviews, and translations published in journals; a film script/novella *Hair o' the Chine*; and one film, *On a Confrontation in Iowa City* (1969). Coover has also published a few essays on authors he admires, such as Samuel Beckett ("The Last Quixote," in *New American Review,* 1970) and Gabriel García Márquez ("The Master's Voice," in *New American Review,* 1977).

Achievements · Coover is one of the authors regularly mentioned in relation to that slippery term "postmodernism." As a result of the iconoclastic and experimental nature of his fictions, Coover's work does not enjoy a widespread audience; his reputation among academics, however, is well established, and the reviews of his works have been consistently positive. Although in the beginning of his career he had to resort to teaching in order to support his family, he soon began to gain recognition, receiving several prizes and fellowships: a William Faulkner Award for best first novel (1966), a Rockefeller Foundation grant (1969), two Guggenheim Fellowships (1971, 1974), an Academy of Arts and Letters award (1975), and a National Book Award nomination for *The Public Burning* (1977). The publisher Alfred A. Knopf's rejection of this novel after initial acceptance for publication brought some notoriety to Coover. Since the novel deals with the trial of Ethel and Julius Rosenberg and presents former president Richard M. Nixon as its central narrator, the publisher thought it would be too controversial. Eventually, *The Public Burning* was published by Viking Press and became a Book-of-the-Month Club selection. Critical studies about Coover started in the late 1970's. Still, in spite of the critical acclaim and the considerable amount of scholarship about his work,

Coover's work remains relatively unknown to the public, and some of his early novels are now out of print.

Biography · Robert Coover was born in Charles City, Iowa. His family soon moved to Indiana and then to Herrin, Illinois. His father managed the local newspaper, the *Herrin Daily Journal*, which prompted Coover's interest in journalism. His college education began at Southern Illinois University (1949-1951), but he transferred to Indiana University, where he received a B.A., with a major in Slavic studies, in 1953. After graduation, Coover was drafted and joined the United States Naval Reserve.

While in Spain, he met Maria del Sans-Mallafré, who became his wife on June 13, 1959. During these years, his interest in fiction started. His first published story, "Blackdamp" (1961), became the seed for his first novel, *The Origin of the Brunists* (1966). He received an M.A. from the University of Chicago in 1965. During the following years, Coover and his family alternated stays in Europe with periods in the United States. The several awards he received during the 1970's made him financially secure and allowed him to continue writing.

Coover has held appointments at Bard College, the University of Iowa, Columbia University, Princeton University, the Virginia Military Institute, and Brown University; he has also been writer-in-residence at Wisconsin State University. In spite of a large amount of time spent abroad (in Europe and in South America) and his outspoken need to take distance from his own country, Coover's production is very "American," since he often bases his fiction on American events, persons, and national myths.

Analysis · Robert Coover's central concern is the human being's need for fiction. Because of the complexity of human existence, people are constantly inventing patterns that give them an illusion of order in a chaotic world. For Coover, any effort to explain the world involves some kind of fiction-making process. History, religion, culture, and scientific explanations are fictional at their core; they are invented narratives through which human beings try to explain the world to themselves. The problem, Coover would say, is that people tend to forget the fictional nature of the fictional systems they create and become trapped by them, making dogmas out of the fictions. The artist's function, then, is to reexamine these fictions, tear them down, and offer new perspectives on the same material, in order to make the reader aware of the arbitrariness of the construct.

Coover's fiction often has been labeled as "metafiction"–that is, fiction about fiction–and indeed most of his works are comments on previously existing fictional constructs. If in his longer works he examines the bigger metaphoric narratives such as religion, history, or politics (which one of the theorists of postmodernism, Jean-François Lyotard, has called "meta-narratives"), in his shorter works Coover turns to smaller constructs, usually literary fictions.

In the prologue to the "Seven Exemplary Fictions" contained in *Pricksongs & Descants*, Coover addresses his admired Miguel de Cervantes as follows:

> But, don Miguel, the optimism, the innocence, the aura of possibility you experienced have been largely drained away, and the universe is closing in on us again. Like you, we, too, seem to be standing at the end of one age and on the threshold of another.

Just as Cervantes stood at the end of a tradition and managed to open a door for a new type of fiction, contemporary authors also confront a changing world in need of new fictional forms that can reflect this world's nature better. Just as Cervantes tried to stress the difference between romance and the real world through the mishaps of Don Quixote, Coover wants to stress the fictionality and arbitrariness of some fictions that hold a tight grip on the reader's consciousness. Like Cervantes, Coover wants to free readers from an uncritical acceptance of untrue or oversimplified ideas that limit and falsify their outlook on life. Fictions, Coover and Cervantes would say, are not there to provide an escape by creating fantasies for the reader. When they do so, Coover continues writing in his prologue, the artist "must conduct the reader to the real, away from mystification to clarification, away from magic to maturity, away from mystery to revelations."

This quotation, coming from an author whose work is usually considered "difficult," might seem somehow odd. How does Coover's fiction clarify, or what does it reveal? His work often presents constantly metamorphosing worlds, which mimic the state of constant change in the real world. Just as the world is continuously changing, Coover's fictions also refuse to present stable, easily describable characters or scenarios. Coover also calls attention to the fictionality of fiction by focusing on the process and the means of creation rather than on the product. As he states in the prologue, the novelist turns to the familiar material and "defamiliarizes" it in order to liberate readers' imagination from arbitrary constraints and in order to make them reevaluate their reactions to those constraints. These are the main strategies of Coover's two collections of stories, *Pricksongs & Descants* and *A Night at the Movies*.

The title of the first collection refers to musical terms, variations played against a basic line (the basic line of the familiar narrative). As one character in one of the stories says, however, they are also "death-cunt and prick-songs," which prepares the reader for the sometimes shocking motifs of death and sex scattered throughout the stories. In *Pricksongs & Descants*, Coover turns to the familiar material of folktales and biblical stories. Using this material offers him the possibility of manipulating the reader's expectations. One of the ways in which Coover forces the reader to look at familiar stories from new perspectives is by retelling them from an unfamiliar point of view. For example, the story "The Brother" is Coover's version of the biblical flood told from the point of view of Noah's brother, who, after helping Noah to build the ark, is left to drown. "J's Marriage" describes how Joseph tries to come to terms with his marriage to the Virgin Mary and his alternating moods of amazement, frustration, and desperation. Some of the stories of the same collection are based on traditional folktales: "The Door" evokes "Little Red Riding Hood," "The Gingerbread House" reminds one of "Hansel and Gretel," "The Milkmaid of Samaniego" is based on the Spanish folktale of the same title; and *Hair o' the Chine*, a novella, mocks the tale of the "Three Little Pigs and the Wolf." Coover subverts, however, the original narratives by stressing the cruelty and the motifs of sex, violence, and death underlying most folktales. Revealing the darker side of familiar stories is in fact one of Coover's recurrent techniques.

In other stories of *Pricksongs & Descants*, Coover experiments with the formal aspects of fiction-making. He reminds the reader of the artificiality of fiction by presenting stories that are repertoires of narrative possibilities. Often, Coover juxtaposes several different beginnings, or potential stories, but leaves them undeveloped. He interweaves the different story lines, some of which are complementary and some of which might be contradictory, as is the case in "Quenby and Ola, Swede and Carl" and in "The Magic Poker." In the "Sentient Lens" section and in "Klee's Dead," Coover explores the possibilities and the limitations of the narrational voice: in the first set of stories, Coover denies the possibility of an objective narrative voice by portraying a camera that constantly interferes with the events of the story; in "Klee's Dead," the supposedly "omniscient" narrator is unable to explain the reasons for Paul Klee's suicide.

In most of the stories of *Pricksongs & Descants*, the figures are types described with a flaunted lack of depth in characterization, which prevents the reader from any possible identification with them. This contributes to the critical distance that Coover thinks is necessary to maintain toward fiction. As Cristina Bacchilega says in her article about Coover's use of the *Märchen* in this collection, while "the *Märchen* is symbolic of development, of a passage from immaturity to maturity, Coover's fictions present rather static characters . . . the only dynamic process allowed is in the reader's new awareness of the world as a construct of fictions." The function of the artist in contemporary society is one of Coover's recurring concerns, which surfaces in "Panel Game," "Romance of Thin Man and Fat Lady," and "The Hat Act," all of which portray cruel and insatiable audiences who, in their thirst for entertainment, do not hesitate to exterminate the artists if their performance does not stand up to their expectations.

In *A Night at the Movies*, Coover probes the nature of filmic fictions, which present a greater danger to be taken for "real" because of the immediacy of filmic images. Coover approaches film from three perspectives. In the stories "Shootout at Gentry's Junction," "Charlie in the House of Rue," "Gilda's Dream," and "You Must Remember This," Coover demythologizes specific films and offers his own version of the story, usually baring the ideology of the original version. In "After Lazarus" and "Inside the Frame," he explores the conventions through which these fictions create an illusion of an independent world on the screen. In "The Phantom of the Movie Palace" and "Intermission," he challenges the ontological status of reality and film by making the characters cross the boundaries that separate these two realms.

"Shootout at Gentry's Junction" is a parody of the ideology and of the form of the Western *High Noon*. Coover parodies the narrative line and the easy identification of good and evil typical of most Westerns. The film celebrates the code of honor and personal integrity typical of the Western hero; abandoned by everybody, the sheriff of the film, played by Gary Cooper, has to fight alone with the villain and his gang. In the story, however, the protagonist is a fastidious, neurotic sheriff who is obsessed with fulfilling the role imposed on him. The villain is Don Pedo, the Mexican bandit, whose major talent is to express himself by expelling intestinal gas. As in the film, the narrative progresses toward the confrontation of the villain and the sheriff. The tight structure of the film, however, is disrupted in the story by giving both characters a different kind of discourse. The sheriff's discourse has a traditional narrative line. It is narrated in the past tense and recurs to formulas taken directly from the visual tradition of the Western. The Mexican's discourse is in the present tense and in broken English, influenced by Spanish. Furthermore, Coover makes the Mexican ubiquitous. Readers never really know where he is—he seems everywhere at the same time, raping the schoolmarm at the local school, cheating at cards in the saloon, and burning papers at the sheriff's office. After shooting the sheriff, the Mexican sets the town on fire and rides into the sunset.

The irreverence of Coover's version of *Casablanca* is even greater.

Casablanca has become the epitome of the romantic melodrama, drawing like the Western upon codes of honor and heroic behavior. In "You Must Remember This," Coover gives his version of what might have happened between frames. Quite literally, Rick and Ilsa fall between frames and make furious love several times. The love story becomes a pornographic movie. The disruption of the moral code of the film creates an avalanche of disruptions in other categories: Rick and Ilsa begin to sense that their senses of time and place are fading, and their identities become increasingly diffused. In the end of the story, the characters melt into nothingness after several desperate attempts to return to the mythic movie.

Other stories in the collection *A Night at the Movies* aim at exposing the artificiality of the technical conventions of film. Written in the form of a film script, "After Lazarus" parodies the notion of the camera as the ultimately objective narrator. In the story, the camera "hesitates," "pauses," "follows back at a discreet distance," and rapidly moves back when frightened. "Inside the Frame" refers in its very title to filmic terms. If films construct a narrative through the sum of frames that all have a reason and a function in the global construct of the story, this story presents several possible beginnings of stories in one single frame. In "Inside the Frame," the reader gets glimpses of what could be potential stories: a woman stepping out of a bus, an Indian with a knife between his teeth, a man praying at a grave, a singing couple, a sleepwalker. There is no development, no explanation of the images. "Lap Dissolves" is a literary imitation of the filmic technique. The story fades from one filmic situation to the next, with the words giving the cues to the transformation of the scenario.

Coover disrupts the ontological boundaries between "reality" and fiction by making the protagonists of "The Phantom of the Movie Palace" and "Intermission" move between them. The mad projectionist of the first story lives in an abandoned movie palace and plays with the reels of film, constructing films by cutting and pasting images of other films. Somehow, his experiments go awry, and he becomes trapped in the fictions he has been creating. The girl of "Intermission" enters a filmic fantasy when the film in the story ends and she steps into the lobby of the movie theater to buy a snack. Outside the theater, she is thrown into a series of situations directly drawn from Hollywood films: she moves from a car race with gangsters, to a tent with Rudolph Valentino, to the sea surrounded by sharks. In what is supposed to be "reality," she becomes a dynamic individual, but back in the cinema she returns to the passivity that Hollywood fictions seem to invite.

In his major collections of stories, Coover elaborates on his fundamental concern, namely the necessity for the individual to distinguish between reality and fiction and to be liberated from dogmatic thinking. In order to do so, Coover emphasizes the self-reflexive, antirealistic elements of his fiction. The result is original, highly engaging, and energetic stories that probe human beings' relationships to the myths that shape their lives.

Other major works

NOVELS: *The Origin of the Brunists*, 1966; *The Universal Baseball Association, Inc., J. Henry Waugh, Prop.*, 1968; *The Public Burning*, 1977; *Gerald's Party*, 1986; *Pinocchio in Venice*, 1991.

PLAY: *A Theological Position*, 1972.

SCREENPLAY: *On a Confrontation in Iowa City*, 1969.

NONFICTION: "The Last Quixote," 1970; "The First Annual Congress of the High Church of Hard Core, Notes from the Underground," 1971; "The Master's Voice," 1977.

Bibliography

Andersen, Richard. *Robert Coover.* Boston: Twayne, 1981. A useful and very accessible introduction to Coover's production up to 1981. Andersen combines plot summary with commentary, helping the reader to make an initial acquaintance with Coover's work. Notes, select bibliography, and index.

Cope, Jackson. *Robert Coover's Fictions.* Baltimore: The Johns Hopkins University Press, 1986. More sophisticated than Richard Andersen's book. Cope supposes that readers know Coover's work and uses several approaches to it, analyzing his techniques, his subject matter, and the critical theories that cast light on Coover's work. Contains index.

Gordon, Lois. *Robert Coover: The Universal Fictionmaking Process.* Carbondale: Southern Illinois University Press, 1983. Like Richard Andersen's book, this volume provides a friendly introduction and overview of Coover's work, placing him in the context of metafictional or postmodernist literature. Notes, select bibliography, and index.

Kenndy, Thomas E. *Robert Coover: A Study of the Short Fiction.* New York: Twayne Publishers, 1992.

McCaffery, Larry. *The Metafictional Muse: The Works of Robert Coover, Donald Barthelme, and William H. Gass.* Pittsburgh: University of Pittsburgh Press, 1982. After describing what he considers a major current in contemporary American fiction, McCaffery discusses the metafictional traits of Coover's work and relates him to other important contemporary American writers.

_____. "Robert Coover on His Own and Other Fictions." *Genre* 14

(Spring, 1981): 45-84. A lively discussion in which Coover examines, among other things, the importance of stories about storytelling, the function of the writer in a world threatened by nuclear apocalypse, the fiction that has influenced his work, and popular culture.

Scholes, Robert. "Metafiction." *The Iowa Review* 1, no. 3 (Fall, 1970): 100-115. Initially theoretical, then descriptive, this article discusses four major metafictional writers: Coover, William H. Gass, Donald Barthelme, and John Barth. Scholes categorizes the different types of metafictional writing and classifies Coover's *Pricksongs & Descants* as "structural" metafiction, since it is concerned with the order of fiction rather than with the conditions of being.

Carlota Larrea

A. E. COPPARD

Born: Folkestone, Kent, England; January 4, 1878
Died: Dunmow, England; January 18, 1957

Principal short fiction · *Adam and Eve and Pinch Me*, 1921 · *Clorinda Walks in Heaven*, 1922 · *The Black Dog*, 1923 · *Fishmonger's Fiddle*, 1925 · *The Field of Mustard*, 1926 · *Count Stephan*, 1928 · *Silver Circus*, 1928 · *The Gollan*, 1929 · *The Higgler*, 1930 · *The Man from Kilsheelan*, 1930 · *Easter Day*, 1931 · *The Hundredth Story of A. E. Coppard*, 1931 · *Nixey's Harlequin*, 1931 · *Crotty Shinkwin, and the Beauty Spot*, 1932 · *Ring the Bells of Heaven*, 1933 · *Dunky Fitlow*, 1933 · *Emergency Exit*, 1934 · *Polly Oliver*, 1935 · *Ninepenny Flute*, 1937 · *These Hopes of Heaven*, 1937 ·*Tapster's Tapestry*, 1938 · *You Never Know, Do You?*, 1939 · *Ugly Anna and Other Tales*, 1944 · *Fearful Pleasures*, 1946 · *Selected Tales from His Twelve Volumes Published Between the Wars*, 1946 · *The Dark-Eyed Lady: Fourteen Tales*, 1947 · *The Collected Tales of A. E. Coppard*, 1948 · *Lucy in Her Pink Jacket*, 1954 · *Simple Day*, 1978

Other literary forms · A. E. Coppard published three slender volumes of poetry, *Hips and Haws* (1922), *Pelagea and Other Poems* (1926), and *Cherry Ripe* (1935), and two collections, *Yokohama Garland* (1926) and *Collected Poems* (1928). In 1957, he published his autobiography, *It's Me, O Lord!*

Achievements · Though not widely known among general readers, Coppard has experienced a resurgence of popularity as a result of the adaptation of several of his stories for *Masterpiece Theatre* on public television. For both his mastery of the short-story form and his sensitive portrayal of English rural life, Coppard is an important figure in the development of the short story as a serious literary form. From a background of poverty and with no formal education, Coppard advanced through a number of clerical and accounting jobs in Oxford, reading and associating with the students there. Becoming increasingly active in political activities and writing for journals, Coppard eventually decided to write professionally. In the 1920's and 1930's, he was considered one of the foremost short-story writers in England. Coppard's stories are frequently compared to those of Anton Chekhov and Thomas Hardy, whose influence Coppard acknowledged, and also to those of his contemporaries H. E. Bates and D. H. Lawrence. Although his poetry has not generated much acclaim, Coppard's prose is eloquently lyrical, its evocation of mood and portrayal of emotion particularly noteworthy.

Biography · Alfred Edgar Coppard's remarkable life contributed to his early success. To such an influential editor-writer as Ford Madox Ford, he was a rustic wise man or gypsy, a character out of one of his own dark country stories. Coppard was born into poverty and attended only four years of elementary school in Brighton. His father was a tailor, his mother a housemaid; when his father died young, Coppard had to help the family survive by taking a series of menial jobs. At age twenty-one, he became a clerk in an engineering firm in Brighton, where he remained for seven years, advancing to cashier. As a teenager and young man he walked the English countryside, absorbing its landscapes and the language of country folk he met in roadside taverns, a favorite setting for many of his later tales. He was a fine athlete and even supplemented his income as a successful professional sprinter. He married in 1906 and a year later took a better position as an accountant for an ironworks in Oxford, a position he held for twelve years. During his years in Oxford he read, often in the Bodleian, associated with students, heard and sometimes met such luminaries as Vachel Lindsay, Aldous Huxley, and William Butler Yeats, and, finally, began to write. He also became involved in Socialist politics and joined the Women's Social and Political Union. Finally, in 1919, having published seven or eight tales in journals such as the *Manchester Guardian* and a few poems in journals such as *The Egoist* (edited by T. S. Eliot), he decided to leave his position at the foundry and become a professional writer. On April 1, 1919, at age forty-one, he moved to a small cottage outside Oxford at Shepherd's Pit, where he lived alone in the woods, becoming aware of "the ignoring docility of the earth" and, finally, publishing his first collec- tion of tales on the second anniversary (*Adam and Eve and Pinch Me*, 1921) of his new career. His first book was well-received and thrust him into prominence as one of the leading English short-story writers. Over the next thirty years his production of tales, poems, and reviews was steady and of high quality. A second marriage, to Winifred May de Kok in 1931, endured, but his reputation as a short-story writer began to wane in the mid-1930's; his last collection of tales (1954) was not even reviewed by the *Times Literary Supplement*. *The Collected Tales*, however, was a clear success, and the autobiography he completed on the eve of his fatal illness in 1957 is a delight.

Analysis · The unique quality of A. E. Coppard's short fiction derives from his powers as a lyrical writer, his sympathetic understanding of the rural, lower-class folk who organically inhabit the English countryside so memo- rably evoked in his tales, and his "uncanny perception," as Frank O'Connor remarked, "of a woman's secretiveness and mystery." Coppard's earliest reviewers and critics emphasized the poetic quality of his tales. The title story from *The Field of Mustard* is one of the great stories in English, and it suggests the full range of Coppard's creative genius, including his lyric portrayal of the English countryside and its folk, especially its women, whose language and life-consciousness seem wedded to the landscape.

Like other lyric short stories, "The Field of Mustard" is nearly plotless. It opens with the suggestion that everything has already happened to the main characters, "three sere disvirgined women from Pollock's Cross." What remains for Coppard is to evoke the quality of these lives and the countryside of which they are a part; the tale proceeds as a kind of lyric meditation on life and death in nature. The women have come to "the Black Wood" in order to gather "dead branches" from the living trees, and on their way home, two of them, Dinah Lock and Rose Olliver, become involved in an intimate conversation that reveals the hopelessness of their lives. Rose, wishing she had children but knowing she never will, cannot understand why Dinah is not happy with her four children. Dinah complains that "a family's a torment. I never wanted mine." Dinah's "corpulence dispossessed her of tragedy," and perhaps because she has had the burden as well as the fulfillment of motherhood, she expressed the bitterness of life in what serves almost as a refrain: "Oh God, cradle and grave is all for we." They are old but their hearts are young, and the truth of Dinah's complaint, "that's the cussedness of nature, it makes a mock of you," is reflected in the world around them: the depleted women are associated with the mustard field and the "sour scent rising faintly from its yellow blooms." Against this natural order, Dinah and Rose wish that "this world was all a garden"; but "the wind blew strongly athwart the yellow field, and the odour of mustard rushed upon the brooding women."

As Dinah and Rose continue their conversation, they complain of their feeble husbands and discover a mutual loss: each had been a lover of Rufus Blackthorn, a local gamekeeper. He was "a pretty man," "handsome," "black as coal and bold as a fox"; and although "he was good to women," he was "a perfect devil," "deep as the sea." Gradually Coppard's pattern of imagery reveals the source of these women's loss to be the very wellspring of life—their love and sexual vitality. The suggestion is explicit in their lover's name, "Blackthorn," who had brought them most in life yet left them now with "old grief or new rancour." This grim reality is suggested earlier when the women meet an old man in the Black Wood; he shows them a timepiece given him by "a noble Christian man," but is met only with Dinah's profane taunt, "Ah! I suppose he slept wid Jesus?" Outraged, the old man calls Dinah "a great fat thing," shouts an obscenity, and leaving them, puts "his fingers to his nose." Dinah's bitter mockery of

Christian love gradually merges with the sour scent of mustard and surfaces transformed in Rose's recollection of how Blackthorn once joked of having slept with a dead man. These women, gathered in "the Black Wood" to collect dead wood from the living trees, have in effect slept with death. The yellow mustard blooms quiver in the wind, yet they are sour. The same "wind hustled the two women close together," and they touch; but, bereft of their sexual vitality, they are left only with Dinah's earlier observation that "it's such a mercy to have a friend at all" and her repeated appeal, "I like you, Rose, I wish you was a man." The tale ends with the women "quiet and voiceless,"

> in fading light they came to their homes. But how windy, dispossessed, and ravaged roved the darkening world! Clouds were borne frantically across the heavens, as if in a rout of battle, and the lovely earth seemed to sigh in grief at some calamity all unknown to men.

Coppard's lyric tales celebrate the oral tradition. His stories are often tales of tales being told, perhaps in a country tavern (as in "Alas, Poor Bollington!"). In some tales an oral narrator addresses the reader directly, and in others the rural settings, the characters, and the events—often of love ending in violence—draw obviously upon the materials of traditional folk ballads. Coppard himself loved to sing ballads and Elizabethan folk songs, and the main characters in these stories are sometimes singers, or their tales are "balladed about." In many tales, Coppard used rhythmic language, poetically inverted constructions, and repeated expressions that function as refrains in ballads. The most explicit example of a tale intended to resound with balladic qualities is "A Broadsheet Ballad," a tale of two laborers waiting in a tavern for the rain to pass. They begin to talk of a local murder trial, and one is moved by the thought of a hanging: "Hanging's a dreadful thing," he exclaims; and at length, with "almost a sigh," he repeats, "Hanging's a dreadful thing." His sigh serves as the tale's refrain and causes his fellow to tell within the tale a longer tale of a love triangle that ended in a murder and an unjust hanging. Finally, the sigh-refrain and the strange narration coalesce in the laborer's language:

> Ah, when things make a turn against you it's as certain as twelve o'clock, when they take a turn; you get no more chance than a rabbit from a weasel. It's like dropping your matches into a stream, you needn't waste the bending of your back to pick them out—they're no good on, they'll never strike again.

Coppard's lyric mode is perfectly suited to his grand theme: the darkness of love, its fleeting loveliness and inevitable entanglements and treacheries. He writes of triangles, entrapping circumstances, and betrayals in which, as often as not, a lover betrays himself or herself out of foolishness, timidity, or blind adherence to custom. Some of his best tales, like "Dusky Ruth" and "The Higgler," dwell on the mysterious elusiveness of love, often as this involves an alluring but ungraspable woman. Men and women are drawn together by circumstances and deep undercurrents of unarticulated feeling but are separated before they consummate their love.

Because of its portrayal of unconsummated love, its treatment of the rural poor, and its poetic atmosphere that arises from the countryside itself, "The Higgler" (the first story in *The Collected Tales*) is fully characteristic of Coppard's best work. It is not simply a tale of unconsummated love, for its main character comes to absorb and reflect the eternal forces of conflict in nature. For Coppard this involves more than man's economic struggle to wrest his living from nature; it involves man's conflict with man in war, his conflict with his lover, his conflict with himself, and ultimately, with his own life source, the mother.

Harvey Witlow is the higgler, a man whose business it is to travel the countryside in a horse-drawn wagon, buying produce from small farms. The story opens with the higgler making his way across Shag Moor, a desolate place where "solitude . . . now . . . shivered and looked sinister." Witlow is shrewd and crafty, "but the season was backward, eggs were scarce, trade was bad"; and he stands to lose the meager business he has struggled to establish for himself since returning from the war, as well as his opportunity to marry. "That's what war does for you," he says. "I was better off working for farmers; much; but it's no good chattering about it, it's the trick of life; when you get so far, then you can go and order your funeral." After this dismal beginning, Witlow is presented with an unexpected opportunity to improve his life in every way; but he is destined to outwit himself, as his name suggests, and to know more fully the "trick of life." As the tale develops, then, the reader watches him miss his opportunity and resume his descent into general desolation.

His chance comes when he stops at the farm of a Mrs. Sadgrove. Here the higgler finds plenty of produce as well as the intriguing possibility of a relationship with Mrs. Sadgrove's daughter, Mary, another of Coppard's alluring, secretive women. Mary's quiet beauty attracts Witlow, but he imagines her to be too "well-up" and "highly cultivated" for him. She shows no interest in him, so he is unprepared when, after several trips to the farm and an invitation to dinner, Mrs. Sadgrove tells him of her poor health and her desire that he should wed Mary and take over the farm. The higgler leaves bewildered. Here is his life's opportunity: the farm is prosperous, and he is far more attracted to Mary than to Sophy, the poor girl he eventually marries; besides, Mary will inherit five hundred pounds on her twenty-fifth birthday. It is simply too good to believe, and after consulting with his mother about his opportunity, Witlow grows increasingly suspicious. The reader has already been told that "mothers are inscrutable beings to their sons, always"; and Witlow is confused by his mother's enthusiasm over his opportunity. Even the natural world somehow conspires to frighten him: "Autumn was advancing, and the apples were down, the bracken dying, the furze out of bloom, and the farm on the moor looked more and more lonely. . . ."

So Witlow begins to avoid the Sadgrove farm and suddenly marries Sophy. Within months, his "affairs had again taken a rude turn. Marriage, alas, was not all it might be; his wife and his mother quarrelled unendingly," and his business fails badly. His only chance seems to be to return to the Sadgrove farm, where he might obtain a loan; but he does so reluctantly, for he knows Mrs. Sadgrove to be a hard woman. She exploits her help and "was reputed to be a 'grinder'"; and he has betrayed her confidence. In an increasingly dark atmosphere of loss, Witlow returns across Shag Moor to the Sadgrove farm, where Mary meets him with the news of her mother's death that day. Now a prolonged, eerie, and utterly powerful scene develops as the higgler agrees to help Mary prepare her mother's body, which lies alone upstairs in a state of rigor mortis. He sends Mary away and confronts the dead mother, whose stiff outstretched arm had been impossible for Mary to manage.

Moments later, in their intimacy near the dead mother, Witlow blurts out, "Did you know as she once asked me to marry you?" Finally Mary reveals that her mother actually opposed the marriage: "The girl bowed her head, lovely in her grief and modesty. 'She was against it, but I made her ask you. . . . I was fond of you–then.'" To his distress and confusion, Mary insists that he leave at once, and he drives "away in deep darkness, the wind howling, his thoughts strange and bitter."

Coppard's vision of life caught in a struggle against itself, of the violence in nature and its mockery of morality, of the deceit among humans and of humans' denial of their true nature–all this is marvelously represented in one of his first and finest tales, "Arabesque: The Mouse." It is a psychological horror story of a middle-aged man who sits alone one night reading Russian novels until he thinks he is mad. He is an idealist who was obsessed by the incompatibilities of property and virtue, justice and sin. He looks at a "print by Utamaro of a suckling child caressing its mother's breasts" and his mind drifts to recall his own mother and then a brief experience with a lover. These recollections merge in a compelling pattern of images that unite finally, and horribly, with an actual experience this night with a mouse. As a child horrified by the sight of some dead larks that had been intended for supper, he sought comfort from his mother and found her sitting by the fire with her bodice open, "squeezing her breasts; long thin streams of milk spurted into the fire with a little plunging noise." Telling him that she was weaning his little sister, she draws him to her breast and presses his face "against the delicate warmth of her bosom." She allows him to do it; "so he discovered the throb of the heart in his mother's breast. Wonderful it was for him to experience it, although she could not explain it to him." They feel his own beat, and his mother assures him his heart is "good if it beats truly. Let it always beat truly, Filip." The child kisses "her bosom in his ecstasy and whisper[s] soothingly: 'Little mother! little mother.'"

The boy forgets the horror of the dead larks bundled by their feet, but the next day his mother is run over by a heavy cart, and before she dies her mutilated hands are amputated. For years the image of his mother's bleeding stumps of arms had haunted his dreams. Into his mind, however, now floats the recollection of an experience with a lovely country girl he had met and accompanied home. It was "dark, dark . . . , the night an obsidian net"; finally in their intimacy she had unbuttoned his coat, and with her hands on his breast asked, "Oh, how your heart beats! Does it beat truly?" In a "little fury of love" he cried "Little mother, little mother!" and confused the girl. At that moment footsteps and the clack of a bolt cause them to part forever.

The sound of the bolt hurls him into the present, where, frightened, he opens his cupboard to find a mouse sitting on its haunches before a snapped trap. "Its head was bowed, but its beadlike eyes were full of brightness, and it sat blinking, it did not flee." Then to his horror he sees that the trap had caught only the feet, "and the thing crouched there holding out its two bleeding stumps humanly, too stricken to stir." He throws the mouse from his window into the darkness, then sits stunned, "limp with pity too deep for tears" before running down into the street in a vain search for the "little philosopher." Later he drops the tiny feet into the fire, resets the trap, and carefully replaces it. "Arabesque: The Mouse" is a masterwork of interwoven imagery whose unity is caught in such details as the mother's heartbeat, the mother's milk streaming with a plunging noise into the fire, the mouse's eyes, and the "obsidian net" of night.

Coppard's characters are sometimes shattered by such thoughts and experiences, but the author never lost his own sense of the natural magnificence and fleeting loveliness in life. It is true that many of his late tales pursue in a more thoughtful and comic manner the natural and psychological forces in life that were simply, but organically and poetically, present in such earlier tales as "The Higgler"; that is, in some of his later stories the reader can too easily see him playing with thoughts about Alfred Adler, Sigmund Freud, and, repeatedly, Charles Darwin (whose prose he admired). Yet the last tale (the title story) of his final volume is one of his best. "Lucy in Her Pink Jacket" is almost a hymn to nature, a song of acceptance in which lovers meet accidentally in a magnificent mountain setting. Their lovemaking is beautiful, natural, and relaxed, and they accept the web of circumstances causing them to part. Coppard's description of his last parting character might serve as our own image of himself: "Stepping out into the bright eager morning it was not long before [he] was whistling softly as he went his way, a sort of thoughtful, plaintive, museful air."

Other major works

POETRY: *Hips and Haws,* 1922; *Pelagea and Other Poems,* 1926; *Yokohama Garland,* 1926; *Collected Poems,* 1928; *Cherry Ripe,* 1935.

NONFICTION: *Rummy: That Noble Game Expounded,* 1933; *It's Me, O Lord!,* 1957.

CHILDREN'S LITERATURE: *Pink Furniture,* 1930.

Bibliography

Bates, H. E. "Katherine Mansfield and A. E. Coppard." In *The Modern Short Story: A Critical Survey.* London: Evensford Productions, 1972. Coppard's contemporary and fellow author of short stories discusses Coppard's role in the development of the modern English short story. Bates discerns an unfortunate influence of Henry James on Coppard's work, which is remarkable in its Elizabethan lyricism and its homage to the oral tradition. Includes an index.

Cowley, Malcolm. "Book Reviews: *Adam and Eve and Pinch Me.*" *The Dial* 71, no. 1 (July, 1921): 93-95. Describes Coppard's careful workmanship, his skillful narration, and his artful blend of fantasy and realism. Cowley notes Coppard's emotional unity, his insight into characters, his animated landscapes, and his role in keeping the short-story form vital.

Ginden, James. "A. E. Coppard and H. E. Bates." In *The English Short Story, 1880-1945: A Critical History,* edited by Joseph M. Flora. Boston: Twayne, 1985. Compares Coppard's and H. E. Bates's treatment of rural life as well as their dedication to the short story as distinguished from other literary forms. Although both authors employed the techniques of the modern short story, Ginden does not consider them "modernists," arguing that their work lacks the reliance on symbol or metaphor and instead stresses anecdote and description.

Lessing, Doris. Introduction to *Selected Stories by A. E. Coppard.* London: Jonathan Cape, 1972. Lessing attributes the general appeal of Coppard's fiction to his exceptional talent for storytelling. Coppard was an expert craftsman, but it is the authentic growth of characters and events that involve the reader.

O'Connor, Frank. *The Lonely Voice: A Study of the Short Story.* New York: World Publishing, 1962, repr. 1985. O'Connor examines Coppard's themes of poverty, personal freedom, and women in the context of other modern short fiction by Irish, English, American, and Russian writers. The two great English storytellers, according to O'Connor, are Coppard and D. H. Lawrence. Though both authors share working-class backgrounds, Coppard is a more deliberate, self-conscious artist, and he betrays feelings of social inadequacy.

Bert Bender
(Revised by *Lou Thompson*)

STEPHEN CRANE

Born: Newark, New Jersey; November 1, 1871
Died: Badenweiler, Germany; June 5, 1900

Principal short fiction · *The Little Regiment and Other Episodes of the American Civil War*, 1896 · *The Open Boat and Other Tales of Adventure*, 1898 · *The Monster and Other Stories*, 1898 · *Whilomville Stories*, 1900 · *Wounds in the Rain*, 1900 · *Last Words*, 1902

Other literary forms · Stephen Crane began his brief writing life as a journalist, and he continued writing for newspapers, notably as a war correspondent, throughout his career, sometimes basing his short stories on events that he had first narrated in press reports. He also wrote raw-edged, realistic novels in which he employed journalistic techniques, most significantly in *Maggie: A Girl of the Streets* (1893) and *The Red Badge of Courage* (1895). By contrast, he composed wry, evocative, often cryptic poems, published in *The Black Riders and Other Lines* (1895) and *War Is Kind* (1899), that seemed to reveal the philosophy behind the world created in his fiction.

Courtesy of the Library of Congress

Achievements · Crane's fiction has proved hard to classify—not, however, because he defies categorization, but because he worked in two nearly incompatible literary styles at once, while being a groundbreaker in both.

On the one hand, he founded the American branch of literary naturalism (this style had originated in France) in his early novels. These works emphasized the sordid aspects of modern life, noted the overpowering shaping influence of environment on human destiny, and scandalously discounted the importance of morality as an effective factor touching on his characters' behavior. In this style, he was followed by writers such as Theodore Dreiser and Frank Norris.

On the other hand, in these same early novels he developed a descriptive style that made him a founder of American impressionism. While the naturalist component of his writing stressed how subjectivity was dominated by social forces, the impressionist component, through coloristic effects and vivid metaphors, stressed the heightened perceptions of individual characters from whose perspectives the story was presented. The man closest to Crane in his own time in developing this impressionist style was Joseph Conrad, though, it will be recognized, this method of drawing from a character's viewpoint became a central tool of twentieth century literature and was prominently employed by authors such as William Faulkner, Virginia Woolf, and Henry James.

Crane took the unusual tack of both playing up his characters' points of view in presenting the world and downplaying the characters' abilities to influence that world. Although this combination of strategies could be made to work satisfactorily, later authors who have taken Crane's path have tended to develop only one of these strands. Moreover, many critics have found Crane's dual emphases to be jarring and incompletely thought through, particularly in his novels. In fact, many have felt that it is only in his short stories that he seemed thoroughly to blend the two manners.

Biography · To some degree, Stephen Crane's life followed a perverse pattern. He was acclaimed for the authenticity of his writings about events that he had never experienced and then spent the remainder of his few years experiencing the events that he had described in prose—often with disastrous consequences.

Born in 1871, in Newark, New Jersey, Crane was the last child in the large family of a Methodist minister, Jonathan Townley Crane. The family moved frequently and, in 1878, came to Port Jervis, New York, in forested Sullivan County, where Crane would set most of his early stories. Two years later, his father died, and his mother began struggling to support the family, doing church work and writing for religious publications.

Crane determined to be a writer early in his life, and though he attended a few semesters at Lafayette College and then Syracuse University, his real interest in his college years was in soaking up the atmosphere of New York City lowlife and writing free-lance articles for newspapers. In 1892, he completed his first novel, *Maggie: A Girl of the Streets*, the story of a young girl driven into streetwalking by a Bowery Romeo. This first novel was so shocking in tone and full of obscenity (in those days, this meant that it contained words such as "hell") that it was rejected by respectable publishers. Borrowing money, Crane printed the book himself, and though it went unread and unsold, it garnered the appreciation of two of the outstanding literary figures of the day, Hamlin Garland and William Dean Howells.

His next book, *The Red Badge of Courage*, a novel about the Civil War, brought him universal acclaim and celebrity status. In the year of the book's publication, however, as if living out his fiction, he defended an unjustly accused prostitute against the corrupt New York City police, just as he had defended the poor prostitute Maggie in prose, and found undeserved blight attached to his name. From then on, life would be made difficult for him in New York City by the angered police force.

He more or less abandoned New York at this point, easily enough since the authority of his army novel had placed him in much demand as a war correspondent. Going to Florida to wait for a ship to Cuba, where a rebellion against the Spanish colonialists was taking place, Crane met Cora Taylor, the madame of a house of ill repute who was to become his common-law wife. The ill-fated ship that he eventually boarded sank, and Crane barely escaped with his life, though, on the positive side, he produced from the experience what many consider his greatest short story, "The Open Boat."

As if to show that he could describe real wars as well as he could imagine them, he began shuttling from battle to battle as a journalist/reporter, first going to the Greco-Turkish War and then back to view the Spanish-American War, ruining his health in the process. Between wars, he stayed in the manorial Brede Place in England, where he became acquainted with a number of other expatriates who lived in the area, including Joseph Conrad, Harold Frederic, and Henry James.

His problems with the police and the irregularity of his liaison with Cora Taylor—she could not get a divorce from her long-estranged husband—would have made it difficult for Crane to live in his homeland, so in 1899, he settled at the manor for good. Sick and beset with financial woes brought on by extravagant living and an openhanded generosity to visitors, he wrote feverishly but unavailingly to clear his debts. He died the next year from tuberculosis, after having traveled to the Continent to seek a cure.

Analysis · Perhaps because his writing career was so short, critics have devoted much space to Stephen Crane's slight, decidedly apprentice series of sketches collectively entitled *The Sullivan County Tales.* One trait that the sketches do have in their favor is that they contain all the facets of style and theme that Crane was to utilize as his writing developed. The reader finds the overbearing power of the environment, the vivid descriptions, the premise that these descriptions reflect the heightened consciousness of a character or characters, and the idea that this very heightening involves a distortion of perception that needs to be overcome for the characters' adequate adjustment to, and comprehension of, reality. Also of significance is that these stories are generally concerned with the actions of four campers and hence reflect not only on individual psychology but also on the psychology of group dynamics. This was also to become a focus of Crane's writing.

In one of the better pieces from this series, "Four Men in a Cave," a quartet of campers decides to explore a cave in order to have something to brag about when they return to the city. Their scarcely concealed fears about the expedition are rendered by Crane's enlivening of stalactites that jab down at them and stalagmites that shoot up at them from crevices. At the end of their path, they find a hermit who invites them to a game of poker, but their fear-stoked imaginations visualize the gamester as a ghoul or Aztec priest. Only later after escaping the cave, in a comic denouement, do they learn of the cave dweller's true identity, that of a mad farmer who took to solitude when he lost his land and wife through gambling. By this time, there seems to be little to brag about, since what has happened has exposed their cowardice and credulity.

The story provides an early example of the rough-and-ready combination of impressionist subjectivity, in how the descriptions in the piece are tinged by the campers' fears, and naturalist objectivity, in how the overwhelming environment of the cave, for part of the story, controls the men's action while dwarfing them. Further, the piece indicates the way, as Crane sees it, emotions can be constructed collectively, as when each camper tells the others how he has misidentified the hermit, adding to the growing hysteria.

In 1894, Crane published a maturer story, "An Experiment in Misery," in which he transposed the narrative of a cave journey into a serious study of urban social conditions. In the originally printed version of the piece, two middle-class men observe tramps and speculate about their motives and feelings. On impulse, the younger man decides to dress as a tramp in order to penetrate into their secrets. (Such a tactic, of disguising oneself to uncover hidden areas of society, was a common practice of crusading reporters at that time.)

In the later, revised version of this story, the one that is more commonly known, Crane removed the beginning and ending that reveal the protagonist to be slumming; yet, though his social origins are obscured, the story still concerns a neophyte who knows nothing of the life of the underclass and who is being initiated into the ways of the Bowery slums. The high point of the tale, corresponding to the cave exploration, is the hero's entrance into an evil-smelling flophouse. He has trouble sleeping in the noisome room for his keyed-up fancy sees morbid, highly romanticized symbols everywhere. He understands the shriek of a nightmare-tossed sleeper as a metaphoric protest of the downtrodden.

Awakening the next morning, the protagonist barely remarks on the stench, and this seems to indicate that, merely through familiarity, some of the falsely romantic pictures that he has entertained about the life of the city's poorest have begun to rub off. Exactly what positive things he has learned and of what value such learning will be to him is never clear and, indeed, as Crane grew, while his stories still turned on the loss of illusions, they began to lose the dogmatic assurance that such a change is necessarily for the good.

The last scene of the sketch, though, does make a more definite point, this one about the nature of groups. The hero has begun to associate with a fellow tramp called the assassin and now, after his initiatory night, seems both adjusted to his new station and accepted by the tramp world, at least insofar as the assassin is willing to regale him with his life story. By abandoning his preconceptions about poverty, the protagonist has quite seamlessly fitted himself into the alien milieu, yet this joining of one community has a negative side effect of distancing him from another. The last tableau has the assassin and the hero lounging on park benches as the morning rush-hour crowd streams by them. Here, soon after the hero has had the comfortable feeling of being accepted in one society, he has the poignant realization that, as a bum, he no longer belongs to the larger American working world. There is even a sly hint, given by the fact that the youth begins employing the same grandiose, romanticized terms in depicting his separation from the business world that he had earlier used to depict the flophouse, that he has embarked on a new course of delusion-building. In other words, his loss of illusions about the reality of tramp life has been counteracted (as if a vacuum needed to be filled) by the imbibing of a new set of illusions about the vast gulf between the classes. Each community one may join seems to have its own supply of false perspectives.

In 1897, after his near death at sea, Crane produced what most name his greatest short story and what some even rank as his supreme achievement, placing it above his novels. This is "The Open Boat." Again there are four men. They are in a small boat, a dinghy, escapees from a sunken vessel, desperately trying to row to shore in heavy seas.

The famed first sentence establishes both the parameters of the fictional world and a new chastening of Crane's style. It reads, "None of them knew the color of the sky." Literally, they are too intent on staying afloat to notice the heavens; figuratively, in this godless universe the men cannot look to the sky for help but must rely on their own muscles and wits, which, against the elements, are little enough. Furthermore, the opening's very dismissal of color descriptions, given that much of Crane's earlier work, such as *The Red Badge of Courage*, depends heavily on color imagery, can be seen as the author's pledge to restrain some of the flashiness of his style.

This restraint is evident not only in a more tempered use of language here but also in the nature of the protagonists' delusions. In works such as the slum experiment, the romanticized preconceptions that determine the protagonist's viewpoint can be seen as trivial products of a shallow culture—that is, as marginal concerns—whereas in the sea story, the men's illusions are necessities of life. The men in the boat want to believe that they must survive, since they have been fighting so hard. If they do not believe this, how can they continue rowing? The point is put wrenchingly at one moment when the men refuse to accept that they will drown, as it seems they will, in the breakers near the shore. Such illusions (about the meaningfulness of valor and effort) obviously have more universal relevance than others with which Crane has dealt, and that is why the story strikes so deep; the illusions also, ingeniously, tie in with the reader's expectations. As much as the reader begins to identify with the four men (and they are sympathetically portrayed), he or she will want them to survive and thus will be on the verge of agreeing to their illusions. Thus, Crane engineers a remarkable and subtle interlocking of readers' and characters' beliefs.

Furthermore, the functionality of the possibly delusive beliefs of the struggling men—that is, the fact that they need to believe that they will make it ashore to keep up the arduous fight for life—helps Crane to a fuller, more positive view of human community. The men in the cave were merely partners in error, but these toilers share a belief system that sustains them in their mutually supportive labor, which the characters themselves recognize as "a subtle brotherhood of men." The men's shared recognition of the supportive structure of human groups gives weight to the story's last phrase, which says, of the three survivors who have reached land, "and they felt that they could then be interpreters."

The story, written in the third person, is given largely from the viewpoint of one of the four, a newspaper correspondent. This is not evident at once, however, since the narrative begins by simply objectively reporting the details of the men's struggle to stay afloat and reproducing their laconic comments. In this way, the group is put first and only later, when the correspondent's thoughts are revealed, does the reader learn of his central-ity as the story begins to be slightly colored by his position. What the focus on his consciousness reveals, aiding Crane in deepening his presentation, is how the subtle brotherhood is felt individually.

After rowing near to the shore but not being able to attract anyone's attention, the crew settles down for a night at sea. While whoever is rowing stays awake, the others sleep like the dead they may soon become, and at this point, the story dwells more intently on the correspondent's outlook as he takes his turn at the oars. The newspaperman reconsiders the beliefs that have been keeping them afloat, seeing the weakness in them and accepting, now that he is alone, the possibility of an ironic death—that is, one coming in sight of shore after their courageous struggle. Yet his existential angst, an acknowledgment that there is no special heavenly providence, neither stops him from his muscle-torturing rowing nor dimin-ishes his revived illusions on the morrow, when they again all breast the waves together.

If this line of reasoning shows him mentally divorcing himself from the collective ideology, another night thought implies that, in another direc-tion, he is gaining a deeper sense of solidarity. He remembers a verse that he had learned in school about a legionnaire dying far from home with only a comrade to share his last moments. The correspondent had thought little of the poem, both because he had never been in extremis (and so saw little to the pathos of the case) and, as Crane notes, had formerly looked cynically at his fellows (and so had found unpalatable or unbelievable the care of one soldier for another). A day's experience in the dinghy has made him keenly aware of the two aspects of experience that he had overlooked or undervalued, and thus has given him a clear understanding of the networks (those of democratic brotherhood) and circumstances (a no-holds-barred fight against an indifferent universe) that underlie the human social world. This understanding can be applied in many ways, not only toward a grasp of group interaction but also toward an interpretation of honest art.

Still, the most telling incident of his lonely watch is not so much any of his thoughts as an action. The boat, the correspondent finds, has become the magnet to a huge shark. Achingly, he wishes that one of his fellow sailors were awake to share his fidgety vigil; yet, he resists any impulse he has to rouse them or even to question aloud whether any of them is conscious for fear that he should waken a sleeper. Even if alone he cannot continue with the group illusion, he can, though alone, effortlessly maintain the group's implicit morality, which holds that each should uncomplainingly shoulder as much of the burden as possible, while never revealing irritation or fear. Much later, the newspaperman learns that another of the four, the captain, was awake and aware of the predatory fish's presence during what had been taken to be the correspondent's moment of isolated anguish. The hidden coexistent alertness of the captain suggests the ongoing mutuality of the group that undergirds even seemingly isolated times of subjectivity.

To bring this story in line with the last one mentioned, it is worth noting that the small group in the boat is contrasted to a group on shore just as, in "An Experiment in Misery," the hoboes were contrasted to the society of the gainfully employed. When the rowers are near the coast on the first day, they vainly hope to attract the ministering attentions of people on land. They do attract their attention, but the people, tourists from a hotel, merrily wave at them, thinking that the men in the dinghy are fishermen. The heedlessness, inanity, and seeming stupidity of the group on shore compare unfavorably with the hard-won, brave alertness of the boatmen, pointing to the fact that the small group's ethical solidarity is not of a type with the weaker unity found in the larger society. The men's deep harmony rather—beautiful as it is—is something that can be found only in pockets. The depicting of the community on the land foreshadows elements of Crane's later, darker pictures of community, as in "The Blue Hotel," where what sustains a group is not a life-enhancing though flimsy hope but a tacitly accepted lie.

In the year that he wrote "The Open Boat" and the next year, Crane was to compose three other brilliant stories, two of which dealt with myths of the Old West. Both these Western tales were written in his mature, unadorned style, and both continued his focus on the belief systems of communities. What is new to them is a greater flexibility in the handling of plot. Previously, he had simply followed his characters through a continuous chronological sequence from start to finish; now, however, he began shifting between differently located character groups and jumping around in time.

In "The Bride Comes to Yellow Sky," the action begins on a train moving through Texas, carrying Yellow Sky's sheriff, Jack Potter, and his new wife back to town. Potter is apprehensive about his reception, since he has married out of town in a whirlwind courtship and none of the townspeople knows of his new status. The scene shifts to the interior of a Yellow Sky saloon, where the gathered, barricaded patrons have other things to be apprehensive about than Potter's marriage. Scratchy Wilson, the local ruffian, has gotten drunk and is shooting in the main street, while, as the bar's occupants admit, the only man able to cow him is the absent sheriff. Scratchy Wilson himself, as the reader learns in another scene shift, not aware of Potter's trip, is truculently looking for the sheriff so that they can engage in a showdown. In truth, the reader, knowing of Potter's imminence, will probably share Wilson's expectation of a gun battle, which is not an unreasonable forecast of the plot's unfolding. Yet, this expectation is founded on a deeper belief, that the West will always be an uncivilized place of outlaws and pistols. A chagrined Scratchy recognizes that this belief is invalid and that an era has passed when he finds that the sheriff has taken a wife. After meeting the couple, he holsters his guns and stalks off toward the horizon.

A tragic variation on similar themes of violence and community beliefs appears in "The Blue Hotel," a story that a few critics rank in importance above "The Open Boat." The tale concerns a fatalistic traveler, the Swede, who stops for the night in a hotel in Nebraska. (This protagonist's name will be picked up by Ernest Hemingway, a Crane admirer, for an equally fatalistic character in his short-story masterpiece "The Killers.") Through the Swede's conversation with the hotel owner, Scully, and other stoppers, it appears that, based perhaps on an immersion in dime novels, the Swede thinks that this town—or, for that matter, any town in the West—is a hotbed of bloodshed and mayhem. After his fears seem to be allayed by the officious owner, who assures him that he is mistaken, the Swede overreacts by becoming boisterous and familiar. This mood of his eventually dissipates when, involved in a game of cards, he accuses the owner's son of cheating. The upshot is that the pair engage in a fistfight, which the Swede wins. He is now triumphant but can, of course, no longer find any welcome at the hotel; so he wanders off to a nearby saloon, in which his even more high-strung and aggressive demonstrations lead to his death at the hands of an icy but violent gambler he had been prodding to drink with him.

At this point, the story seems a grim meditation on the truth or falsity of myths. What seemed to be the manifestly absurd belief of the Swede has been proven partially true by his own death. Yet, it appears this truth would never have been exposed except for the Swede's own pushy production of the proper circumstances for Western violence to emerge. There is, however, another turn of the cards. A final scene is described in which, months later, two of the hotel's card players, witnesses of the dispute between the Swede and Scully's son, discuss events of that fateful evening. One of them, the Easterner, claims that the whole group collected at the hotel that night is responsible for what led to the death since they all knew that the owner's son was cheating but did not back up the Swede when he accused the youth.

In one way, this final episode indicates that perhaps the Swede's suspicions were accurate in yet another sense; the whole town is made up, metaphorically, of killers in that the community is willing to sacrifice an outsider to maintain its own dubious harmony. From this angle, though, this Western town's particular violence merely crystallizes and externalizes any hypocritical town's underlying psychic economy. (Crane depicted this economy more explicitly in his novella *The Monster*.) In another way—and here the increasing complexity of Crane's thought on community is evident—even after the final episode, it still appears that the Swede's murder has some justification.

There are two points to be made in this connection. For one, throughout the story, Crane represents the frailty of human existence as it is established on the prairies in the depths of winter. The story begins by underlining the presumptuousness of Scully's hotel's bright blue color, not so much as it may be an affront to the other, staider buildings in town, but in its assertiveness against the grimness of the white wastes of nature surrounding and swamping the little burg. The insignificance of human beings measured against the universe is explicitly stated by Crane in an oft-quoted passage. He speaks of humans clinging to a "whirling, fire-smitten, ice-locked, disease-stricken, space-lost bulb." He goes on to say that the "conceit of man" in striving to prevail in such conditions is "the very engine of life." It is true that they all killed the Swede in some sense, but the fragility of the human community, it may be surmised, demands that its members all practice respect and forbearance toward one another so that a common front can be presented against uncaring nature. If anyone consistently violates this unwritten code, as the Swede does, he must be eliminated for group self-preservation. It is significant in this light that the Swede, who demands a grudge match with the owner's son, would take the men away from the large, red-hot stove (symbol of the warmth of peaceful intercourse and home comfort) outside to fight in subzero weather. To restate this, for his own egotistical purposes, the Swede would drag everyone into a much greater exposure to a harsh environment than life in the community, were it running harmoniously, would ever make necessary.

The second point to be made is that Crane's portrait of the gambler, which interrupts the narrative at a high point and which, thus, seems at first sight a cumbersome miscalculation by the author, allows the reader a fuller understanding of the place of an outsider in this Western society. If the reader was only given the Swede's treatment to go by, he or she would be forced to conclude that, whatever the necessity of the visitor's expulsion, this town has little tolerance for aberrant personalities. Yet, such a position has to be modified after Crane's presentation of the gambler, whose disreputable calling excludes him from the city's better social functions but whose behavior in other areas—he bows to the restrictions put on him with good grace and is a charitable family man who will not prey on the better citizens—conforms enough to standards to allow him to be generally accepted. Intervening at this point, Crane's portrayal of this second (relative) outsider is used to indicate that the community will permit in its midst a character who has not followed all of its rules, provided such a character does not, as the Swede does, insistently and continuously breach the accepted norms.

All this taken together does not, certainly, excuse a murder. What it does show is that Crane's understanding of how a community sustains itself has expanded beyond the understanding that he had at the time of the sea story. He indicates that the guiding principle of mutual support found in the dinghy has remained operative, even in a far less threatened situation, while adding that violations of this principle can lead to less happy consequences than might have been foreseen in the earlier story.

Finally, in "Death and the Child," Crane produced an excellent story about war, the topic which had been both the most consistent and the least successful subject of his short pieces. The intertwined themes of the effect of illusions and the ways that an individual can be integrated into, or excluded from, a community, the most important themes of Crane's work, are again central. In this piece, the character who nurses illusions is Peza, a journalist who has decided to join the Greek side during the Greco-Turkish War, motivated by unrealistic ideas about the glories of classical Greece and the adventure of fighting. Once he reaches the battle lines, however, he finds it impossible to join the other combatants.

He is displeased by the nonchalance of the troops, who refuse to strike heroic poses, but what actually ends up turning him away from solidarity is his realization that to become part of the group he must accept not only a largely humdrum life but also the possibility of a prosaic death. In other words, it is not coming down to earth with the common men that ultimately scares him but the understanding that he may have to come down under the earth (into a grave) with them.

The story exhibits what had become the traits of Crane's mature style. He writes with a terse, crisp, subdued prose that is occasionally shot through with startling or picturesque imagery, this imagery being the residue of his initial, more flowery style. Crane also exhibits a mastery of plotting. This is brought out by the careful joining of Peza's emotional states to his gyrations around the battle camp as well as by the story's final encounter, where Peza comes upon an abandoned child, who, too young to comprehend war, still has a clearer view of reality than the distraught journalist. This skill at plotting is not something that Crane possessed from the beginning, which brings up a last point.

It might be said that there is a chronological distinction between Crane's interests and his method of narration. While his thematic concerns were constant throughout his career, though as he grew older his attention to how a community was created and sustained grew in weight, his ability to construct complex plots is one that he picked up during the course of his creative life. There are authors who advance little after their first books, but in Crane's case, it can definitely be said that there was a promise for the future that his short life never redeemed.

Other major works

NOVELS: *Maggie: A Girl of the Streets,* 1893, 1896; *The Red Badge of Courage,* 1895; *George's Mother,* 1896; *The Third Violet,* 1897.

POETRY: *The Black Riders and Other Lines,* 1895; *War Is Kind,* 1899.

NONFICTION: *The Great Battles of the World,* 1901; *The War Dispatches of Stephen Crane,* 1964; *The Correspondence of Stephen Crane,* 1988.

Bibliography

Benfey, Christopher. *The Double Life of Stephen Crane.* New York: Knopf, 1992.

Berryman, John. *Stephen Crane.* New York: William Sloane Associates, 1950. This combined biography and interpretation has been superseded as a biography, but it continues to be an absorbing Freudian reading of Crane's life and work. Berryman, himself a major American poet, eloquently explains the patterns of family conflict that appear in Crane's fiction. Furthermore, Berryman's wide-ranging interests allow him to tackle such large topics as Crane's influence on the birth of the short story, a form which, though existing earlier, came to prominence only in the 1890's. Includes notes and index.

Colvert, James B. *Stephen Crane.* New York: Harcourt Brace Jovanovich, 1984. This short biography by a notable Crane scholar has as one of its emphases the inclusion of many photographs and illustrations. These not only show Crane and his friends but also depict some of the scenes that Crane described in his writing. Chronology, notes.

Dooley, Patrick. *Stephen Crane: An Annotated Bibliography of Secondary Scholarship.* New York: G. K. Hall, 1992. Replaces Stallman's bibliography for secondary scholarship.

Halliburton, David. *The Color of the Sky: A Study of Stephen Crane.* Cambridge, England: Cambridge University Press, 1989. Though somewhat thematically disorganized, the author's philosophical grounding and ability to look at Crane's works from unusual angles make for many provocative readings. In his discussion of "The Blue Hotel," for example, he finds much more aggression directed against the Swede than may at first appear, coming not only from seemingly benign characters but also from the layout of the town. Notes, index.

Nagel, James. Stephen Crane and Literary Impressionism. University Park: Pennsylvania State University Press, 1980. Nagel carefully delineates what he considers Crane's application of impressionist concepts of painting to fiction, which involved Crane's "awareness that the apprehension of reality is limited to empirical data interpreted by a single human intelligence." This led the writer to stress the flawed visions of men and women and a depiction of the dangers of this natural one-sidedness in works such as Maggie: A Girl of the Streets, as well as depictions of characters who transcended this weakness through an acceptance of human inadequacies in such works as "The Open Boat." Notes, index.

Stallman, R. W. *Stephen Crane: A Biography.* New York: George Braziller, 1968. This definitive biography involves a thorough sifting of all the circumstances surrounding Crane's major fiction, a sifting that is especially impressive in the case of "The Open Boat." Stallman also gives the reader a feeling for Crane's times. Contains a meticulous bibliography (Stallman later composed a book-length bibliography), extensive notes, an index, and appendices that include contemporary reviews of Crane's work and obituaries.

Wertheim, Stanley. *The Crane Log: A Documentary Life of Stephen Crane, 1871-1900.* New York: G. K. Hall, 1994.

Wertheim, Stanley, and Paul Sorrentino, eds. *The Correspondence of Stephen Crane.* New York: Columbia University Press, 1988.

Wolford, Chester L. *Stephen Crane: A Study of the Short Fiction.* Boston: Twayne, 1989. This overly brief but useful look at Crane's short fiction provides Wolford's sensitive readings as well as commentary on the major points that have been raised in critical discussions of the Crane pieces. In describing "The Bride Comes to Yellow Sky," for example, Wolford explains his view of how the story fits into the archetypical patterns of the passing of the West narratives, while also exploring why other critics have seen Crane's story as a simple parody. About half of the book is given over to selected Crane letters and extractions from other critics' writings on Crane's short pieces. Includes a chronology, bibliography, and index.

James Feast

WALTER DE LA MARE

Born: Charlton, Kent, England; April 25, 1873
Died: Twickenham, Middlesex, England; June 22, 1956

Principal short fiction · *Story and Rhyme: A Selection*, 1921 · *The Riddle and Other Stories*, 1923 · *Ding Dong Bell*, 1924 · *Broomsticks and Other Tales*, 1925 · *Miss Jemima*, 1925 · *Readings*, 1925-1926 (2 volumes) · *The Connoisseur and Other Tales*, 1926 · *Told Again: Traditional Tales*, 1927 · *Old Joe*, 1927 · *On the Edge*, 1930 · *Seven Short Stories*, 1931 · *The Lord Fish*, 1933 · *The Nap and Other Stories*, 1936 · *The Wind Blows Over*, 1936 · *Animal Stories*, 1939 · *The Picnic*, 1941 · *The Best Stories of Walter de la Mare*, 1942 · *The Old Lion and Other Stories*, 1942 · *The Magic Jacket and Other Stories*, 1943 · *The Scarecrow and Other Stories*, 1945 · *The Dutch Cheese and Other Stories*, 1946 · *Collected Stories for Children*, 1947 · *A Beginning and Other Stories*, 1955 · *Ghost Stories*, 1956

Other literary forms · In addition to his numerous volumes of short fiction, Walter de la Mare published poetry, novels, anthologies of various kinds, collections of essays, one play, and scores of essays, reviews, and articles published separately. In the United States, de la Mare is better known as a children's writer than he is for the other genres in which he worked.

Achievements · De la Mare's remarkable literary career spans more than five decades. The English novelist, poet, dramatist, short-story writer, critic, essayist, and anthropologist is best known today as a writer infused with a Romantic imagination. He has often been compared to William Blake and Thomas Hardy because of similarities in thematic development of mortality and visionary illumination. Often labeled as an escapist because of his retreat from reality, de la Mare's work touches on dreams, fantasy worlds, emotional states, and transcendent pursuits. Best known in the United States for his children's literature, he has produced numerous volumes of prose and verse in the genre. All of his work is suffused by a childlike quality of imagination. De la Mare's writings have still not received the attention they deserve. He lived a quiet, uneventful life, always reluctant to impart information about himself. No biography of the writer has as yet been written. Throughout his life de la Mare wrote poetry. It is this work that represents his truest and most lasting literary achievement. In 1948, de la Mare received the Companion of Honour and in 1953, the Order of Merit. During the next three years he also received honorary degrees from five colleges, including Oxford and Cambridge.

Biography · Walter de la Mare was born on April 25, 1873, in Charlton, Kent, the son of well-to-do parents, James Edward de la Mare and Lucy Sophia Browning de la Mare. In her book *Walter de la Mare* (1966), Doris Ross McCrosson said that de la Mare's life "was singularly and refreshingly uneventful." De la Mare was educated at St. Paul's Cathedral Choir School in London, where he was the founder and editor of the school magazine, *The Choristers' Journal.* In 1890, at the age of seventeen, de la Mare began working as a bookkeeper at the Anglo-American Oil Company in London, a position he held for almost twenty years. While working as a bookkeeper, de la Mare began writing stories, essays, and poetry, many of which were published in various magazines. For a while, de la Mare wrote under the pseudonym "Walter Ramal." Soon after the publication of his first books, he was granted a civil list pension by the British government amounting to one hundred pounds a year. Thereafter, he devoted himself entirely to literature and writing. De la Mare died at home on June 22, 1956, at the age of eighty-three. He is buried at St. Paul's Cathedral.

Analysis · Walter de la Mare's stories take the form both of wish fulfillment and nightmare projections. Believing that the everyday world of mundane experience is a veil hiding a "real" world, de la Mare used dream forms as a means of piercing the veil as well as a means of suggesting that between dream and reality looms, as de la Mare said, "no impassable abyss." Because of their hallucinatory character, dreams merge with states of madness, travel to mysterious realms, childhood visions. The surfaces of de la Mare's stories belie an underlying reality; rendering the texture of everyday experience with exquisite detail, he built his surfaces with such lucidity that a reader is often surprised to find a horror beneath that which is apparently placid or a joy beneath that which is apparently mundane.

"The Riddle" starts like a fairy tale with such lightness and grace that one might expect a "happy ever after" ending. Soon, however, it becomes apparent that the quavering voice of the grandmother betokens something more than age, and the gifts she presents to her seven grandchildren become something more than sugar plums. Although it is never made explicit, one may assume that the grandchildren have come to live with their grandmother because of the death of their parents. The aged woman says to the children ". . . bring me smiling faces that call back to my mind my own son Harry." The children are told they may come in the presence of their grandmother twice a day—in the morning and in the evening. The rest of the time they have the run of the house with the exception of the large spare bedroom where there stands in a corner an old oak chest, older than the aged woman's own grandmother.

The chest, of course, represents death. It is later revealed to be decorated as a coffin and it attracts the children one by one. Harry is first. Opening the chest, he finds something strangely seductive that reminds him of his mother, so he climbs in and the lid miraculously closes. When the other children tell their grandmother of Harry's disappearance, she responds, "Then he must be gone away for a time. . . . But remember, all of you, do not meddle with the oak chest."

Now it becomes apparent that the grandmother, herself so close to death that she seems more feeble every day, is also to be identified with the oak chest, and that rather than a good fairy dispensing sugar plums she is a wicked witch seducing the children to their death. Ann is the last child to be called to the chest, and she walks as if in a dream and as if she were being guided by the hand. One paragraph more ends the story. With the children all gone, the grandmother enters the spare room, but her eyesight is too dim for her to see, and her mind is a tangled skein of memories which include memories of little children.

"The Orgy: An Idyll" seems an entirely different kind of story. Rather than being set in a house with myriad rooms suggesting something of the Gothic, "The Orgy" is set mainly in a large and elegant department store in London; rather than beginning with a "once upon a time" element, it opens on a bright May morning, crisp, brisk, scintillating. Details of the great packed street down which Philip walks leave readers no doubt that here is the world of their own experience. Before the action is ended, however, it becomes clear that the story is an extravaganza. Philip is engaged in a buying orgy, charging everything that strikes his fancy to the account of his uncle who has just disinherited him, and the orgy is a fanciful idyll of the wish fulfillment variety. Philip's desire for revenge projected into bright, hallucinatory images is carried into action in exactly the way the uncle will understand—to the tune of "a couple of hundred thousand pounds," a considerable amount of money in 1931, the year the story was published.

"In the Forest" is a brilliant exercise in point of view restricted to the mind of a small boy in such a way that the childlike behavior and lack of perception characteristic of the very young take on the aura of nightmare. At no time does de la Mare vary the focus; no words are used that a child could not know; no insight is offered that a child could not understand. Although the child occasionally feels a twinge of guilt because he has not obeyed his mother, he is completely impervious to the horror of the action going on around him.

The story opens when the boy's father is leaving to go to war. The boy is half asleep and is moving in and out of consciousness. It is the advent of the fall of the year, and a storm has brought down leaves that are still green from the trees. Although the leaves are still green, it is getting cold. The boy asks his father to bring him a gun back from the war and notices without comment that his father, instead of leaving immediately, keeps coming back to say good-bye. Unaware of the anguish being suffered by his father and mother, the boy asks his mother if she is glad his father is going to the war. The mother does not answer, but the boy's simple statement makes the point. "But she was crying over the baby, so I went out into the forest till dinner."

Later the boy chops wood, an activity that causes him to be hot and excited, and then he brings the logs into the house. The wind is roaring as if it is angry, more leaves are falling, and the weather is cold and misty. The boy finds his mother asleep with the baby in her arms, and the baby, too, is asleep, although, as the boy notices, the baby scarcely seems to be breathing. The boy falls asleep by the warm hearth and stays there all night. In the morning he rushes out, glad that his father is gone, because now he can do just as he pleases. Visiting the snares, he finds a young rabbit caught by one leg and, imitating his father, kills the hare with a crack on the neck and carries it to the house by the hind legs. Later he wonders how "they would carry back" his father's body "if he was killed in the war."

Because the baby is crying, the boy chooses to spend his days in the forest until one day when he tells his mother he is going to "bring her some fish for dinner!" The dialogue that follows is the first that occurs in the story. The mother tells the boy that the baby is very ill and tries to get him to touch and hold his baby brother, asking: "Do you love it?" The boy shakes his head and persists: "I think I should *like* to go fishing mother . . . and I promise you shall have the biggest I catch." Then, denying the mother's plea that he go for the doctor, the boy runs out saying, "It's only crying."

He catches no fish and believes the fish would not bite because he has been wicked, so he goes home, and now for the first time he hears cannons on the other side of the forest. When he gets home, he finds his mother angry, calling him a coward, and the baby dead. The next day he consents to his mother's request that he go for the sexton, but as he is on his way he hears a rifle sound and "a scream like a rabbit," and he is frightened and runs home. Since his mother has already called him a coward, however, he lies to her, telling her the sexton was gone. Now the mother decides she must take the dead baby to the graveyard herself, and once again she addresses her son: "Won't you kiss your little brother, Robbie?"

Alone, the boy eats more than he should and builds the fire up so high that its noise drowns out any outside noises. Alone, he believes he is in a dream "that would never come to an end." He does not cry, but he feels angry at being left alone, and he is afraid. He also feels guilty about the amount of food he has consumed. He fears his mother's return and yet longs for her, feeling that he loves her and is sorry for his wickedness.

The next thing he knows, it is broad daylight. His mother has still not returned, but he hears a groan at the doorway. It is his father with a "small hole" at the back of his shoulder; dark, thick blood covers the withered leaves on which he lies. The boy tries to give his father water and tells him about the baby, "but he didn't show that he could hear anything." Then the boy hears his mother coming back and runs out to tell her "that it was father." The story ends as abruptly as it begins, but the point of view so neatly restricted and the image patterns masterfully arranged create the tenor and vehicle of an Everyman's Freudian nightmare. The subtly stated but powerfully conveyed theme delineates an Oedipal pattern that raises the story from an isolated and factual experience to an overwhelming and communal dream having mythic proportions.

"An Ideal Craftsman" is just as powerful. Although the story makes use of a young boy as protagonist, point of view is different from that found in "In the Forest." This time de la Mare allows an omniscient narrator to move in and out of the consciousness of the two major characters. Once again, however, a horror is present, foreshadowed from the beginning of the story; once again the aura of dream is cast over the entire story; and once again death, this time murder, is the focal point of the story.

For a short-story writer of such consummate skill, de la Mare has attracted almost no critical attention, and what books have been written about him concentrate more on his other writings than on his pieces of short fiction. This lack of attention is a great pity. In her book *Walter de la Mare*, McCrosson devotes only one chapter of some twenty pages to de la Mare's short-story craft, but her summary of his achievement is accurate:

> His preoccupation with good and evil puts him on a level with Haw-thorne and Conrad; his mastery of suspense and terror is equal to Poe's; the subtlety of his characterizations occasionally rivals James'. And the range of his portrayals is impressive: children, old maids, the demented, old idealists and young pessimists, artists, business men, dandys, young women in love–all of whom share in the mysterious and sometimes maddening business called living.

Other major works

NOVELS: *Henry Brocken,* 1904; *The Return,* 1910; *The Three Mulla-Mulgars,* 1910 (reprinted as *The Three Royal Monkeys: Or, The Three Mulla-Mulgars,* 1935); *Memoirs of a Midget,* 1921; *At First Sight: A Novel,* 1928.

PLAY: *Crossings: A Fairy Play,* 1921.

POETRY: *Songs of Childhood,* 1902; *Poems,* 1906; *The Listeners and Other Poems,* 1912; *A Child's Day: A Book of Rhymes,* 1912; *Peacock Pie: A Book of Rhymes,* 1913; *The Sunken Garden and Other Poems,* 1917; *Motley and Other Poems,* 1918; *Flora: A Book of Drawings,* 1919; *Poems 1901 to 1918,* 1920; *Story and Rhyme,* 1921; *The Veil and Other Poems,* 1921; *Down-Adown-Derry: A Book of Fairy Poems,* 1922; *Thus Her Tale,* 1923; *A Ballad of Christmas,* 1924; *Stuff and Nonsense and So On,* 1927; *Self to Self,* 1928; *The Snowdrop,* 1929; *News,* 1930; *Poems for Children,* 1930; *Lucy,* 1931; *Old Rhymes and New,* 1932; *The Fleeting and Other Poems,* 1933; *Poems 1919 to 1934,* 1935; *This Year, Next Year,* 1937; *Memory and Other Poems,* 1938; *Haunted,* 1939; *Bells and Grass,* 1941; *Collected Poems,* 1941; *Collected Rhymes and Verses,* 1944; *The Burning-Glass and Other Poems,* 1945; *The Traveller,* 1946; *Rhymes and Verses: Collected Poems for Young People,* 1947; *Inward Companion,* 1950; *Winged Chariot,* 1951; *O Lovely England and Other Poems,* 1953; *The Complete Poems,* 1969.

NONFICTION: *Rupert Brooke and the Intellectual Imagination,* 1919; *The Printing of Poetry,* 1931; *Lewis Carroll,* 1932; *Poetry in Prose,* 1936; *Pleasures and Speculations,* 1940; *Chardin, J.B.S. 1699-1779,* 1948; *Private View,* 1953.

ANTHOLOGIES: *Come Hither,* 1923; *The Shakespeare Songs,* 1929; *Christina Rossetti's Poems,* 1930; *Desert Islands and Robinson Crusoe,* 1930; *Stories from the Bible,* 1930; *Early One Morning in the Spring,* 1935; *Animal Stories,* 1939; *Behold, This Dreamer!,* 1939; *Love,* 1943.

Bibliography

Atkins, John. *Walter de la Mare: An Exploration.* London: C & J Temple, 1947. A slim volume of appreciation by Atkins, who concentrates on de la Mare's stories and on two of the novels, neglecting the verse, which he considers inferior. The study is a rambling discourse without a solid structure and is not recommended for newcomers to de la Mare.

Duffin, Henry Charles. *Walter de la Mare: A Study of His Poetry.* London: Sidgwick & Jackson, 1949. The author focuses on de la Mare's verse. He considers him a sublime visionary poet of exceptional lucidity whose excessive creative energies are diminished in the prose stories, which he also considers delightful. His main thesis is that de la Mare's poetry neither criticizes nor escapes life, but rather heightens it.

Hopkins, Kenneth. *Walter de la Mare.* 1953. Rev. ed. London: Longmans, Green, 1957. This slim volume touches on de la Mare's life and his prose and verse writings. The author, who is an ardent admirer of de la Mare, briefly examines all of his major writings. A useful but limited introduction to de la Mare. Supplemented by a select bibliography.

McCrosson, Doris Ross. *Walter de la Mare*. New York: Twayne, 1966. A good critical introduction to de la Mare. McCrosson examines at length the author's total literary output, concentrating particularly on the novels, which she feels not only have been neglected but also contain the clearest statement of his vision of life. The writer points out that de la Mare's fascinating quest into the mysteries of life never coalesced into a coherent vision. Complemented by a chronology and a select bibliography.

Megroz, R. L. *Walter de la Mare: A Biographical and Critical Study*. London: Hodder & Stoughton, 1924. Megroz conducted the first study of de la Mare's work, "treading what is almost virgin soil," as he phrased it. The author professes his deep admiration for de la Mare, sketches a brief biography, comments on personal impressions, and then devotes his study to the poetry. His book is less a critical examination of de la Mare and more an appreciation.

Mary Rohrberger
(Revised by *Terry Theodore*)

ISAK DINESEN

Baroness Karen Blixen-Finecke

Born: Rungstedlund, Denmark; April 17, 1885
Died: Rungstedlund, Denmark; September 7, 1962

Principal short fiction · *Seven Gothic Tales*, 1934 · *Vinter-Eventyr*, 1942 (*Winter's Tales*, 1942) · *Sidste Fortællinger*, 1957 (*Last Tales*, 1957) · *Skæbne-Anekdoter*, 1958 (*Anecdotes of Destiny*, 1958) · *Ehrengard*, 1963 · *Efterladte Fortællinger*, 1975 (*Carnival: Entertainments and Posthumous Tales*, 1977)

Other literary forms · In addition to her numerous tales and stories, Isak Dinesen wrote many letters and essays. She is particularly well known, however, for her narrative *Den afrikanske Farm* (1937; *Out of Africa*, 1937), which tells of her years in Kenya (a sequel was published in 1960). After her death, two volumes of letters, written while in Africa, were published, as were her essays.

Achievements · Dinesen has a special position in modern literature in that she is a major author in two languages. Although a native of Denmark, she wrote in both English and Danish, creating her tales as original works in both tongues. Popular with the critics as well as the general public, she was appointed an honorary member of the American Academy of Arts and Letters in 1957 and was repeatedly mentioned as a candidate for the Nobel Prize in Literature. Her initial success came in the English-speaking world. With time, however, she became successful also at home, where her magnetic personality and storytelling gifts gradually captivated the public. Aided by the medium of radio, she became a veritable cultural institution in Denmark. Since her death, her critical reputation has steadily grown both at home and abroad, and she has come to be considered a modern master of short fiction.

Biography · Isak Dinesen's life may be divided into three parts, namely her childhood and youth, her time in Africa, and her years as a recognized writer. Her parents came from very different social backgrounds. From her father, Wilhelm Dinesen, a landed proprietor, she inherited a love of adventure, nature, and storytelling. Her mother, on the other hand, came from a bourgeois family of merchants and attempted to foster a sense of

duty, obligation, and guilt in her three daughters. Karen Christenze (Isak is a pseudonym that she assumed at the beginning of her writing career) was her father's favorite daughter and thereby was able to avoid some of her mother's puritanical manacles. At the age of ten, however, her father's suicide turned her youth into a period of mostly joyless desperation. Early she began writing stories and short plays, for which she had been prepared by an unsystematic private education. She also studied art and traveled abroad with her mother, sisters, and aunt.

The second period in Dinesen's life began in 1914, when she married her first cousin, the Baron Bror Blixen-Finecke, and with him settled down to manage a coffee plantation outside Nairobi, in British East Africa. Her husband infected her with syphilis and proved himself a poor manager of the plantation; the couple was separated in 1921 and divorced four years later. Living in what was then known as Kenya as the manager of a different, and larger, coffee farm, Dinesen cultivated a friendship with Denys Finch Hatton, whom she had met in 1918. A confirmed bachelor, Finch Hatton had no desire to marry Dinesen, which grieved her. Dinesen's African life came to an end in 1931, when the coffee farm had to be sold and Denys died in the crash of his private plane.

Dinesen returned to Denmark in a state of abject poverty. Supported by her family and inspired by the success of a few stories, which years earlier had been published under the pen name Oceola, she set out to create a new life for herself as a writer. Other stories, written during her African sojourn, existed in draft form, and some of these gradually became perfected and included in *Seven Gothic Tales*, the English-language edition of which became both a critical and a popular success. Her autobiographical narrative *Out of Africa* established her as a major presence on the literary scene both in Denmark and in the English-language world, and the following books were also enthusiastically received. An indication of Dinesen's popularity in the United States is the fact that five of her titles were chosen as Book-of-the-Month Club selections. Living at her birthplace, Rungsted lund, north of Copenhagen, Denmark, she gathered her admirers around her and tended her literary reputation.

During most of her adult life, Dinesen was plagued by illness, which was exacerbated by much strenuous travel abroad and the entertainment of numerous guests at home. After a particularly taxing summer, she died at her home on September 7, 1962.

Analysis · Isak Dinesen reacted against the psychological and social realism of contemporary Danish literature and looked back to the Romantic storytellers for inspiration. Like them, she preferred the longer, drawn-out tale to the short story proper, and authorial narration, often with overtly present narrators, is a hallmark of her narratives. Her chosen form therefore often struck her contemporaries as old-fashioned. This was also the case with her thematic concerns, for her stories take place mostly in the century between 1770 and 1870 and express the ethos of a bygone age. She speaks in favor of such aristocratic values as duty, honor, and justice, but she also rejects the Christian dualistic worldview and questions the role of religion and the place of women in contemporary bourgeois society. Above all, however, the role of art in human life constitutes a central theme of her authorship. Through art, a unified vision is possible, and such a monistic perception of reality is, for Dinesen, a primary source of meaning in general and of comfort in difficult times.

"Aben" ("The Monkey"), a long story from *Seven Gothic Tales*, is a good example of Dinesen's "gothic" or fantastic narratives that also exhibits many of her thematic concerns. Its setting is a noble milieu in northern Germany in the 1830's; its theme is the nature of love. Boris, a young lieutenant in the Prussian Royal Guards, has become involved in a homosexual scandal in the capital and is seeking the aid of his maiden aunt, Cathinka, the Prioress of Cloister Seven, a convent for spinsters of noble blood. In order to escape dishonor and almost certain death, Boris has resolved to marry, thus hoping to lay to rest the rumors of his homosexual involvement with other members of his regiment. His aunt, who is well acquainted with the various noble families of the land, is being asked to select a suitable mate for him. The fantastic element of the story is found in the relationship between the Prioress and her little gray monkey, to which she has a mysterious bond and with which she, from time to time and in accordance with traditional Scandinavian folk belief in shape-shifting, exchanges her identity. The monkey is connected with the idea of love through the love goddess of an ancient Baltic people, the Wends. The goddess looks like a beautiful woman from the front and like a monkey from the back. Through this image, Dinesen argues against the Judeo-Christian distinction between the hetero-erotic, which is acceptable to society, and the homo-erotic, which is not. Speaking in favor of a monistic outlook on human sexuality, Dinesen, through the similarity between the Wendish love goddess and the Janus face, problematizes the distinction between normal and abnormal sexuality. The text actually foregrounds the question of how it can be determined which side is the front and which is the back of the goddess, and the implied answer is that no such determination can be made on objective grounds.

There is, nevertheless, a recognition on Dinesen's part that people have to live up to the expectations of their society if they are to get along in life.

Boris has certain duties to his family, and despite his sexual difference from the norm, he is obligated to repress his desires and to force himself to marry. The Prioress, who at this time and in a mysterious way is possessed by aspects of her monkey's personality, chooses as his bride the only daughter of a neighbor, a tall and strong young woman named Athena, whom Boris has known since childhood. Her father welcomes Boris as a suitor and says that he would delight in seeing the young man's features in the faces of his grandchildren. Athena rejects him, however, and states unequivocally that she will never marry; she will not, in other words, yield to her duty to her family. There is a strong implication in the text that Athena is as troubled by her gender role as Boris is by his.

Athena's rejection infuriates the Prioress, who arranges a supper of seduction during which Athena gets drunk. As the girl goes to her room, the Prioress gives Boris an aphrodisiac to help him complete his conquest, and he struggles with Athena, who knocks out two of his teeth. Boris interprets this as a symbolic castration and feels that he has been freed from his obligation to have a normal conjugal relationship with her, should they get married. She has won his battle with traditional sexuality for him, and he therefore triumphantly kisses her with his bloody mouth. The significance of this perverted and ironic image of defloration is not lost on Athena, who, in horror and disgust, loses her consciousness. Boris does not touch her further.

The next morning, Athena is told by the Prioress that she is now most likely pregnant and that her only hope of avoiding dishonor is to marry Boris. Together, they then watch as the Prioress, who all along has been in the grip of the personality of the monkey, reasserts her own true self through an intense struggle with the little animal. This astonishing event affects Athena deeply, and she resigns herself to marrying Boris, with the proviso, however, that she is to have dominion in their relationship. Athena's and Boris's union is thus marked by the back side of the love goddess in several ways. Erotically, they are misfits in that they both look on heterosexuality with revulsion. Psychologically and emotionally, their union is a result of a power struggle, touched by the fantastic, rather than a consequence of the usual process of falling in love. Morally, their marriage represents a surrender to the expectations of their families, but it is unlikely that they will do their real duty and have children. Socially, their marriage will also be out of the ordinary, as, in opposition to the patriarchal norm of their time and place, the wife will rule the roost with the consent of her husband. Dinesen thus problematizes one of the fundamental oppositions of human life, namely that between male and female, and offers a critique of both sex roles and Christian dualism.

While the stories in *Seven Gothic Tales* touch on the fantastic and frequently present challenges to the reader, those of *Winter's Tales* are more traditional, and therefore also more accessible, narratives. Written during the German occupation of Denmark, they are tales for difficult times, in which the possibility of reconciliation and restoration is held dear.

"Den unge Mand med Nelliken" ("The Young Man with the Carnation"), which introduces the English-language edition of the collection, is a powerful expression of Dinesen's theory of art. Its protagonist, Charlie Despard, is a young English writer who, while born and reared in circumstances of great poverty, has transmuted the pain of his childhood experiences into his first novel, with which he has had tremendous success. Because of his newfound reputation as a writer, he has been able to marry a beautiful young woman from a family of means, and outwardly he has every reason to be happy, which indeed, for a time, he has been. As Dinesen indicates through his name, however, he is now in despair, for he has found that art has failed him. He has nothing more to say as a writer, while at the same time he feels that life holds no joys for him. His is not simply a bad case of writer's block, though, but a case of someone who, because of his erstwhile happiness, has lost his ability to create. The story tells about how Charlie comes to terms with his situation and regains his creativity.

While traveling on the Continent, Charlie and his wife have been separated for a few days but have planned to meet at a hotel in Amsterdam. Charlie arrives last and goes to his wife's room, where he finds her asleep with her door unlocked. Shortly after his arrival, someone else tries to open the door, and when Charlie gets out of bed to investigate, he finds a young man who, wearing a carnation, is obviously on his way to a rendezvous. Charlie's first reaction is envy, for he believes the young man to have found the happiness which he, himself, is lacking. He then experiences a shock at his wife's infidelity, feels sorry for himself, writes her a brief note, and leaves in search of that happiness which he sensed in the face of the young man with the carnation.

During the next few hours, his mind is in turmoil, and he walks along the waterfront, contemplating his situation. He is then found by some sailors who believe him to be thinking of suicide and who therefore invite him to come with them to a tavern. The men spend the night telling one another stories, and Charlie's tales indicate that he now suffers from no loss of creativity; the experience of the night has given him the pain which is needed by the artist. His regained creativity gives him the strength to face his wife, and he returns to the hotel only to find that he, the previous night, had entered the wrong room. Dinesen's imagery shows that Charlie the fiction writer interprets his experience as a kind of resurrection, which is followed by a dialogue with God. Charlie is told by God that he had been created in order to write, and that it is God who wants him to tell his stories and who therefore gave him the pain of the previous evening. He is promised, however, that God will not measure out any more distress to him than what is needed for his art. Charlie accepts the idea that pain is a necessary condition of creativity and realizes that it is the young man with the carnation who is to be pitied, rather than himself.

Dinesen's theory of art is thus basically a romantic one, in which the joys of life are viewed as inferior to art and therefore fundamentally incompatible with creative endeavor. The artist is required to sacrifice normal human happiness for the privilege of being able to commune with the divine, which is the essence of artistic creation.

Another significant aspect of "The Young Man with the Carnation" is the concept of duty, which manifests itself as Charlie's obligation to God to be a writer of stories. In "Sorg-Agre" ("Sorrow-Acre"), the next story in *Winter's Tales,* duty is a central motif that contributes much to the story's theme. "Sorrow-Acre" tells about a young Dane named Adam who has spent several years in England, but who, at the beginning of the story, has just returned home to his ancestral estate, only to find himself in conflict with his uncle, the ruler of the manor. Adam represents the beginnings of a new social order and serves as the embodiment of the ideas of the French Revolution, while his uncle advocates a traditional, aristocratic view of life. The three intertwined plots of the story are played out against the backdrop of life on this semifeudal Danish country estate in the late 1700's.

The first plot concerns the uncle's dealings with Anne-Marie, the mother of a young man who has been accused of a crime. There is little proof in the case, and the uncle admits that he has no basis for making a judgment about the man's guilt or innocence. When Anne-Marie begs for the freedom of her son, however, he offers her a bargain: if she can cut a certain rye field in the course of one day, her son will receive his freedom. The outward drama of the story concerns Anne-Marie's superhuman attempt at harvesting the field, which is normally three days' work for a man. She succeeds but at the end dies from exhaustion.

The second plot line concerns the relationship between Adam and his uncle. Adam finds his uncle's action barbarous and threatens to leave because of his sense of outrage. The uncle defends himself by referring to the divine principle of arbitrary power, saying that because he is essentially like a god in his relationship to his serflike farm workers, his actions should not be questioned. While the drama in the rye field may seem like a tragedy to most mortals, the unresolved question of the young man's innocence or guilt adds a divinely comic flavor to Anne-Marie's attempt to buy his freedom. A nobleman may approach the divine by accepting and appreciating the comic aspects of human life. The uncle would himself, he says, like nothing better than to be in a position where he might be able to buy himself a son at the cost of his own life, thus ensuring the succession of the family line. He has lost his only son and has recently, in his rather advanced age, married the young lady who was intended to be his son's bride.

The third strand of the plot involves the relationship between Adam and his uncle's young wife. It is very much against Adam's interests that his uncle should receive an heir, for if the uncle were to die childless, Adam would inherit the estate. It has been prophesied by a gypsy, however, that Adam's posterity is to possess the estate, and it is becoming clear to Adam that he has a duty to the family to give his uncle a legal heir. The young wife's attitude toward Adam would clearly facilitate such an unspoken arrangement.

All the main characters in this tale thus exemplify the principle of duty, particularly as it concerns the continuation of a family line. Adam recognizes that he has been brought back to Denmark by fate and that he must play his part in the drama of his family. He is reconciled to his uncle, who begs him to stay; the uncle surely knows that Adam is essential to the success of his project. The uncle's young wife knows that she has been brought into the family expressly for the purpose of providing an heir. Anne-Marie, whose death is a powerful reminder of a person's duty to his or her descendants, sets a powerful example of commitment to one's family.

Dinesen sees a connection between duty and the concept of justice, for it is a paramount duty of human beings to strive to be just. Her idea of justice is most clearly expressed in "Skibsdrængens Fortælling" ("The Sailor-Boy's Tale"), a rather simple story that is also found in *Winter's Tales*. Like "The Monkey," "The Sailor-Boy's Tale" presupposes that the reader is familiar with folk beliefs related to shape-shifting, the idea that a human being may temporarily take on the form of an animal. The story tells about a young sailor boy named Simon, who, during a storm in the Mediterranean, climbs the mainmast of his ship in order to free a peregrine falcon that has become caught in the rigging. Before Simon sets it free, the falcon pecks his thumb sufficiently hard to draw blood, and Simon retaliates by hitting it on the head. This incident proves to be significant to Dinesen's portrait of justice and its operation.

Two years later, Simon's ship has come to the herring markets in the town of Bodø in northern Norway, where Simon meets and falls in love with a young girl named Nora. One evening, when he is on his way to a meeting with the girl, he runs into an overly friendly Russian sailor, whose behavior has homosexual overtones. Simon, who does not want to be late for his meeting with the girl, stabs and kills the Russian, after which he is pursued by the dead man's shipmates. While hiding in the crowd at a dance, an old pagan Lapp woman named Sunniva shows up, says that Simon is her son, and tells him to come home with her. Sunniva wipes off his bloody knife on her skirt and, while hiding Simon when the Russian sailors come looking for him, cuts her thumb to explain the presence of blood. She then arranges for safe passage for him back to his ship, at which point she reveals that she is the falcon that Simon released during the storm in the Mediterranean. She has rescued him both because she likes him and because of her sense of justice, for he deserves to be paid back for helping her. In order to completely settle her accounts with him, she then boxes his ear in return for his blow to her head while she was in the shape of the falcon.

Sunniva also explains to Simon that she admires his devotion to the girl Nora, and that the females of the earth hold together. Referring to men as their sons, she indicates that the world is really run by women, who are bound together with a matriarchal compact. Sunniva's pagan matriarchy gestures at Dinesen's questioning of both traditional sex roles and the Christian religion.

Dinesen's rather gentle critique of Christianity in "The Sailor-Boy's Tale" becomes relentlessly satirical in "Heloise" ("The Heroine"), in which she casts a woman stripper in the role of the Christian savior. A young Englishman named Frederick Lamond, together with a company of French travelers, is caught in a German border town at the time of the Franco-Prussian war. A student of religious philosophy, Frederick is at the time writing a treatise on the doctrine of the Atonement. When the German army marches into town, he and the other stranded travelers are accused of espionage. A famous messianic prophecy from the Book of Isaiah, which is quoted in Frederick's manuscript, is read as a code by the Germans and forms the main proof of their accusation.

One of the travelers is a woman named Heloise, whose rare beauty greatly impresses one of the German officers. Realizing that the accusation of espionage may not have much merit, he offers the travelers a bargain: if Heloise will appear before him in the nude, they will be permitted to continue to France; otherwise, they will be shot. Heloise turns to the company and leaves the decision in their hands, and they all vote to refuse the German's demand. The officer, who respects the courage of both Heloise and her companions, then decides to let them go after all, and he apologizes to Heloise, whom he terms a heroine, by sending her a big bouquet of roses.

Six years later, Frederick is in Paris in order to attend some lectures in his field. Entertained by a friend, he is taken to a music hall, where the most beautiful woman in Paris is appearing nude in a show. It turns out that the woman is Heloise, whom Frederick still remembers well. They meet and reminisce after the show, and Heloise explains what in her opinion was at stake in the dramatic incident six years earlier. It was not only the lives of the travelers, she says, which hung in the balance, but their ability to live with their consciences. It would have cost her very little to comply with the German's demand; for her, it would have been a professional matter, not one of conscience. The other travelers, however, would have never gotten over it if Heloise were to have bought their freedom at the cost of exposing her body. Frederick now understands that her heroism did not consist in standing up to the German officer's demands but in looking after the welfare of her companions' souls. Heloise, who through the imagery in the story has been carefully presented as a kind of Christ-figure, now appears, to both Frederick and the reader, as a full-blown savior.

Portraying a stripper as someone who saves people from guilt constitutes a truly ironic comment on traditional Christian religion. Casting a woman in such a position undercuts the traditional conception of women's roles as well. "The Heroine," through its overt questioning of central religious and social norms, therefore becomes one of Dinesen's most radical stories.

Heloise's parting comment to Frederick is that she wishes that he might have seen her perform six years earlier, when her beauty was at its fullest. Heloise has the temperament of an artist in that art, in her case the beauty of her body, gives meaning to her life. A similar commitment is held by the title character in "Babettes Gæstebud" ("Babette's Feast") from *Anecdotes of Destiny*, who, like Heloise, is French. Babette is a famous Parisian chef who had to flee her country at the time of the Paris Commune. She finds her way to a small Norwegian fishing village, where she, for the next fourteen years, lives as a maid in the home of two spinsters. These two sisters are the daughters of a minister who founded a pietistic religious society, and who, because of his asceticism, rejected his daughters' suitors. Years after his death, his daughters live solely for their father's memory and religious ideals.

Babette regularly plays the French lottery and chances to win ten thousand francs, which she wishes to spend on a French dinner at the centenary of the minister's birth. The various foreign dishes are disconcerting to the guests, who are all members of the minister's sect; only one of them, the former suitor of one of the daughters, is able to appreciate Babette's culinary artistry. When, at the end of the dinner, the two sisters learn that the utterly exhausted Babette has spent all of her money on the project, they cannot understand her motivation, but Babette states that she has done it for her own sake: she is an artist who craves excellence in her field of endeavor.

Like Babette, Dinesen placed high demands on herself. She felt a strong sense of duty and loyalty to the artist within her, thus her tales are exquisitely crafted but not numerous. She relentlessly pursued her unitary vision, subtly criticizing those aspects of life which went against the grain of her thought, such as the dualism of received religion and traditional sex roles. Through her authorship she prepared a literary feast that continues to be enjoyed by numerous readers.

Other major works

NOVEL: *Gengældelsens Veje*, 1944 (*The Angelic Avengers*, 1946; written under the pseudonym Pierre Andrézel).

NONFICTION: *Den afrikanske Farm*, 1937 (*Out of Africa*, 1937); *Skygger paa Græsset*, 1960 (*Shadows on the Grass*, 1960); *Essays*, 1965; *Breve fra Afrika 1914-1931*, 1978 (*Letters from Africa 1914-1931*, 1981); *Daguerreotypes, and Other Essays*, 1979; *Samlede essays*, 1985.

Bibliography

Anastasia, Olga, ed. *Isak Dinesen: Critical Views*. Athens: Ohio University Press, 1993.

Bjørnvig, Thorkild. *The Pact: My Friendship with Isak Dinesen*. Translated from the Danish by Ingvar Schousboe and William Jay Smith. Baton Rouge: Louisiana State University Press, 1983. This short book offers Bjørnvig's account of his friendship with Dinesen, from their first meeting in 1948 to their definitive parting in 1954. Written by an accomplished poet, the volume is interesting in its own right as well as for the insight into Dinesen which it provides.

Johannesson, Eric O. *The World of Isak Dinesen*. Seattle: University of Washington Press, 1961. From the theoretical perspective of the New Criticism, Johannesson offers brief but close analyses of Dinesen's tales, concluding that the art of storytelling is the author's central theme and the basis for her worldview. The book serves as an excellent introduction to Dinesen's work. Contains a good bibliography as well as an index.

Juhl, Marianne, and Bo Hakon Jørgensen. *Diana's Revenge: Two Lines in Isak*

Dinesen's Authorship. Translated from the Danish by Anne Born. Odense, Denmark: Odense University Press, 1985. This volume contains two sophisticated scholarly and critical essays of considerable length. Juhl's contribution, "Sex and Consciousness," is informed by feminist theory. Jørgensen, in "The Ways of Art," discusses the relationship between Dinesen's sensuality and her art. Their book, which includes a good bibliography, is particularly strong in its discussion of Dinesen's use of classical symbols.

Langbaum, Robert Woodrow. *The Gayety of Vision: A Study of Isak Dinesen's Art*. New York: Random House, 1964. In an extensive study that will serve as a suitable introduction to Dinesen for the experienced reader, Langbaum places her within the Western literary tradition. A major claim is that by dissolving the distinction between fact and value, Dinesen is able to achieve a unified vision of the beauty, sadness, and gaiety of life. Good bibliography, index.

Migel, Parmenia. *Titania: The Biography of Isak Dinesen*. New York: Random House, 1967. The work of a writer rather than that of a scholar, Migel's biography truly represents a labor of love. Migel, a friend of Dinesen, promised Dinesen that she would be her biographer once Dinesen had died. The resulting volume is aimed at an audience of Dinesen devotees but will be of interest to others as well. Bibliography, index.

Stambaugh, Sara. *The Witch and the Goddess in the Stories of Isak Dinesen: A Feminist Reading*. Ann Arbor: UMI Research Press, 1988. Stambaugh offers a feminist-inspired examination of the portraits of women which are found in Dinesen's texts. The strength of her brief study is the recognition of the centrality of gender for an understanding of Dinesen's work; its weakness is its lack of theoretical sophistication. The book has a complete scholarly apparatus.

Thurman, Judith. *Isak Dinesen: The Life of a Storyteller*. New York: St. Martin's Press, 1982. Thurman's biography constitutes the fullest treatment of Dinesen's life and work in any language. Meticulously researched and highly readable, it provides an account of the writer's life, brief analyses of her works, and extensive discussion of the relationship between her life and works. Addressed to both scholars and an educated nonspecialist audience, it contains scholarly notes, a select bibliography, and a useful index.

Jan Sjåvik

FYODOR DOSTOEVSKI

Born: Moscow, Russia; November 11, 1821
Died: St. Petersburg, Russia; February 9, 1881

Principal short fiction · *Sochineniya*, 1860 (2 volumes) · *Polnoye sobraniye sochineniy*, 1865-1870 (4 volumes) · *Povesti i rasskazy*, 1882 · *A Christmas Tree and a Wedding, and an Honest Thief*, 1917 · *White Nights and Other Stories*, 1918 · *An Honest Thief and Other Stories*, 1919 · *The Short Novels of Dostoevsky*, 1945

Other literary forms · In addition to short fiction, Fyodor Dostoevski wrote novels, nonfiction, criticism, and *Yevgeniya Grande* (1844), a translation of Honoré de Balzac's novel *Eugénie Grandet* (1833). In his own time, Dostoevski was exceptionally influential, especially through *Dnevnik pisatelya* (1876-1877, 1800-1881; *The Diary of a Writer*, 1949), a series of miscellaneous writings that he published occasionally in St. Petersburg. Dostoevski also wrote a series of essays on Russian literature, some *feuilletons*, and the well-known travelogue "Zimniye zametki o letnikh vpechatleniyakh" (1863; "Winter Notes on Summer Impressions," 1955). His most famous contribution in his own time was his speech in Alexander Pushkin's honor, given on the occasion of the dedication of a monument to Pushkin in 1880.

Achievements · In the world literature of the nineteenth century, Dostoevski has few rivals. Some of his characters have penetrated literary consciousness and produced a new generation in the works of prominent twentieth century authors such as Jean-Paul Sartre and Jorge Luis Borges. He initiated psychological realism, inspiring both Friedrich Wilhelm Nietzsche and Sigmund Freud. His novels are read in translation in twenty-six languages. Dosto-

Courtesy of the Library of Congress

271

evski was originally suppressed in the Soviet Union, only to reemerge as even more influential in the second half of the twentieth century, finding a whole new generation of admirers in his transformed homeland. Even though his style is markedly nineteenth century, Dostoevski still seems quite modern today.

Biography · Fyodor Mikhailovich Dostoevski was born on November 11, 1821, in a small Moscow public hospital, where his father, Dr. Mikhail Andreevich Dostoevski, worked. He was the second son to the doctor and Marya Fyodorovna (née Nechaeva). One year after his mother's death, in 1837, Fyodor enrolled in the St. Petersburg Academy for Military Engineers. He completed his studies at the academy even after his father had died of a stroke in 1839, thanks to the inheritance of the Dostoevski estate.

Like so many writers' attempts, Dostoevski's first foray into the literary world was through translation—in his case, of Balzac's *Eugénie Grandet*, appearing in print in 1844. His first original work was a novel in letters, *Bednye lyudi* (1846; *Poor Folk*, 1887), which met with immediate success, creating quite a literary sensation even before its publication. The great critic Vissarion Belinsky hailed it with such enthusiasm that the novice writer was propelled into early fame.

Dostoevski followed this initial success with *Dvoynik* (1846; *The Double*, 1917). It was met more coolly, was considered an artistic failure, and was generally unpopular. The failure of *The Double*, as seen today, is quite ironic, since it contains many of the thematic occupations that eventually made Dostoevski famous. His next novel, *Netochka Nezvanova* (1849; English translation, 1920), was fated never to be completed. Most novels then appeared in journals and were serialized; this was the case with all Dostoevski's novels. After the first three installments of *Netochka Nezvanova* appeared in 1849, Dostoevski was arrested for participating in a secret anti-czarist society, the Petrashevsky Circle. He and thirty-two of his associates were arrested, imprisoned for eight months, and sentenced to death. At precisely the moment that his comrades were facing the firing squad, the sentence was commuted to hard labor. Dostoevski spent four years in hard labor at Omsk, followed by three years of exile from the capital.

He married Marya Isaeva in 1857, while still in Siberia. He was beginning to suffer from epilepsy, however, and she was also sickly. They returned to St. Petersburg in 1859, and shortly thereafter his works began again to appear in print. Life, however, did not return to normal. In 1864, his brother died, leaving him a second family to support. His wife, too, died the same year. Strapped financially, Dostoevski accepted an advance payment, agreeing to deliver a novel to a publisher that same year—or else forfeit the profits from all of his subsequent works. He succeeded in completing *Igrok* (1866; *The Gambler*, 1887), satisfying this publisher thanks to his stenographer, Anna Snitkina, whom he married in 1867. They left Russia for a few years, returning in 1871. The novels that he wrote while abroad established him as an important writer but not as a popular or successful one. In fact, during his life, he met with very little recognition.

The one shining exception to this neglect came at the dedication of a monument to Pushkin, in 1880. Thousands of people greeted his speech enthusiastically. He died only a few months later, in 1881, when an even larger crowd attended his funeral.

Analysis · Fyodor Dostoevski's works fall into two periods that coincide with the time before his imprisonment and following it. The seven-year hiatus in his creative output between 1849 and 1857 corresponds to the four years that he spent in prison and the three subsequent years during which he was banished in Siberia. The first period produced primarily shorter novels and short stories, many of which have never been translated into English; the latter period is represented more by the great novels, the epithet denoting both significance and size, as well as by *The Diary of a Writer*, which also contains several new short stories.

In Dostoevski's works, complex structures are created that introduce fundamentally antipodal constructs and that produce, among other effects, a mythologization of the antagonistic elements. Thus, the city, often the St. Petersburg of Dostoevski's present, contrasts with the countryside. The squalor of poverty permeates St. Petersburg with sounds and smells in Dickensian realistic fashion, as opposed to the quaint, provincial quiet of the country. Usually, problems or actual troublemakers come from the city, or, if one leaves the provinces for the city, one may become "infected" with urban discontent and return to plague the countryside. In another prevalent dichotomy, the "man of the forties" (that is, the optimistic believer in the Enlightenment) often clashes with the "man of the sixties" (that is, the atheistic and/or nihilistic revolutionary). This conflict often is positioned generationally, and it is seldom clear whether the representative of either generation should prevail.

Often throughout Dostoevski's works, men of a higher social class, although not necessarily a very high class, interact most significantly with women who are socially inferior, usually powerless or "compromised." The relationship takes on many different attitudes in the various works, but in almost every case, the woman turns out to be of greater virtue or higher moral and spiritual constitution than the man who, nevertheless, from his privileged position in society, usually fares better than the woman.

Perhaps most important of all the themes in his work is the belief in God versus atheism. If there is no God, many of Dostoevski's characters realize, then either every human being is a God or every human being is nothing at all. This conflict can, and sometimes does, take place within a single person as well as between two characters. Atheism usually appears in its most extreme state–that is, in the belief that since there is no God, the human being must be God. While Dostoevski's proponents of atheism are strong-willed, disciplined, and morbidly dedicated, in Dostoevski's world they need to accept the existence of God as their only chance for peace or, in the final analysis, for existing in the world at all. While free will is interpreted by these radical proponents as the ability to become gods, the submission to the will of the divine God is the only means toward happiness. Those who fail to redeem themselves through God either perish or are subject to enormous spiritual and psychological torment. Such conflict forms the crux of more than one novel in Dostoevski's latter period, and it will be the treatment of this element in Dostoevski's work that will earn for him recognition as the founder of existentialism in literature. Ironically from the point of view of Dostoevski's beliefs, it is his existential writings rather than his metaphysical ones that constitute his most profound influence on world literature in the twentieth century.

Most of Dostoevski's short stories are simpler works than the novels, both in terms of the psychology of the characters and in terms of structure. One of his best-known short stories, "Belye nochi" ("White Nights"), is subtitled "A Sentimental Story from the Diary of a Dreamer." The unnamed protagonist of this work meets a young woman, Nastenka, by chance one evening along the embankment. When they have the opportunity to speak to each other, they find that they have much in common: neither of them is able to enjoy a life of his or her own, and both of them, because of varying circumstances, are confined to their own abodes, occupied most of the time in daydreaming. Nastenka is physically restrained by her grandmother by being pinned to her skirt; the male protagonist is confined by his abject poverty and the inertia of unsociability to his quarters, with the green wallpaper and the spiderwebs. At the end of the story, Nastenka, nevertheless, is able to escape her fate thanks to the offices of the young boarder, who has taken pity on her, but she has had to wait an entire year; it is precisely at the end of this year that she meets the protagonist, whom, she claims, she would certainly love, and does in fact love, but as she truly still loves the other, she must relinquish. Nastenka leaves, imploring the protagonist not to blame her, knowing that he cannot blame her because he loves her. The protagonist feels that, somehow, this "moment" that they have shared is enough love to sustain him for a lifetime of dreaming. This story, unusual in the oeuvre of Dostoevski, does not involve the motif of the abused young woman, and the rejected young man seems quite content with his fate. Unlike most of Dostoevski's women, Nastenka has succeeded in meeting an honorable man who seemingly keeps his word, making her a singular female in the works of Dostoevski.

More in keeping with Dostoevski's image of the abused, victimized woman is the young girl in "Elka i svad'ba" ("A Christmas Tree and a Wedding"). The first-person narrator relates how he notices the indecent attention of a "great man" of society toward an eleven-year-old girl playing with dolls, who has been promised a huge dowry during one family's Christmas party. The "great man" is interested only in the fabulous dowry and bides his time. Five years later, the narrator notices a wedding taking place in the church and focuses on the face of the very young bride, "pale and melancholy," her eyes perhaps even red from "recent weeping" and her look of "childish innocence," where could be detected "something indescribably naive . . . mutely begging for mercy." He recognizes the young girl of a few years before and also the "great man," who is now the groom. The narrator concludes that it was a "good stroke of business." In this story, the theme of the helpless woman completely at the mercy of rapacious, evil men plays a major role, and the fate of the young girl in "A Christmas Tree and a Wedding," for all her money, bodes much worse than that of the impoverished Nastenka.

Perhaps Dostoevski's best-known short story, "Son smeshnogo che-loveha" ("The Dream of a Ridiculous Man") presents more of the most typical Dostoevskian philosophy of any short story. In it, a petty clerk who has realized that he has no reason to live believes that he should commit suicide to put an end to his ridiculous existence. Just when he decides to do so, a young girl accosts him and seemingly tries to engage his assistance. He pushes her aside, but his action causes him great shame, and he feels deep pity for the young girl. The experience of these two emotions causes him to postpone his suicide, if only for a few hours. Meanwhile, he falls asleep, and in his dream he shoots himself. Then, after he is dead and buried, he is transported to an Earth-like planet inhabited by people who only love. Unfortunately, he corrupts the entire population, causing wars, antipathies, and alienation. Upon awakening, the man feels that he has undergone a revelation and must preach his new religion, trying to con-vince people that it is possible to live in harmony together and to love sincerely people other than oneself.

In "The Dream of a Ridiculous Man," many themes from Dostoevski's mature novels appear: whether one is a zero or a human, whether there is an afterlife, suffering as the only condition for the possibility of love, and suicide as a means of investing significance to human action, as well as many more. It is in the great novels that the complex world wherein the actions of all Dostoevski's creations take place, including the short works. To read a short story without a fundamental background in other seminal works–for example *Zapiski iz podpolya* (1864; *Notes from the Underground,* 1918)–would very likely lead to a trap that could trivialize what are, by themselves, minor works such as the short stories. If, however, the short stories are contextualized within the entire oeuvre of Dostoevski over both his major periods, they form several interesting transitional points between many of his philosophical designs.

The young girls, usually victimized by poverty and evil men, seem to be an outgrowth of an early novel, *Poor Folk,* and a continuing motif throughout the later period. Here, an orphan serf girl is pressured into a marriage that will doubtless cause her endless degradation and possibly physical harm. The paradoxical "spiteful man" of *Notes from the Underground* is the model of the "little clerk" who, nevertheless, has been influenced by German romantic philosophy and against logical positivism. His voice and "spite" reverberate almost palpably in the short stories as well as in the great novels. The theme of life as suffering and love or compassion as life's greatest suffering is developed throughout the great novels, which, when used as a backdrop for the short works, provides a glimpse into the motivations of many of the protagonists.

Dostoevski's short stories clearly have a place of their own in Russian literature. Together, they form a miniature portrait of the most compelling people in Dostoevski's world. Reading them, along with the longer works, gives the discriminating reader an insight into one of the most powerful and intricate minds of the nineteenth century.

Other major works

NOVELS: *Bednye lyudi,* 1846 (*Poor Folk,* 1887); *Dvoynik,* 1846 (*The Double,* 1917); *Netochka Nezvanova,* 1849 (English translation, 1920); *Unizhennye i oskorblyonnye,* 1861 (*Injury and Insult,* 1886; better known as *The Insulted and Injured,* 1887); *Zapiski iz myortvogo doma,* 1861-1862 (*Buried Alive: Or, Ten Years of Penal Servitude in Siberia,* 1881; better known as *The House of the Dead,* 1915); *Zapiski iz podpolya,* 1864 (*Letters from the Underworld,* 1913; better known as *Notes from the Underground,* 1918); *Igrok,* 1866 (*The Gambler,* 1887); *Prestupleniye i nakazaniye,* 1866 (*Crime and Punishment,* 1886); *Idiot,* 1868 (*The Idiot,* 1887); *Vechny muzh,* 1870 (*The Permanent Husband,* 1888; better known as *The Eternal Husband,* 1917); *Besy,* 1871-1872 (*The Possessed,*

1913; also as *The Devils*, 1953); *Podrostok*, 1875 (*A Raw Youth*, 1916); *Bratya Karamazovy*, 1879-1880 (*The Brothers Karamazov*, 1912); *The Novels*, 1912 (12 volumes).

NONFICTION: "Zimniye zametki o letnikh vpechatleniyakh," 1863 ("Winter Notes on Summer Impressions," 1955); *Dnevnik pisatelya*, 1876-1877, 1880-1881 (2 volumes, partial translation as *Pages from the Journal of an Author; The Diary of a Writer*, 1949); *Pisma*, 1928-1959 (4 volumes); *Iz arkhiva F. M. Dostoyevskogo: "Prestupleniye i nakazaniye,"* 1931 (*The Notebooks for "Crime and Punishment,"* 1967); *Iz arkhiva F. M. Dostoyevskogo: "Idiot,"* 1931 (*The Notebooks for "The Idiot,"* 1967); *Zapisnyye tetradi F. M. Dostoyevskogo*, 1935 (*The Notebooks for "The Possessed,"* 1968); *F. M. Dostoyevsky: Materialy i issledovaniya*, 1935 (*The Notebooks for "The Brothers Karamazov,"* 1971); *Dostoevsky's Occasional Writings*, 1963; *F. M. Dostoyevsky v rabote nad romanom "Podrostok,"* 1965 (*The Notebooks for "A Raw Youth,"* 1969); *Neizdannyy Dostoyevsky: Zapisnyye knizhki i tetradi 1860-1881 gg.*, 1971 (3 volumes; *The Unpublished Dostoevsky: Diaries and Notebooks, 1860-1881*, 1973-1976); *F. M. Dostoyevsky ob iskusstve*, 1973; *Selected Letters of Fyodor Dostoyevsky*, 1987.

TRANSLATION: *Yevgeniya Grande*, 1844 (of Honoré de Balzac's novel *Eugénie Grandet*).

MISCELLANEOUS: *Polnoe sobranie sochinenii v tridtsati tomakh*, 1972- (30 volumes).

Bibliography

Catteau, Jacques. *Dostoevsky and the Process of Literary Creation*. Translated by Audrey Littlewood. Cambridge, England: Cambridge University Press, 1989. This excellent book offers detailed textual analysis and factual information on Dostoevski. The categories that form the subheadings range from "Time and Space in the World of the Novels" to ones such as "Money." Catteau provides a thematic overview of the pressures and inspirations that motivated Dostoevski. The volume includes ninety-five pages of notes and bibliography, as well as an index.

Frank, Joseph. *Dostoevsky: The Seeds of Revolt, 1821-1849*. Princeton, N.J.: Princeton University Press, 1976.

_____. *Dostoevsky: The Years of Ordeal, 1850-1859*. Princeton, N.J.: Princeton University Press, 1983.

_____. *Dostoevsky: The Stir of Liberation, 1860-1865*. Princeton, N.J.: Princeton University Press, 1986.

_____. *Dostoevsky: The Miraculous Years, 1865-1871*. Princeton, N.J.: Princeton University Press, 1995. These four volumes are the most significant and important English-language biographies.

Grossman, Leonid. *Dostoevsky: A Biography*. Translated by Mary Mackler.

New York: Bobbs-Merrill, 1975. Grossman was himself a good writer, and his critical work reads very well. There are moments of suspense and drama, but most of all, one senses the care and consideration taken by the author on Dostoevski's behalf. Generally, Grossman's volume covers Dostoevski's life and works, creative product, and critical reception. Includes detailed notes and an index.

Kjetsaa, Geir. *Fyodor Dostoevsky: A Writer's Life*. Translated by Siri Hustvedt and David McDuff. New York: Viking, 1987. By far the best work on Dostoevski's life: very thorough and very interesting. Kjetsaa debunks the myth of Dostoevski's father's murder definitively; his access to archives closed to previous scholars provides him the unambiguous evidence. His viewpoint is, appropriately, to shed light on the creation of Dostoevski's fiction, citing letters and notes as artistic points of departure for Dostoevski. The thorough, up-to-date bibliography of thirty pages will direct future scholars to his resources. Some illustrations, index.

Leatherbarrow, William J. Fedor Dostoevsky: A Reference Guide. Boston: G. K. Hall, 1990.

Mochulsky, K. V. *Dostoevsky: His Life and Work*. Translated by Michael Minihan. Princeton, N.J.: Princeton University Press, 1967. This book's title may slightly mislead the reader into thinking that the author is somehow isolating Dostoevski's life from his work. Mochulsky, however, informs the reader in his preface that "the life and work of Dostoevsky are inseparable. He lived in literature." Thus, rather than making a large work consisting of two major parts, Mochulsky interweaves biography and literary analysis brilliantly. His style is engaging and very accessible. This book is regularly recommended for undergraduates by many teachers of courses on Dostoevski.

Wasiolek, Edward. *Dostoevsky: The Major Fiction*. Cambridge: Massachussetts Institute of Technology Press, 1964. In this interesting and comprehensive work, Wasiolek not only addresses virtually all Dostoevski's fiction but also introduces much of the contemporary political polemics. He also includes a well-balanced assessment of many important subsequent literary critical opinions, which is interwoven in his analysis of the individual works. Includes notes about the first publication of Dostoevski's works as well as a detailed bibliography presenting both general subject headings (for example, a work's reception in the West) and writing apropos an individual work.

Christine Tomei

ARTHUR CONAN DOYLE

Born: Edinburgh, Scotland; May 22, 1859
Died: Crowborough, England; July 7, 1930

Principal short fiction · *Mysteries and Adventures*, 1889 (also as *The Gully of Bluemansdyke and Other Stories*) · *The Captain of Polestar and Other Tales*, 1890 · *The Adventures of Sherlock Holmes*, 1892 · *My Friend the Murderer and Other Mysteries and Adventures*, 1893 · *The Great Keinplatz Experiment and Other Stories*, 1894 · *The Memoirs of Sherlock Holmes*, 1894 · *Round the Red Lamp: Being Fact and Fancies of Medical Life*, 1894 · *The Exploits of Brigadier Gerard*, 1896 · *The Man from Archangel and Other Stories*, 1898 · *The Green Flag and Other Stories of War and Sport*, 1900 · *The Adventures of Gerard*, 1903 · *The Return of Sherlock Holmes*, 1905 · *Round the Fire Stories*, 1908 · *The Last Galley: Impressions and Tales*, 1911 · *One Crowded Hour*, 1911 · *His Last Bow*, 1917 · *Danger! and Other Stories*, 1918 · *Tales of the Ring and Camp*, 1922 (also as *The Croxley Master and Other Tales of the Ring and Camp*) · *Tales of Terror and Mystery*, 1922 (also as *The Black Doctor and Other Tales of Terror and Mystery*) · *Tales of Twilight and the Unseen*, 1922 (also as *The Great Keinplatz Experiment and Other Tales of Twilight and the Unseen*) · *Three of Them*, 1923 · *The Dealings of Captain Sharkey and Other Tales of Pirates*, 1925 · *Last of the Legions and Other Tales of Long Ago*, 1925 · *The Case-Book of Sherlock Holmes*, 1927 · *The Maracot Deep and Other Stories*, 1929 · *The Final Adventures of Sherlock Holmes*, 1981 · *Uncollected Stories: The Unknown Conan Doyle*, 1982

Other literary forms · Arthur Conan Doyle's more than one hundred published works include novels, autobiography, political treatises, plays adapted from his fiction, and works on spiritualism as well as his short stories, for which he is best known. His character Sherlock Holmes has been the subject of innumerable films, plays, and radio scripts and has become the archetype of the conventional detective hero.

Achievements · While Doyle was not the first to write short stories featuring a detective with great analytical powers, and while he acknowledged his debt to such writers as Edgar Allan Poe and Émile Gaboriau, who had written tales of intelligent amateur detectives solving crimes through logical deduction, in Sherlock Holmes, Doyle created a character who has entered the popular imagination like no other. Sherlock Holmes is perhaps the most famous and popular character in detective fiction, if

Courtesy of the Library of Congress

not in all modern fiction. Doyle's stories were a strong influence on writers such as Ellery Queen, Agatha Christie, John Dickson Carr, and the many others who create tightly constructed puzzles for their detectives to solve with clearly and closely reasoned analysis. Societies such as the Baker Street Irregulars have sprung up around the world to study Doyle's stories, and the name of Sherlock Holmes has become synonymous with deduction, while "Elementary, my dear Watson" is a catchphrase even among those who have never read the stories.

Biography · Arthur Conan Doyle was born in Scotland of devout Irish Catholic parents and educated by the Jesuits in England and Austria. He was graduated from the medical school at the University of Edinburgh and first went to sea as a ship's surgeon on a whaler to the Arctic, later on a West African passenger liner. He opened an office in Southsea, England, and because of a dearth of patients, began writing to fill his leisure time and to supplement his income. He had previously published a few short stories anonymously, and in 1887 completed *A Study in Scarlet*, a novelette in which Sherlock Holmes, as the central character, appears for the first time. Urged on by his American editor, he wrote *The Sign of Four* (1890) and a series of Sherlock Holmes stories which appeared in the *Strand Magazine*. The popularity of Holmes enabled Doyle to give up the practice of medicine, but since the author desired to be known as a historical romancer, the character was "killed off" in a struggle with his archenemy, Professor Moriarty, in the story "The Final Problem." Ten years later, yielding to pressure from his publishers and the public, he resurrected Holmes, first in *The Hound of the Baskervilles* (1901-1902) and later in another series of short stories. Doyle was knighted in 1902 for his political service and principally for his publications defending the conduct of the British in the Boer War. Having left Catholicism, he turned to spiritualism and devoted the rest of his life to psychic research and propagandizing his beliefs.

Analysis · In spite of his desire to be acknowledged as a writer of "serious" literature, Arthur Conan Doyle is destined to be remembered as the creator of a fictional character who has taken on a life separate from the literary works in which he appears. Sherlock Holmes, as the prototype of almost all fictional detectives, has become a legend not only to his devotees but also to those who have not even read the works in which he appears, the detective being immortalized by reputation and through the media of movies, television, and radio.

Doyle claimed that the character of Sherlock Holmes was based upon his memories of Dr. Joseph Bell, a teacher of anatomy at the University of Edinburgh, whose diagnostic skills he had admired as a student of medicine. Bell, however, disclaimed the honor and suggested that Doyle himself possessed the analytical acumen that more closely resembled the skills of Sherlock Holmes. Regardless of the disclaimers and acknowledgments, there is little doubt that Doyle owed a large debt to Edgar Allan Poe and other predecessors in detective fiction, such as Émile Gaboriau and François Eugène Vidocq. Doyle records that he was familiar with *Mémoires* (1828-1829; *Memoirs of Vidocq, Principal Agent of the French Police*, 1828-1829) and had read Gaboriau's *Monsieur Lecoq* (1880). It is the influence of Poe, however, that is most in evidence in the character of Holmes and in many of his plots.

Poe's character of C. Auguste Dupin bears remarkable similarities to the Sherlock Holmes character. Both Holmes and Dupin, for example, are eccentrics; both are amateurs in the detective field; both have little regard for the official police; and both enter into investigations, not because of any overwhelming desire to bring a culprit to justice but out of the interest that the case generates and the challenge to their analytical minds. In addition, both have faithful companions who serve as the chroniclers of the exploits of their respective detective friends. While Dupin's companion remains anonymous and the reader is unable to draw any conclusions about his personality, Dr. Watson, on the other hand, takes on an identity (although always in a secondary role) of his own. The reader shares with Watson his astonishment at Holmes's abilities. In effect, Watson becomes a stand-in for the reader by asking the questions that need to be asked for a complete understanding of the situation.

Generally, the Sherlock Holmes stories follow a similar pattern: there is usually a scene at the Baker Street residence, at which time a visitor appears and tells his or her story. After Holmes makes some preliminary observations and speculates upon a possible solution to the puzzle, Holmes and Watson visit the scene of the crime. Holmes then solves the mystery and explains to Watson how he arrived at the solution. "The Adventure of the Speckled Band" follows this formula, and it is apparent that Poe's "The Murders in the Rue Morgue" had a direct influence upon this "locked room" mystery. The murder, the locked room, and the animal killer are all variations upon the ingredients in the first case in which C. Auguste Dupin appears. Even the reference to the orangutan on the grounds of the Manor House would appear to be an allusion to the murderer in Poe's story. The Gothic romance influence is also apparent in this adventure of Sherlock Holmes: there is the mysterious atmosphere and the strange, looming manor house; and there is the endangered woman threatened by a male force. Changing the murderer from the ape of Poe's story to a serpent in Doyle's story suggests at least symbolically the metaphysical (or supernatural) struggle between the forces of good and evil.

Typically, this story as well as all the Holmes stories ends with the solution to the mystery. Sherlock Holmes acknowledges that, by driving the snake back into the room where Dr. Roylott, the murderer, is waiting, he is indirectly responsible for his death; yet he matter-of-factly states that it is not likely to weigh heavily upon his conscience. The mystery has been solved; that has been the detective's only interest in the case. Because of this single-minded interest on the part of the detective, what happens to the criminal after discovery is no longer relevant. If the criminal is to stand trial, the story ends with the arrest and no more is heard of him. There are no trials, no dramatic courtroom scenes, and no reports of executions or prison sentences which had been popular in earlier detective stories and which were to regain immense popularity in the future.

While the solution to the "ingenious puzzle" is the prime concern for the detective and certainly of interest to the reader, it is Sherlock Holmes's character with his multifaceted personality and his limitations which makes Doyle's stories about the detective's adventures so re-readable. Holmes, for example, is an accomplished musician, a composer as well as an instrumentalist; he is an expert in chemical research and has educated himself to be an authority on blood stains; he is the author of innumerable monographs on such esoteric subjects as different types of tobacco, bicycle tire impressions, and types of perfume; and he is an exceptionally fine pugilist.

His limitations, however, are what make Sherlock Holmes so attractive to the reader. He is sometimes frighteningly ignorant; for example, after Dr. Watson has explained the Copernican system to him, he responds: "Now that I know it. . . . I shall do my best to forget it"; he considers this information trivial, since it is not useful, and he feels that retaining it will crowd practical knowledge out of his mind. Holmes can also make erroneous judgments, and, perhaps most appealing of all, he can fail as a detective. It is this capacity for the detective to fail or to be outwitted that is perhaps Doyle's most significant contribution to the detective-fiction genre. Whereas Holmes's predecessors such as Lecoq and Dupin are presented as unerring in their conclusions and infallible in solving their cases, Doyle's hero demonstrates his fallibility early in his career. It is in the first of the Sherlock Holmes short stories, "A Scandal in Bohemia," without doubt Doyle's version of Edgar Allan Poe's "The Purloined Letter," that this very human fallibility is revealed. Both stories deal with the need to recover items that are being used to blackmail a person of royal heritage. In both cases, attempts to find the items have failed and the detectives are called upon for assistance; and in both stories, a ruse is used to discover the whereabouts of the incriminating items.

While the debt to Poe is large in this story, "A Scandal in Bohemia" also displays some significant departures that establish the work as Doyle's own, artistically. The scenes in the streets of London are conveyed with convincing detail to capture effectively "the spirit of the place" of Victorian England. The characters in Poe's Dupin stories are lightly drawn, and the central interest for these tales is not in the people but in what happens to them. While the characters in Poe's stories talk about matters which are only relevant to the mystery at hand, the direct opposite is true in Doyle's story. The people in the Holmes story are interesting and full of dramatic movement, and Holmes's conversations with Watson and the others are filled with comments which are not related to the case.

In addition, Doyle introduces the device of disguises in "A Scandal in Bohemia." The King of Bohemia, wearing a small face mask to hide his identity, visits Holmes in his lodgings; his disguise, however, is immediately penetrated by the detective. Sherlock Holmes also assumes a disguise in the story that is so convincing and successful that even his close friend Dr. Watson is unable to recognize him. It is the skill of Irene Adler, Holmes's antagonist in the story, in assuming another identity that leads to the detective's being foiled. Holmes's failure in this story, however, in no way detracts from him. On the contrary, this failure and his others (such as in "The Yellow Face") serve only to make him more convincing and more three-dimensional as a human being than the always successful C. Auguste Dupin. Holmes loses no status through his errors; instead, he gains in the light of his past and future successes.

While there will always be disagreement among Sherlock Holmes aficionados about which of the many short stories is best, there is broad agreement that one of the best-constructed stories by Arthur Conan Doyle is the second short story in the first series, "The Red-Headed League." Doyle himself ranked the story very high when he was queried, and the Victorian reading public's response attested to its popularity. This story also introduces one of the recurring themes of the short stories: that of the *Doppelgänger*, or double. The dual nature of the world and of personalities is developed in parallel manners throughout the unraveling of the mystery of Jabez Wilson's involvement with the Red-Headed League. The contemplative side of Holmes is repeatedly contrasted with his energized side, just as the orderliness of Victorian England is seen in stark relief against "the half that is evil." Repeatedly, when there is a lull in the chase or a mystery has been solved, Sherlock Holmes retreats to his contemplative side to forget at least temporarily "the miserable weather and the still more miserable ways of our fellowmen."

"The Red-Headed League" follows the traditional formula of a Sherlock Holmes story. Holmes is visited at his flat by Jabez Wilson, who relates his problem. Wilson, the owner of a small pawnshop, has been working for the Red-Headed League for eight weeks, until abruptly and under mysterious circumstances, the League has been dissolved. He qualified for the position because of his red hair and his only duties were to remain in a room and copy the *Encyclopædia Britannica*. He has been able to perform these chores because his assistant, Vincent Spaulding, was willing to work in the pawnshop for half-wages. He has come to Sherlock Holmes because he does not want to lose such a position without a struggle.

Holmes and Watson visit the pawnshop and Spaulding is recognized by the detective as being in reality John Clay, a master criminal and murderer. The detective is able to infer from the circumstances that the opposite of what is expected is true. He concludes that it is not the presence of Jabez Wilson in the room performing a meaningless "intellectual" task for the League that is important; rather, it is his absence from the pawnshop that gives his alter ego assistant the opportunity to perform the "physical" task of tunneling from the cellar into the nearby bank. Setting a trap, Holmes, Watson, and the police are able to capture Clay and his confederates in their criminal act.

The double theme of the story is also reinforced in Jabez Wilson's account of the applicants lining up to apply for the position with the Red-Headed League. He describes the crowd lining up on the stair; those in anticipation of employment ascending the stairs with hope; those who have been rejected descending in despair, forming a "double" stream. John Clay, Holmes's antagonist in this story, is the first in a long line of adversaries of the detective who serve in effect as *Doppelgängers* of the sleuth. Clay has an aristocratic background and possesses royal blood. Holmes also has illustrious ancestors, being descended from country squires, and his grandmother is described as being "the sister of Vernet, the French artist." Clay is well educated and urbane, characteristics Holmes repeatedly shows throughout his adventures. Clay is described as being "cunning" in mind as well as skillful in his fingers, again a reflection of the detective's characteristics. Clay is also gracious in his defeat and expresses admiration for the ingenuity displayed by the victorious Holmes. He is truly a worthy adversary for the detective and the direct mirror image of Sherlock Holmes.

Other great master criminals and, in effect, doubles for the great detective are Colonel Sebastian Moran of "The Adventure of the Empty House," Van Bork of "His Last Bow," and, the most famous of them all, Professor Moriarty, who is described in "The Final Problem" as the "Napoleon of crime" and the "organizer of half that is evil and of nearly all that is undetected in this great city." In essence, "The Final Problem" is a departure from the formula that characterizes the previous twenty-two Holmesian short stories, basically because Doyle intended that this would be the final work in which his detective would appear. Tiring of his creation and motivated by the desire to pursue his other literary interests, he has Watson record the demise of his friend. The story has no ingenious puzzle for the detective to unravel but instead is a detailed account of Sherlock Holmes's confrontation with his nemesis. For years, Holmes, who could "see deeply into the manifold wickedness of the human heart" and who could "leave his body at will and place himself into the mind and soul" of others, had been unable to penetrate the veil that shrouded the power "which for ever stands in the way of the law, and throws its shield over the wrongdoer." In this manner, Doyle almost casually proposes a conspiracy theme in this story which, in the hands of other writers, becomes one of the overriding characteristics of the detective fiction and thriller genres.

It is the character of Professor Moriarty, however, which commands the interest of the reader, particularly when seen as a reflection of Holmes. Professor Moriarty's career, like Holmes's, "has been an extraordinary one. He is a man of good birth and excellent education, endowed by Nature with a phenomenal mathematical faculty. At the age of twenty-one he wrote a treatise upon the Binomial Theorem, which has had a European vogue." When the Professor visits Holmes at his flat, his physical appearance is described as "extremely tall and thin, his forehead domes out in a white curve, and his two eyes are deeply sunken in his head. He is clean shaven, pale, and ascetic looking." To Holmes, his appearance is quite familiar, even though he has never met the man before. It is entirely likely that Holmes's immediate recognition is intended to suggest that the detective, for the first time in his life, is viewing in the flesh the side of his nature which his great intellect has refused to allow him to acknowledge.

Even though Dr. Watson had made special efforts to characterize Holmes as being almost totally devoid of emotion in his previous chronicles of Holmes's adventures, there are many instances in which there are outbursts of extreme feelings on the part of the detective. Holmes fluctuates between ennui and expressions of delight. He is often impulsive and compassionate. He is patient and deferential to his female clients. He is moved to indignation and intends to exact a form of revenge in "The Five Orange Pips." In this story, "The Final Problem," he shows a level of nervousness and caution which is almost akin to fear in response to the threat that the malevolent genius Moriarty poses toward his person. Professor Moriarty is too much like himself for the detective to remain scientifically detached. There is no doubt that Holmes is totally conscious of the significance of the parallels that exist between the two when the Professor states:

> It has been a duel between you and me, Mr. Holmes. You hope to place me in the dock. I tell you that I will never stand in the dock. You hope to beat me. I tell you that you will never beat me. If you are clever enough to bring destruction upon me, rest assured that I shall do as much to you.

Holmes, with Watson, flees this enemy whom he acknowledges as "being quite on the same intellectual plane" as himself. Then, at Reichenbach Falls, he is inevitably forced to come face-to-face once again with his other self. Sidney Paget, the illustrator of many of the original publications in the *Strand Magazine*, depicts the struggle between Holmes and Moriarty just before their dual plunge into the chasm as being entwined together.

Thus, the culmination of Holmes's illustrious career, as originally intended by Doyle, was brought about in an entirely satisfactory symbolic and literary manner. Holmes, who could idly concede, "I have always had an idea that I could have made a highly efficient criminal," and "Burglary was always an alternative profession had I cared to adopt it," had resisted those impulses. In "The Final Problem" he could say: "In over a thousand cases I am not aware that I have ever used my powers upon the wrong side." The detective, however, was keenly aware throughout this story that "if he could be assured that society was freed from Professor Moriarty he would cheerfully bring his own career to a conclusion." With the death of Moriarty, he achieves that end. While "London is the sweeter for [my] presence," the destruction of the other side of his nature in Professor Moriarty makes it all the more so. The death of Sherlock Holmes along with his nemesis is comparable to self-destruction.

When Doyle "killed off" his detective hero, he was in no way prepared for the public reaction that followed. He resisted almost continuous pressure from his publishers and the public until 1902, when he finally relented and resurrected Holmes in *The Hound of the Baskervilles* and later in the story "The Adventure of the Empty House." In this story, a lieutenant of Professor Moriarty, Colonel Sebastian Moran, is the culprit and functions as the alter ego for Holmes. One of the more subtle acknowledgments of the double theme in this story is the use by Holmes of a wax model of himself to mislead his adversaries. Similar to "The Final Problem," the story of the return of Sherlock Holmes does not follow the usual formula for the previous works, but the rest in the series adheres rather closely. When the stories are read in sequence, however, one can understand why the mere presence of the detective, however contrived his survival, would be cause for rejoicing by his followers. Even a lapse of more than ten years since his last appearance (three years within the stories) has in no way diminished his skill or intellectual capacity. Sherlock Holmes remains all that he was before his showdown with Professor Moriarty. The dialogue between the characters is as crisp as ever; the scenes are portrayed as vividly as before; the careful construction of the plots and the unraveling of the mysteries are as provocative as ever; and the imagination of the author is very much in evidence. There is evidence, however, of Doyle's reluctance to take his hero as seriously as he had before. The story "The Adventure of the Dancing Men," for example, is extremely contrived, almost totally dependent upon cartoons as a cipher, and the reader is left with a feeling of dissatisfaction. The stories in the first series after the "death" of Sherlock Holmes are nevertheless of generally high quality and possess many memorable scenes which remain after the mysteries have been solved.

There is agreement that the quality of the Sherlock Holmes stories published in the two collections, *His Last Bow* and *The Case-Book of Sherlock Holmes*, is significantly diminished. Published in 1917 and 1927 respectively, the books demonstrate that Doyle was tired of his detective, as the works were written casually and almost impatiently. The onset of World War I in the title story of *His Last Bow* is pointed out by Jacques Barzun as being "perhaps symbolic of the end of a world of gaslight and order in which Holmes and Watson could function so predictably." The stories in *The Case-Book of Sherlock Holmes*, published only a few years before Doyle's death, possess some fine moments, but there is a singular failure on the part of the author to re-create the vividness of the Victorian world that had lifted the previous series of short stories out of the ordinary and enabled the reader to accept and admire so readily the reasoning powers of Sherlock Holmes.

Despite the uneven quality of these works, it is a tribute to Doyle's ability that Sherlock Holmes remains a memorable character. Although Watson informs the reader that Holmes's knowledge of formal philosophy is nil, he is a philosopher in his own way. Holmes has probed the most abstract of understandings–ranging from the motivation of humans to the nature of the universe–from the study of the physical world. He possesses a peculiar morality akin to the John Stuart Mill variety: evil is doing harm to others. When he seeks justice, he inevitably finds it; justice in the social and structured sense. Holmes has little regard for the laws of man; he recognizes that they do not always serve the purposes of justice, so at times he rises above them and often ignores them. For him, the distinction between right and wrong is absolute and beyond debate. It was Doyle's skill in infusing such depth into his character that makes Holmes greater than Dupin and Lecoq.

Other major works

NOVELS: *A Study in Scarlet*, 1887; *The Mystery of Cloomber*, 1888; *The Firm of Girdlestone*, 1889; *Micah Clarke*, 1889; *The Sign of Four*, 1890 (first pb. as *The Sign of the Four*); *Beyond the City*, 1891; *The Doings of Raffles Haw*, 1891; *The White Company*, 1891; *The Great Shadow*, 1892; *The Refugees*, 1893; *The*

Parasite, 1894; *The Stark Munro Letters,* 1895; *The Surgeon of Gaster Fell,* 1895; *Rodney Stone,* 1896; *The Tragedy of the Koroska,* 1897 (also as *A Desert Drama*); *Uncle Bernac,* 1897; *A Duet, with an Occasional Chorus,* 1899, revised 1910; *The Hound of the Baskervilles,* 1901-1902 (serial), 1902 (book); *Sir Nigel,* 1906; *The Lost World,* 1912; *The Poison Belt,* 1913; *The Valley of Fear,* 1915; *The Land of Mist,* 1926.

PLAYS: *Foreign Policy,* 1893; *Jane Annie: Or, the Good Conduct Prize,* 1893 (with J. M. Barrie); *Waterloo,* 1894 (also as *A Story of Waterloo*); *Halves,* 1899; *Sherlock Holmes,* 1899 (with William Gillette); *A Duet,* 1903; *Brigadier Gerard,* 1906; *The Fires of Fate,* 1909; *The House of Temperley,* 1909; *The Pot of Caviare,* 1910; *The Speckled Band,* 1910; *The Crown Diamond,* 1921; *Exile: A Drama of Christmas Eve,* 1925; *It's Time Something Happened,* 1925.

POETRY: *Songs of Action,* 1898; *Songs of the Road,* 1911; *The Guards Came Through and Other Poems,* 1919; *The Poems: Collected Edition,* 1922.

NONFICTION: *The Great Boer War,* 1900; *The War in South Africa: Its Causes and Conduct,* 1902; *The Case of Mr. George Edalji,* 1907; *Through the Magic Door,* 1907; *The Crime of the Congo,* 1909; *The Case of Oscar Slater,* 1912; *Great Britain and the Next War,* 1914; *In Quest of Truth, Being a Correspondence Between Sir Arthur Conan Doyle and Captain H. Stansbury,* 1914; *To Arms!,* 1914; *The German War: Some Sidelights and Reflections,* 1915; *Western Wanderings,* 1915; *The Origin and Outbreak of the War,* 1916; *A Petition to the Prime Minister on Behalf of Robert Casement,* 1916(?); *A Visit to Three Fronts,* 1916; *The British Campaign in France and Flanders,* 1916-1919 (6 volumes); *The New Revelation,* 1918; *The Vital Message,* 1919; *Our Reply to the Cleric,* 1920; *Spiritualism and Rationalism,* 1920; *A Debate on Spiritualism,* 1920 (with Joseph McCabe); *The Evidence for Fairies,* 1921; *Fairies Photographed,* 1921; *The Wanderings of a Spiritualist,* 1921; *The Coming of the Fairies,* 1922; *The Case for Spirit Photography,* 1922 (with others); *Our American Adventure,* 1923; *My Memories and Adventures,* 1924; *Our Second American Adventure,* 1924; *The Early Christian Church and Modern Spiritualism,* 1925; *Psychic Experiences,* 1925; *The History of Spiritualism,* 1926 (2 volumes); *Pheneas Speaks: Direct Spirit Communications,* 1927; *What Does Spiritualism Actually Teach and Stand For?,* 1928; *A Word of Warning,* 1928; *An Open Letter to Those of My Generation,* 1929; *Our African Winter,* 1929; *The Roman Catholic Church: A Rejoinder,* 1929; *The Edge of the Unknown,* 1930; *Arthur Conan Doyle on Sherlock Holmes,* 1981; *Essays on Photography,* 1982; *Letters to the Press,* 1984.

TRANSLATION: *The Mystery of Joan of Arc,* 1924 (by Léon Denis).

EDITED TEXTS: *D. D. Home: His Life and Mission,* 1921 (by Mrs. Douglas Home); *The Spiritualist's Reader,* 1924.

ANTHOLOGY: *Dreamland and Ghostland,* 1886.

Bibliography

Carr, John Dickson. *The Life of Sir Arthur Conan Doyle.* London: John Murray, 1949. One of the first biographies of Doyle not written by a relative. Carr's straight-forward biography gives a good overview of Doyle's life. Carr quotes copiously from Doyle's letters, but there is very little discussion of the stories. Includes a list of sources and an index.

Edwards, Owen Dudley. *The Quest for Sherlock Holmes: A Biographical Study of Arthur Conan Doyle.* Edinburgh: Mainstream Publishing, 1983. This dense, scholarly biography attempts to display the social, historical, and scientific background on which Doyle drew to create Sherlock Holmes. Edwards does not discuss the stories much except to place them in a historical and biographical context. Contains a discussion of sources, an index, and illustrations.

Hodgson, John A., ed. *Sherlock Holmes: The Major Stories with Contemporary Critical Essays.* Boston: Bedford Books of St. Martin's Press, 1994.

Jaffee, Jacqueline A. *Arthur Conan Doyle.* Boston: Twayne, 1987. Jaffee's solid work combines biography and a critical discussion of Doyle's stories and novels. Contains three chapters on the Sherlock Holmes stories, which closely examine the tales. Supplemented by an index, a bibliography of Doyle's work, and an annotated bibliography.

Knight, Stephen. *Form and Ideology in Crime Fiction.* London: Macmillan, 1980. Knight's work includes a chapter on *The Adventures of Sherlock Holmes* as well as a discussion of Doyle's work in chapters on various themes, styles, and structures of detective fiction. He focuses on Doyle's use of science and logic and examines style and structure in a close reading of several stories. The index lists topics discussed as well as names and titles so that the student can compare Doyle's treatment of various subjects with that of other authors.

Priestman, Martin. *Detective Fiction and Literature: The Figure on the Carpet.* London: Macmillan, 1990. Priestman discusses the differences and similarities of detective and conventional fiction and provides an introduction to the social, structural, and psychological implications of crime fiction. He includes two chapters on the Sherlock Holmes stories, which provide close readings of several stories.

Symons, Julian. *Conan Doyle: Portrait of an Artist.* London: Andre Deutsch, 1979. Symons, a recognized expert in the history of detective fiction, has produced a readable popular biography of Doyle. There is some discussion of the Sherlock Holmes stories in the context of Doyle's life. Includes illustrations, a bibliography, and an index.

Robert W. Millett
(Revised by *Karen M. Cleveland Marwick*)

WILLIAM FAULKNER

Born: New Albany, Mississippi; September 25, 1897
Died: Oxford, Mississippi; July 6, 1962

Principal short fiction · *These Thirteen,* 1931 · *Doctor Martino and Other Stories,* 1934 · *Go Down, Moses,* 1942 · *The Portable Faulkner,* 1946, 1967 · *Knight's Gambit,* 1949 · *Collected Short Stories of William Faulkner,* 1950 · *Big Woods,* 1955 · *Three Famous Short Novels,* 1958 · *Uncollected Stories of William Faulkner,* 1979

Other literary forms · William Faulkner published nearly twenty novels, two collections of poetry, and a novel-drama, as well as essays, newspaper articles, and illustrated stories. His early work has been collected and his University of Virginia lectures transcribed. As a screenwriter in Hollywood, he was listed in the credits of such films as *The Big Sleep* (1946), *To Have and Have Not* (1944), and *Land of the Pharaohs* (1955).

Achievements · Faulkner is best known for his novels, particularly *The Sound and the Fury* (1929), *Absalom, Absalom!* (1936), and *As I Lay Dying* (1930), all of which have been translated widely. *A Fable* (1954) and *The Reivers* (1962) won Pulitzer Prizes, and *A Fable* and the *Collected Short Stories* won National Book Awards. Faulkner received the Nobel Prize in 1949.

Film versions have been made of several of his works: *Sanctuary* (1961), *Intruder in the Dust* (1949), *The Sound and the Fury,* (1959), *The Reivers* (1969), and *Pylon* (1957; or *Tarnished Angels*). Others (*Requiem for a Nun,* 1951, and "Barn Burning") have been filmed for television.

Such attention attests to the fact that Faulkner has been one of the most influential writers in the twentieth century–both in the United States, where his work suggested to an enormous generation of Southern writers the valuable literary materials that could be derived from their own region, and in Europe, particularly in France. He has had a later, but also profound, effect on Latin American fiction, most noticeably in the work of Colombian writer Gabriel García Márquez, who seeks, like Faulkner did, to create a fictive history of a region and a people. Faulkner's work has also been well received in Japan, which he visited as a cultural ambassador in 1955.

Biography · William Faulkner spent most of his life in Mississippi, although as a young man he went briefly to Paris and lived for a time in New Orleans, where he knew Sherwood Anderson. He trained for the Royal

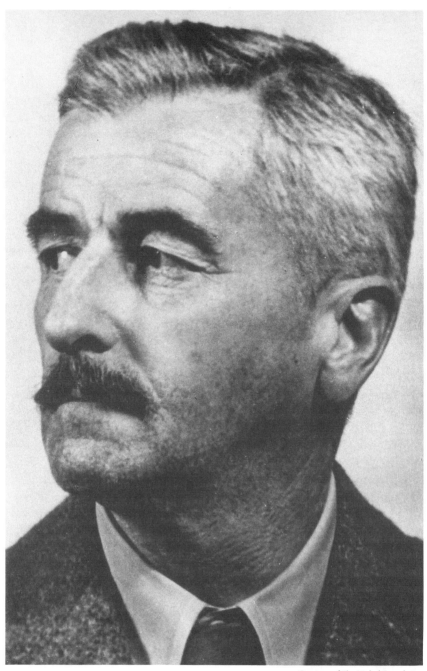

Courtesy of The Nobel Foundation

Air Force in Canada during World War I, but the war was over before he saw action. He attended the University of Mississippi in Oxford for a year, where he published poems and reviews in a campus periodical; and after dropping out, he worked for a time in the university post office. He married Estelle Oldham, and they had a daughter, Jill. Except for periodic and often unhappy stays in Hollywood to work on film scripts—in order to support a large number of dependents—Faulkner lived and wrote in Oxford, where he had available to him in the town and surrounding countryside the prototypes for the characters that inhabit his major works. In the late 1950's, he accepted a position as a writer-in-residence at the University of Virginia and traveled to Japan on behalf of the Department of State. Although his literary reputation waned in the 1940's, when virtually all of his earlier works were out of print, Faulkner's stature as a writer grew after 1946, when Malcom Cowley published *The Portable Faulkner*, and especially after 1950, when he accepted the Nobel Prize, when his collected stories were published, and when his novels began to be reprinted. Faulkner drove himself harder physically as he grew older, and he was troubled throughout his life with alcohol binges into which he would often fall after completing a book. These factors contributed to his death in 1962.

Analysis · William Faulkner has been credited with having the imagination to see, before other serious writers saw, the tremendous potential for drama, pathos, and sophisticated humor in the history and people of the South. In using this material and, in the process, suggesting to others how it might be used, he has also been credited with sparking the Southern Renaissance of literary achievement that has produced much of the United States' best literature in the twentieth century.

In chronicling the tragedy of Southern history, he delineated a vision tempered by his historical perspective that has freed the region from the popular conception of its character as possessing a universal gentility and a pervasive aristocracy, and he portrayed realistically a population often idealized and caricatured in songs, movies, and pulp fiction. In undercutting the false idealizations, Faulkner often distorted the stereotypes and rendered them somewhat grotesque in the interest of bringing them to three-dimensional life; and he attempted to show in the political and social presumptions of the South the portent of its inevitable destruction—first through war and then through an insidious new social order based on commercial pragmatism and shortsighted lust for progress. In this sense, the New South is shown to have much in common with mainstream America.

Faulkner's themes are often conveyed in an elaborate Baroque style noted for its long, difficult sentences that challenge the reader to discern the speaker, the time, and even the subject of the narrative. Faulkner makes considerable use of stream-of-consciousness interior monologues, and his frequent meshings of time reinforce his conviction that the past and present are intricately interwoven in the human psyche.

"A Rose for Emily," frequently anthologized and analyzed, is probably Faulkner's best-known story. Because of its elements of mystery, suspense, and the macabre, it has enjoyed a popular appeal. That Emily Grierson, an aging Southern belle, murders the lover who spurned her and sleeps beside his decaying body for a number of years is only the most sensational aspect of the story. What is more interesting to the serious reader of Faulkner is the interplay between Emily Grierson and the two generations of townspeople who attempt to cope with her—one the old guard and the other a new generation with "modern ideas."

The opening paragraphs of the story inform the reader that when Miss Emily died, the whole town turned out for her funeral. She was a "fallen monument . . . a tradition, a duty and a care; a sort of hereditary obligation upon the town." The townspeople, who are by the time of Emily's death mostly of a younger generation than her own, have never been able to incorporate her into their community. For them, as well as for their fathers, she has stood as an embodiment of an older ideal of Southern woman-hood—even though in her later years she has grown obese, bloated, and pale as dough. The older generation, under the mayoralty of Colonel Sartoris ("who fathered the edict that no Negro woman should appear on the streets without an apron"), has relieved Miss Emily of her taxes and has sent its children to take her china painting classes "in the same spirit that they were sent to church on Sunday with a twenty-five-cent piece for the collection plate." The new generation, however, is not pleased with the accommodations its fathers made with Miss Emily; it tries to impose taxes upon her and it no longer sends its children to take her lessons. Miss Emily has been encouraged in her ways by the old guard, however; she refuses to pay the town's taxes, telling the representatives of the new generation to "see Colonel Sartoris," who has been dead for ten years. The town is unable to handle Emily; it labels her "insane" and likewise comes to see her as the ghost of a feminine ideal out of the past. She becomes a recluse, living alone in her house with her black servant; and in her claim to privilege and impunity, she stands as a reminder to the town of the values—and sins—of its fathers, which are visited upon the third generation.

It is tempting to think of Miss Emily as merely a decadent and perverse relic of the South's antebellum past; indeed, this is how the story has often been read. Such a neat interpretation, however, would seem to be defeated by the time element in the story. Emily lives in a house spiraled and cupolaed in the architectural style of the 1870's, on a once-elegant street that has been altered by industry and commercial development. Although the rickety town fathers of the Civil War era come to her funeral dressed in their dusty uniforms and even believe that she was of their own generation and that they had danced with her when she was a young woman, clearly Emily is not of that generation; she is of the postwar South. She has not lingered as a relic from a warped racist culture; she has instead been created by defeated members of that culture who have continued to yearn after a world they have lost, a world that might well have existed largely in their imaginations, but a concept so persistent that the newer generation, for all its modern ideas, is powerless to control it. The reader is told that the town had long thought of Emily and her dead father "as a tableau, Miss Emily a slender figure in white in the background, her father a spraddled silhouette in the foreground, his back to her and clutching a horsewhip, the two of them framed by the backflung front door." It is clear that the newer generation of the twentieth century has adopted certain popular ideas about the old South. This "tableau" could serve as the dust jacket for any number of romantic novels set in the plantation days.

Thus, the two generations are complicit in ignoring the real Emily and creating and maintaining the myth of Emily as an exemplum of Southern womanhood from a lost age, just as the town aldermen—"three graybeards and one younger man, a member of the rising generation"—have conspired to cover up Emily's horrible crime. When the smell of the corpse of Emily's decaying lover, Homer Barron, had become so strong that it could no longer be ignored by the town, the aldermen had scattered lime around Emily's house secretly at night, although they knew she had recently purchased arsenic from the druggist and that Barron had disappeared; and when the smell went away, so did the town's concern about the matter. The old guard cannot bear, and does not wish, to accept the grim essence of the dream it has spun; the new generation, under the influence of the old, grudgingly accepts its burden of the past, but then wrenches it into a romantic shape that obscures the "fat woman in black" (overindulgent, moribund) that is Emily Grierson.

The story, then, is a comment on the postbellum South which inherited the monstrous code of values, glossed over by fine words about honor and glory, that characterized the slave era; that postbellum South learns to ignore the unsavory elements of its past by ignoring Emily the recluse and murderess and by valorizing the romantic "tableau." This is, however, a complex matter. The new generation—a generation excluded from the nominal code of honor, valor, and decorum that the old Confederates believed to have sustained them and excluded from the benefits that were to be gained from the slave system of the "glorious" old South—sees the Griersons as "high and mighty," as holding themselves "a little too high for what they really were." The new generation, pragmatic and small-minded, for the most part, has inherited a landscape sullied by cotton gins and garages. Miss Emily Grierson, as a privileged person and as a reminder of what the older generation forfeited in its defeat, is a goad in the minds of the uncharitable newer generation, which, when she does not marry, is "vindicated." When it hears the rumor that she has inherited nothing but the decaying house from her father, it is glad: "At last they could pity Miss Emily." Miss Emily out of sight, destitute, "insane," and deprived too of the lost legacy of the old South can be recreated as a fictional heroine in white, part of the backdrop against which the popularized hero, her father, stands with his horsewhip—a faceless silhouette, cruel and powerful, an "ancestor" who can be claimed by the dispossessed generation as its own.

The incestuous image of the father and daughter suggests the corrupt nature of the new South which, along with the corrupt nature of the old South, is a favorite Faulknerian concern. Granted, the "tableau" on the face of it appears to be the cover of a romantic novel, and in that sense it seems to be merely a popular rendering of history; but it is the townspeople who arrange *father and daughter* in the lurid scene. It is the men of the new generation who black out the distinguishing features of Emily's dead father in their creation of the tableau, leaving a dark masculine space (more, one would guess, in the shape of foreman Homer Barron than of Mr. Grierson) into which they can dream themselves, as masters of a glorious age, as potent heroes for whom the wispy heroine wanes in the background. The newer generation has the "modern ideas" bred of the necessity of surviving in the defeated, industrialized South; but in its attitudes toward Emily Grierson, it reveals the extent to which the old decadent values of the fathers have been passed along.

The narrator of the story, one of the townspeople himself, has proved unreliable. While it is true that Emily seems to be "a tradition, a duty, a care, . . . an hereditary obligation," a relic of the past miraculously sprung into being in spite of the disparity between her time and the historical time with which she is associated, the narrator only inadvertently reveals the truth of the matter: that both generations of the town are guilty of the desires and misplaced values that not only allow Miss Emily the murderess to come into being, but which also lead them to cover her crime and enshrine her in a tableau into which they, in their basest longings, can insert themselves. There is an incestuousness to all of this, an unhealthy interbreeding of values that allows each generation to perform despicable acts in the process of maintaining its ideas of what it would like to be. It is true that Emily is a "fallen monument"; but what the narrator fails to spell out explicitly is that the monument has been erected not only by the historical grandeur of her family, but also by the dispossessed generations that interpret her to their own ends. The monument is toppled by death, not by an ethical evolution in the town. The narrator is redeemed to some extent by "his" pity for Emily and by the recognition that the town, by driving her into mad isolation, has treated her badly.

As for Emily herself, she would seem to represent the worst elements of her neighbors, carried to their extreme conclusions. As the antebellum masters of the slaves presumed an all-powerfulness that allowed them to believe that they could own people, so does Miss Emily presume. Alive, Homer Barron–the outsider, the Yankee, a curious vitality in the pallid town–is outside Miss Emily's control. Dead, however, she can own him, can dress his corpse like a groom, can sleep beside him perhaps every night at least until her hair turns gray. As the new generation can blind itself to unpleasant truths about its history and itself, so can Emily become lost in delusion: her father, dead for three days, is proclaimed not dead and she refuses to bury him; Homer's corpse is a "groom" (and, perhaps in some further depraved vision, connected with the dead father). Emily represents not only the decadence of Colonel Sartoris' racist era, but also the decadence of the "modern" generation's use of that era. Thus "A Rose for Emily," often dismissed as Faulkner's ghost story, proves to be a clear expression of a recurring motif in Faulkner's works: the complexity of the connections between the present and the past.

These connections are explored in a less sensational manner in "The Bear." This story, which Faulkner also made the centerpiece of his novel *Go Down, Moses*, is another of the most anthologized, most studied pieces of Faulkner's short fiction. Composed of five sections (although often only four are printed in anthology versions, the long and complex fourth section being omitted), "The Bear" covers the history of Isaac (Ike) McCaslin, heir to the land and to the shame of his slave-owner grandfather, L. P. C. McCaslin, who committed incest with his illegitimate daughter, thereby driving her mother to suicide. After discovering this horrifying ghost in old plantation ledgers, Ike feels bound to repudiate the inheritance that has descended to him from his grandfather–even though the repudiation costs him his wife and any hope of progeny–in an attempt to expiate his inherited guilt and to gain a measure of freedom from the vicious materialism that brought the slavery system into being. Thus he allows his patrimony to pass to his cousin McCaslin Edmonds, who plays devil's advocate in Ike's attempt to understand the South and his own place in it, the tragedy of the blacks and of his own class, and the significance of what he possesses without inheriting: an instinctual knowledge of nature and an infallible sense of what is just.

"The Bear" may be seen as a hunting story, part of the *Big Woods* collection that includes "The Bear Hunt" and "Race at Morning." As a hunting story it is concerned with Ike's maturing, with his pilgrimage year after year to the hunting grounds where he and a group of adult hunters stalk the ancient bear, Old Ben, an enduring symbol of nature. Ike's guide and teacher is Sam Fathers, an aging Indian who still holds a sure instinct for the truths to be found in nature, and under whose tutelage Ike comes to form a system of values that later will lead him to renounce his inheritance. From Sam, Ike acquires a sense of nature's terms and of humanity's need to meet her on her own terms—of the necessity of according dignity to the force of nature and to all creatures through whom it courses. To meet the embodiment of that force in Old Ben, Ike must leave behind the instruments of civilization: the gun, the compass, the watch. Eventually Ike is able to track down Old Ben with regularity, but even when he encounters the bear and is armed, he refuses to shoot it.

It would seem that the proof of nature's endurance, represented in the bear, is of paramount concern to Ike. When Old Ben is finally killed and Sam Fathers dies, the ritual of the hunt is over for Ike. Yet two years later, he returns to the woods and sees in its organic and deathless elements, which have incorporated the remains of Old Ben and Sam Fathers, a proof of nature's dualistic power to absorb death and bring forth new life from it. This force is at the same time awesome and terrifying, and it must be revered and confronted if humanity is to live meaningfully. Even as Ike makes this last pilgrimage, however, a lumber company hacks away at the forest and a train cuts through the wilderness, underscoring the idea of the damage a materialistic civilization can do to even the most powerful aspects of nature. Faulkner shows an era of United States history passing— an era of abundance and of human appreciation of what nature requires from humanity in their mutual interest.

When "The Bear" is examined from the point of view of the intricate fourth section, it goes beyond being merely a hunting story to comment profoundly on the passing age and that which is replacing it. The scene shifts from the vast wilderness of nature to the intense confines of Ike McCaslin's consciousness, which struggles to find a way to atone for the sins of his ancestors and of his class. The entanglement of past and present here is more complex than it is in "A Rose for Emily," for Ike must face the knowledge that bloods mingled in the past—black and white, slave and owner—have in the present flowed in grossly inequitable courses to the present, as reflected in the sufferings of his mixed-blood relatives. Therefore, he renounces his patrimony, he sets out to redress old wrongs with his black relatives, and he seeks to give full recognition to the brotherhood he shares with these relatives by recognizing the strengths they contribute to his family and to Southern society—the virtues of "pity and tolerance and forbearance and fidelity and love of children."

In contrast to the self-serving generation of postbellum townspeople in "A Rose for Emily," Ike—also of that era—is a man of conscience. This is not to suggest, however, that Ike is particularly "modern" in his ideas; rather he has modeled himself on older examples of integrity, not only Sam Fathers but also his father and his uncle, who had turned over their own inherited house to their slaves and built a humbler cabin for themselves. In Ike's own case, the personal sacrifices to integrity and conscience have been enormous—his wife's love; his hope of a son to carry on his mission; living alone and ultimately uncertain that his sacrifice will bear fruit beyond his limited scope to influence events. Nevertheless, Faulkner illustrates through his invention of Ike McCaslin the extent to which idealism can flourish, even when constantly challenged by the grimmest vestiges of past evils.

"Barn Burning" is an inversion of "The Bear" in that its protagonist, ten-year-old Sarty Snopes, is seeking the world that Ike McCaslin wishes to repudiate. Not of the landed class, but the son of a tenant farmer who is always on the move because arson is his means of creating justice, Sarty associates the landed gentry with a "peace and dignity" and a civilized justice that is the direct opposite of the "fear and terror, grief and despair" that characterizes his life with his father, Ab Snopes. Ab uses fire as a weapon against the ruling class that he sees as the shaper of his economic fate, and he exhorts Sarty to be true to the blood ties which Ab sees as the only protection for his kind against the forces of an exploitative aristocracy. Sarty, however, rejects the "old blood" that he has not chosen for what seems to him a higher concept of fairness, and he longs to be free of his family and the turmoil it generates in his life.

For Sarty, Major DeSpain is the antithesis of Ab. DeSpain owns the farm on which Ab has most recently contracted to work. To Sarty, DeSpain and his columned house, as big as a courthouse, represent not what Ab sees, the sweat of black and white people to produce someone else's wealth, but the peace and dignity for which Sarty yearns and a system of justice that operates on principles of law rather than on personal revenge. Sarty's view is based on a naïve trust in civilization that blinds his inexperienced eyes to the inescapable connections between wealth and the mechanism of civilization.

Ab provokes a confrontation with DeSpain by deliberately tracking horse manure on an expensive rug. A series of moves and countermoves by Ab and DeSpain brings the pair to the point where, although DeSpain cannot begin to recover his loss from Ab, the local court nevertheless rules that Ab must take responsibility, within his means, for his act. This is enough to satisfy Ab yet again that the social system only works in behalf of the rich, and he sets out that night to redress this wrong by burning DeSpain's barn. Sarty cannot bear to allow this injustice, and so he is torn between real loyalty to his family and commitment to an ideal of justice. Specifically, he must decide whether to support his father's crime through silence or to betray the familial bond and warn DeSpain. Sarty chooses the ideal, warns DeSpain even as the barn begins to burn, and then flees the scene, unsure whether the shots he hears wound any of his family. Having made his choice, Sarty must set out alone to forge his own life.

"Barn Burning" offers a helpful picture of how Faulkner sees the economics of the postbellum South, where the poor whites remain the underclass rivals of black sharecroppers. Faulkner shows in other works how a new social order eventually evolved in which the descendants of Ab Snopes slip into the defeated, genteel society like silent bacteria and take over its commerce, coming finally to own the mansions that had previously belonged to the DeSpains and Compsons and Sartorises. Again and again Faulkner reiterates that it was the corrupt systems of slavery and of the plantation that ultimately ensured the fall of the Old South. Yet his view of Snopeses—violent, relentless, insidious men and inert, cowlike women, who by their numbers and crafty pragmatism will wrench the land and the wealth from the depleted gentility—is hardly positive.

In fact, "Barn Burning" is singular in that it is perhaps the only example of Faulkner's fiction in which the Snopeses are depicted sympathetically without first being made to appear ridiculous. As is often the case, Faulkner is extremely sensitive to the young boy caught in a painful rite of passage—as true for Sarty Snopes as it is for Ike McCaslin, Lucius Priest, Chick Mallison, and others not of the threatening Snopes clan. Moreover, "Barn Burning" makes an interesting case for Ab Snopes as the pitiable creation of the landed aristocracy, who seeks dignity and integrity for himself, although his only chance of achieving either would seem to lie in the democratic element of fire as the one defense available to all, regardless of social class. In this story, Ab is placed in the company of Wash Jones, Joe Christmas, and other members of the underclass that Faulkner views with sympathy and whose portrayals are in themselves indictments of the civilization that has forced them to desperate means.

While none of these examples quite suggests the very humorous ends to which Faulkner often turns his Southern materials, it should be remembered that he was highly aware of the potential for comedy in all the situations described here and that even such delicate matters as the tensions between the races and the revolution in the social order are, in Faulkner's hands, as frequently the catalysts of tall tales and satire as they are of his most somber and lyrical prose. It is true that "A Rose for Emily" hints at a typically Faulknerian humor in that a whole town is turned on its end by the bizarre behavior of one of its citizens; but the grotesque nature of Miss Emily's secret smothers the promise of comedy in the story. Those seeking to experience Faulkner's comic voice are better served by reading such stories as "Shingles for the Lord," "Mule in the Yard," and "Spotted Horses."

In any case, whatever the mode Faulkner adopted in creating his Yoknapatawpha County and thereby recreating the South, he produced a stunning body of work, and in both matter and style, his works have had an equally stunning impact on modern letters.

Other major works

NOVELS: *Soldiers' Pay*, 1926; *Mosquitoes*, 1927; *Sartoris*, 1929; *The Sound and the Fury*, 1929; *As I Lay Dying*, 1930; *Sanctuary*, 1931; *Light in August*, 1932; *Pylon*, 1935; *Absalom, Absalom!*, 1936; *The Unvanquished*, 1938; *The Wild Palms*, 1939; *The Hamlet*, 1940; *Intruder in the Dust*, 1948; *Requiem for a Nun*, 1951; *A Fable*, 1954; *The Town*, 1957; *The Mansion*, 1959; *The Reivers*, 1962.

SCREENPLAYS: *Today We Live*, 1933; *To Have and Have Not*, 1945; *The Big Sleep*, 1946; *Faulkner's MGM Screenplays*, 1982.

POETRY: *The Marble Faun*, 1924; *A Green Bough*, 1933.

NONFICTION: *New Orleans Sketches*, 1958; *Faulkner in the University*, 1959; *Faulkner at West Point*, 1964; *Essays, Speeches and Public Letters*, 1965; *The Faulkner-Cowley File: Letters and Memories, 1944-1962*, 1966 (Malcolm Cowley, editor); *Lion in the Garden*, 1968; *Selected Letters*, 1977.

MISCELLANEOUS: *The Faulkner Reader*, 1954; *William Faulkner: Early Prose and Poetry*, 1962; *The Wishing Tree*, 1964; *Mayday*, 1976.

Bibliography

Bassett, John E. *Faulkner in the Eighties: An Annotated Critical Bibliography.* Metuchen, N.J.: Scarecrow Press, 1991.

Blotner, Joseph. *Faulkner: A Biography.* 2 vols. New York: Random House, 1964, 1974; 1-volume edition, 1984. This extensive but readable two-volume biography is the major source for details about Faulkner's life. It contains many photographs and a useful index.

Brooks, Cleanth. *William Faulkner: The Yoknapatawpha County.* New Haven, Conn.: Yale University Press, 1963. Brooks has written several excellent books on Faulkner, but this venerable classic of Faulkner criticism is one of the best introductions, treating Faulkner's characteristic themes, historical and social background, and offering detailed readings of the major novels and stories. His carefully prepared notes, appendices, and character index can be immensely helpful to beginning readers trying to make sense of mysterious events and complex family relations.

Broughton, Panthea. *William Faulkner: The Abstract and the Actual.* Baton Rouge: Louisiana State University Press, 1974. Of several fine critical studies that attempt to see Faulkner whole and understand his worldview, this is one of the best, especially for readers just beginning to know Faulkner. Broughton sees the tension between the ideal and the actual as central to understanding the internal and external conflicts about which Faulkner most often writes.

Carothers, James. *William Faulkner's Short Stories.* Ann Arbor, Mich.: UMI Research Press, 1985. This study gives special attention to interrelations among the short stories and between the stories and the novels. Carothers offers balanced and careful readings of the stories and a useful bibliography.

Gray, Richard J. *The Life of William Faulkner.* Cambridge, Mass.: Blackwell Press, 1994.

Hoffman, Frederick, and Olga W. Vickery, eds. *William Faulkner: Three Decades of Criticism.* New York: Harcourt, Brace, 1960. Though there are more recent collections of critical essays on Faulkner, this volume remains one of the most useful. It contains the important *The Paris Review* interview of 1956, the Nobel Prize address, and twenty-two essays, many of them seminal, on Faulkner's work and life.

Howe, Irving. *William Faulkner: A Critical Study.* 3d rev. ed. Chicago: Chicago University Press, 1975.

McHaney, Thomas. *William Faulkner: A Reference Guide.* Boston: G. K. Hall, 1976. Though somewhat difficult to use, this guide provides an admirably complete annotated listing of writing about Faulkner through 1973. Because Faulkner is a world-class author, a tremendous amount has been written since 1973. A good source of information about later writing is *American Literary Scholarship: An Annual.*

Minter, David. *William Faulkner: His Life and Work.* Baltimore: The Johns Hopkins University Press, 1980. Shorter and less detailed than Joseph Blotner's biography, this volume gives more attention to exploring connections between Faulkner's life and his works.

Wagner-Martin, Linda, ed. *William Faulkner: Four Decades of Criticism.* East Lansing: Michigan State University Press, 1973.

Constance Pierce (Revised by *Terry Heller*)

F. SCOTT FITZGERALD

Born: St. Paul, Minnesota; September 24, 1896
Died: Hollywood, California; December 21, 1940

Principal short fiction · *Flappers and Philosophers,* 1920 · *Tales of the Jazz Age,* 1922 · *All the Sad Young Men,* 1926 · *Taps at Reveille,* 1935 · *The Stories of F. Scott Fitzgerald,* 1951 · *Afternoon of an Author,* 1958 · *Babylon Revisited and Other Stories,* 1960 · *The Pat Hobby Stories,* 1962 · *The Apprentice Fiction of F. Scott Fitzgerald, 1907-1917,* 1965 · *The Basil and Josephine Stories,* 1973 · *Bits of Paradise, 1974* · *The Price Was High: The Last Uncollected Stories of F. Scott Fitzgerald,* 1979

Other literary forms · Four novels, four short-story collections, and a play make up the nine F. Scott Fitzgerald books published in his lifetime. They were issued in uniform editions by Scribner's with a British edition of each. His short stories were widely anthologized in the 1920's and 1930's in collections such as *The Best Short Stories of 1922, Cream of the Jug,* and *The Best Short Stories of 1931. The Vegetable: Or, From President to Postman* (1923) was produced at the Apollo Theatre in Atlantic City, and, while Fitzgerald was under contract to MGM, he collaborated on such film scripts as *Three Comrades, Infidelity, Madame Curie,* and *Gone with the Wind.* There have been numerous posthumous collections of his letters, essays, notebooks, stories, and novels; and since his death there have been various stage and screen adaptations of his work, including film versions of *The Great Gatsby* (1925) and *Tender Is the Night* (1934).

Courtesy of the Library of Congress

303

Achievements · Fitzgerald, considered "the poet laureate of the Jazz Age," is best remembered for his portrayal of the "flapper" of the 1920's, a young woman who demonstrated scorn for conventional dress and behavior. Fitzgerald's fiction focuses on young, wealthy, dissolute men and women of the 1920's. His stories written for popular magazines such as the *Saturday Evening Post* and, later, *Esquire* were very much in demand. Fitzgerald's literary reputation, however, is chiefly based on the artistry of stories such as "Babylon Revisited" and "The Rich Boy," as well as the novel *The Great Gatsby*. In this important novel, Fitzgerald uses rich imagery and symbolism to portray lives of the careless, restless rich during the 1920's and to depict Jay Gatsby as the personification of the American dream, the self-made man whose quest for riches is also a futile quest for the love of the shallow, spoiled Daisy.

Biography · F. Scott Fitzgerald was educated at St. Paul Academy and at the Newman School in Hackensack, New Jersey. While attending Princeton University he wrote for the *Princeton Tiger* and *Nassau Literary Magazine*. He left Princeton without a degree, joined the army, and was stationed near Montgomery, Alabama, where he met Zelda Sayre. In 1920, they were married in New York City before moving to Westport, Connecticut. Their only child, Frances Scott Fitzgerald, was born in 1921. In the mid-1920's the Fitzgeralds traveled extensively between the United States and Europe, meeting Ernest Hemingway in Paris in 1925. The decade of the 1930's was a bleak one for the Fitzgeralds; Zelda had several emotional breakdowns and Scott sank into alcoholism. They lived variously in Montgomery and on the Turnbull estate outside Baltimore. Fitzgerald went to Hollywood for the second time in 1931. After that they lived for a time in Asheville, North Carolina, where Zelda was hospitalized and where Fitzgerald wrote the Crack-up essays for *Esquire*. In 1937, Fitzgerald met Sheila Graham while he was living in Hollywood and writing under contract to MGM. He began writing *The Last Tycoon* in 1939 and died, before it was completed, on December 21, 1940, at the age of forty-four.

Analysis · F. Scott Fitzgerald was a professional writer who was also a literary artist. In practical terms this meant that he had to support himself by writing short stories for popular magazines in order to get sufficient income, according to him, to write decent books. Indeed, most of the money that Fitzgerald earned by writing before he went to Hollywood in 1937 was earned by selling stories to magazines. In his twenty-year career as a writer, he published 164 magazine stories; other stories were never published. All but eight of the stories that originally appeared in magazines became available in hardcover editions.

As one would expect of a body of 164 stories written in a twenty-year period mainly for popular consumption, the quality of the stories is uneven. At the bottom of this collection are at least a dozen stories, most of them written for *Esquire* during the last years of his life, which have few redeeming qualities; at the top of the list are at least a dozen stories which rank among the best of American short stories. One should not, however, be led to believe that these, as well as the hundred or more "potboilers" in the middle, do not serve a useful role in his development as an artist. Fitzgerald in the 1920's was considered the best writer of quality magazine fiction in America, and his stories brought the highest prices paid by slick magazines; the *Saturday Evening Post,* for example, paid him four thousand dollars per story even during the Depression. Dorothy Parker commented that Fitzgerald could write a bad story, but that he could not write badly. Thus each story, no matter how weak, has the recognizable Fitzgerald touch—that sparkling prose which Fitzgerald called "the something extra" that most popular short stories lacked. Fitzgerald also learned at the beginning of his career that he could use the popular magazines as a workshop for his novels, experimenting in them with themes and techniques which he would later incorporate into his novels. An understanding of a Fitzgerald story should take into account this workshop function of the story as well as its artistic merits.

Fitzgerald's career as a writer of magazine fiction breaks logically into three periods: 1919-1924, years during which he shopped around for markets and published stories in most of the important periodicals of the times; 1925-1933, the central period characterized by a close association with the *Saturday Evening Post*—a relationship which almost precluded his publication of stories in other magazines; and 1934-1940, a period beginning with the publication of his first *Esquire* story and continuing through a subsequent relationship with that magazine which lasted until his death. During the first of these periods, Fitzgerald published thirty-two stories in ten different commercial magazines, two novels (*This Side of Paradise,* 1920, and *The Beautiful and Damned,* 1922), two short-story collections (*Flappers and Philosophers* and *Tales of the Jazz Age*), and one book-length play (*The Vegetable*). In the second period, during which *The Great Gatsby* and a third short-story collection (*All the Sad Young Men*) appeared, he enjoyed the popular reputation he had built with readers of the *Saturday Evening Post* and published forty-seven of the fifty-eight stories which appeared during this nine-year period in that magazine; the remaining eleven stories were scattered throughout five different magazines. In the final period, Fitzgerald lost the large *Saturday Evening Post* audience and gained the *Esquire* audience, which was smaller and quite different. Of the forty-four Fitzgerald stories to appear between 1934 and his death, twenty-eight appeared in *Esquire*. In addition to *Tender Is the Night*, which was completed and delivered before Fitzgerald's relationship with *Esquire* began, Fitzgerald published his final short-story collection (*Taps at Reveille*); he also drafted *The Last Tycoon* (1941) during the *Esquire* years. Twelve stories, nine of which have appeared in *Esquire*, have been published since his death.

An obvious conclusion may be drawn about Fitzgerald's professional career: he was at his best artistically in the years of his greatest popularity. During the composition of *The Great Gatsby*, Fitzgerald's commercial fiction was in such demand that large magazines such as the *Saturday Evening Post*, *Hearst's*, and *Metropolitan* competed for it. *Tender Is the Night* was written during the time when Fitzgerald's popularity with slick magazine readers was at its all-time high point; for example, in 1929 and 1930, important years in the composition of *Tender Is the Night*, he published fifteen stories in the *Saturday Evening Post*. In sharp contrast to the 1925-1933 stories, which are characteristic of an even, high quality, and many of which are closely related to two novels of this period, the stories of the *Esquire* years are, in general, undistinguished. In addition, with minor exceptions, the stories written in this final period have little relation to Fitzgerald's last "serious" work, *The Last Tycoon*. The *Esquire* years thus constitute a low point from both a popular and an artistic standpoint. They are years during which he lost the knack of pleasing the large American reading public and at the same time produced a comparatively small amount of good artwork.

In the first two years of Fitzgerald's storywriting, his sensitivity to audience tastes was naïve. "May Day" and "The Diamond as Big as the Ritz," not only the two best stories from these years but also two of the best stories in the Fitzgerald canon, were written for sale to mass-circulation magazines. Both, however, were too cynical about American values to be acceptable to a large, middle-American audience. By 1922 and the publication of "Winter Dreams" in *Metropolitan*, Fitzgerald had learned how to tailor his stories for slick magazine readers while at the same time using them to experiment with serious subjects and themes that he would later use in longer works.

Viewed in association with *The Great Gatsby*, "Winter Dreams" provides an excellent illustration of Fitzgerald's method of using his stories as a proving ground for his novels. In a letter to Maxwell Perkins, Fitzgerald describes "Winter Dreams" as a "sort of 1st draft of the Gatsby idea," and indeed, it contains sufficient similarities of theme and character to be called a miniature of *The Great Gatsby*. Parallels between Dexter Green and Jay Gatsby are striking: both men have made a total commitment to a dream, and both of their dreams are hollow. Dexter falls in love with wealthy Judy Jones and devotes his life to making the money that will allow him to enter her social circle; his idealization of her is closely akin to Gatsby's feelings for Daisy Buchanan. Gatsby's idealized conception of Daisy is the motivating force that underlies his compulsion to become successful, just as Dexter's conception of Judy Jones drives him to amass a fortune by the time he is twenty-five. The theme of commitment to an idealized dream that is the core of "Winter Dreams" and *The Great Gatsby* and the similarities between the two men point up the close relationship between the story and the novel. Because "Winter Dreams" appeared three years before *The Great Gatsby*, its importance in the gestation of the novel cannot be overemphasized.

Important differences in Fitzgerald's methods of constructing short stories and novels emerge from these closely related works. Much of the effectiveness of *The Great Gatsby* lies in the mystery of Gatsby's background, while no such mystery surrounds the early life of Dexter Green. In "Winter Dreams," Dexter's disillusionment with Judy occurs suddenly; when he learns that she is no longer pretty, the "dream was gone. Something had taken it from him . . . the moonlit veranda, and gingham on the golf links and the dry sun and the gold color of her neck's soft down. . . . Why these things were no longer in the world!" Because his enchantment could be shattered so quickly, Dexter's commitment to Judy is not of the magnitude of Gatsby's commitment to Daisy. Gatsby's disenchantment could only occur gradually. When he is finally able to see Daisy, "the colossal significance of the green light . . . vanished forever," but his "count of enchanted objects" had only diminished by one. Even toward the end of the novel, there is no way of knowing that Gatsby is completely disenchanted with Daisy. Nick says that "perhaps he no longer cared." The "perhaps" leaves open possibilities of interpretation that are closed at the end of "Winter Dreams." While Dexter can cry at the loss of a dream, Gatsby dies, leaving the reader to guess whether or not he still held on to any fragment of his dreams about Daisy. The expansiveness of the novel obviously allowed Fitzgerald to make Gatsby and his dream believable while he could maintain the mystery of Gatsby's past and the origins of his dream. Fitzgerald could not do this as well with Dexter in "Winter Dreams." The point is that in writing "Winter Dreams" Fitzgerald was giving shape to his ideas about Jay Gatsby, and, after creating the story, he could better see the advantages of maintaining the sense of mystery that made Gatsby a more memorable character than his counterpart in "Winter Dreams."

Like "Winter Dreams," "The Rich Boy," published a year after *The Great Gatsby*, clearly illustrates the workshop function that the stories served. The story's rich boy, Anson Hunter, falls in love with the beautiful and rich Paula Legendre, but he always finds some reason for not marrying her, although he maintains that his love for her never stops. Anson, the bachelor, ironically becomes an unofficial counselor to couples with marital difficulties and, in his role as protector of the family name, puts an end to an affair that his aunt is having. Paula marries another man, divorces him, and, when Anson encounters her late in the story, he finds her happily remarried and pregnant. Paula, whose revered place has been jeopardized by her pregnancy, finally dies in childbirth, symbolically taking with her Anson's youth. He goes on a cruise, disillusioned that his only real love is gone. Yet he is still willing to flirt with any woman on the ship who will affirm the feeling of superiority about himself that he cherishes in his heart.

In "The Rich Boy," then, Fitzgerald uses many of the themes—among them, lost youth and disillusionment in marriage—that he had covered in previous stories; in addition, he uses devices such as the narrator-observer point of view that had been successful in *The Great Gatsby*, and he pulls from the novel subjects such as the idealization of a woman who finally loses her suitor's reverence. "The Rich Boy" also blends, along with the themes he had dealt with before, new topics that he would later distill and treat singly in another story, just as he first deals explicitly with the rich-are-different idea in "The Rich Boy" and later focuses his narrative specifically on that idea in "Six of One." Finally, particularly in the use of the theme of bad marriages in "The Rich Boy," there are foreshadowings of *Tender Is the Night* and the stories which cluster around it.

The best of these *Tender Is the Night* cluster stories is "Babylon Revisited," which earned Fitzgerald his top *Saturday Evening Post* price of four thousand dollars and which is generally acclaimed as his finest story. "Babylon Revisited" represents a high point in Fitzgerald's career as a short-story writer: it is an artistically superior story which earned a high price from a commercial magazine. In the story's main character, Charlie Wales, Fitzgerald creates one whose future, in spite of his heroic struggle, is prescribed by his imprudent past, a past filled with heavy drinking and irresponsibility. He is destined to be haunted by reminders of his early life, embodied by Lorraine and Duncan, drinking friends from the past; to be judged for them by Marion, his dead wife's sister who, like Charlie's conscience personified, is disgusted by his past and demands punishment; and to be denied, for his penance, any right to fill the emptiness of his life with his daughter Honoria, who is in Marion's custody and who is the only really meaningful thing left. Fitzgerald fashions Charlie as a sensitive channel through which the reader can simultaneously view both Paris as it existed for expatriate wanderers before the Depression and the now-dimmed Paris to which Charlie returns.

The contrast is masterfully handled in that the course of Charlie's emotional life closely parallels the changing mood of the city–a movement from a kind of unreal euphoria to a mood of loss and melancholy. The contrast at once heightens the reader's sense of Charlie's loneliness in a ghost town of bad memories and foreshadows his empty-handed return to Prague, his present home. All of Charlie's present misery has resulted, in Fitzgerald's precise summary, from his "selling short" in the boom–an allusion to the loss of his dead wife Helen. Charlie, however, refuses to be driven back to alcohol, even in the face of being denied his daughter Honoria. Although he might easily have done so, Fitzgerald avoids drawing the reader into a sentimental trap of identification with Charlie's plight, the responsibility for and consequences of which must finally be borne only by Charlie. As he later did in Dick Diver's case in *Tender Is the Night*, Fitzgerald has shown in "Babylon Revisited" how one man works his way into an existence with *nada* at the core; how he manages to dissipate, "to make nothing out of something," and thus prescribe for himself a future without direction. It is also in the creation of this mood of Charlie's isolation that the artistic brilliance of the story, as well as its kinship to *Tender Is the Night*, lies.

The popular thrust of "Babylon Revisited" is a dual one in which Fitzgerald plays on what were likely to be ambivalent feelings of popular readers toward Charlie. On the one hand, he is pictured first as an expatriate about whose resolution to remain abroad American audiences may have been skeptical. On the other, Charlie appears to have reformed and obviously loves his daughter. Marion, by contrast, is depicted as a shrew, and the reader is left to choose, therefore, between the punishment of a life sentence of loneliness for a penitent wrongdoer and the granting of his complete freedom and forgiveness rendered against the better judgment of the unsympathetic Marion. Fitzgerald guarantees that the reader will become emotionally involved by centering the story around the highly emotional relationship between a father and his daughter. Because Charlie is, in fact, guilty, to let him go free would be to let wrongdoing go unpunished–the strictest kind of violation of the Puritan ethic. To deprive Charlie of Honoria, however, would be to side with the unlikable Marion. Fitzgerald, then, resolves the conflict in the only satisfactory way–by proposing a compromise. Although Marion keeps Honoria for the moment, Charlie may be paroled, may come back and try again, at any time in the future.

The story, therefore, is successful on three major counts: it served as a workshop in which Fitzgerald shaped the mood of *Tender Is the Night*; it entertained with the struggle against unfair odds of a well-intentioned father for the affection of his daughter; and it succeeded on the mythic level, suggested in the title, as a story in which all ingredients conspire to lead to Charlie's exile–an isolation from the city that has fallen in the absence of a now-reformed sinner, carrying with it not only the bad but also the good which Charlie has come to salvage.

About four years after the publication of "Babylon Revisited," Fitzgerald had lost the knack of writing *Saturday Evening Post* stories, and he began writing shorter pieces, many of which are sketches rather than stories, for *Esquire*. *Esquire*, however, was not a suitable medium to serve a workshop function as the *Saturday Evening Post* had been. On the one hand, it did not pay enough to sustain Fitzgerald through the composition of a novel; even if it had, it is difficult to imagine how Fitzgerald would have experimented in the framework of short *Esquire* pieces with the complex relationships that he was concurrently developing in *The Last Tycoon*. Moreover, there is the question of the suitability of Fitzgerald's *The Last Tycoon* material, regardless of how he treated it, for *Esquire*: the Monroe Stahr-Kathleen relationship in *The Last Tycoon*, for example, and certainly also the Cecelia-Stahr relationship, would have been as out of place in *Esquire* as the *Esquire* story of a ten-year binge, "The Lost Decade," would have been in the *Saturday Evening Post*. In short, *Esquire* was ill-suited to Fitzgerald's need for a profitable workshop for *The Last Tycoon*, and it is difficult to read the *Esquire* pieces, particularly the Pat Hobby stories about a pathetic movie scriptwriter, without realizing that every hour Fitzgerald spent on them could have been better spent completing *The Last Tycoon*. From a practical standpoint, it is fair to say that the small sums of income for which Fitzgerald worked in writing the *Esquire* stories may have interfered with the completion of his last novel, whereas the high prices Fitzgerald earned from the *Saturday Evening Post* between 1925 and 1933 provided the financial climate which made it possible for him to complete *Tender Is the Night*.

Indeed, if the *Esquire* stories in general and the Pat Hobby stories in particular, close as they were in terms of composition to *The Last Tycoon*, marked the distance Fitzgerald had come in resolving the professional writer-literary artist dichotomy with which he had been confronted for twenty years, any study of the function of the stories in Fitzgerald's overall career would end on a bleak note. Two stories, "Discard" and "Last Kiss," neither of which was published in Fitzgerald's lifetime, indicate, however, that he was attempting to re-create the climate of free exchange between his stories and novels characteristic especially of the composition period of *Tender Is the Night*. "Last Kiss" provides a good commentary on this attempt. When the story appeared in 1949, the editors remarked in a headnote that the story contained "the seed" that grew into *The Last Tycoon*. The claim is too extravagant for the story in that it implies the sort of relationship between the story and the novel that exists between "Winter Dreams" and *The Great Gatsby*, a relationship that simply does not exist in this case. There are, however, interesting parallels.

Fitzgerald created in "Last Kiss" counterparts both to Monroe Stahr and Kathleen in the novel. Jim Leonard, a thirty-five-year-old producer in "Last Kiss," is similar to Stahr in that he possesses the same kind of power: when the budding starlet, Pamela Knighton, meets Leonard, her agent's voice tells her: "This *is* somebody." In fact, on the Hollywood success ladder he is in Fitzgerald's words "on top," although like Stahr he does not flaunt this fact. Although Pamela is fundamentally different from Kathleen in her self-centered coldness, they also share a resemblance to "pink and silver frost" and an uncertainty about Americans. Kathleen is no aspiring actress; but her past life, like Pamela's, has an aura of mystery about it. Moreover, the present lives of both are complicated by binding entanglements: Pamela's to Chauncey Ward, and Kathleen's to the nameless man she finally marries. There are other parallels: the first important encounter between Leonard and Pamela, for example, closely resembles the ballroom scene during which Stahr becomes enchanted by Kathleen's beauty. In fact, the nature of Leonard's attraction to Pamela is similar to that of Stahr's to Kathleen; although there is no Minna Davis lurking in Leonard's past as there is in Stahr's, he is drawn to Pamela by the kind of romantic, mysterious force which had finally, apart from her resemblance to Minna, drawn Stahr to Kathleen. Moreover, both attachments end abruptly with the same sort of finality: Pamela dies leaving Jim with only film fragments by which to remember her, and Kathleen leaves Stahr when she marries "the American."

That these parallels were the seeds of *The Last Tycoon* is doubtful. The important point, however, is that "Last Kiss" is a popular treatment of the primary material that Fitzgerald would work with in the novel: Jim's sentimental return to the drugstore where he had once seen Pamela and his nostalgic remembrance of their last kiss earmark the story for a popular audience which, no doubt, Fitzgerald hoped would help pay his bills during the composition of the novel. Fitzgerald was unable to sell the story, probably because none of the characters generate strong emotion. It is sufficiently clear from "Last Kiss," however, that Fitzgerald was regaining his sense of audience. In the process of demonstrating how well he understood Hollywood, the story also captured much of the glitter that is associated with it in the popular mind. In order to rebuild the kind of popular magazine workshop that he had had for *Tender Is the Night*, it remained for him to subordinate his understanding of Hollywood to the task of re-creating its surface. If he had continued in the direction of "Last Kiss," he would perhaps have done this and thus returned to the kind of climate which had in the past proven to be most favorable for his serious novel work—one in which he wrote handfuls of stories for popular magazines while the novel was taking shape. It is also possible that he might have used such stories to make *The Last Tycoon* something more than a great fragment.

Regarding the role of the stories in Fitzgerald's career, one can finally state that they functioned as providers of financial incentive, as proving grounds for his ideas, as workshops for his craft, and as dictators of his popular reputation. The problem for the serious student of Fitzgerald's works is whether he should examine the popular professional writer who produced some 164 stories for mass consumption or limit his examination of Fitzgerald to his acclaimed works of art, such as "Babylon Revisited," "The Rich Boy," *The Great Gatsby*, and *Tender Is the Night*. To do one to the exclusion of the other is to present not only a fragmented picture of Fitzgerald's literary output but also a distorted one. Just as the stories complement the novels, so do the novels make the stories more meaningful, and the financial and emotional climate from which they all came illuminate the nature of their interdependence.

Other major works

NOVELS: *This Side of Paradise*, 1920; *The Beautiful and Damned*, 1922; *The Great Gatsby*, 1925; *Tender Is the Night*, 1934; *The Last Tycoon*, 1941.

PLAY: *The Vegetable: Or, From President to Postman*, 1923.

NONFICTION: *The Crack-Up*, 1945; *The Letters of F. Scott Fitzgerald*, 1963; *Letters to His Daughter*, 1965; *Thoughtbook of Francis Scott Fitzgerald*, 1965; *Dear Scott/Dear Max: The Fitzgerald-Perkins Correspondence*, 1971; *As Ever, Scott Fitzgerald*, 1972; *F. Scott Fitzgerald's Ledger*, 1972; *The Notebooks of F. Scott Fitzgerald*, 1978.

MISCELLANEOUS: *Afternoon of an Author: A Selection of Uncollected Stories and Essays*, 1958.

Bibliography

Bloom, Harold, ed. *F. Scott Fitzgerald: The Great Gatsby*. New Haven, Conn.: Chelsea House, 1986. A short but important collection of critical essays. This book provides an introductory overview of Fitzgerald scholarship (five pages), as well as readings from a variety of perspectives on Fitzgerald's fiction.

Bruccoli, Matthew J. *Some Sort of Epic Grandeur*. New York: Harcourt Brace Jovanovich, 1981. In this outstanding biography, a major Fitzgerald scholar argues that Fitzgerald's divided spirit, not his lifestyle, distracted him from writing. Bruccoli believes that Fitzgerald both loved and hated the privileged class that was the subject of his fiction.

_____, ed. *New Essays on "The Great Gatsby."* Cambridge, England: Cambridge University Press, 1985. This short but important collection includes an introductory overview of scholarship, plus interpretive essays on Fitzgerald's best-known novel.

Donaldson, Scott. *Fool for Love: F. Scott Fitzgerald*. New York: Congden and Weed, 1983.

Eble, Kenneth. *F. Scott Fitzgerald*. Rev. ed. Boston: Twayne, 1977. A clearly written critical biography, this book traces Fitzgerald's development from youth through a "Final Assessment," which surveys scholarship on Fitzgerald's texts.

Gervais, Ronald J. "The Socialist and the Silk Stockings: Fitzgerald's Double Allegiance." *Mosaic* 15 (June, 1982): 79-82. In this useful article, Gervais explores the tension of Fitzgerald's use of individualism and his Marxist inclinations, with some biographical data.

Higgins, John A. *F. Scott Fitzgerald: A Study of the Stories*. Jamaica, N.Y.: St. Johns University Press, 1971.

Kuehl, John Richard. *F. Scott Fitzgerald: A Study of the Short Fiction*. New York: Twayne Publishers, 1991.

Lee, A. Robert, ed. *Scott Fitzgerald: The Promises of Life*. New York: St. Martin's Press, 1989. An excellent collection of essays by Fitzgerald scholars, this book includes an introduction that surveys scholarship on the texts. Topics addressed include Fitzgerald's treatment of women, his notion of the decline of the West, his "ethics and ethnicity," and his use of "distortions" of the imagination.

Miller, James E., Jr. *F. Scott Fitzgerald: His Art and His Technique*. New York: New York University Press, 1964. An expanded version of *The Fictional Technique of Scott Fitzgerald*, originally published in 1957, this book emphasizes Fitzgerald's technique, focusing on the impact of the "saturation vs. selection" debate between H. G. Wells and Henry James; it also adds critical commentary and interpretations of the later works.

Roulston, Robert. *The Winding Road to West Egg: The Artistic Development of F. Scott Fitzgerald*. Lewisburg, Penn.: Bucknell University Press, 1995.

Bryant Mangum
(Revised by *Mary Ellen Pitts*)

E. M. FORSTER

Born: London, England; January 1, 1879
Died: Coventry, England; June 7, 1970

Principal short fiction · *The Celestial Omnibus and Other Stories,* 1911 · *The Eternal Moment and Other Stories,* 1928 · *The Collected Tales of E. M. Forster,* 1947 · *The Life to Come and Other Stories,* 1972 · *Arctic Summer and Other Fiction,* 1980

Other literary forms · E. M. Forster wrote six novels, one of which (*Maurice,* 1971) was published posthumously because of its homosexual theme. He also wrote travel books, essays, reviews, criticism, biography, and some poetry. Together with Eric Crozier he wrote the libretto for the four-act opera *Billy Budd* (1951), adapted from Herman Melville's famous work.

Achievements · As a novelist of rare distinction and one of the great literary figures of the twentieth century, Forster enjoyed international recognition and received many literary awards and honors. In 1921, as private secretary to the Maharajah of Dewas State Senior, he was awarded the Sir Tukojirao Gold Medal. The publication of *A Passage to India* (1924) brought him much acclaim, including the Femina Vie Heureuse Prize and the James Tait Black Memorial Prize in 1925. In 1927, he was elected Fellow of King's College, Cambridge, and he delivered Clark Lectures at Trinity College. In 1937, the Royal Society of Literature honored him with the Benson Medal. In 1945, he was made Honorary Fellow, King's College, Cambridge, where he remained until his death in 1970. In 1953, he was received by Queen Elizabeth II as a Companion of Honor. Between 1947 and 1958, several universities, including Cambridge, conferred on him the honorary degree of LL.D. In 1961, the Royal Society of Literature named him a Companion of Literature. He attained the greatest recognition when, on his ninetieth birthday, on January 1, 1969, he was appointed to the Order of Merit by Queen Elizabeth II.

Biography · Edward Morgan Forster was born in London on January 1, 1879. He was the great-grandson of Henry Thornton, a prominent member of the Evangelical Clapham Sect and a member of parliament. His father, an architect, died early, and he was brought up by his mother and his great-aunt, Marianne Thornton (whose biography he published in 1956). He received his early education at Tonbridge School, but he did not like the public school atmosphere. His bitter criticism of the English public school system appears in his portrayal of Sawston School in his first two novels, *Where Angels Fear to Tread* (1905) and *The Longest Journey* (1907). From Tonbridge, Forster went on to the University of Cambridge–thanks to the rich inheritance left by his aunt, Marianne Thornton, who died when he was eight–where he came under the influence of Goldworthy Lowes Dickinson (whose biography he wrote in 1934) and quickly began to blossom as a scholar, writer, and humanist.

After graduating from King's College, Cambridge, Forster traveled, with his mother, to Italy and Greece in 1901. His first short story, "Albergo Empedocle," was published in 1903. Between 1903 and 1910, he published four novels, nine short stories, and other nonfictional items. His travels to Greece and Italy led to his representation of life in those countries as being less repressive than life in England. During World War I, he served as a volunteer with the Red Cross in Alexandria, Egypt. His stay there resulted in *Alexandria: A History and a Guide* (1922) and *Pharos and Pharillon* (1923). His two visits to India, the first in 1912 in company of Goldworthy Lowes Dickinson and the second in 1921 as private secretary to the Maharajah of Dewas State Senior, provided him material for his masterpiece novel *A Passage to India* (1924) and *The Hill of Devi* (1953). With *A Passage to India*, Forster's reputation was established as a major English novelist of the twentieth century. He made a third visit to India in 1945 to attend a conference of Indian writers at Jaipur. He then wrote, "If Indians had not spoken English my own life would have been infinitely poorer." He visited the United States in 1947 to address the Symposium on Music Criticism at Harvard and again in 1949 to address the American Academy of Arts and Letters.

Though Forster stopped publishing fiction after 1924, he continued to produce significant nonfiction writing to the end. In a statement at the beginning of B. J. Kirkpatrick's *A Bibliography of E. M. Forster* (1965), Forster said: "The longer one lives the less one feels to have done, and I am both surprised and glad to discover from this bibliography that I have written so much." He died on June 7, 1970, at the age of ninety-one. Throughout his life he kept his faith in liberal humanism, in the sanctity of personal relationships, and, above all, in individualism. His charismatic personality and his personal warmth have led many people to believe that the man was greater than his books.

Analysis · All of Forster's best-known and most anthologized stories appeared first in two collections, *The Celestial Omnibus* and *The Eternal Moment.* The words "celestial" and "eternal" are especially significant because a typical Forster story features a protagonist who is allowed a vision of a better life, sometimes momentarily only. Qualifications for experiencing this epiphany include a questioning mind, an active imagination, and a dissatisfaction with conventional attitudes. The transformation resulting from the experience comes about through some kind of magic that transports him through time—backward or forward—or through space—to Mt. Olympus or to heaven. Whether his life is permanently changed, the transformed character can never be the same again after a glimpse of the Elysian Fields, and he is henceforth suspect to contemporary mortals.

Forster termed his short stories "fantasies," and when the discerning reader can determine the point at which the real and the fantastic intersect, he will locate the epiphany, at the same time flexing his own underused imaginative muscles. Perhaps "The Machine Stops," a science-fiction tale about a world managed by a computer-like Machine that warns men to "beware of first-hand ideas," was at the time of its writing (1909) the most fantastic of Forster's short fiction, but its portrayal of radio, television, and telephones with simultaneous vision seems now to have been simply farsighted.

Forster frequently uses a narrator who is so insensitive that he ironically enhances the perception of the reader. In "Other Kingdom," for example, when Mr. Inskip finds it "right" to repeat Miss Beaumont's conversation about a "great dream" to his employer, the reader correctly places the tutor on the side of unimaginative man, rather than in the lineup of Dryads to which the young lady will repair. When the narrator of "The Story of a Panic" boasts that he "can tell a story without exaggerating" and then unfolds a tale about a boy who obviously is visited by Pan and who finally bounds away to join the goat-god, the reader knows that he must himself inform the gaps of information. When the same narrator attributes the death of the waiter Gennaro to the fact that "the miserable Italians have no stamina. Something had gone wrong inside him," the reader observes the disparity between the two statements and rightly concludes that Gennaro's death has a supernatural cause—that he had been subjected to the same "panic" as had Eustace, and that only the latter had passed the test.

In *Aspects of the Novel* (1927), Forster suggests that fiction will play a part in the ultimate success of civilization through promotion of human sympathy, reconciliation, and understanding. In each of the short stories the protagonist gets a finger-hold on the universal secret, but he sometimes loses his grip, usually through the action of someone too blind, materialistic, or enslaved by time to comprehend the significance of the moment.

If, as Forster himself declares, the emphasis of plot lies in causality, he allows the reader an important participation, because the causes of transformation are never explicit, and the more mundane characters are so little changed by the miraculous events taking place around them that they are not puzzled or even aware that they occur.

In "The Eternal Moment," the stiffly insensitive Colonel Leyland, Miss Raby's friend and traveling companion, is just such a character. While Miss Raby is determined to accept the responsibility for the commercialization of the mountain resort Vorta engendered by her novel, Colonel Leyland can understand her feelings no more readily than can Feo, the uneducated waiter who is the immediate object of Miss Raby's search. While Miss Raby ostensibly has returned to the village to see how it has been affected by tourism since she made it famous, she also is drawn to the spot because it was the scene of the one romantic, although brief, interlude of her life. For twenty years she has recalled a declaration of passionate love for her by a young Italian guide whose advances she had rejected. This memory has sustained her because of its reality and beauty. She finds the once rustic village overgrown with luxury hotels, in one of which Feo, her dream-lover, is the stout, greasy, middle-aged, hypocritical concierge. Miss Raby, whose instincts have warned her that the progress of civilization is not necessarily good, sees that "the passage of a large number of people" has corrupted not only the village and its values, but also Feo. Observing that "pastoral virtues" and "family affection" have disappeared with the on-slaught of touristry, she accosts the embarrassed peasant who had once offered her flowers. In a scene that is the quintessence of a human failure to communicate, Feo believes that she is attempting to ruin him, while she is actually appealing to him to help the old woman who owns the only hotel untouched by modernity. Colonel Leyland, who cannot bear the thought, much less the reality, of such intimate contact with a member of the lower class, gives up his idea of marrying Miss Raby. The rich novelist, whose entire life has been enriched by the "eternal moment" when she briefly and in imagination only had spanned class barriers, asks Feo if she can adopt one of his children. Rebuffed, she will live alone, able perhaps to blot out reality and relive the happiness that the memory of the "eternal moment" has brought her.

Another misunderstood protagonist is Eustace, the fourteen-year-old English boy considered a misfit by the group of tourists with whom he is seeing Italy. Listless and pampered, bad-tempered and repellent, Eustace dislikes walking, cannot swim, and appears most to enjoy lounging. Forced to go to a picnic, the boy carves from wood a whistle, which when blown evokes a "catspaw" of wind that frightens all of the other tourists into running. When they return to their picnic site in search of Eustace, they find him lying on his back, a green lizard darting from his cuff. For the first time on the trip the boy smiles and is polite. The footprints of goats are discerned nearby as Eustace races around "like a real boy." A dazed hare sits on his arm, and he kisses an old woman as he presents her with flowers. The adults, in trying to forget the encounter, are cruel to Eustace and to Gennaro, a young, natural, ignorant Italian fishing lad, who is a "stop-gap" waiter at the inn, and who clearly understands the boy's experience. As Eustace and Gennaro attempt to flee to freedom from human responsibility, the waiter is killed, the victim of a society which in its lack of understanding had attempted to imprison Eustace, oblivious to his miraculous change, or at least to its significance. He has turned into an elfin sprite of the woods, to which he escapes forever, leaving behind him Forster's customary complement of complacent, nonplussed tourists.

No Pan, but a Dryad is Evelyn Beaumont of "Other Kingdom." Mr. Inskip, who narrates the tale, has been hired as a tutor of the classics by handsome, prosperous, and pompous Harcourt Worters. Inskip's charges are Worters' fiancée Miss Evelyn Beaumont and his ward Jack Ford. When Worters announces that he has purchased a nearby copse called "Other Kingdom" as a wedding gift for Evelyn, she dances her gleeful acceptance in imitation of a beech tree. On a celebratory picnic Evelyn asks Jack to stand in a position that will hide the house from her view. She is dismayed to learn that Worters plans to build a high fence around her copse and to add an asphalt path and a bridge. Evelyn values the fact that boys and girls have been coming for years from the village to carve their initials on the trees, and she notes that Worters finds blood on his hands when he attempts to repeat the romantic ritual. Upon hearing that Worters has obtained Other Kingdom by taking advantage of a widow, she realizes that he is a selfish person who views her as one of his possessions to be enjoyed. Broken in spirit, she apparently agrees to his plan of fencing in the copse, but she dances away "from society and life" to be united with other wood nymphs and likely with Ford, who knows intuitively that she is a free spirit that can never be possessed.

While Eustace in "Story of a Panic" is a Pan-figure, Evelyn a Dryad, and Harcourt Worters a prototype of Midas, Mr. Lucas of "The Road from Colonus" is associated with Oedipus. The tale's title is reminiscent of Sophocles' play, and Ethel, Mr. Lucas' daughter, represents Antigone. As do Miss Raby, Eustace, and Evelyn Beaumont, Mr. Lucas enters into a special union with nature and mankind. Riding ahead of his daughter and her friends, he finds the "real Greece" when he spies a little inn surrounded by a grove of plane trees and a little stream that bubbles out of a great hollow tree. As he enters this natural shrine, he for the first time sees meaning to his existence, and he longs to stay in this peaceful spot. The other tourists, however, have schedules and appointments to adhere to, and they forcibly carry Mr. Lucas away from the scene of his revelation. That night the plane tree crashes to kill all occupants of the inn, and Mr. Lucas spends his remaining days fussing about his neighbors and the noises of civilization, especially those made by the running water in the drains and reminiscent of the pleasant, musical gurgles of the little stream in Greece.

More fortunate than Mr. Lucas is the boy who rides "The Celestial Omnibus" from an alley where an old, faded sign points the way "To Heaven." After the driver Sir Thomas Browne delivers the boy across a great gulf on a magnificent rainbow to the accompaniment of music, and back home to his nursery, the boy's parents refuse to believe his tale. Mr. Bons, a family friend, attempts to prove the boy is lying by offering to make a repeat journey with him. On this trip the driver is Dante. Even though Mr. Bons is finally convinced that the boy has actually met Achilles and Tom Jones, he wants to go home. When Mr. Bons crawls out of the omnibus shrieking, "I see London," he falls and is seen no more. His body is discovered "in a shockingly mutilated condition," and the newspaper reports that "foul play is suspected." The boy is crowned with fresh leaves as the dolphins awaken to celebrate with him the world of imagination. Mr. Bons, when accosted with this world, rejected it so violently that he suffered physical pain.

In all of these "fantasies," a gulf separates reality from illusion, and the latter is clearly to be preferred. If a person must inhabit the real world, one can bear its existence and even love its inhabitants if one is among the fortunate few receptive to a special kind of vision.

Other major works

NOVELS: *Where Angels Fear to Tread*, 1905; *The Longest Journey*, 1907; *A Room with a View*, 1908; *Howards End*, 1910; *A Passage to India*, 1924; *Maurice*, 1971.

PLAY: *Billy Budd*, 1951 (libretto, with Eric Crozier).

NONFICTION: *Alexandria: A History and a Guide*, 1922; *Pharos and Pharillon*, 1923; *Aspects of the Novel*, 1927; *Goldsworthy Lowes Dickinson*, 1934; *Abinger Harvest—A Miscellany*, 1936; *Virginia Woolf*, 1942; *Development of English Prose Between 1918 and 1939*, 1945; *Two Cheers for Democracy*, 1951; *The Hill of Devi*, 1953; *Marianne Thornton: A Domestic Biography, 1797-1887*, 1956; *Commonplace Book*, 1978.

Bibliography

Furbank, Philip N. *E. M. Forster: A Life*. New York: Harcourt Brace Jovan-
    ovich, 1978. In this authorized biography of E. M. Forster, Furbank
    successfully recreates an authentic, intimate, and illuminating portrait

of the man behind the writer and controversial public figure. The wealth of new material contained in this biography makes it an indispensable source of Forster's life, times, and work.

Herz, Judith Scherer. *The Short Narratives of E. M. Forster*. New York: St. Martin's Press, 1988.

Lago, Mary. *E. M. Forster: A Literary Life*. New York: St. Martin's Press, 1995.

McConkey, James. *The Novels of E. M. Forster*. Ithaca, N. Y.: Cornell University Press, 1957. Using the fictional criteria and terminology that Forster expounded in *Aspects of the Novel*, McConkey offers insightful close reading of Forster's novels and some of his short stories. His exposition of Forster's theories and practices is illuminating. Includes a select bibliography of critical studies on Forster.

McDowell, Frederick P. W. *E. M. Forster*. Rev. ed. Boston: Twayne, 1982. A brilliant, well-balanced, and compendious overview of Forster's life, times, career, work, and achievement. This book contains a useful chronology, a select bibliography, and an index. It also offers a concise and perceptive analysis of Forster's short stories.

Stape, J. H., ed. *E. M. Forster: Interviews and Recollections*. New York: St. Martin's Press, 1993.

Stone, Wilfred. *The Cave and the Mountain: A Study of E. M. Forster*. Stanford, Calif.: Stanford University Press, 1966. A well-researched and scholarly book. Contains a vast amount of useful information about Forster's background, career, esthetics, and work. Includes a detailed and illuminating chapter on the short stories. Using psychological and Jungian approaches, Stone offers insightful and masterly critiques of Forster's fiction. Supplemented by notes and a comprehensive index.

Thomson, George H. *The Fiction of E. M. Forster*. Detroit: Wayne State University Press, 1967. Thomson presents a critical study of Forster's novels and short stories in terms of their symbolical and archetypal aspects. He argues that Forster's symbols "achieve archetypal significance and mythic wholeness" through "the power of ecstatic perception" in his work. Complemented by notes and a valuable appendix on the manuscripts of *A Passage to India*.

Trilling, Lionel. *E. M. Forster: A Study*. Norfolk, Conn.: New Directions, 1943. A pioneer study, instrumental in establishing Forster's reputation. This book assesses Forster's artistic achievement in terms of his liberal humanism and moral realism.

Wilde, Alan, ed. *Critical Essays on E. M. Forster*. Boston: G. K. Hall, 1985.

Sue L. Kimball
(Revised by *Chaman L. Sahni*)

MAVIS GALLANT

Born: Montreal, Canada; August 11, 1922

Principal short fiction · *The Other Paris*, 1956 · *My Heart Is Broken: Eight Stories and a Short Novel*, 1964 · *An Unmarried Man's Summer*, 1965 · *The Pegnitz Junction*, 1973 · *The End of the World and Other Stories*, 1974 · *From the Fifteenth District: A Novella and Eight Short Stories*, 1979 · *Home Truths*, 1981 · *Overhead in a Balloon*, 1985 · *In Transit*, 1988 · *Across the Bridge*, 1993 · *The Collected Stories of Mavis Gallant*, 1996

Other literary forms · Journalist and essayist as well as a writer of fiction, Mavis Gallant has chronicled various social and historical events, such as the case of Gabrielle Russier, a young high school teacher in Marseille who was driven to suicide by persecution for having become involved with one of her students. *Paris Notebooks: Essays and Reviews* (1986) is a collection of essays in which Gallant offers observations relating to the many years spent in France, scrutinizing French culture and life in general. Her accounts of the student revolt in 1968 are particularly riveting.

Achievements · Gallant's stature as a writer of short fiction is unsurpassed. The elegant simplicity of her pieces is an unchanging trait of her work and was in fact recognized in her first published piece, "Madeleine's Birthday" for which *The New Yorker* paid six hundred dollars in 1951. In 1981, Gallant was awarded Canada's Governor General's Award for fiction for *Home Truths*. The often somber tone of her work is strengthened by the combination of acute lucidness and understated stylistic richness. Gallant is a remarkable observer. She succeeds in creating worlds that are both familiar and foreign, appealing yet uninviting. Her mastery in the restrained use of language and in her incomparable narrative powers make her undeniably one of the world's greatest fiction writers.

Biography · Born in Montreal in 1922, Mavis Gallant (née Mavis de Trafford Young), an only child, was placed in a Catholic convent school at the age of four. She attended seventeen schools: Catholic schools in Montreal, Protestant ones in Ontario, as well as various boarding schools in the United States. After the death of her father, Gallant lived with her legal guardians in New York, a psychiatrist and his wife. At the age of eighteen, Gallant returned to Montreal. After a short time working for the

National Film Board of Canada in Ottawa during the winter of 1943-1944, Gallant accepted a position as reporter with the *Montreal Standard*, which she left in 1950. In 1951, Gallant began contributing short-fiction stories to *The New Yorker*. In the early 1950's, she moved to Europe, living in London, Rome, and Madrid, before settling in Paris in the early 1960's. It was through her travels and experiences in France, Italy, Austria, and Spain that she observed the fabric of diverse societies. During the initial years of her life in Europe, Gallant lived precariously from her writings, ultimately becoming an accomplished author, depicting loners, expatriates, and crumbling social structures. Gallant settled in Paris, working on a history of the renowned Dreyfus affair in addition to her work in fiction.

Analysis · As the title story of Mavis Gallant's first collection, "The Other Paris" strikes the pitch to which the others that follow it are tuned. Most of these stories are about young Americans in Europe just entering into a marriage, uncertain about what they should feel, unsure of their roles, and unable to find appropriate models around them for the behavior that they think is expected of them. The young protagonists in the stories grope through their ambivalences, looking for guidance in others who seem more sure of themselves, or clutching written words from some absent sibling—advice recorded in a letter, or written down by themselves about appropriate responses to their present situation. In the other stories in which a parent is present, the other parent, usually ill or divorced, is absent, and the rules of conduct become equally tenuous because of that absence. The European stories are set in the early 1950's, when the devastations of the recent war are still being felt. Refugee figures haunt the fringes.

"The Other Paris" refers to the romantic illusions generated by films about that city which Carol feels she is missing. She is about to be married to Howard Mitchell, with whom she works in an American government agency, and with whom she is not yet in love. She keeps remembering her college lectures on the subject to reassure herself. Common interests and similar economic and religious backgrounds were what mattered. "The illusion of love was a blight imposed by the film industry, and almost entirely responsible for the high rate of divorce." Carol waits expectantly for the appropriate emotions to follow the mutuality of their backgrounds: their fathers are both attorneys, Protestants, and from the same social class. In Carol's mind, the discovery of that mysterious "other Paris" is linked with the discovery of love. She believes the Parisians know a secret, "and if she spoke to the right person, or opened the right door, or turned down an unexpected street, the city would reveal itself and she would fall in love." She tries all the "touristy" things, such as listening to carols at the

Place Vendôme, but everything has been commercialized. Newsreel cameras and broadcast equipment spoil the atmosphere she seeks. Plastic mistletoe with "cheap tinsel" is tied to the street lamps.

Odile invites her to a private concert. Excitedly Carol thinks that she has finally gained entrance into the aristocratic secrets that are hidden from foreigners. Instead of the elegant drawing room she had anticipated, it is an "ordinary, shabby theatre" on an obscure street, nearly empty except for a few of the violinist's relatives. Odile, Howard's secretary, is thin, dark, seldom smiles, and often sounds sarcastic because of her poor English. She is involved with Felix, pale, ill, hungry, and without papers, who sells things on the black market. He is twenty-one, she is more than thirty years old, and Carol finds the gap in their ages distasteful. They have no common interests, no mitigating mutual circumstances; yet, one night in Felix's dark, cluttered room, she discovers that they love each other. The thought makes her ill. In that dusty slum, with revulsion, she discovers that, at last, she has "opened the right door, turned down the right street, glimpsed the vision." On this paradox, that the sordid reality reveals the romantic illusion, the story closes with a time shift to the future in which Carol is telling how she met and married Howard in Paris and making it "sound romantic and interesting," believing it as it had never been at all.

"Autumn Day" is another initiation story of a nineteen-year-old who follows her Army husband to Salzburg. She has a list of instructions: "Go for walks. Meet Army wives. Avoid people on farm." She attributes her unhappiness, her failure to feel like a wife, to the fact that they have no home. They are boarding in a farmhouse from which she takes dutiful long walks under the lowering Salzburg skies, gray with impending snow. An American singer practices a new setting of the poem "Herbsttag" (Autumn Day), whose most haunting line, which the narrator feels had something to do with her, is "who does not yet have a home, will never have one." She feels that the poet had understood her; it was exactly the life she was leading, going for lonely walks. She slides a note under the singer's door, asking if they might meet. After a complicated day in which she has had to listen to two sets of confessions, Laura's and Mrs. de Kende's, she returns to the farmhouse to find the singer had invited her to lunch and had returned to America. Walt, her bewildered husband, finds her crying. He tries, timidly, to console her by insisting that they "will be all right" when they get their own apartment. She wonders if her present mood is indeed temporary or whether all their marriage will be like this.

Your girlfriend doesn't vanish overnight. I know, now, what a lot of wavering goes on, how you step forward and back again. The frontier is invisible; sometimes you're over without knowing it. I do know that some change began then, at that moment, and I felt an almost unbearable nostalgia for the figure I was leaving behind.

It is in depicting these border states of consciousness that Gallant excels. Her portraits of girls who are trying to become women without having internalized a strong role model are moving because the portrayal of their inner sense of being lost is augmented by the setting; it is externalized into the girls' awareness of being foreigners alone in a strange country. The psychic territory has been projected outward into an alien land. Both Carol and Cissy have heard music which they feel contains some secret knowledge that can help them understand their feeling of having been somehow left out, excluded from a love they would like to feel. Both accommodate themselves to lives which are less than the songs promised they might be. "Autumn Day" closes with Cissy's ritually repeating the magic formula, like an incantation, like a figure in a fairy tale casting a spell over her own anxiety, "We'll be all right, we'll be all right, we'll be all right."

"Poor Franzi" is also set in Salzburg and in the same wavering space. The young American Elizabeth is engaged to the grandson (Franzi) of Baron Ebendorf, an Austrian aristocrat who dies in the course of the story. Because Franzi refuses to go to the funeral, Elizabeth feels obligated to attend. A party of American tourists serves as choric voices. They insinuate that the young Austrian has become engaged to the American girl simply to escape from the country. They gossip about his failure to visit the old woman in her last illness, and his refusal to pay for the funeral, and his having burned her will. Her landlady, "out of helplessness and decency," had arranged for the last rites, which she could ill-afford, a peasant paying homage to a noble line.

Elizabeth's nearsightedness is a physical correlative of her failure to see her fiancé's faults, which are obvious to everyone else. "Blind as a bat!" the other Americans mutter as she walks straight past them. She gazes at the edge of the horizon, but her myopia prevents her from distinguishing whether she is seeing clouds or mountains. She sees Franzi in this same suffused haze. Instead of the cynicism and selfishness his behavior so clearly outlines, there is a fuzzy aura blurred by her feeling of having to be protective of his great grief. Poor thing, he is all alone now; he must never suffer again. The soft shapes, "shifting and elusive," which better eyes than hers saw as the jutting rocks of the Salzburg mountains, become an emblem of her emotional condition. The story closes on this ambiguous haze. "What will happen to me if I marry him? she wondered; and what would become of Franzi if she were to leave him?"

Other major works

NOVELS: *Green Water, Green Sky*, 1959; *Its Image on the Mirror*, 1964; *A Fairly Good Time*, 1970.

PLAY: *What Is to Be Done*, 1982.

NONFICTION: *The Affair of Gabrielle Russier*, 1971; *Paris Notebooks: Essays and Reviews*, 1986.

Bibliography

Besner, Neil. *The Light of Imagination: Mavis Gallant's Fiction*. Vancouver: University of British Columbia Press, 1988. An extremely thorough analysis of Gallant's fiction from *The Other Paris* to *Overhead in a Balloon*. Includes a biographical review as well as a useful critical bibliography.

Hatch, Ronald. "Mavis Gallant." In *Canadian Writers Since 1960: First Series*. Vol. 53 in *Dictionary of Literary Biography*, edited by W. H. New. Detroit: Gale Research, 1986. A thorough general introduction to Gallant's fiction up to, and including, *Home Truths*. Supplemented by a bibliography of interviews and studies.

Jewison, Don. "Speaking of Mirrors: Imagery and Narration in Two Novellas by Mavis Gallant." *Studies in Canadian Literature* 10, nos. 1, 2 (1985): 94-109. A study of *Green Water, Green Sky* and *Its Image on the Mirror*. Focuses on the importance of mirrors from the perspective of imagery as well as of narration.

Keefer, Janice Kulyk. *Reading Mavis Gallant*. Toronto: Oxford University Press, 1989. A comprehensive study of Gallant's fiction and journalism. Discusses the prison of childhood and the world inhabited by women, in addition to Gallant's conception of memory.

Smythe, Karen. *Figuring Grief: Gallant, Munro, and the Poetics of Elegy*. Montreal, Canada: McGill-Queen's University Press, 1992.

_____. "The Silent Cry: Empathy and Elegy in Mavis Gallant's Novels." *Studies in Canadian Literature* 15, no. 2 (1990): 116-135. A study discussing the ways in which the reader is forced to become involved in the emotional and empathetic elements present in *Green Water, Green Sky*; *Its Image on the Mirror*; and *A Fairly Good Time*.

Ruth Rosenberg
(Revised by *Kenneth W. Meadwell*)

GABRIEL GARCÍA MÁRQUEZ

Born: Aracataca, Colombia; March 6, 1928

Principal short fiction · *La hojarasca,* 1955 (novella; *Leaf Storm and Other Stories,* 1972) · *El coronel no tiene quien le escriba,* 1961 (novella; *No One Writes to the Colonel and Other Stories,* 1968) · *Los funerales de la Mamá Grande,* 1962 · *Relato de un náufrago . . . ,* 1970 (*The Story of a Shipwrecked Sailor . . . ,* 1986) · *La increíble y triste historia de la Cándida Eréndira y de su abuela desalmada,* 1972 (*Innocent Eréndira and Other Stories,* 1978) · *Ojos de perro azul,* 1972 · *Todos los cuentos de Gabriel García Márquez,* 1975 (*Collected Stories,* 1984) · *Crónica de una muerte anunciada,* 1981 (novella; *Chronicle of a Death Foretold,* 1982) · *Collected Novellas,* 1990 · *Doce cuentos peregrinos,* 1992 (*Strange Pilgrims: Twelve Stories,* 1993)

Other literary forms · Besides his short fiction, including short stories and novellas, Gabriel García Márquez's fictional work includes full-length novels. His masterpiece and best-known novel is the epic *Cien años de soledad* (1967; *One Hundred Years of Solitude,* 1970). In addition, during his long career as a journalist, he has written numerous articles, essays, and reports on a variety of topics, particularly relating to Latin American life and politics but also including a book of his observations during a trip to eastern Europe in 1957.

Achievements · In 1967, García Márquez's highly acclaimed novel *One Hundred Years of Solitude* appeared and was immediately recognized by critics as a masterpiece of fiction. As a work of high literary quality, this novel was unusual in that it also enjoyed tremendous popular success both in Latin America and in translation throughout the world. This work made García Márquez a major figure–perhaps *the* major figure–of contemporary Latin American literature.

García Márquez's work has been praised for bringing literary fiction back in contact with real life in all of its richness. His combination of realism and fantasy known as Magical Realism *(realismo mágico)* sets the stage for a full spectrum of Latin American characters. His stories focus on basic human concerns, and characters or incidents from one work are often integrated into others, if only with a passing reference.

In recognizing his work with the Nobel Prize in Literature in 1982, the Nobel committee compared the breadth and quality of his work to that of such great writers as William Faulkner and Honoré de Balzac.

Biography · Gabriel García Márquez was born in Aracataca, a town near the Atlantic coast of Colombia, on March 6, 1928. His parents, Luisa Santiaga and Gabriel Eligio Márquez, sent him to live with his maternal grandparents for the first eight years of his life. He attended school in Barranquilla and Zipaquirá, followed by law studies at the Universidad Nacional in Bogotá.

His first short story was published in 1947 in the Bogotá newspaper *El Espectador*. The literary editor praised the work, and in the next five years several more short fictions were also published. When his studies were interrupted by political violence in 1948, García Márquez transferred to the Universidad de Cartagena, but he never received his degree. Instead, he began his career as a journalist, writing for *El Universal*. He soon had a daily column and became friends with the writers and artists of the "Barranquilla group." In 1950, he moved to Barranquilla and in 1954 to Bogotá, continuing his work as a journalist. During this time, he also published *Leaf Storm and Other Stories* and received a prize from the Association of Artists and Writers of Bogotá.

In 1955, he was sent to Geneva, Switzerland, as a European correspondent. When *El Espectador* closed in January, 1956, he spent a period of poverty in Paris, working on *La mala hora* (1962; *In Evil Hour*, 1979) and writing free-lance articles. In the summer of 1957, he traveled through eastern Europe, then moved to Caracas, Venezuela, as a journalist. With the prospect of a steady job, he married Mercedes Barcha in March, 1958.

Interested since his university days in leftist causes, García Márquez worked for the Cuban news agency Prensa Latina in Bogotá after Fidel Castro came to power in 1959, then in Havana, Cuba, and later New York. After leaving the agency, he moved to Mexico City, where he worked as a journalist and film scriptwriter with Carlos Fuentes during the period 1961-1967. In 1962, *In Evil Hour* was published and won the Esso Literary Prize in Colombia. That same year, a collection of stories, *Los funerales de la Mamá Grande* also appeared. Then, in a spurt of creative energy, García Márquez spent eighteen months of continuous work to produce his best-selling novel *One Hundred Years of Solitude*, which won book prizes in Italy and France in 1969. In order to be able to write in peace after the tremendous success of this book, he moved to Barcelona, Spain, where he met Peruvian author Mario Vargas Llosa. In 1972, he won both the Rómulo Gallego Prize in Venezuela and the Neustadt International Prize for Literature. The money from both prizes was donated to political causes.

García Márquez left Barcelona in 1975 and returned to Mexico. That same year, *El otoño del patriarca* (1975; *The Autumn of the Patriarch*, 1975), about the life of a Latin American dictator, was published, and in 1981, his

Chronicle of a Death Foretold appeared. His news magazine, *Alternativa,* founded in 1974 in Bogotá to present opposing political views, folded in 1980, but García Márquez continued his activism by writing a weekly column for Hispanic newspapers and magazines. His Nobel Prize speech in 1982 made a strong statement about conditions in Latin America yet sounded the note of hope in the face of oppression.

García Márquez has continued his literary production since receiving the Nobel Prize, publishing *El amor en los tiempos del cólera* in 1985 (*Love in the Time of Cholera,* 1988) and *El general en su laberinto* in 1989 (*The General in His Labyrinth,* 1990), based on the life of Simón Bolívar.

Analysis · Gabriel García Márquez's fiction is characterized by a thread of common themes, events, and characters that seem to link his work together into one multifaceted portrayal of the experiences of Latin American life. From the influences of his early childhood, when he learned from his grandmother how to tell the most fantastic stories in a matter-of-fact tone, to his later observations of the oppression and cruelties of politics, García Márquez captures the everyday life of the amazing people of coastal Colombia, with its Caribbean flavor, as well as the occasional resident of the highlands of Bogotá. He has an eye for the details of daily life mixed with humor and an attitude of acceptance and wonder. His characters experience the magic and joy of life and face the suffering of solitude and isolation but always with an innate dignity. García Márquez's vision touches real life with its local attitudes and values, and in the process it also reveals a criticism of politics, the church, and U.S. imperialism, as they contribute to the Latin American experience.

García Márquez's earliest stories have a bizarre, almost surreal, tone, reminiscent of Franz Kafka. Collected in *Ojos de perro azul,* these stories represent an experimental phase of García Márquez's development as a writer and as such are disappointing to readers who have first read his mature work. "La tercera resignación" ("The Third Resignation"), for example, deals with the thoughts and fears of a young man in his coffin. "Nabo, el negro que hizo esperar a los ángeles" ("Nabo, the Black Man Who Made the Angels Wait") tells of a man who is locked in a stable because he goes insane after being kicked in the head by a horse.

In "Isabel viendo llover en Macondo" ("Monologue of Isabel Watching It Rain in Macondo"), published the same year as his first novella, *Leaf Storm,* García Márquez captures the atmosphere of a tropical storm through the eyes of his protagonist. Here, the world of Macondo, used in *Leaf Storm* as well and made world-famous in *One Hundred Years of Solitude,* is presented amid the suffocating oppressiveness of tropical weather. Here as later, nature itself is often a palpable force in the fiction of García Márquez–often exaggerated and overwhelming in order to reflect the reality of Latin American geography and the natural forces within it. The theme of solitude is reflected in the imagery as well as in the personal relationship of Isabel and Martin: "the sky was a gray, jellyish substance that flapped its wings a hand away from our heads."

After demonstrating his ability to capture the tropical atmosphere, García Márquez shows himself capable of capturing a portrait in words with his well-structured novella *No One Writes to the Colonel.* The central character is a dignified man with a deep sense of honor who has been promised a military pension. Every Friday, he goes to the post office to wait for mail that never comes, and then he claims that he really was not expecting anything anyway. He is a patient man, resigned to eternal waiting and hope when there is no reason to expect that hope to be fulfilled. "For nearly sixty years–since the end of the last civil war–the colonel had done nothing else but wait. October was one of the few things which arrived." His other hope is his rooster, which belonged to his son, who was executed for handing out subversive literature, but since he is too poor to feed the rooster, some townspeople work out an arrangement to provide food until after the big fight. The political background is introduced subtly as the story opens with the funeral of the first person to die of natural causes in this town for a long time. Violence, censorship, and political repression are a given, as is the pervasive poverty. The colonel continues passing out the literature in his son's place and waiting for his pension. His dignity sustains him in the face of starvation.

The image of dignity is developed again in the first story of *Los funerales de la Mamá Grande*, entitled "La siesta del martes" ("Tuesday Siesta") and also set in Macondo. Said to be García Márquez's favorite, it tells of a woman and her young daughter who arrive by train in the stifling heat at siesta time. The woman asks the priest to be allowed to visit her son in the cemetery. The young man was shot for being a thief, but she proudly claims him as her own with quiet self-control: "I told him never to steal anything that anyone needed to eat, and he minded me."

The title story, "Los funerales de la Mamá Grande" ("Big Mama's Funeral"), still set in Macondo, breaks the tone of the other stories into a technique of hyperbole, which García Márquez later used in *One Hundred Years of Solitude* to good effect. The opening sentence sets the tone: "This is, for all the world's unbelievers, the true account of Big Mama, absolute sovereign of the Kingdom of Macondo, who lived for ninety-two years, and died in the odor of sanctity one Tuesday last September, and whose funeral was attended by the Pope."

The panorama and parody of the story mention Mama's power and property in high-sounding phrases, many from journalism. The pageantry is grandiose to the point of the absurd for this powerful individual, a prototype of the patriarch who appears in García Márquez's later work. She is a legend and local "saint," who seemed to the local people to be immortal; her death comes as a complete surprise. The story criticizes the manipulation of power but also skillfully satirizes the organized display or public show that eulogizes the holders of power with pomp and empty words. The story ends when the garbage men come and sweep up on the next day.

Fantastic elements characterize the collection entitled *Innocent Eréndira and Other Stories.* Two of the stories, "Un señor muy viejo con unas alas enormes" ("A Very Old Man with Enormous Wings") and "El ahogado más hermoso del mundo" ("The Handsomest Drowned Man in the World"), have adult figures who are like toys with which children, and other adults, can play. With the second story, García Márquez also tries a technique of shifting narrators and point of view to be used later in the novel *The Autumn of the Patriarch.*

A political satire is the basis for another story, "Muerte constante más allá del amor" ("Death Constant Beyond Love"). The situation that forms the basis for the satire is also incorporated into the longer "Innocent Eréndira." Geographically, in this collection García Márquez has moved inland to the barren landscape on the edge of the Guajiro desert. Here, he sets a type of folktale with an exploited granddaughter, a green-blooded monster of a grandmother, and a rescuing hero named Ulises. Combining myth, allegory, and references from other works, García Márquez weaves a story in which "the wind of her misfortune" determines the life of the extraordinarily passive Eréndira. Treated as a slave and a prostitute by her grandmother, Eréndira persuades Ulises to kill the evil woman–who turns out to be amazingly hard to kill. Throughout the story, García Márquez demonstrates the ability to report the most monstrous things in a matter-of-fact tone. Some critics have pointed out that the exaggeration that seems inherent in many of his tales may have its roots in the extraordinary events and stories that are commonplace in his Latin American world.

In *Chronicle of a Death Foretold,* García Márquez blends his experience in journalism with his mastery of technique to tell a story based on an actual event that took place in 1955 in Sucre, where he lived at the time. Using records and witness testimony, he unfolds his story on the lines of a detective story. The incident is based on the revenge taken by Angela Vicario's brothers on their friend Santiago Nasar, who supposedly took Angela's virginity (although some doubt is cast on this allegation). The story is pieced together as the townspeople offer their memories of what happened, along with excuses for not having warned the victim. Tension builds as the reader knows the final outcome but not how or why it will occur. The use of dreams (ironically, Nasar's mother is an interpreter of dreams), the feeling of fatalism, and submission to the code of honor, all of which form a part of this society's attitudes, play a central role in the novella, as do García Márquez's use of vision and foreshadowing. Although the basis for the story is a journalistic report of a murder, the actual writing captures the themes of love and death as well as the complex interplay of human emotions and motives in a balanced and poetic account, which reveals García Márquez's skill as a writer.

García Márquez's body of work portrays a complete reality breaking out of conventional bounds. Characters from one story regularly show up or are mentioned in another, while his complex mix of fantasy and reality reveals a consummate storyteller capable of bringing to his work the magic of his non-European world. His impact as a writer lies in the fact that although his work describes the Latin American experience of life, it also goes beyond to reveal a universal human experience.

Other major works

NOVELS: *La mala hora,* 1962, revised 1966 (*In Evil Hour,* 1979); *Cien años de soledad,* 1967 (*One Hundred Years of Solitude,* 1970); *El otoño del patriarca,* 1975 (*The Autumn of the Patriarch,* 1975); *El amor en los tiempos del cólera,* 1985 (*Love in the Time of Cholera,* 1988); *El general en su laberinto,* 1989 (*The General in His Labyrinth,* 1990); *Del amor y otros demonios,* 1994 (*Of Love and Other Demons,* 1995).

NONFICTION: *La novela en América Latina: Diálogo,* 1968 (with Mario Vargas Llosa); *Cuando era feliz e indocumentado,* 1973; *Chile, el golpe y los gringos,* 1974; *Crónicas y reportajes,* 1976; *Operación Carlota,* 1977; *Periodismo militante,* 1978; *De viaje por los países socialistas,* 1978; *Obra periodística: Textos costeños,* 1981 (volume 1); *Entre cachacos I,* 1982 (volume 2); *Entre cachacos II,* 1982 (volume 3); *De Europa y América, 1955-1960,* 1983 (volume 4); *El olor de la guayaba: Conversaciones con Plinio Apuleyo Mendoza,* 1982 (*The Fragrance of the Guava: Plinio Apuleyo Mendoza in Conversation with Gabriel García Márquez,* 1983; also known as *The Smell of Guava,* 1984); *La aventura de Miguel Littín, clandestino en Chile,* 1986 (*Clandestine in Chile: The Adventures of Miguel Littín,* 1987).

Bibliography

Bell-Villada, Gene H. *García Márquez: The Man and His Work.* Chapel Hill: University of North Carolina Press, 1990. This well-written book traces the forces that have shaped the life and work of García Márquez and analyzes his short fiction as well as his novels. Includes an index, and a fine selected bibliography of sources in English and Spanish, as well as a listing of works by García Márquez and of available English translations.

McMurray, George R., ed. *Critical Essays on Gabriel García Márquez.* Boston: G. K. Hall, 1987. A collection of book reviews, articles, and essays covering the full range of García Márquez's fictional work. Very useful for an introduction to specific novels and collections of short stories. Also includes an introductory overview by the editor and an index.

_____. *Gabriel García Márquez.* New York: Frederick Ungar, 1977. The first full-length study of García Márquez in English and still an accessible introduction to his life and works. The author traces García Márquez's development from his "early gropings" through his novel *The Autumn of the Patriarch.* A useful chronology, some plot summaries, a bibliography, and an index are provided.

McNerney, Kathleen. *Understanding Gabriel García Márquez.* Columbia: University of South Carolina Press, 1989. An overview addressed to students and non-academic readers. After an introduction on Colombia and a brief biography, the five core chapters explain his works in depth. Chapters 1 through 3 discuss three novels, chapter 4 focuses on his short novels and stories, and chapter 5 reviews the role of journalism in his work. Includes a select, annotated bibliography of critical works and an index.

McQuirk, Bernard, and Richard Cardwell, eds. *Gabriel García Márquez: New Readings.* Cambridge, England: Cambridge University Press, 1987. A collection of twelve essays in English by different authors reflecting a variety of critical approaches and covering García Márquez's major novels as well as a selection of his early fiction: *No One Writes to the Colonel, Innocent Eréndira,* and *Chronicle of a Death Foretold.* Also includes a translation of García Márquez's Nobel address and a select bibliography.

Minta, Stephen. *Gabriel García Márquez: Writer of Colombia.* New York: Harper & Row, 1987. After a useful first chapter on Colombia, the book traces García Márquez's life and work. Minta focuses his discussion on the political context of the *violencia* in *No One Writes to the Colonel* and *In Evil Hour.* Includes two chapters on "Macondo" as García Márquez's fictional setting and another chapter with individual discussions of *The Autumn of the Patriarch, Chronicle of a Death Foretold,* and *Love in the Time of Cholera.* Includes a select bibliography by chapter and an index.

Williams, Raymond L. *Gabriel García Márquez.* Boston: Twayne, 1984.

Susan L. Piepke

HAMLIN GARLAND

Born: West Salem, Wisconsin; September 14, 1860
Died: Hollywood, California; March 4, 1940

Principal short fiction · *Main-Travelled Roads: Six Mississippi Valley Stories,*
1891 · *Prairie Folks,* 1893 · *Wayside Courtships,* 1897 · *Other Main-Travelled*
Roads, 1910 · *They of the High Trails,* 1916 · *The Book of the American Indian,*
1923

Other literary forms · Hamlin Garland's more than fifty published works
include nearly every literary type—novels, biography, autobiography, essays, dramas, and poems. His best and most memorable novels are *Rose of*
Dutcher's Coolly (1895), similar in plot to the later Theodore Dreiser novel,
Sister Carrie (1900), and *Boy Life on the Prairie* (1899), chronicling the social
history of Garland's boyhood. One book of essays, *Crumbling Idols* (1894),
presents his theory of realism ("veritism"). His autobiographical quartet, *A*
Son of the Middle Border (1917), *A Daughter of the Middle Border* (1921),
Trail-Makers of the Middle Border (1926), and *Back-Trailers from the Middle*
Border (1928), recounts the story of his family. *A Daughter of the Middle Border*
won the Pulitzer Prize for 1922. These books contain episodes that are
treated in greater detail in some of his short stories.

Achievements · Garland's work stands at an important transition point
from Romanticism to realism, playing a role in ushering in the new literary
trend. His best works are important for their depiction of a segment of
society seldom delineated by other writers and for the relationship they
show between literature and its socioeconomic environment. He used
American themes—rather than Americanized European themes—and commonplace characters and incidents that turned the American writer away
from his colonial complex, even away from the New England tradition of
letters. His realism emancipated the American Midwest and West and the
American farmer particularly from the romanticized conception that kept
their story from being told before. Like Walt Whitman, Garland wanted
writers to tell about life as they knew it and witnessed it. His realism
foreshadowed the work of young writers such as Stephen Crane, E. W.
Howe, and Harold Frederic. His naturalistic inclination, apparent in his
belief that environment is crucial in shaping men's lives, preceded the
naturalistic writing of Crane, Frank Norris, and Dreiser. Aside from their

value as literature, Garland's best stories are a comprehensive record of an otherwise relatively unreported era of American social history. Much read in his prime, he enjoyed considerable popularity even while antagonizing, with his merciless word pictures, the very people about whom he wrote. Garland was awarded honorary degrees from the University of Wisconsin, the University of Southern California, Northwestern University, and Beloit College. In 1918, he was elected to the board of directors of the American Academy of Arts and Letters. He won the Pulitzer Prize for Biography and Autobiography in 1922.

Biography · Of Scotch-Irish descent, Hannibal Hamlin Garland moved with his family from Wisconsin, where he was born in West Salem on September 14, 1860, to an Iowa farm while still a child. Years spent on the farm made him seek escape through a career in oratory. To this end, he attended Cedar Valley Seminary from which he was graduated in 1881. He held a land claim in North Dakota for a year, but mortgaged it for the chance to go East and enroll in Boston University. He succeeded in getting to Boston but was unable to attend the university; however, he embarked on a self-directed program of reading in the holdings of the Boston Public Library. While in Boston, he began writing, his first attempts being lectures, then stories and books. It was around this time also that he joined the Anti-Poverty Society and became an active reformer. He read Henry George and embraced the Single Tax theory as a solution to some of the many contemporary social problems.

Donald Pizer, along with many scholars, divides Garland's career into three general phases: a period of political and social reform activity that coincides with his most memorable fiction set in the Middle West (1884-1895); a period of popular romance-writing in which his settings shifted from the Midwest to the Rocky Mountains (1896-1916); and a period of increasing political and social conservatism, during which he wrote his major autobiographical works (1917-1940). In 1899, Garland married Zulime Taft, and they became parents of daughters born in 1904 and 1907. His list of acquaintances and friends grew to include such literary figures as William Dean Howells, Eugene Field, Joseph Kirkland, Edward Eggleston, Frank Norris, Stephen Crane, George Bernard Shaw, and Rudyard Kipling.

He lived the last years of his life in Hollywood, where he could be near his married daughter. In these later years, he turned more seriously to a lifelong fascination with the occult, producing two books on the subject. He died of cerebral hemorrhage in Hollywood on March 4, 1940.

Analysis · Hamlin Garland's most enduring short stories are those dealing with the Middle Border (the prairie lands of Iowa, Wisconsin, Minnesota, Nebraska, and the Dakotas). Collected for the most part in four books, they touch on nearly every subject of everyday life, from birth through youth, adulthood, courtship, and marriage, to death. They deal with the unromantic life of harassed generations on the farms and in the small towns of the prairie. Garland's belief that an author must write of "what is" with an eye toward "what is to be" causes him alternately to describe, prophesy, suggest, and demand. Although often subtle in his approach, he is sometimes, when championing the cause of the farmer, more the reformer than the artist. Social protest is the single most recurrent theme in his work. "A Stopover at Tyre" and "Before the Low Green Door" show with some skill the unrelenting drudgery of the farmer's life.

"Under the Lion's Paw," Garland's most anthologized story, is his most powerful statement of protest. In it, one man, Tim Haskins, like thousands of struggling farmers, is exploited by another man, representative of scores of other land speculators. Haskins, through months of arduous labor, pushing his own and his wife's energies to their limits, has managed to make the dilapidated farm he is renting a productive place of which he can be proud. He has begun to feel confident that he can buy the farm and make a success of it. The owner, however, has taken note of the many physical improvements Haskins has made and recognizes its increased value. Thus, when Haskins talks to the owner about buying the place, he is astonished to learn that the purchase price has doubled and the rent has been increased. Haskins is "under the lion's paw," caught in untenable circumstances that will hurt him no matter what he does. If he gives up the farm, as his angry indignation dictates, he will lose all the money and time he has invested in the farm's improvements. If he buys, he will be under a heavy mortgage that could be foreclosed at any time. If he continues to rent at the higher fee, all his work will almost literally be for the owner's benefit, not for himself and his family. The personally satisfying alternative of simply striking the man dead is wildly considered by Haskins momentarily until the thought of the repercussions to his family brings him to his senses, and he agrees to buy on the owner's terms. The situation in itself is cruel. Garland clearly shows that it is even worse when one realizes that the exploitation of Haskins is only one of thousands of similar cases.

"Lucretia Burns," another social protest story, is longer and has more action and a more complex major character than the similar "Before the Low Green Door." Although some of its impact is diminished by its tiresome discussions on reform and by its weak denouement, Garland has created in Lucretia an unforgettable character who makes the story praiseworthy. Lucretia is a strong personality who had "never been handsome, even in her days of early childhood, and now she was middle-aged, distorted with work and childbearing, and looking faded and worn." Her face is "a pitifully worn, almost tragic face—long, thin, sallow, hollow-eyed. The mouth had long since lost the power to shape itself into a kiss. . . ." She has reached a point of desperation that calls for some kind of action: confrontation (with her husband), capitulation, or a mental breakdown. She chooses to renounce her soul-killing existence and operate on a level of bare subsistence, with no more struggling to "get ahead" or do what is expected. When the spirit of rebellion overcomes her, she simply gives in to her chronic weariness and refuses to do more than feed her children and the husband for whom she no longer cares.

For a successful conclusion to this powerful indictment against the farm wife's hopeless life, Garland had several choices. Unfortunately, he chose the ineffectual ending in which a dainty, young, idealistic schoolteacher persuades Lucretia to give life another try. The reader, having seen Lucretia's determination to stop the drudgery in her life forever, is dissatisfied, knowing it would have taken a great deal more than a sympathetic stranger to convince Lucretia that her life was worth enduring.

This kind of lapse is not Garland's only flaw. Occasionally, he leads on his readers, telling them what they should think about a character. In "A Sociable at Dudleys," for example, he describes the county bully: "No lizard revelled in the mud more hideously than he. . . . His tongue dropped poison." Garland apparently abhorred the "vileness of the bully's whole life and thought." Moreover, in most of the stories, one can tell the heroes from the villains by the Aryan features and Scottish names of the former and the dark, alien looks of the latter. His heroes are further categorized into two prevailing physical types: either they are tall, imposing, strong, even powerful and handsome (Tim Haskins is an older, more worn version of this type); or they are stocky, sturdy, ambitious, cheerful, and optimistic counterparts of the young Hamlin Garland as he described himself in *A Son of the Middle Border*. Will Hannan of "A Branch Road" falls into this category.

"A Branch Road" develops another favorite theme of Garland—a romantic one in which boy meets girl; misunderstanding separates them; and then adversity reunites them. Although this plot is well-worn today, in the late 1800's and early 1900's, the reading public still liked it, and Garland occasionally catered to the larger reading public. "A Branch Road," a novelette, is long enough for the author to develop character, setting, and plot in a more leisurely, less personal manner than in some of his other stories on the same theme, such as "A Day of Grace," "A Sociable at

Dudleys," and "William Bacon's Man." In "A Branch Road," young Will Hannan and Agnes Dingman have fallen in love. Will is ecstatic when he goes to the Dingman farm to help with the threshing, secure in his belief that she cares as much for him as he for her.

Once at the farm, however, listening to the other men, both young and older, making casual, joking comments about Agnes' prettiness and her attraction to most of the young swains in the county, Will becomes apprehensive that they will notice her obvious preference for him and make light of his deep private feelings. To prevent this, he repays her smiling attentions to him with curt words and an aloof manner. Agnes is hurt and confused by this, not understanding his masculine pride and sensitivity to ridicule. She responds by keeping up a light-hearted demeanor by smiling and talking to the other men, who are delighted, a response that makes Will rage inwardly. The day is a disaster for Will, but because he is to take Agnes to the fair in a few days, he is confident that he will be able to set things right then.

On the morning of the day of the fair, however, the hopeful lover sets out early, but promptly loses a wheel from his buggy, requiring several hours of delay for repair. By the time he gets to Agnes' house, she has gone to the fair with Will's rival, Ed Kinney. Will is so enraged by this turn of events that he cannot think. Dominated by his pride and jealous passion, blaming her and considering no alternatives, he leaves the county, heading West, without a word of farewell or explanation to Agnes.

Seven years later he returns to find Agnes married to Ed Kinney, mother of a baby, daughter-in-law to two pestering old people, and distressingly old before her time. Will manages to speak privately to her and learns how he and she had misunderstood each other's actions on that day long ago. He finds she had indeed loved him. He accepts that it is his fault her life is now so unhappy, that she is so abused and worn. In defiance of custom and morality, he persuades her to leave her husband and go away with him. They flee taking her baby with them.

In outline, this is the familiar melodrama of the villain triumphing over the fair maiden while the hero is away; then, just in time, the hero returns to rescue the heroine from the villain's clutches. Actually, however, Garland avoids melodrama and even refrains from haranguing against farm drudgery. He avoids the weak denouement and chooses instead a rather radical solution to the problem: the abduction of a wife and baby by another man was a daring ending to an American 1890's plot. Yet Garland makes the justice of the action acceptable.

Will Hannan, a very sensitive young man living among people who seem coarse and crude, is propelled through the story by strong, understandable emotions: love, pride, anger, fear of humiliation, remorse, pity, and guilt. Love causes the anger that creates the confusion in his relationship with Agnes. Pride and fear of humiliation drive him away from her. Remorse pursues him all the time he is away and is largely responsible for his return. Pity and guilt make him steal Agnes away from the life to which he feels he has condemned her. Many of Garland's other stories do not have the emotional motivation of characters that "A Branch Road" has (in all fairness, most are not as long); nor are Garland's characters generally as complex. He seems less concerned with probing a personality's reaction to a situation than with describing the consequences of an act.

The theme of the return of the native to his Middle Border home is used in several stories, among them "Up the Coolly," "Mrs. Ripley's Trip," and "Among the Corn Rows." Less pessimistic and tragic and more sentimental than these is "The Return of a Private," an elaboration of Garland's father's return from the Civil War as told in the first chapter of *A Son of the Middle Border*. The story describes the sadness which old war comrades feel as they go their separate ways home. It describes the stirring emotions which the returning soldier feels as he nears his home and sees familiar landmarks; when he first catches sight of the homestead; when he sees his nearly disbelieving wife and the children who hardly remember him. They are tender scenes, but Garland the artist cannot contain Garland the reformer, who reminds the reader of the futility facing the soldier, handicapped physically from war-connected fever and ague and handicapped financially by the heavy mortgage on his farm. The soldier's homecoming is shown as one tiny, bright moment in what has been and will continue to be an endless cycle of dullness and hardship. Garland obviously empathizes with the character and shows the homecoming as a sweet, loving time; but as with so many of his stories, "The Return of a Private" is overcast with gloom.

Garland's stories show the ugly and the beautiful, the tragic with the humorous, the just with the unjust. He tries always to show the true, reporting the speech and dress of the people accurately, describing their homes and their work honestly. Truth, however, is not all that he seeks; he wants significance as well. To this end, his stories show the effects of farm drudgery on the men and women, of the ignorant practices of evangelists, of the thwarted ambitions of the youth because of circumstances beyond their control. Garland does not always suppress his reformer's instincts, and so in some stories he offers solutions. In his best stories, however, he simply shows the injustice and moves the reader, by his skillful handling of details, to wish to take action. Although his stories are often bitter and depressing, there is a hopefulness and optimism in Garland that compels him to bring them to a comparatively happy ending. In his best stories, he does for the Middle Border what Mary E. Wilkins Freeman does for New England, brings the common people into rich relation with the reader and shows movingly the plights of the less fortunate among them, especially women.

Other major works

NOVELS: *A Member of the Third House*, 1892; *Jason Edwards: An Average Man*, 1892; *A Little Norsk*, 1892; *A Spoil of Office*, 1892; *Rose of Dutcher's Coolly*, 1895; *The Spirit of Sweetwater*, 1898 (reissued as *Witch's Gold*, 1906); *Boy Life on the Prairie*, 1899; *The Eagle's Heart*, 1900; *Her Mountain Lover*, 1901; *The Captain of the Gray-Horse Troop*, 1902; *Hesper*, 1903; *The Light of the Star*, 1904; *The Tyranny of the Dark*, 1905; *The Long Trail*, 1907; *Money Magic*, 1907 (reissued as *Mart Haney's Mate*, 1922); *The Moccasin Ranch*, 1909; *Cavanagh, Forest Ranger*, 1910; *Victor Ollnee's Discipline*, 1911; *The Forester's Daughter*, 1914.

PLAY: *Under the Wheel: A Modern Play in Six Scenes*, 1890.

POETRY: *Prairie Songs*, 1893.

NONFICTION: *Crumbling Idols: Twelve Essays on Art*, 1894; *Ulysses S. Grant: His Life and Character*, 1898; *Out-of-Door Americans*, 1901; *A Son of the Middle Border*, 1917; *A Daughter of the Middle Border*, 1921; *Trail-Makers of the Middle Border*, 1926; *The Westward March of American Settlement*, 1927; *Back-Trailers from the Middle Border*, 1928; *Roadside Meetings*, 1930; *Companions on the Trail: A Literary Chronicle*, 1931; *My Friendly Contemporaries: A Literary Log*, 1932; *Afternoon Neighbors*, 1934; *Joys of the Trail*, 1935; *Forty Years of Psychic Research: A Plain Narrative of Fact*, 1936.

Bibliography

Kaye, Frances. "Hamlin Garland's Feminism." In *Women and Western Literature*, edited by Helen Winter Stauffer and Susan Rosowski. Troy, N.Y.: Whitston, 1982. Kaye discusses Garland's deliberate feminism, identifying him as the only male author of note at the end of the nineteenth century who spoke in favor of women's rights, suffrage, and equality in marriage.

McCullough, Joseph. *Hamlin Garland*. Boston: Twayne, 1978. This study follows Garland through his literary career, dividing it into phases, with major attention to the first phase of his reform activities and the midwestern stories. A primary bibliography and a select, annotated secondary bibliography are included.

Nagel, James, ed. *Critical Essays on Hamlin Garland*. Boston: G. K. Hall, 1982. Nagel's introduction surveys the critical responses to Garland's work. This volume is especially rich in reviews of Garland's books, and it also includes twenty-six biographical and critical essays.

Pizer, Donald. *Hamlin Garland's Early Work and Career.* Berkeley: University of California Press, 1960. Pizer treats in careful detail Garland's intellectual and artistic development during the first phase of his literary and reformist career, from 1884 to 1895. He discusses Garland's development of his creed, his literary output, and reform activities in society, theater, politics, and the arts. Pizer includes a detailed bibliography of Garland's publications during these years.

Silet, Charles. *Henry Blake Fuller and Hamlin Garland: A Reference Guide.* Boston: G. K. Hall, 1977. This volume contains a comprehensive annotated guide to writing about Garland through 1975. For information about scholarly writing on Garland after 1975, see *American Literary Scholarship: An Annual.*

Silet, Charles, Robert Welch, and Richard Boudreau, eds. *The Critical Reception of Hamlin Garland, 1891-1978.* Troy, N.Y.: Whitston, 1985. This illustrated volume contains thirty-three essays that illustrate the development of Garland's literary reputation from 1891 to 1978. The introduction emphasizes the difficulty critics have had trying to determine the quality of Garland's art.

Taylor, Walter. *The Economic Novel in America.* Chapel Hill: University of North Carolina Press, 1942. Taylor examines Garland's work in the context of fiction that reflects economic issues and trends. In Garland's literary career he sees a reflection of the fall of pre-Civil War agrarian democracy with the halting of the advance of the frontier and the decline of populism.

Jane L. Ball
(Revised by *Terry Heller*)